MARVEL
BLACK WIDOW
PRELUDE

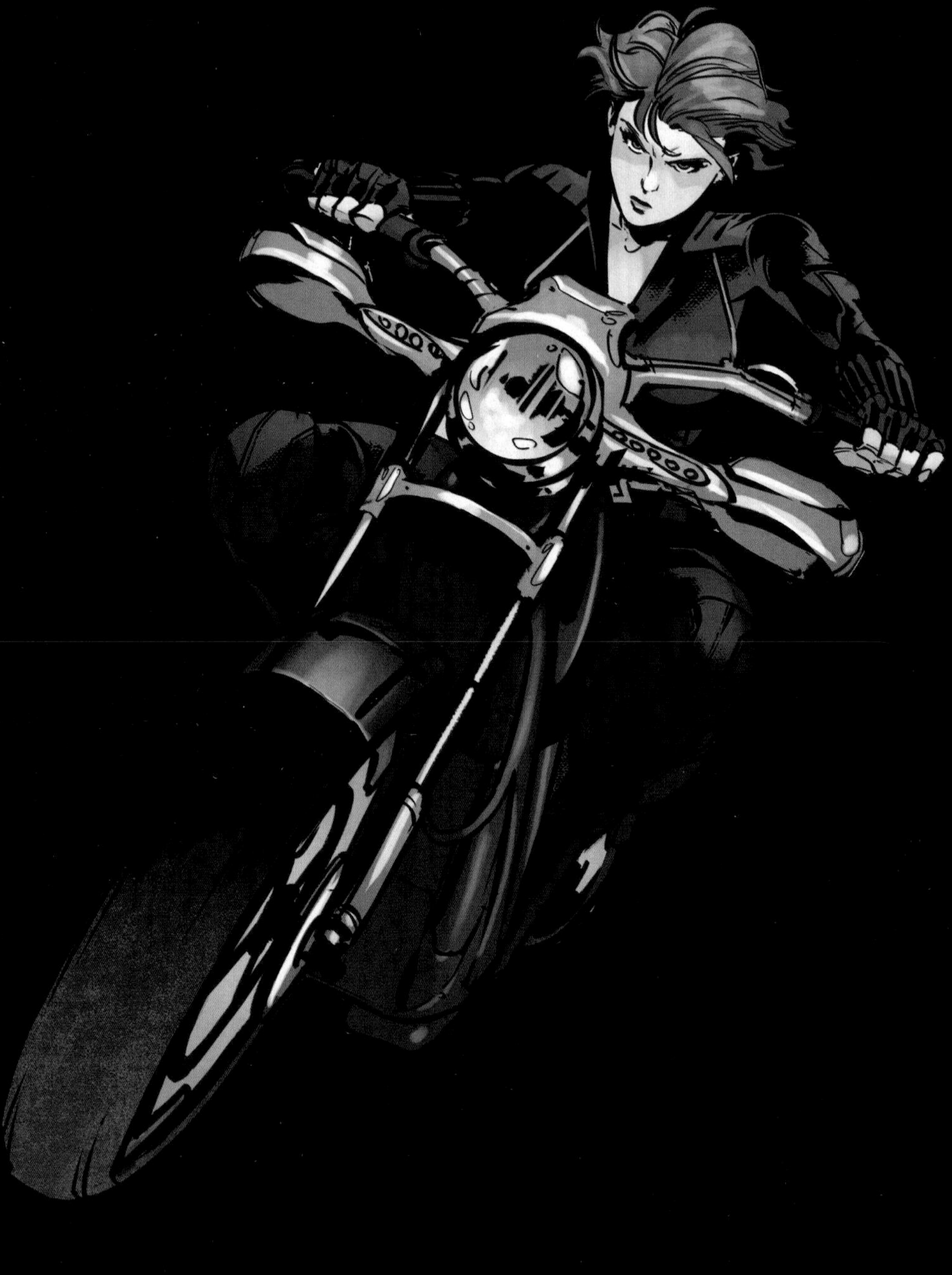

WRITER: **PETER DAVID**
ARTIST: **CARLOS VILLA**
COLOR ARTIST: **CHRIS SOTOMAYOR**
LETTERER: **VC'S TRAVIS LANHAM**
ASSISTANT EDITOR: **MARTIN BIRO**
EDITOR: **MARK BASSO**

FOR MARVEL STUDIOS
DIRECTOR, PRODUCTION & DEVELOPMENT: **BRIAN CHAPEK**
MANAGER, PRODUCTION & DEVELOPMENT: **KYANA F. DAVIDSON**
PRESIDENT: **KEVIN FEIGE**

COLLECTION EDITOR: **JENNIFER GRÜNWALD**
ASSISTANT MANAGING EDITOR: **MAIA LOY**
ASSISTANT MANAGING EDITOR: **LISA MONTALBANO**
EDITOR, SPECIAL PROJECTS: **MARK D. BEAZLEY**
VP PRODUCTION & SPECIAL PROJECTS: **JEFF YOUNGQUIST**
SVP PRINT, SALES & MARKETING: **DAVID GABRIEL**
EDITOR IN CHIEF: **C.B. CEBULSKI**

MARVEL'S BLACK WIDOW PRELUDE. Contains material originally published in magazine form as MARVEL'S BLACK WIDOW PRELUDE (2019) #1-2, AVENGERS (1963) #43 and #196, TALES OF SUSPENSE (1959) #52-53, and THE WEB OF BLACK WIDOW (2019) #1. First printing 2020. ISBN 978-1-302-92108-8. Published by MARVEL WORLDWIDE, INC., a subsidiary of MARVEL ENTERTAINMENT, LLC. OFFICE OF PUBLICATION: 1290 Avenue of the Americas, New York, NY 10104. © 2020 MARVEL No similarity between any of the names, characters, persons, and/or institutions in this magazine with those of any living or dead person or institution is intended, and any such similarity which may exist is purely coincidental. **Printed in Canada.** KEVIN FEIGE, Chief Creative Officer; DAN BUCKLEY, President, Marvel Entertainment; JOHN NEE, Publisher; JOE QUESADA, EVP & Creative Director; TOM BREVOORT, SVP of Publishing; DAVID BOGART, Associate Publisher & SVP of Talent Affairs; Publishing & Partnership; DAVID GABRIEL, VP of Print & Digital Publishing; JEFF YOUNGQUIST, VP of Production & Special Projects; DAN CARR, Executive Director of Publishing Technology; ALEX MORALES, Director of Publishing Operations; DAN EDINGTON, Managing Editor; SUSAN CRESPI, Production Manager; STAN LEE, Chairman Emeritus. For information regarding advertising in Marvel Comics or on Marvel.com, please contact Vit DeBellis, Custom Solutions & Integrated Advertising Manager, at vdebellis@marvel.com.

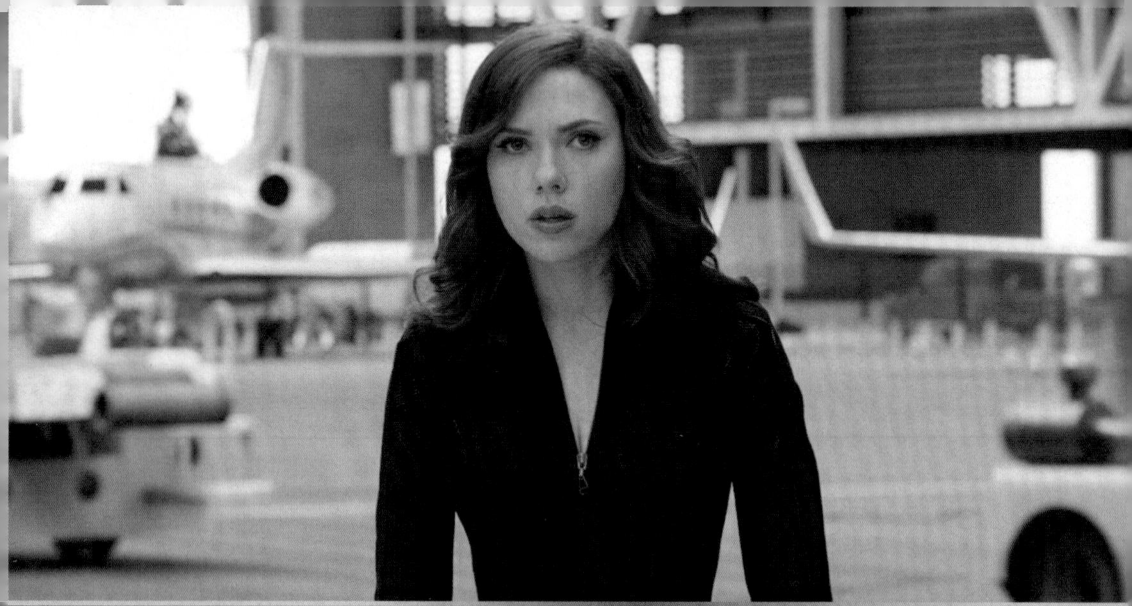

MARVEL'S BLACK WIDOW PRELUDE #1

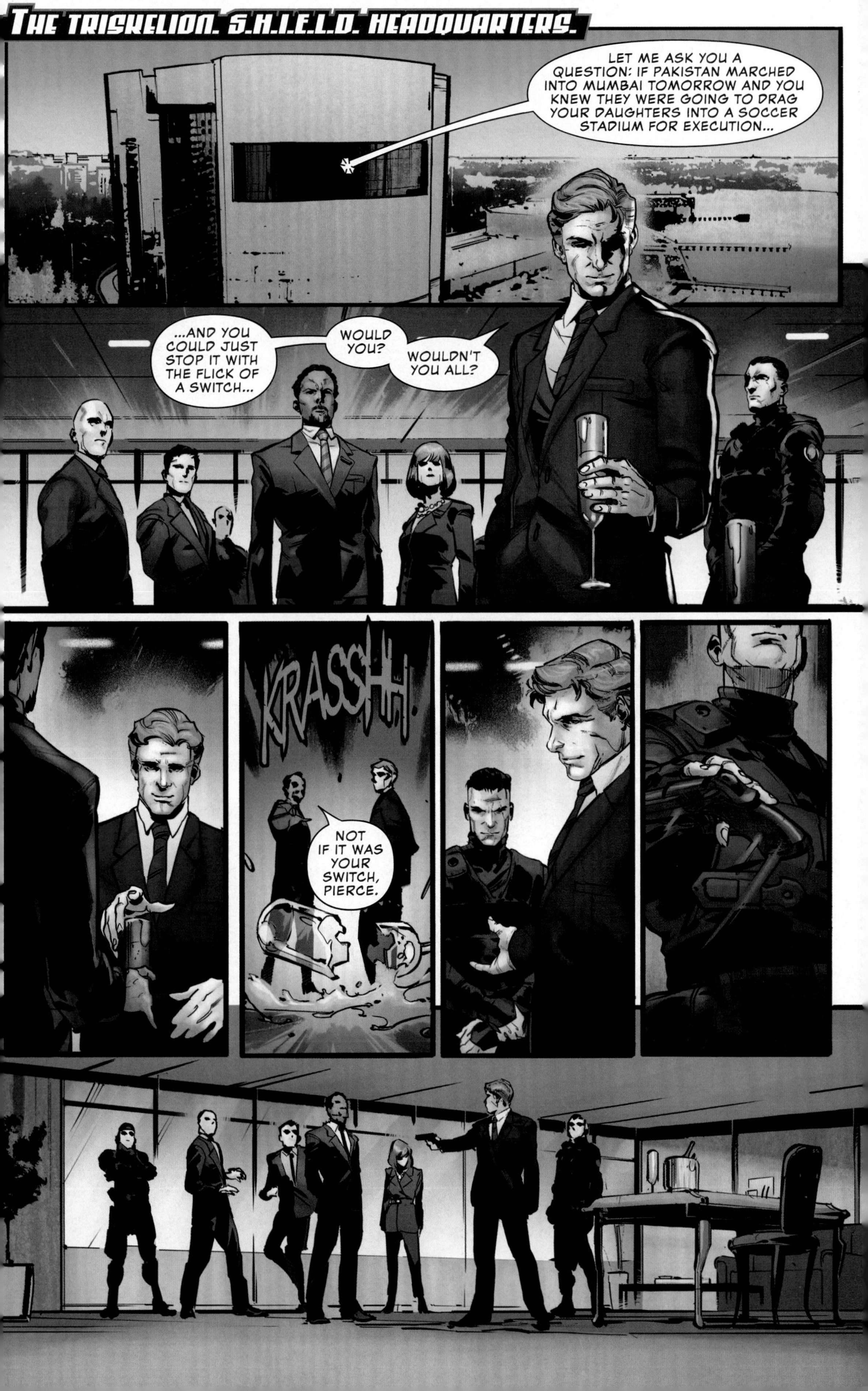
THE TRISKELION. S.H.I.E.L.D. HEADQUARTERS.
LET ME ASK YOU A QUESTION: IF PAKISTAN MARCHED INTO MUMBAI TOMORROW AND YOU KNEW THEY WERE GOING TO DRAG YOUR DAUGHTERS INTO A SOCCER STADIUM FOR EXECUTION...
...AND YOU COULD JUST STOP IT WITH THE FLICK OF A SWITCH...
WOULD YOU?
WOULDN'T YOU ALL?
KRASSHH
NOT IF IT WAS YOUR SWITCH, PIERCE.

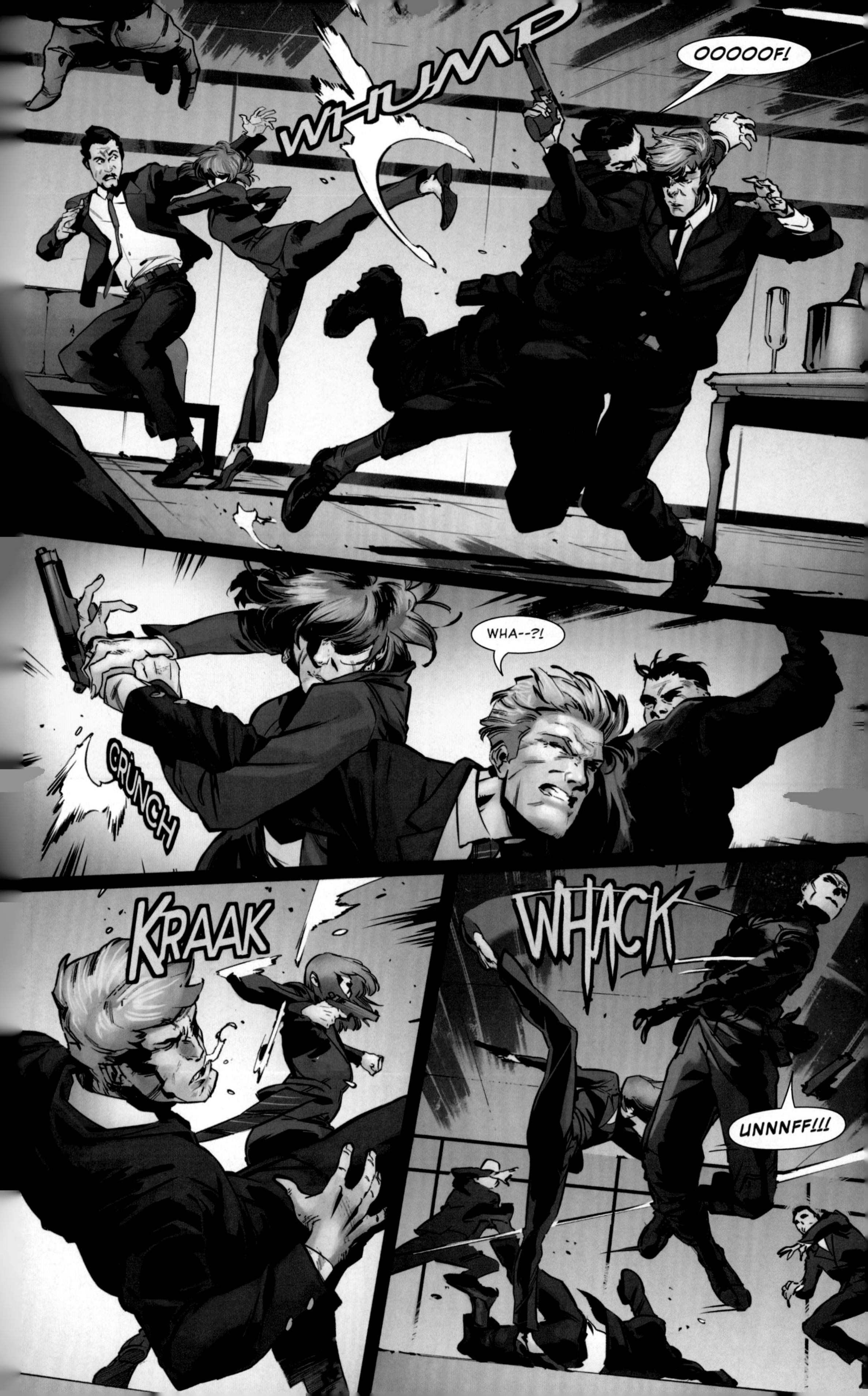

WHUMP
OOOOOF!
WHA--?!
CRUNCH
KRAAK
WHACK
UNNNFF!!!

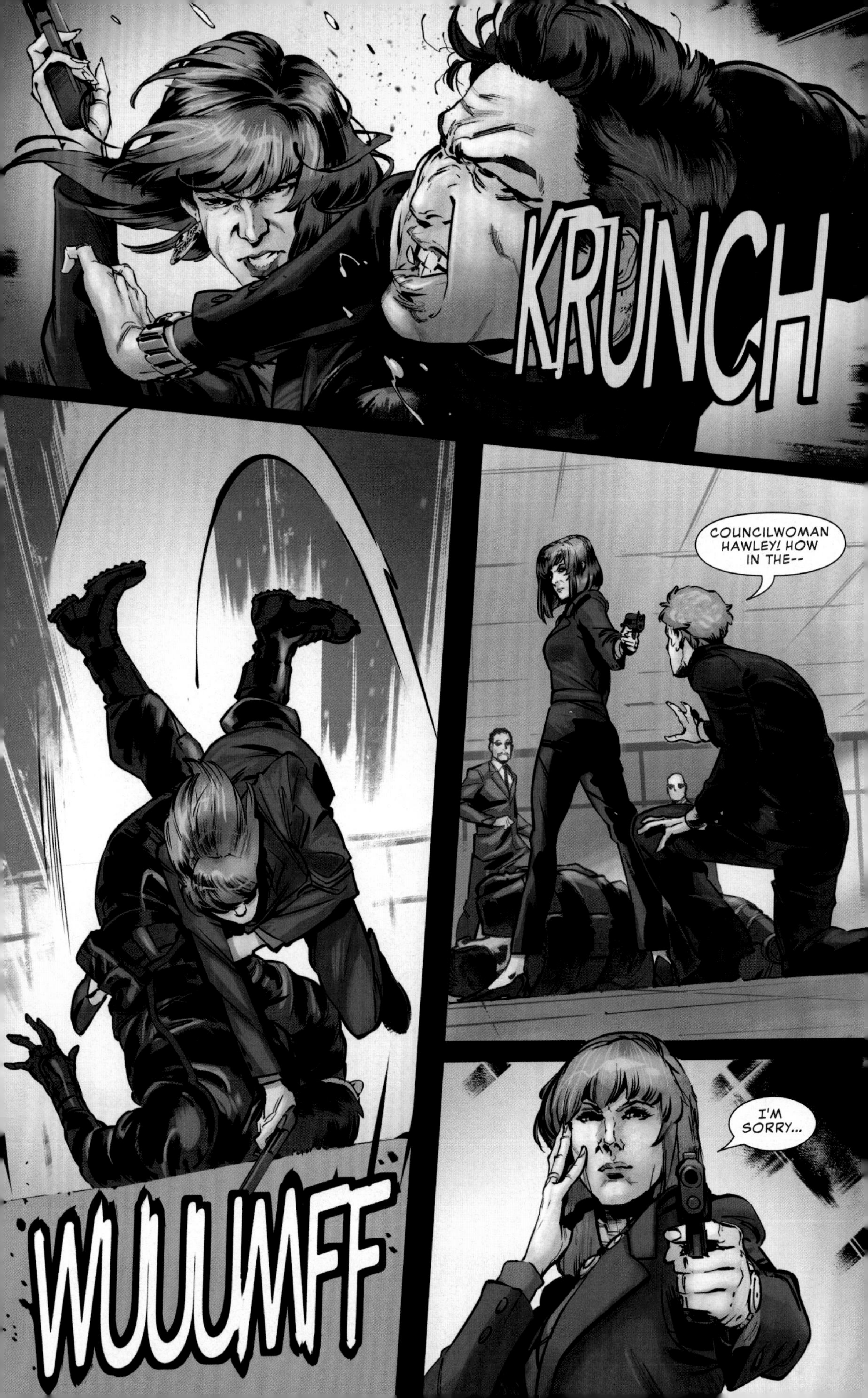
KRUNCH
WUUUMFF
COUNCILWOMAN HAWLEY! HOW IN THE--
I'M SORRY...

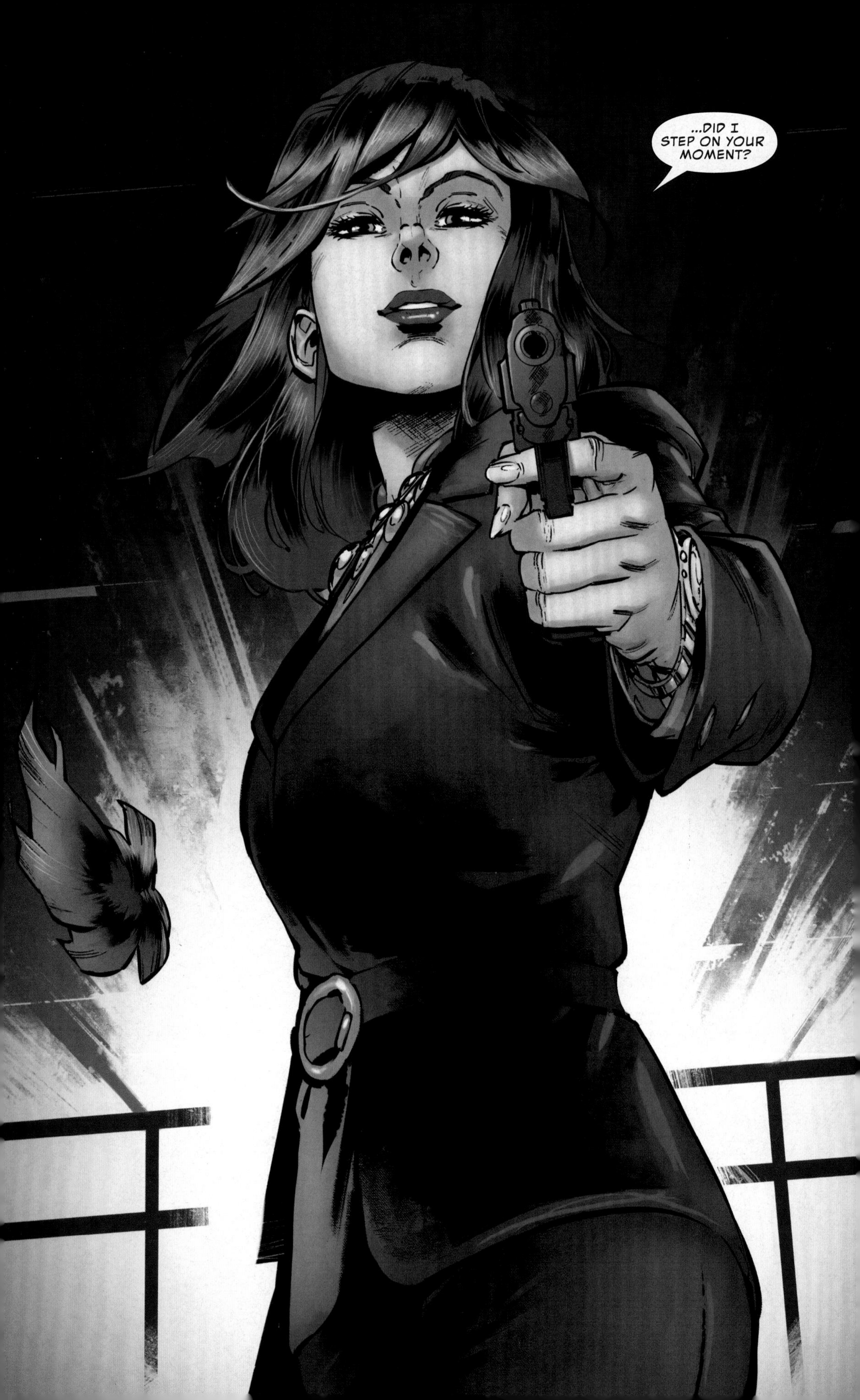
...DID I STEP ON YOUR MOMENT?

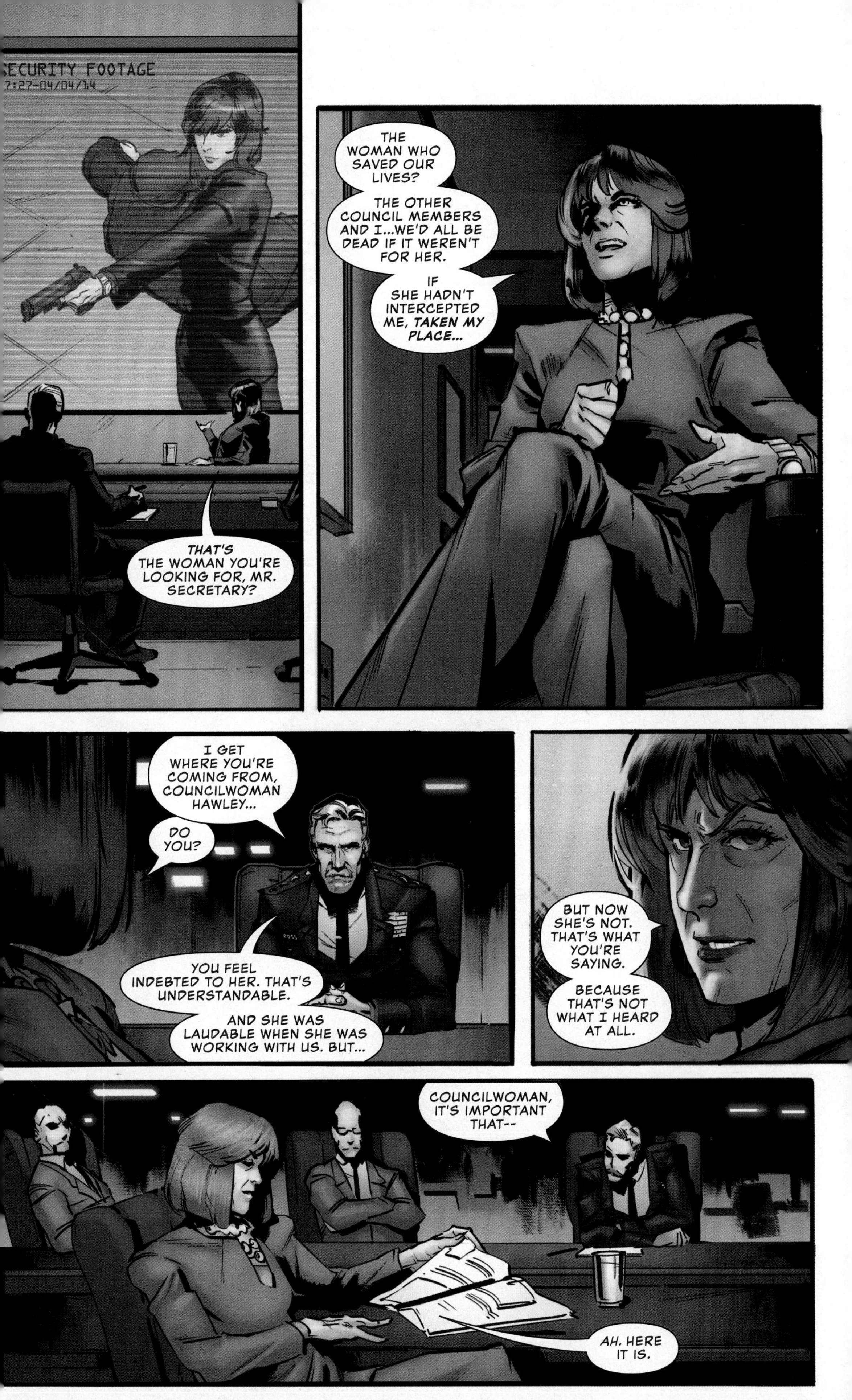

SECURITY FOOTAGE
7:27-04/04/14
THAT'S THE WOMAN YOU'RE LOOKING FOR, MR. SECRETARY?
THE WOMAN WHO SAVED OUR LIVES?
THE OTHER COUNCIL MEMBERS AND I...WE'D ALL BE DEAD IF IT WEREN'T FOR HER.
IF SHE HADN'T INTERCEPTED ME, TAKEN MY PLACE...
I GET WHERE YOU'RE COMING FROM, COUNCILWOMAN HAWLEY...
DO YOU?
YOU FEEL INDEBTED TO HER. THAT'S UNDERSTANDABLE.
AND SHE WAS LAUDABLE WHEN SHE WAS WORKING WITH US. BUT...
BUT NOW SHE'S NOT. THAT'S WHAT YOU'RE SAYING.
BECAUSE THAT'S NOT WHAT I HEARD AT ALL.
COUNCILWOMAN, IT'S IMPORTANT THAT--
AH. HERE IT IS.

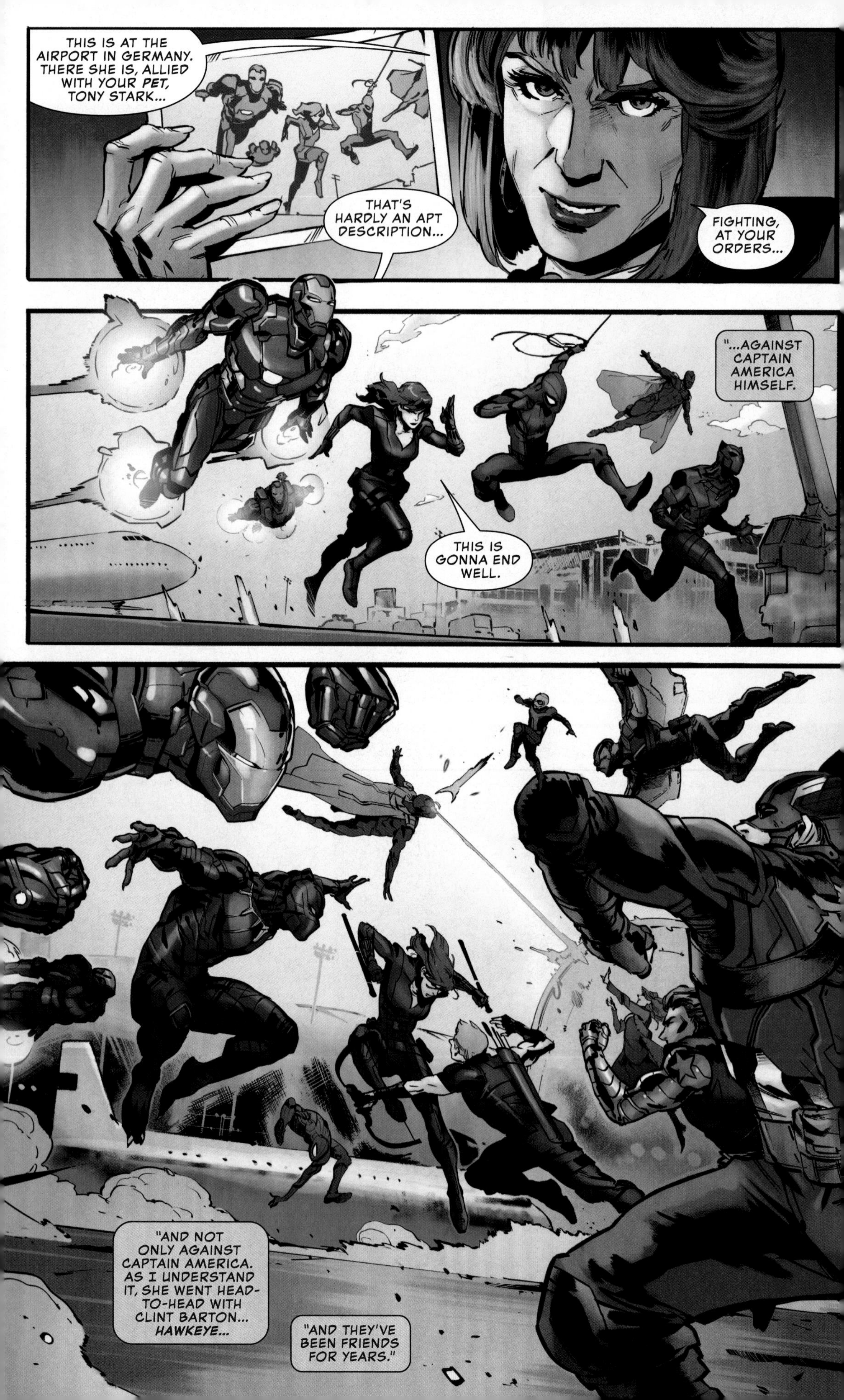
THIS IS AT THE AIRPORT IN GERMANY. THERE SHE IS, ALLIED WITH YOUR *PET,* TONY STARK...
THAT'S HARDLY AN APT DESCRIPTION...
FIGHTING, AT YOUR ORDERS...
"...AGAINST CAPTAIN AMERICA HIMSELF.
THIS IS GONNA END WELL.
"AND NOT ONLY AGAINST CAPTAIN AMERICA. AS I UNDERSTAND IT, SHE WENT HEAD-TO-HEAD WITH CLINT BARTON... *HAWKEYE...*
"AND THEY'VE BEEN FRIENDS FOR YEARS."

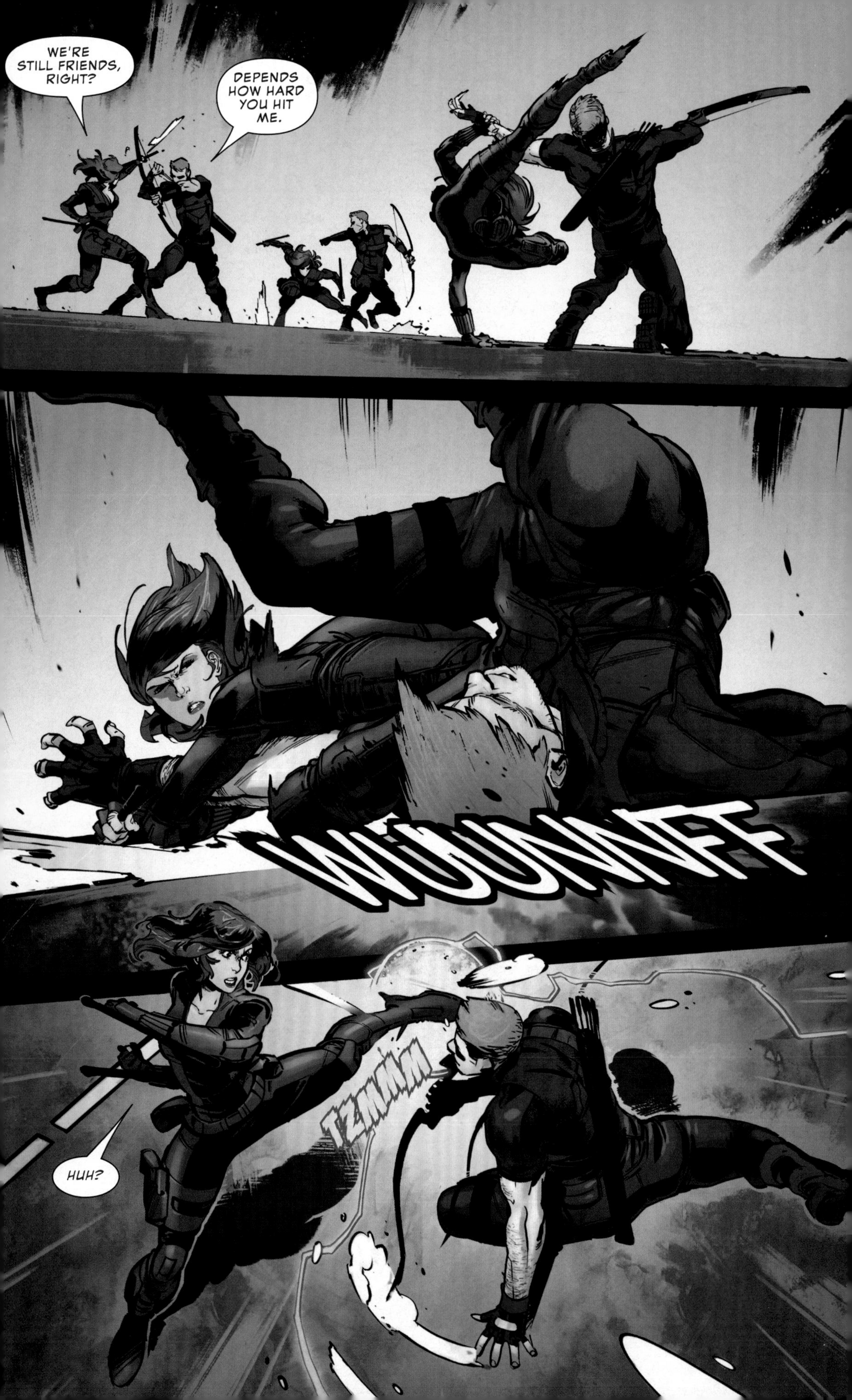
WE'RE STILL FRIENDS, RIGHT?
DEPENDS HOW HARD YOU HIT ME.
WUUNFF
TZMMM
HUH?

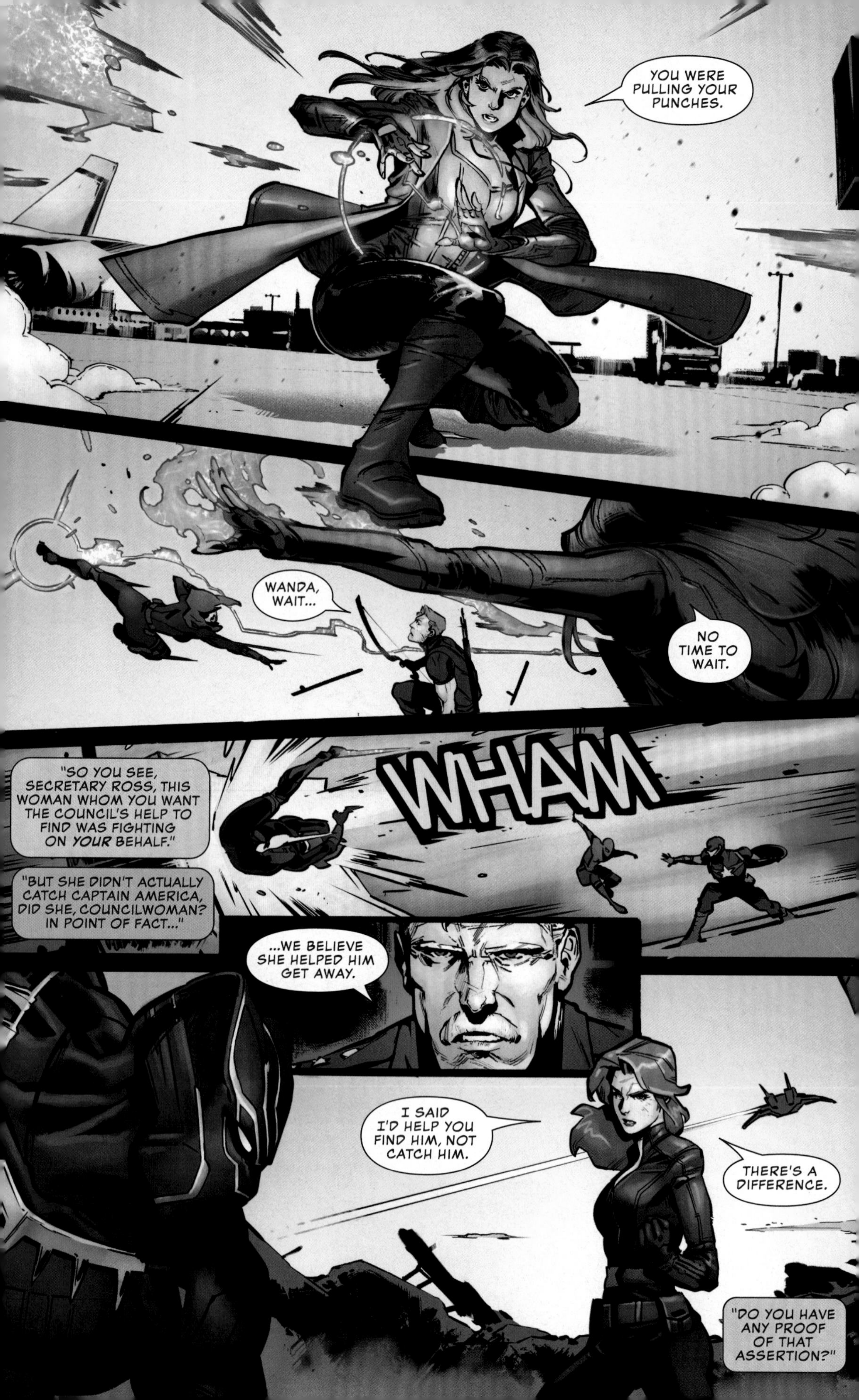
YOU WERE PULLING YOUR PUNCHES.
WANDA, WAIT...
NO TIME TO WAIT.
WHAM
"SO YOU SEE, SECRETARY ROSS, THIS WOMAN WHOM YOU WANT THE COUNCIL'S HELP TO FIND WAS FIGHTING ON YOUR BEHALF."
"BUT SHE DIDN'T ACTUALLY CATCH CAPTAIN AMERICA, DID SHE, COUNCILWOMAN? IN POINT OF FACT..."
...WE BELIEVE SHE HELPED HIM GET AWAY.
I SAID I'D HELP YOU FIND HIM, NOT CATCH HIM.
THERE'S A DIFFERENCE.
"DO YOU HAVE ANY PROOF OF THAT ASSERTION?"

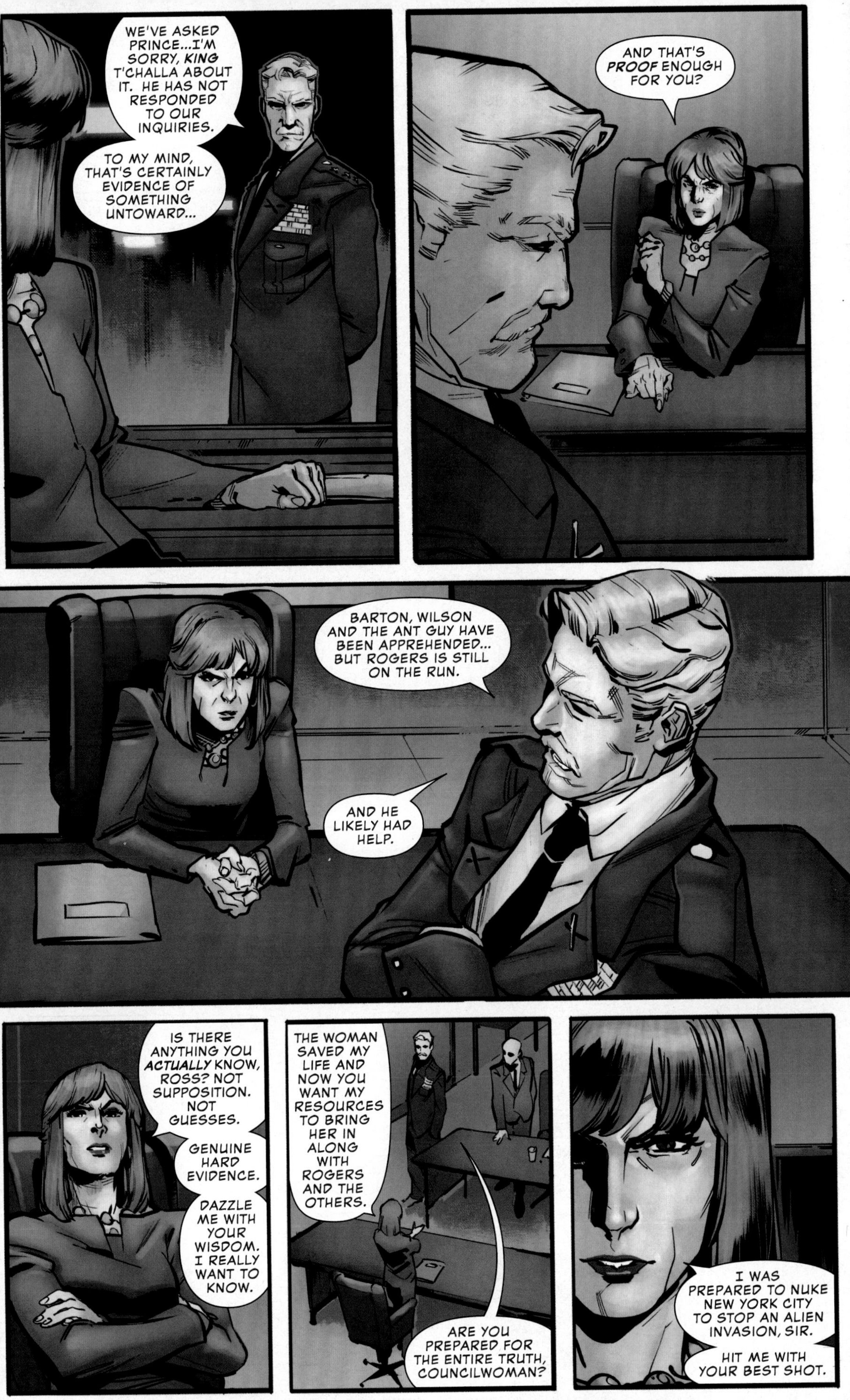
WE'VE ASKED PRINCE...I'M SORRY, *KING* T'CHALLA ABOUT IT. HE HAS NOT RESPONDED TO OUR INQUIRIES.
TO MY MIND, THAT'S CERTAINLY EVIDENCE OF SOMETHING UNTOWARD...
AND THAT'S *PROOF* ENOUGH FOR YOU?
BARTON, WILSON AND THE ANT GUY HAVE BEEN APPREHENDED... BUT ROGERS IS STILL ON THE RUN.
AND HE LIKELY HAD HELP.
IS THERE ANYTHING YOU *ACTUALLY* KNOW, ROSS? NOT SUPPOSITION. NOT GUESSES.
GENUINE HARD EVIDENCE.
DAZZLE ME WITH YOUR WISDOM. I REALLY WANT TO KNOW.
THE WOMAN SAVED MY LIFE AND NOW YOU WANT MY RESOURCES TO BRING HER IN ALONG WITH ROGERS AND THE OTHERS.
ARE YOU PREPARED FOR THE ENTIRE TRUTH, COUNCILWOMAN?
I WAS PREPARED TO NUKE NEW YORK CITY TO STOP AN ALIEN INVASION, SIR.
HIT ME WITH YOUR BEST SHOT.

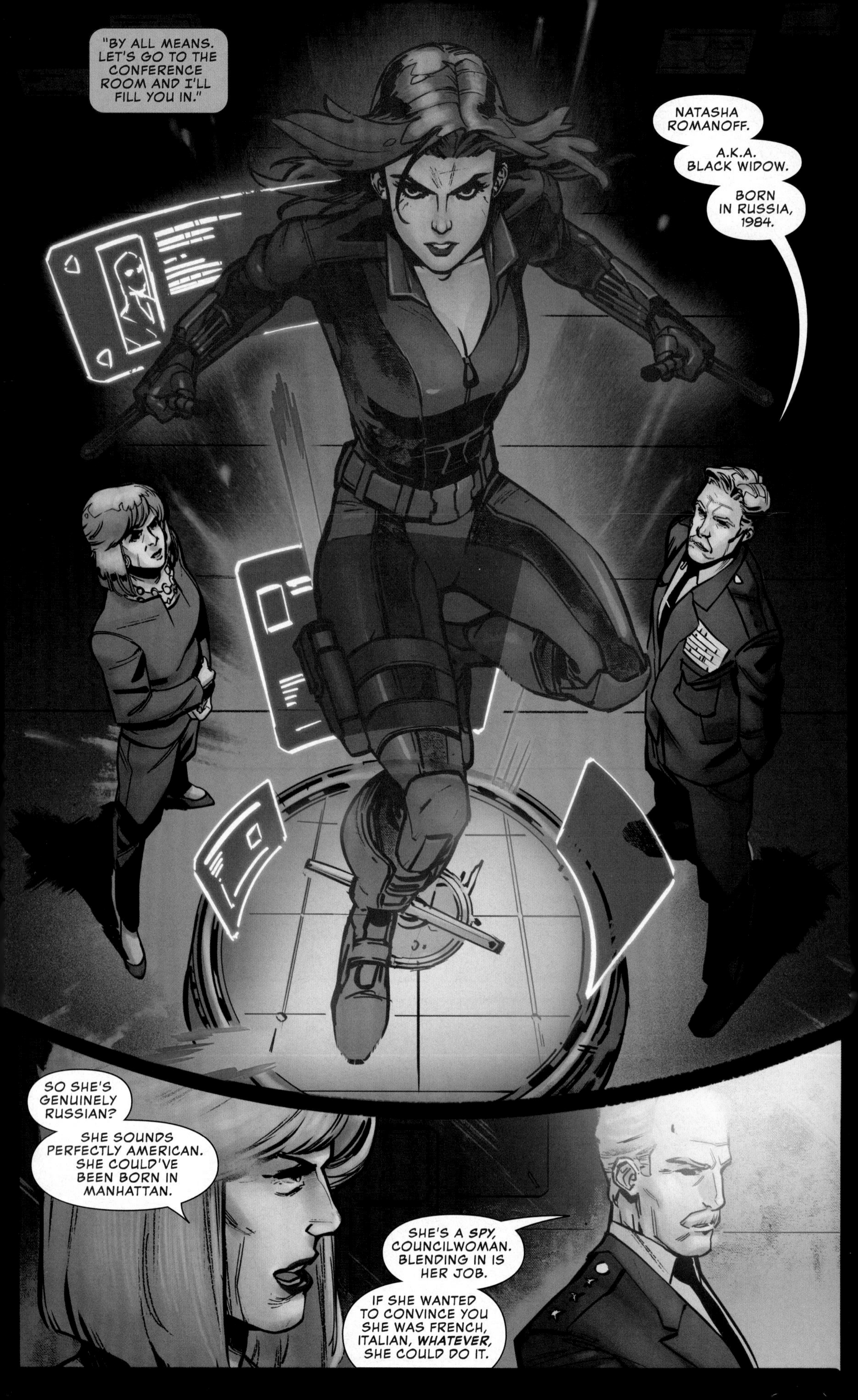
"BY ALL MEANS. LET'S GO TO THE CONFERENCE ROOM AND I'LL FILL YOU IN."
NATASHA ROMANOFF.
A.K.A. BLACK WIDOW.
BORN IN RUSSIA, 1984.
SO SHE'S GENUINELY RUSSIAN?
SHE SOUNDS PERFECTLY AMERICAN. SHE COULD'VE BEEN BORN IN MANHATTAN.
SHE'S A *SPY*, COUNCILWOMAN. BLENDING IN IS HER JOB.
IF SHE WANTED TO CONVINCE YOU SHE WAS FRENCH, ITALIAN, ***WHATEVER***, SHE COULD DO IT.

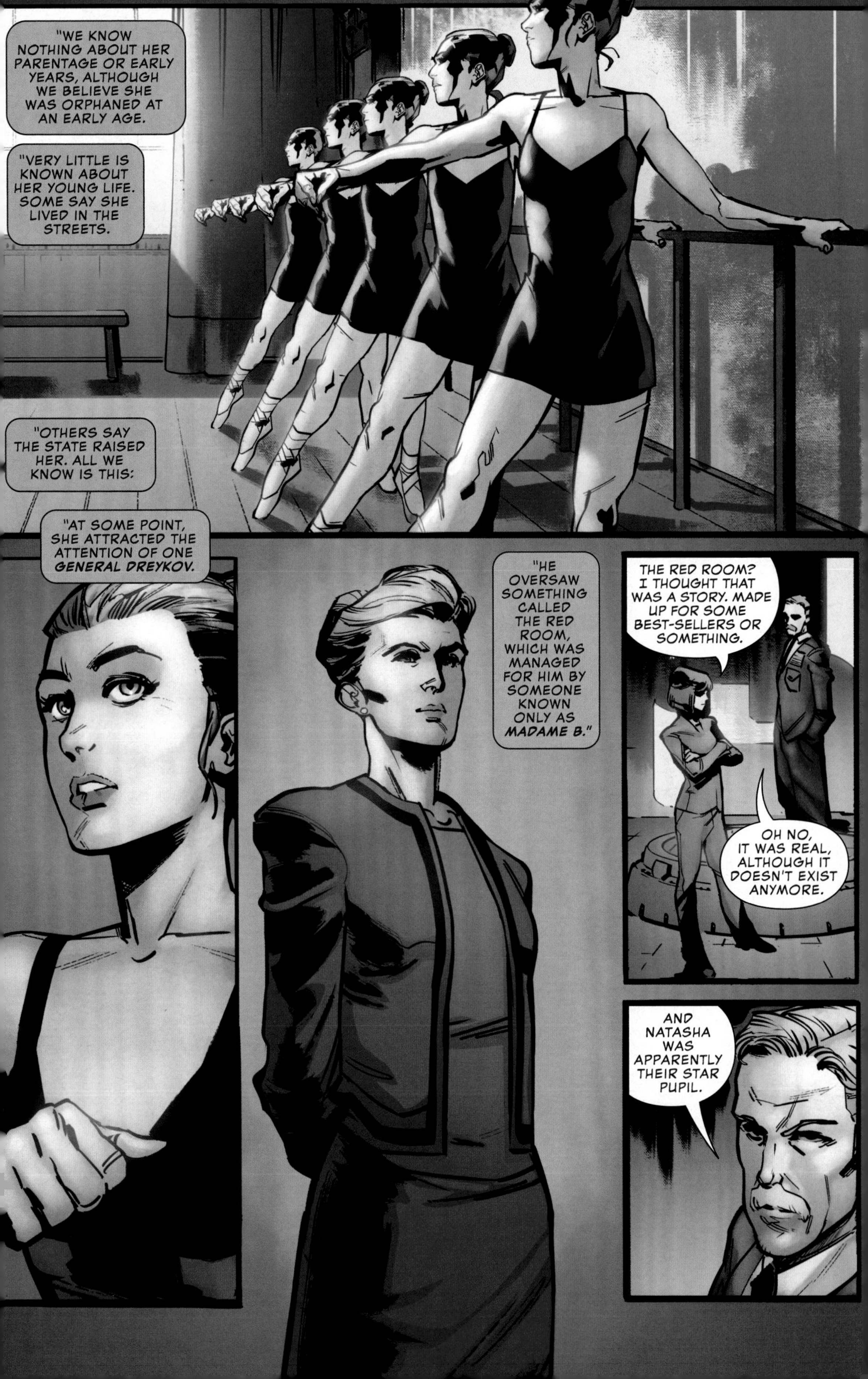
"WE KNOW NOTHING ABOUT HER PARENTAGE OR EARLY YEARS, ALTHOUGH WE BELIEVE SHE WAS ORPHANED AT AN EARLY AGE.
"VERY LITTLE IS KNOWN ABOUT HER YOUNG LIFE. SOME SAY SHE LIVED IN THE STREETS.
"OTHERS SAY THE STATE RAISED HER. ALL WE KNOW IS THIS:
"AT SOME POINT, SHE ATTRACTED THE ATTENTION OF ONE *GENERAL DREYKOV.*
"HE OVERSAW SOMETHING CALLED THE RED ROOM, WHICH WAS MANAGED FOR HIM BY SOMEONE KNOWN ONLY AS *MADAME B.*"
THE RED ROOM? I THOUGHT THAT WAS A STORY. MADE UP FOR SOME BEST-SELLERS OR SOMETHING.
OH NO, IT WAS REAL, ALTHOUGH IT DOESN'T EXIST ANYMORE.
AND NATASHA WAS APPARENTLY THEIR STAR PUPIL.

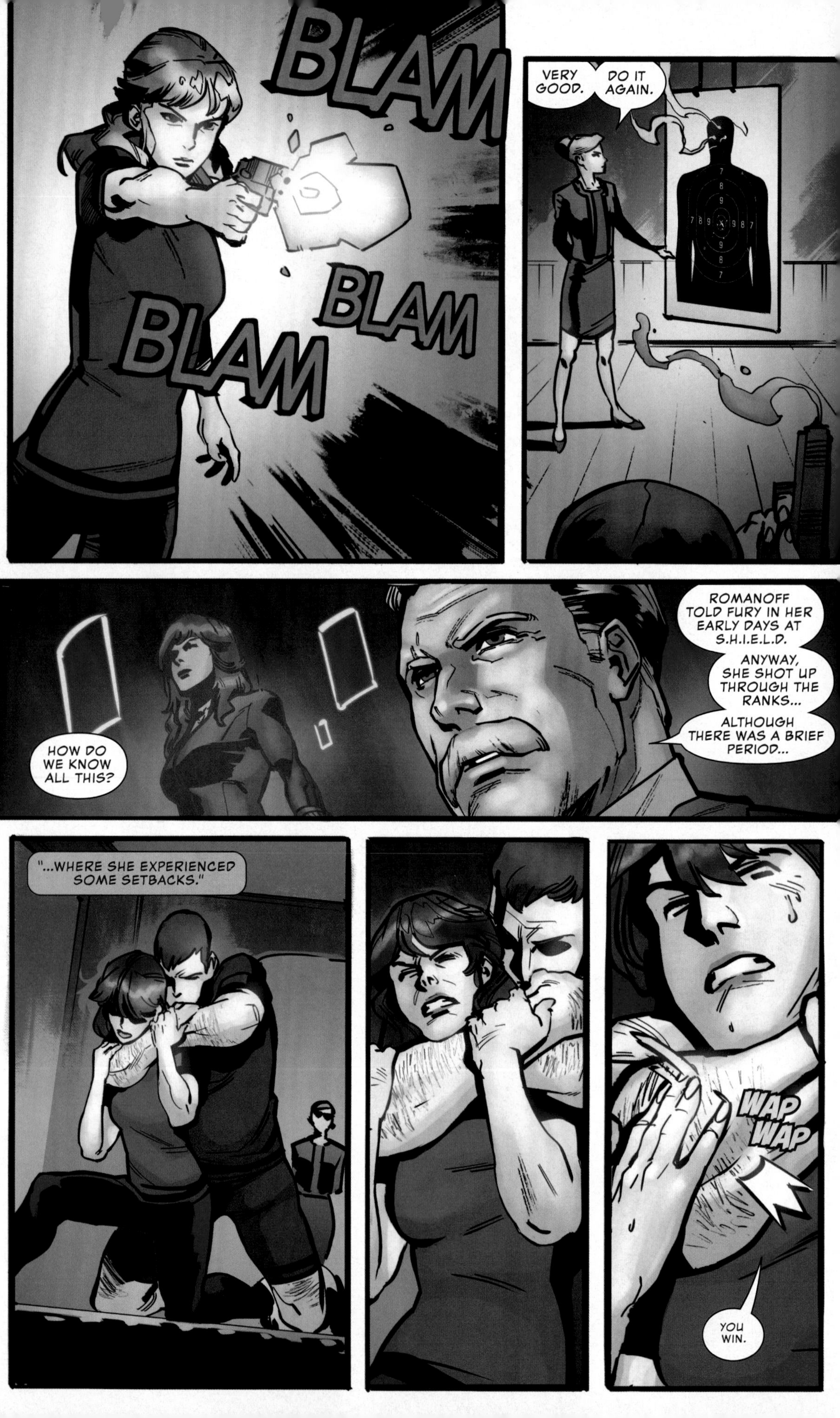
BLAM
BLAM
BLAM
VERY GOOD.
DO IT AGAIN.
HOW DO WE KNOW ALL THIS?
ROMANOFF TOLD FURY IN HER EARLY DAYS AT S.H.I.E.L.D.
ANYWAY, SHE SHOT UP THROUGH THE RANKS...
ALTHOUGH THERE WAS A BRIEF PERIOD...
"...WHERE SHE EXPERIENCED SOME SETBACKS."
WAP
WAP
YOU WIN.

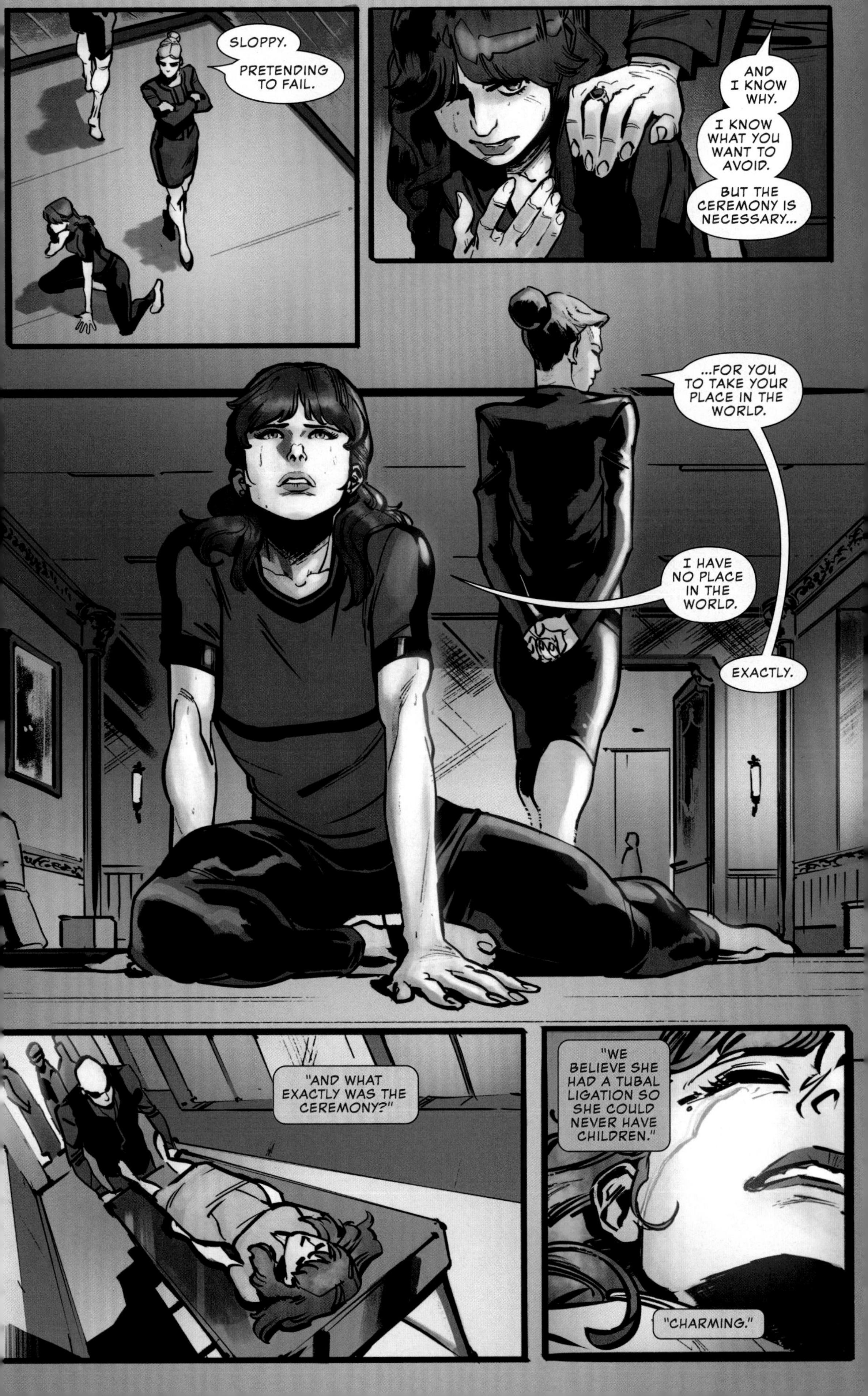
SLOPPY.
PRETENDING TO FAIL.
AND I KNOW WHY.
I KNOW WHAT YOU WANT TO AVOID.
BUT THE CEREMONY IS NECESSARY...
...FOR YOU TO TAKE YOUR PLACE IN THE WORLD.
I HAVE NO PLACE IN THE WORLD.
EXACTLY.
"AND WHAT EXACTLY WAS THE CEREMONY?"
"WE BELIEVE SHE HAD A TUBAL LIGATION SO SHE COULD NEVER HAVE CHILDREN."
"CHARMING."

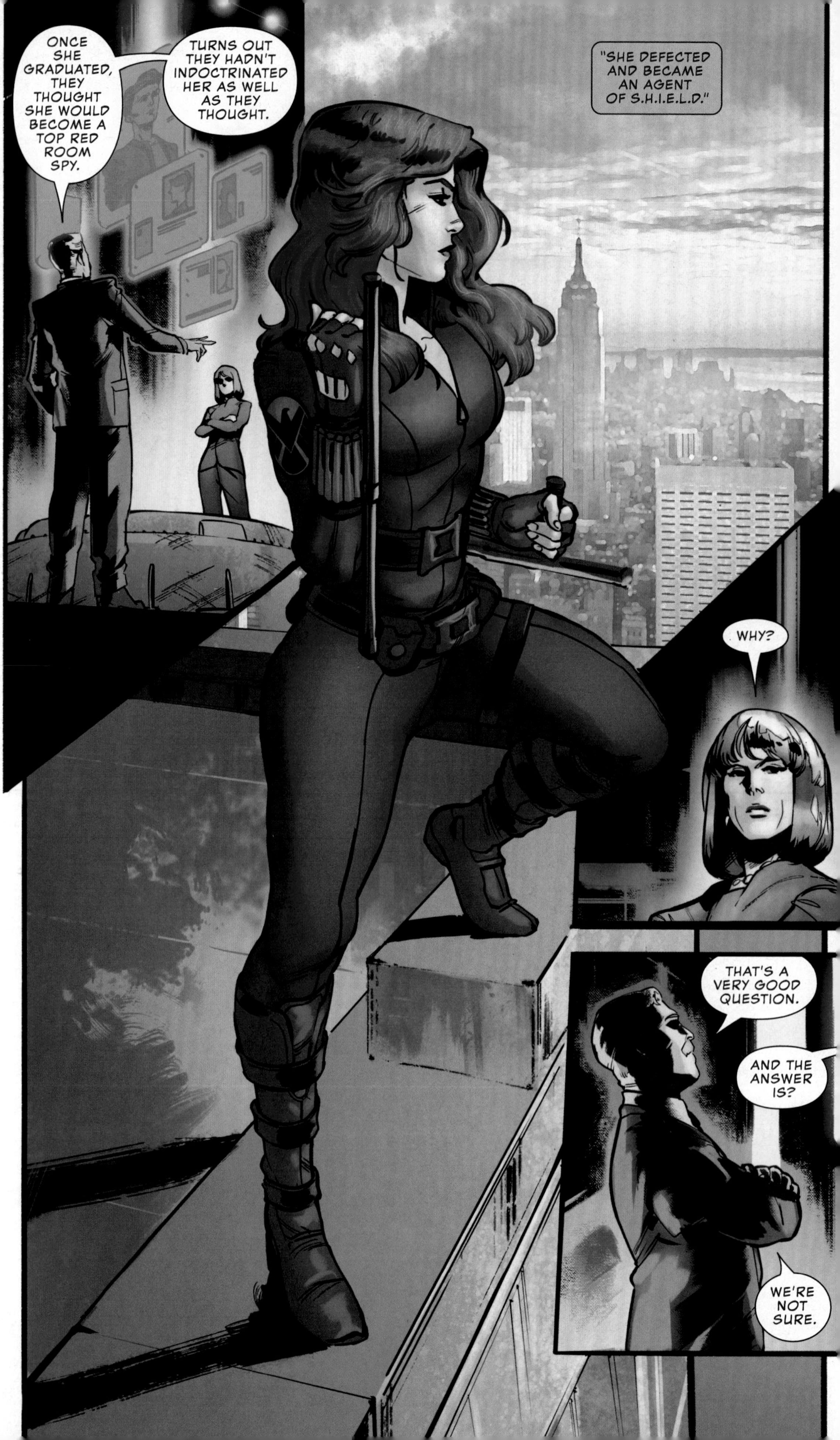
ONCE SHE GRADUATED, THEY THOUGHT SHE WOULD BECOME A TOP RED ROOM SPY.
TURNS OUT THEY HADN'T INDOCTRINATED HER AS WELL AS THEY THOUGHT.
"SHE DEFECTED AND BECAME AN AGENT OF S.H.I.E.L.D."
WHY?
THAT'S A VERY GOOD QUESTION.
AND THE ANSWER IS?
WE'RE NOT SURE.

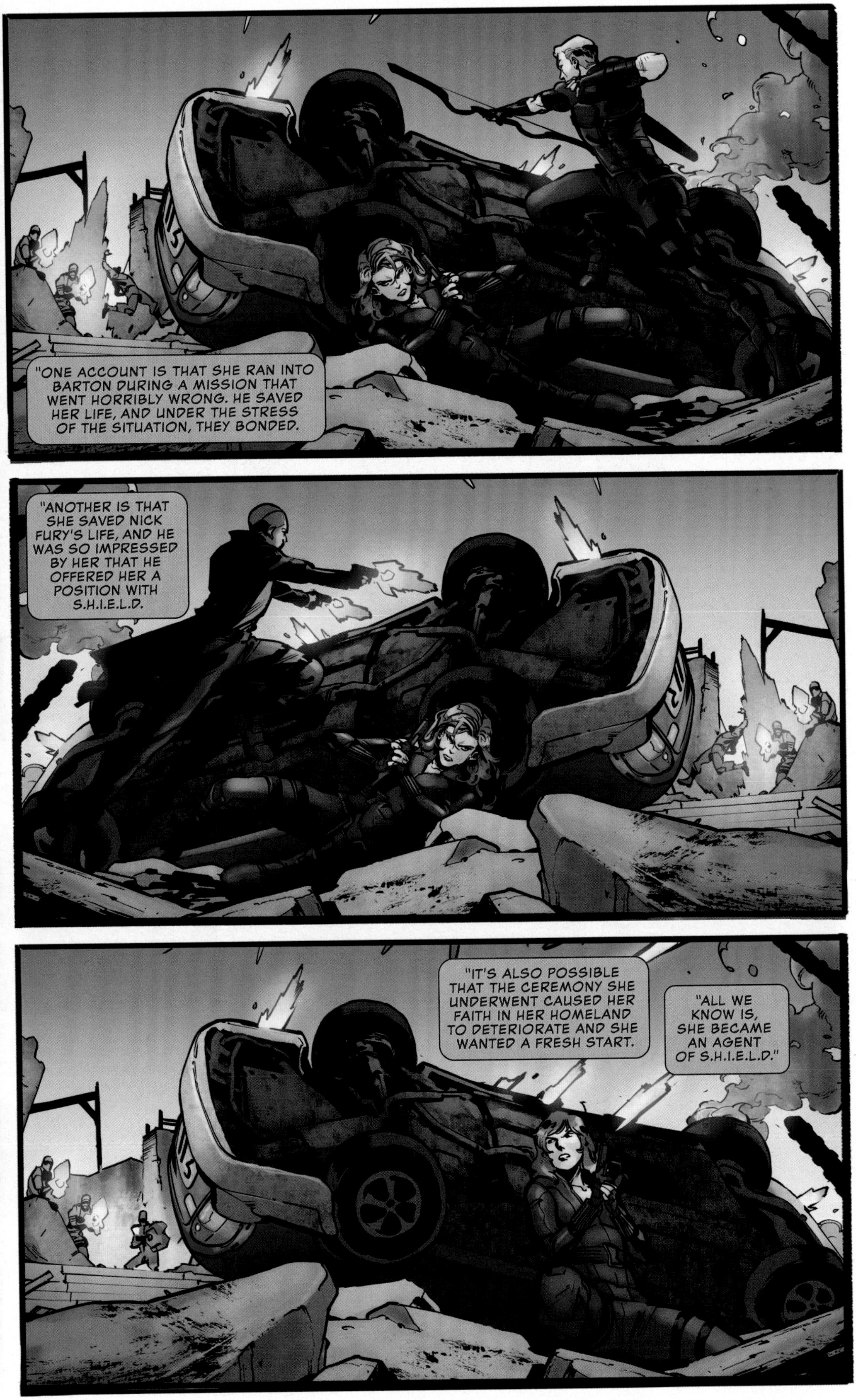
"ONE ACCOUNT IS THAT SHE RAN INTO BARTON DURING A MISSION THAT WENT HORRIBLY WRONG. HE SAVED HER LIFE, AND UNDER THE STRESS OF THE SITUATION, THEY BONDED.
"ANOTHER IS THAT SHE SAVED NICK FURY'S LIFE, AND HE WAS SO IMPRESSED BY HER THAT HE OFFERED HER A POSITION WITH S.H.I.E.L.D.
"IT'S ALSO POSSIBLE THAT THE CEREMONY SHE UNDERWENT CAUSED HER FAITH IN HER HOMELAND TO DETERIORATE AND SHE WANTED A FRESH START.
"ALL WE KNOW IS, SHE BECAME AN AGENT OF S.H.I.E.L.D."

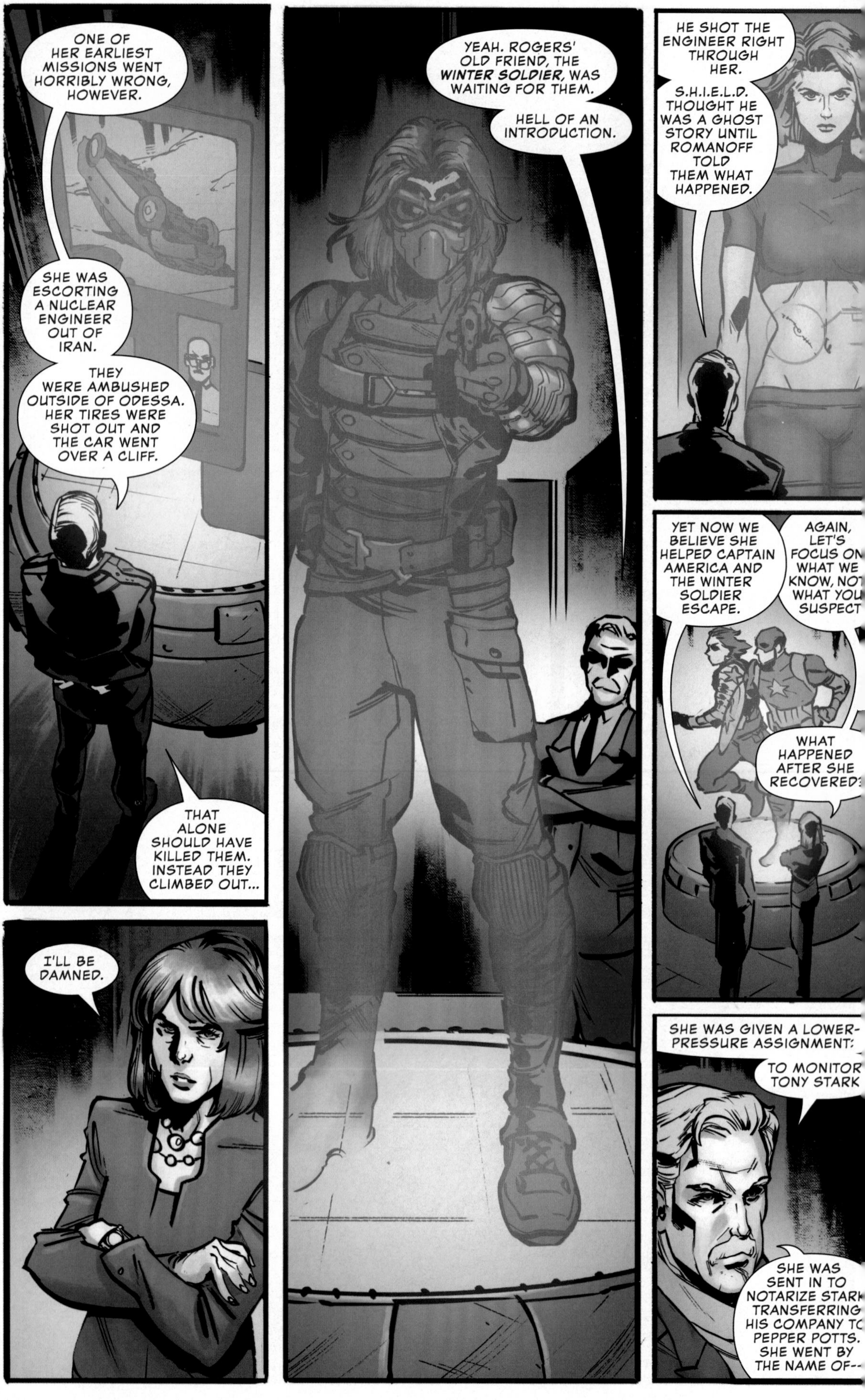
ONE OF HER EARLIEST MISSIONS WENT HORRIBLY WRONG, HOWEVER.
SHE WAS ESCORTING A NUCLEAR ENGINEER OUT OF IRAN.
THEY WERE AMBUSHED OUTSIDE OF ODESSA. HER TIRES WERE SHOT OUT AND THE CAR WENT OVER A CLIFF.
THAT ALONE SHOULD HAVE KILLED THEM. INSTEAD THEY CLIMBED OUT...
I'LL BE DAMNED.
YEAH. ROGERS' OLD FRIEND, THE *WINTER SOLDIER*, WAS WAITING FOR THEM.
HELL OF AN INTRODUCTION.
HE SHOT THE ENGINEER RIGHT THROUGH HER.
S.H.I.E.L.D. THOUGHT HE WAS A GHOST STORY UNTIL ROMANOFF TOLD THEM WHAT HAPPENED.
YET NOW WE BELIEVE SHE HELPED CAPTAIN AMERICA AND THE WINTER SOLDIER ESCAPE.
AGAIN, LET'S FOCUS ON WHAT WE KNOW, NOT WHAT YOU SUSPECT
WHAT HAPPENED AFTER SHE RECOVERED?
SHE WAS GIVEN A LOWER-PRESSURE ASSIGNMENT:
TO MONITOR TONY STARK
SHE WAS SENT IN TO NOTARIZE STARK TRANSFERRING HIS COMPANY TO PEPPER POTTS. SHE WENT BY THE NAME OF--

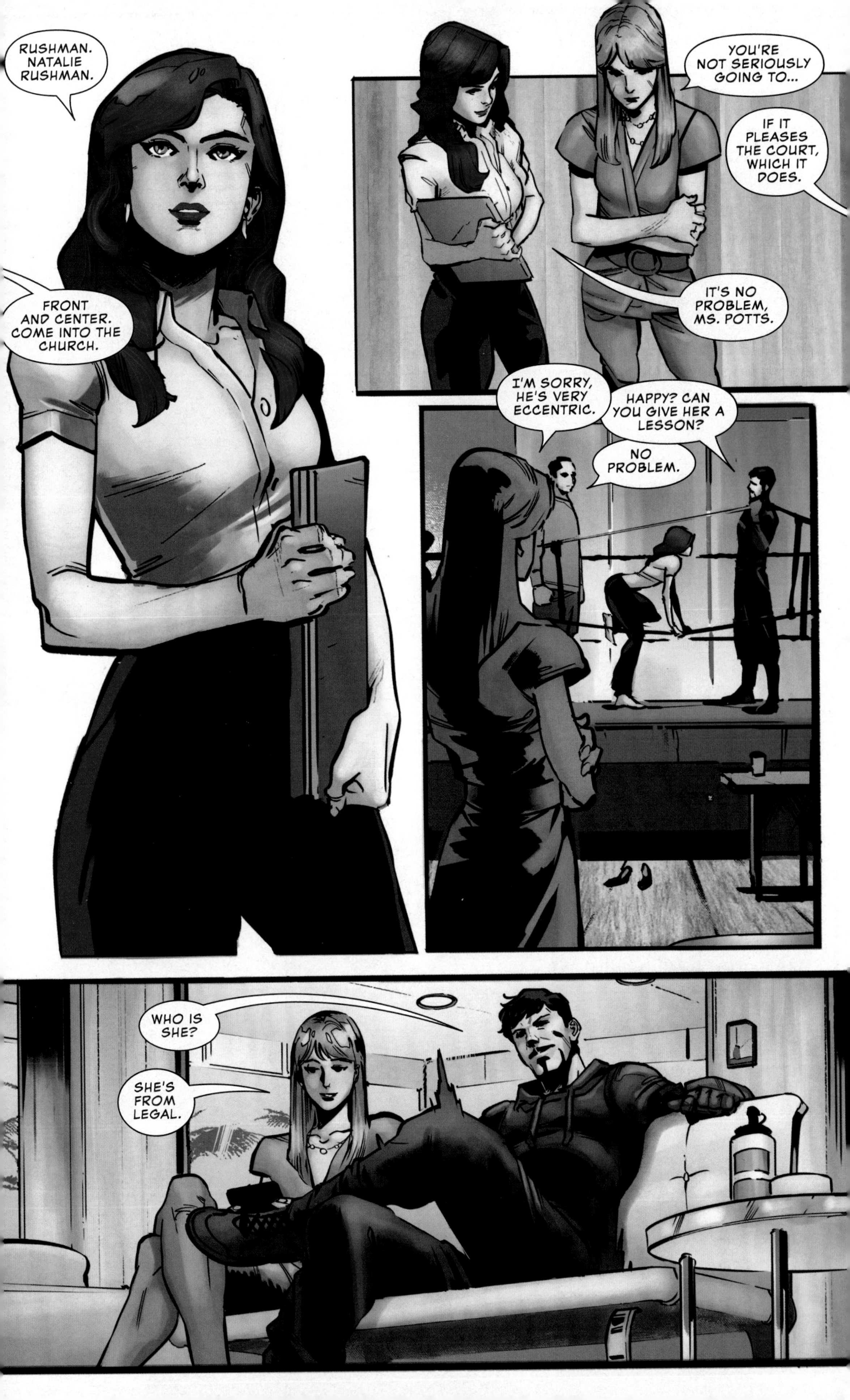
RUSHMAN. NATALIE RUSHMAN.
FRONT AND CENTER. COME INTO THE CHURCH.
YOU'RE NOT SERIOUSLY GOING TO...
IF IT PLEASES THE COURT, WHICH IT DOES.
IT'S NO PROBLEM, MS. POTTS.
I'M SORRY, HE'S VERY ECCENTRIC.
HAPPY? CAN YOU GIVE HER A LESSON?
NO PROBLEM.
WHO IS SHE?
SHE'S FROM LEGAL.

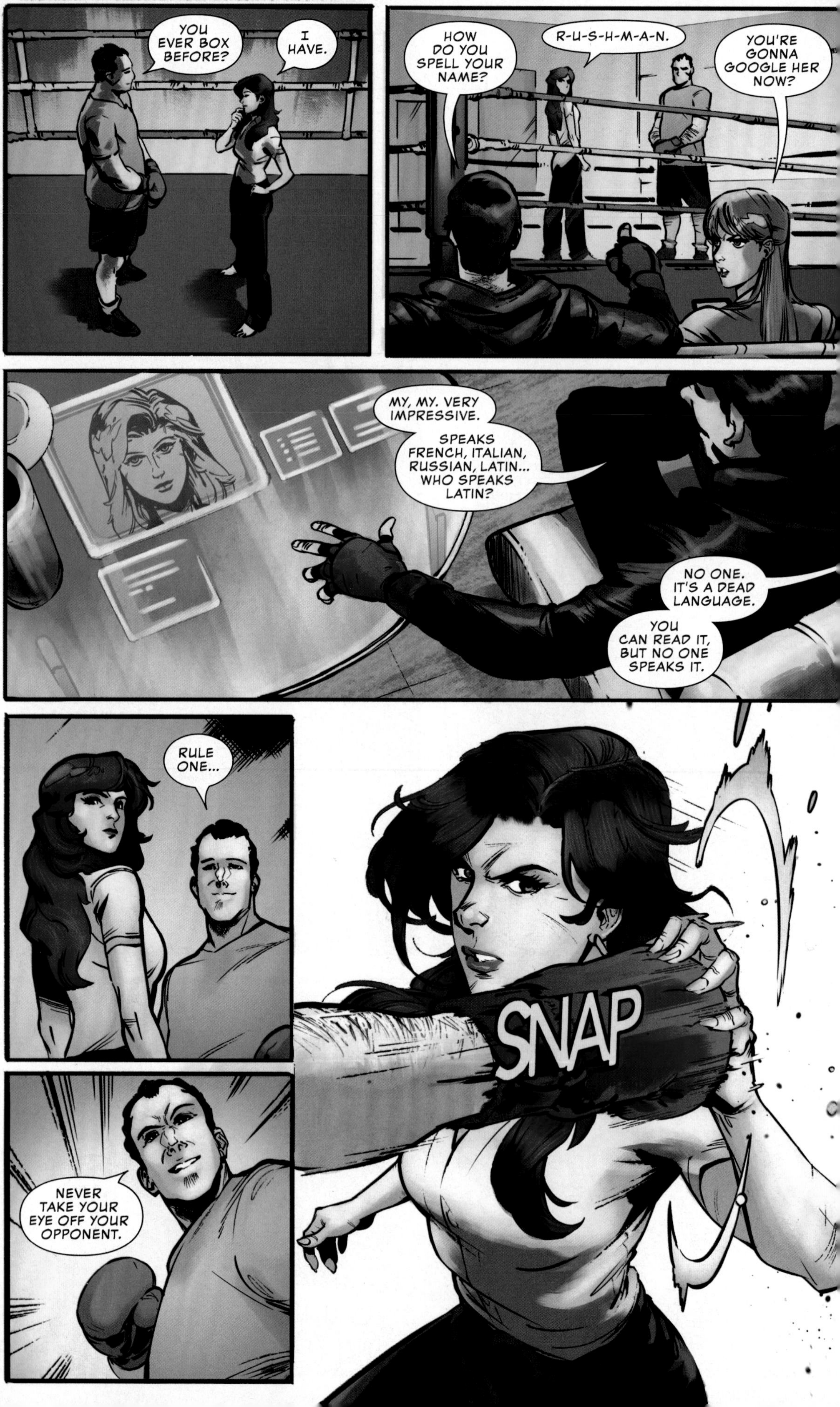

YOU EVER BOX BEFORE?
I HAVE.
HOW DO YOU SPELL YOUR NAME?
R-U-S-H-M-A-N.
YOU'RE GONNA GOOGLE HER NOW?
MY, MY. VERY IMPRESSIVE.
SPEAKS FRENCH, ITALIAN, RUSSIAN, LATIN... WHO SPEAKS LATIN?
NO ONE. IT'S A DEAD LANGUAGE.
YOU CAN READ IT, BUT NO ONE SPEAKS IT.
RULE ONE...
NEVER TAKE YOUR EYE OFF YOUR OPPONENT.
SNAP

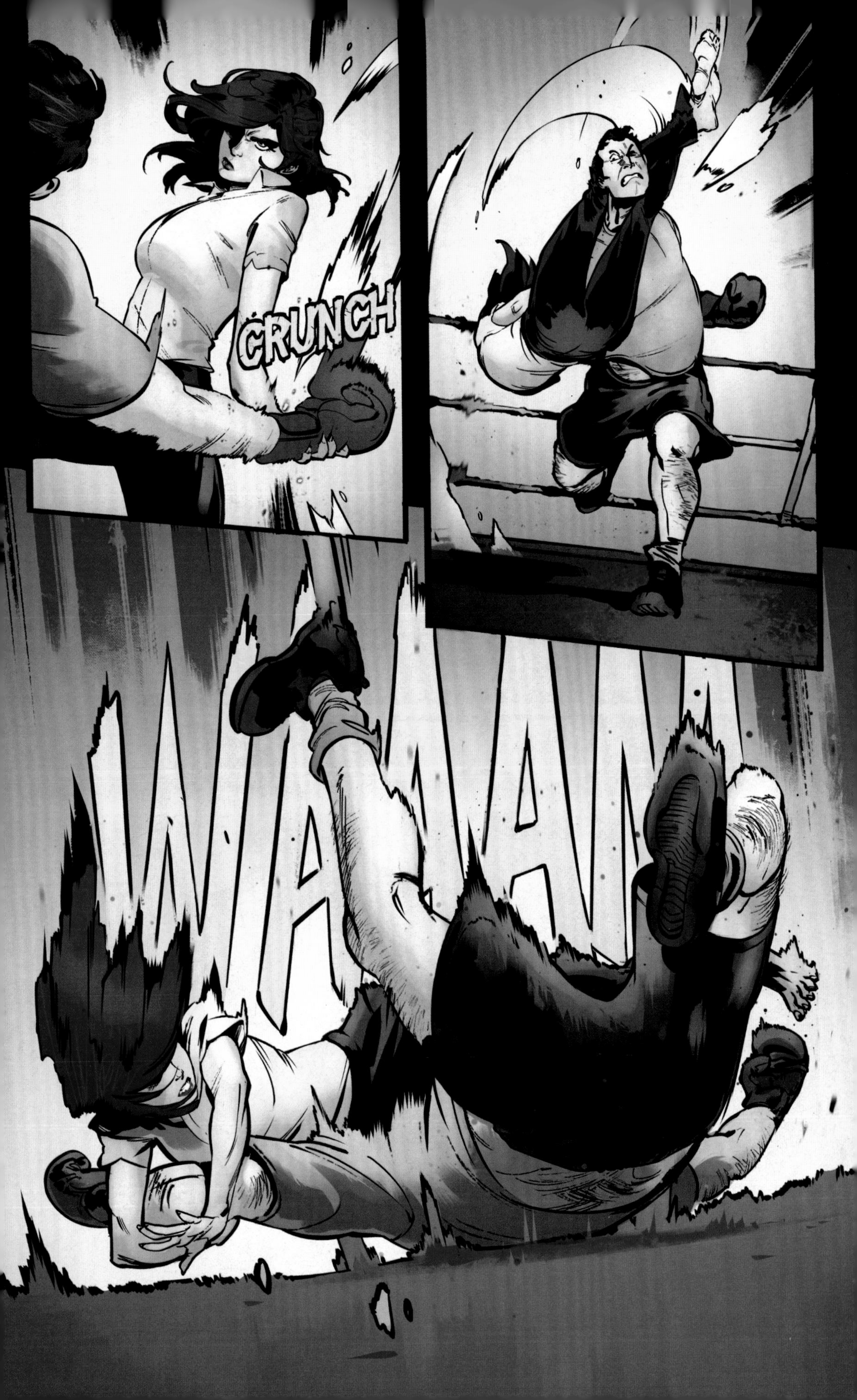
CRUNCH

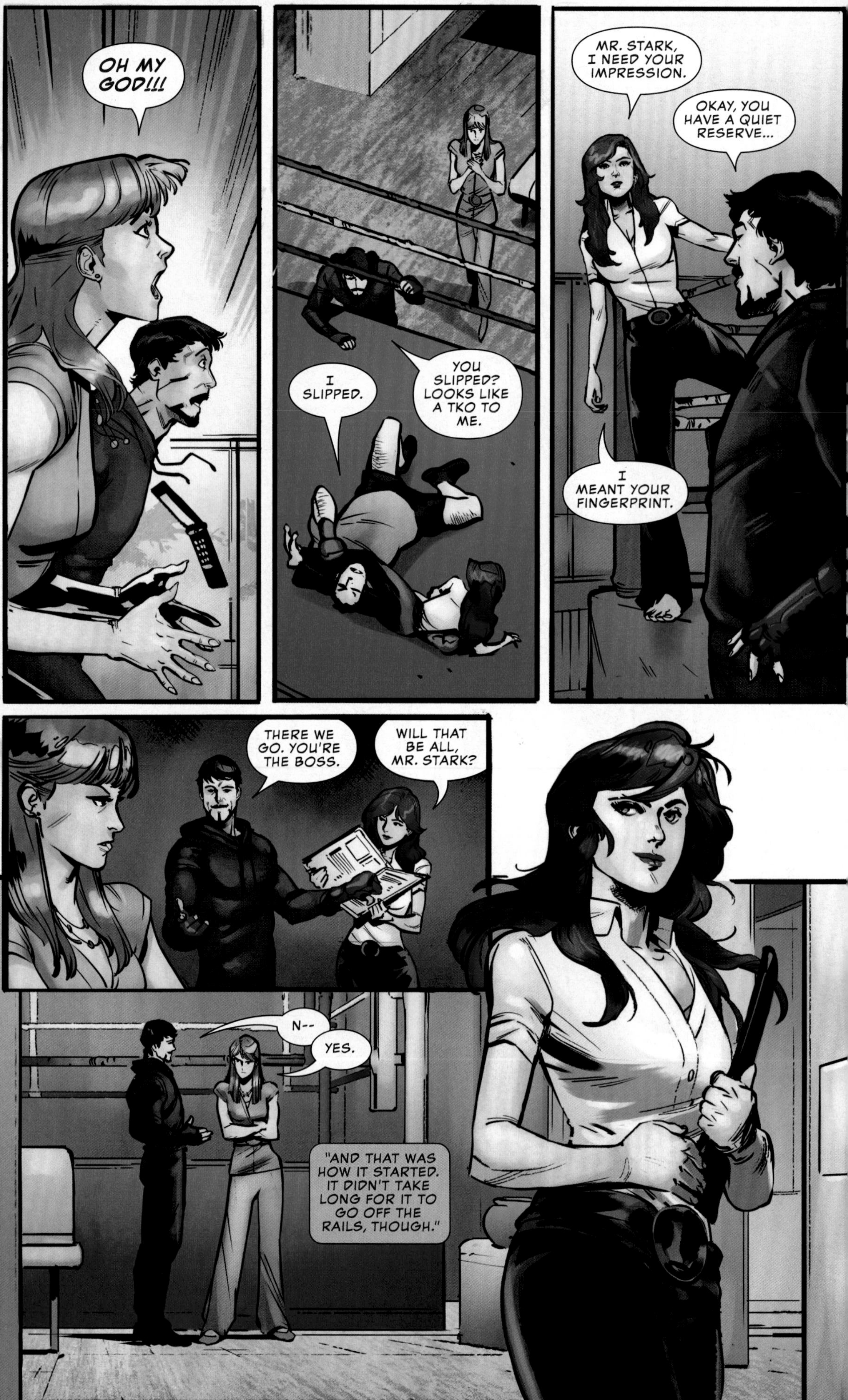
OH MY GOD!!!
I SLIPPED.
YOU SLIPPED? LOOKS LIKE A TKO TO ME.
MR. STARK, I NEED YOUR IMPRESSION.
OKAY, YOU HAVE A QUIET RESERVE...
I MEANT YOUR FINGERPRINT.
THERE WE GO. YOU'RE THE BOSS.
WILL THAT BE ALL, MR. STARK?
N--
YES.
"AND THAT WAS HOW IT STARTED. IT DIDN'T TAKE LONG FOR IT TO GO OFF THE RAILS, THOUGH."

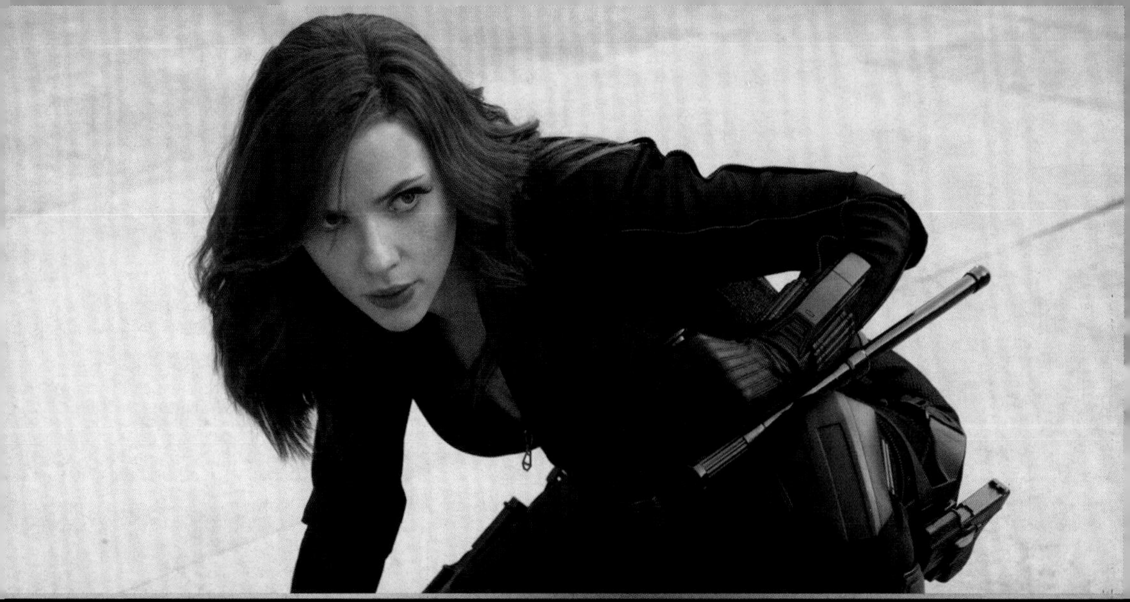

MARVEL'S BLACK WIDOW PRELUDE #2

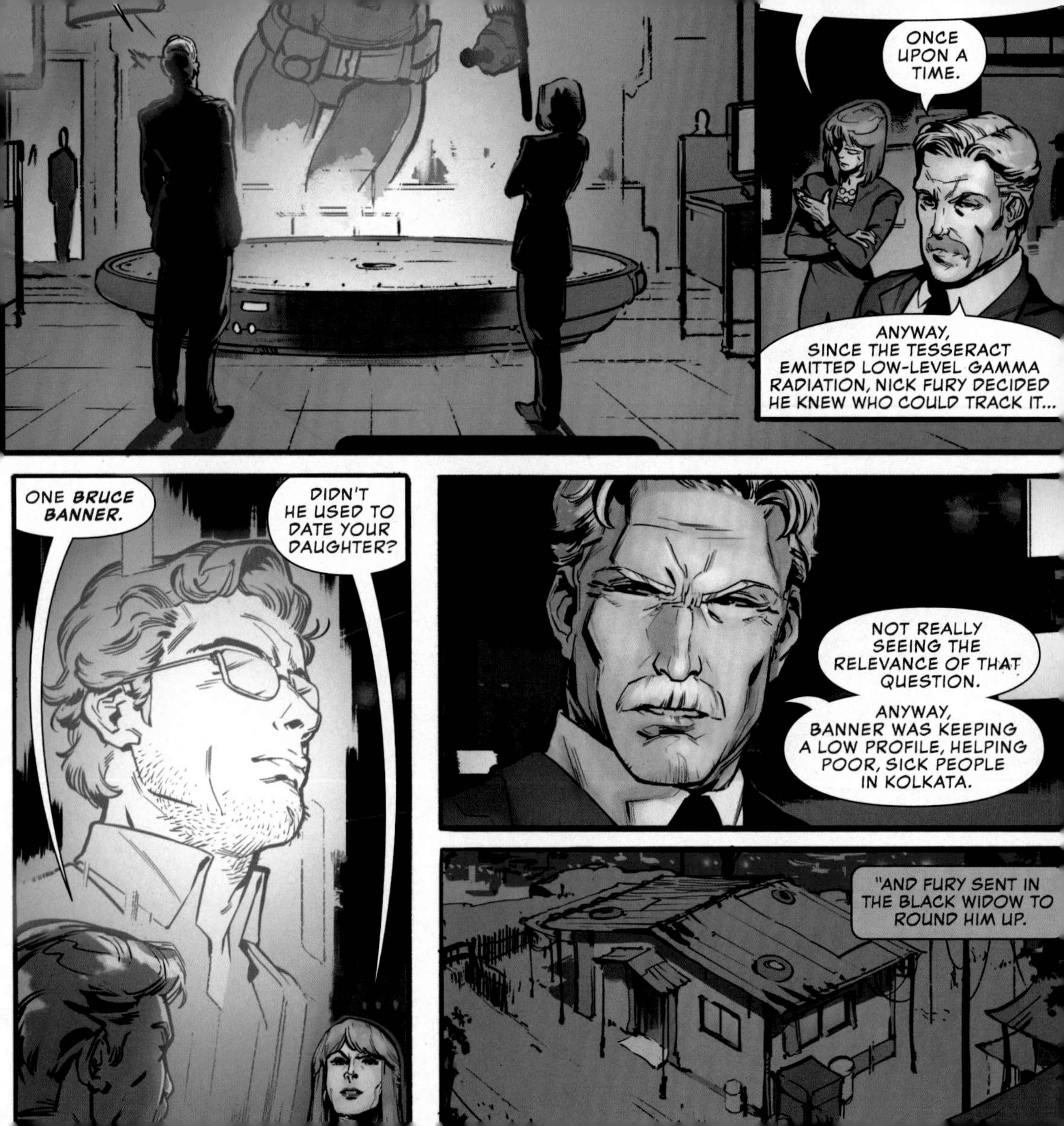
ONCE UPON A TIME.
ANYWAY, SINCE THE TESSERACT EMITTED LOW-LEVEL GAMMA RADIATION, NICK FURY DECIDED HE KNEW WHO COULD TRACK IT...
ONE BRUCE BANNER.
DIDN'T HE USED TO DATE YOUR DAUGHTER?
NOT REALLY SEEING THE RELEVANCE OF THAT QUESTION.
ANYWAY, BANNER WAS KEEPING A LOW PROFILE, HELPING POOR, SICK PEOPLE IN KOLKATA.
"AND FURY SENT IN THE BLACK WIDOW TO ROUND HIM UP.

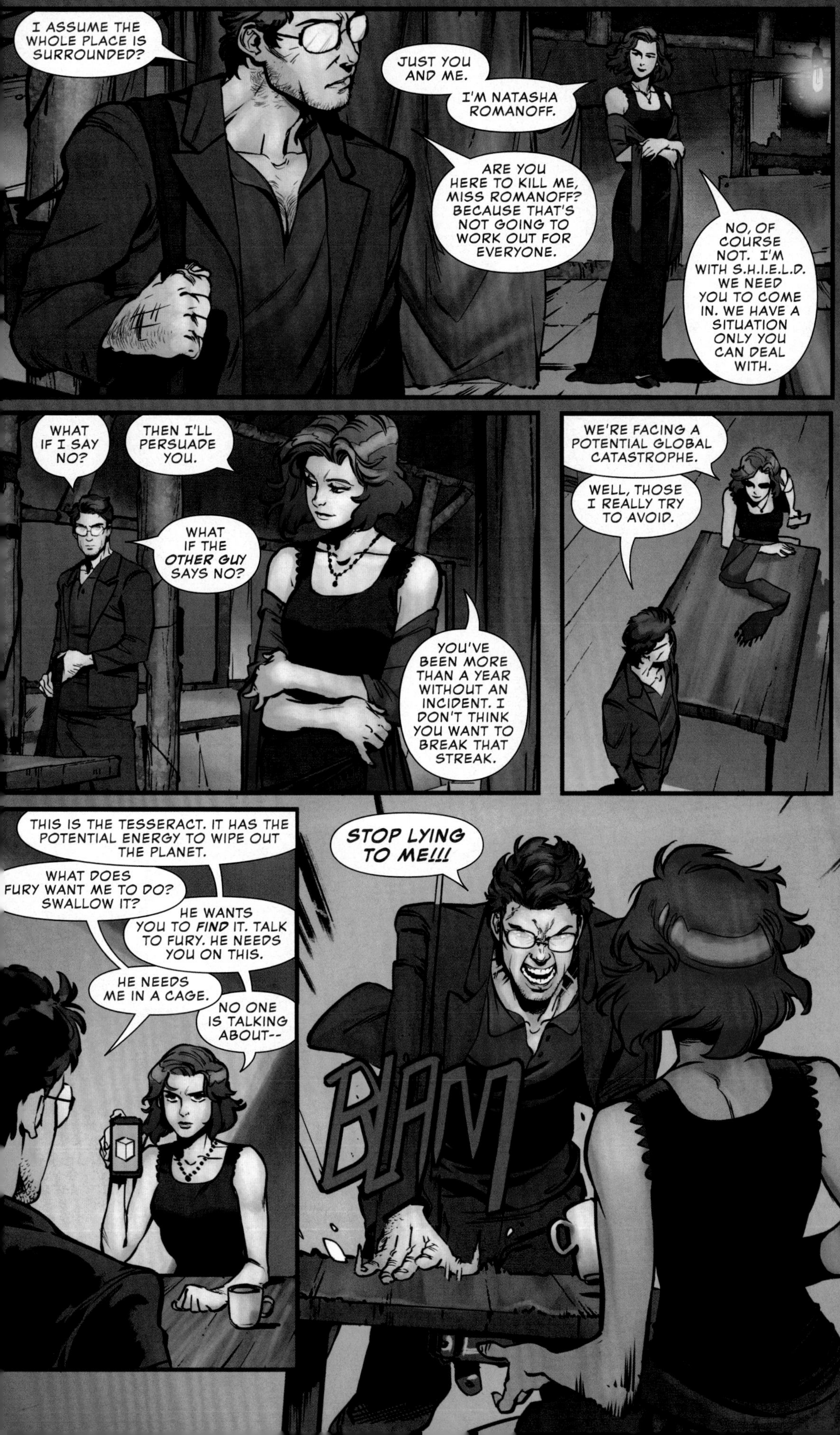
I ASSUME THE WHOLE PLACE IS SURROUNDED?
JUST YOU AND ME.
I'M NATASHA ROMANOFF.
ARE YOU HERE TO KILL ME, MISS ROMANOFF? BECAUSE THAT'S NOT GOING TO WORK OUT FOR EVERYONE.
NO, OF COURSE NOT. I'M WITH S.H.I.E.L.D. WE NEED YOU TO COME IN. WE HAVE A SITUATION ONLY YOU CAN DEAL WITH.
WHAT IF I SAY NO?
THEN I'LL PERSUADE YOU.
WHAT IF THE *OTHER GUY* SAYS NO?
YOU'VE BEEN MORE THAN A YEAR WITHOUT AN INCIDENT. I DON'T THINK YOU WANT TO BREAK THAT STREAK.
WE'RE FACING A POTENTIAL GLOBAL CATASTROPHE.
WELL, THOSE I REALLY TRY TO AVOID.
THIS IS THE TESSERACT. IT HAS THE POTENTIAL ENERGY TO WIPE OUT THE PLANET.
WHAT DOES FURY WANT ME TO DO? SWALLOW IT?
HE WANTS YOU TO *FIND* IT. TALK TO FURY. HE NEEDS YOU ON THIS.
HE NEEDS ME IN A CAGE.
NO ONE IS TALKING ABOUT--
STOP LYING TO ME!!!
BLAM

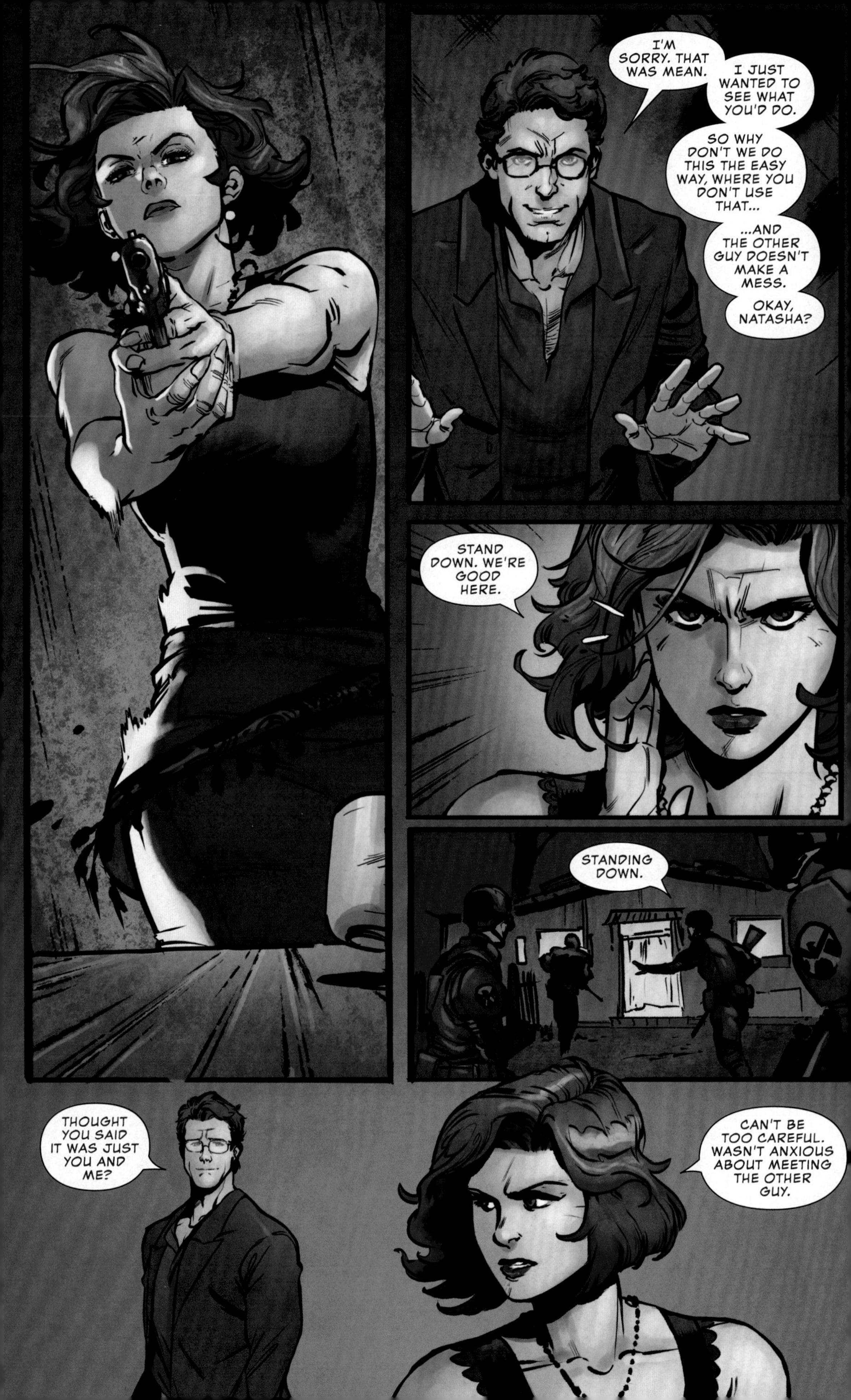
I'M SORRY. THAT WAS MEAN.
I JUST WANTED TO SEE WHAT YOU'D DO.
SO WHY DON'T WE DO THIS THE EASY WAY, WHERE YOU DON'T USE THAT...
...AND THE OTHER GUY DOESN'T MAKE A MESS.
OKAY, NATASHA?
STAND DOWN. WE'RE GOOD HERE.
STANDING DOWN.
THOUGHT YOU SAID IT WAS JUST YOU AND ME?
CAN'T BE TOO CAREFUL. WASN'T ANXIOUS ABOUT MEETING THE OTHER GUY.

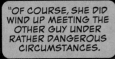

"OF COURSE, SHE DID WIND UP MEETING THE OTHER GUY UNDER RATHER DANGEROUS CIRCUMSTANCES.

"BANNER APPARENTLY HARBORED DISTRUST FOR HER, AND THAT BORE ITSELF OUT WHEN HIS GREEN ALTER EGO, THE *HULK*, EMERGED WHILE SHE AND THE OTHER AVENGERS WERE ON THE S.H.I.E.L.D. HELICARRIER.

"ANYONE ELSE, THE HULK WOULD HAVE TORN APART. BUT AS SHE'S PROVEN REPEATEDLY, THE BLACK WIDOW IS HARDLY ANYONE ELSE.

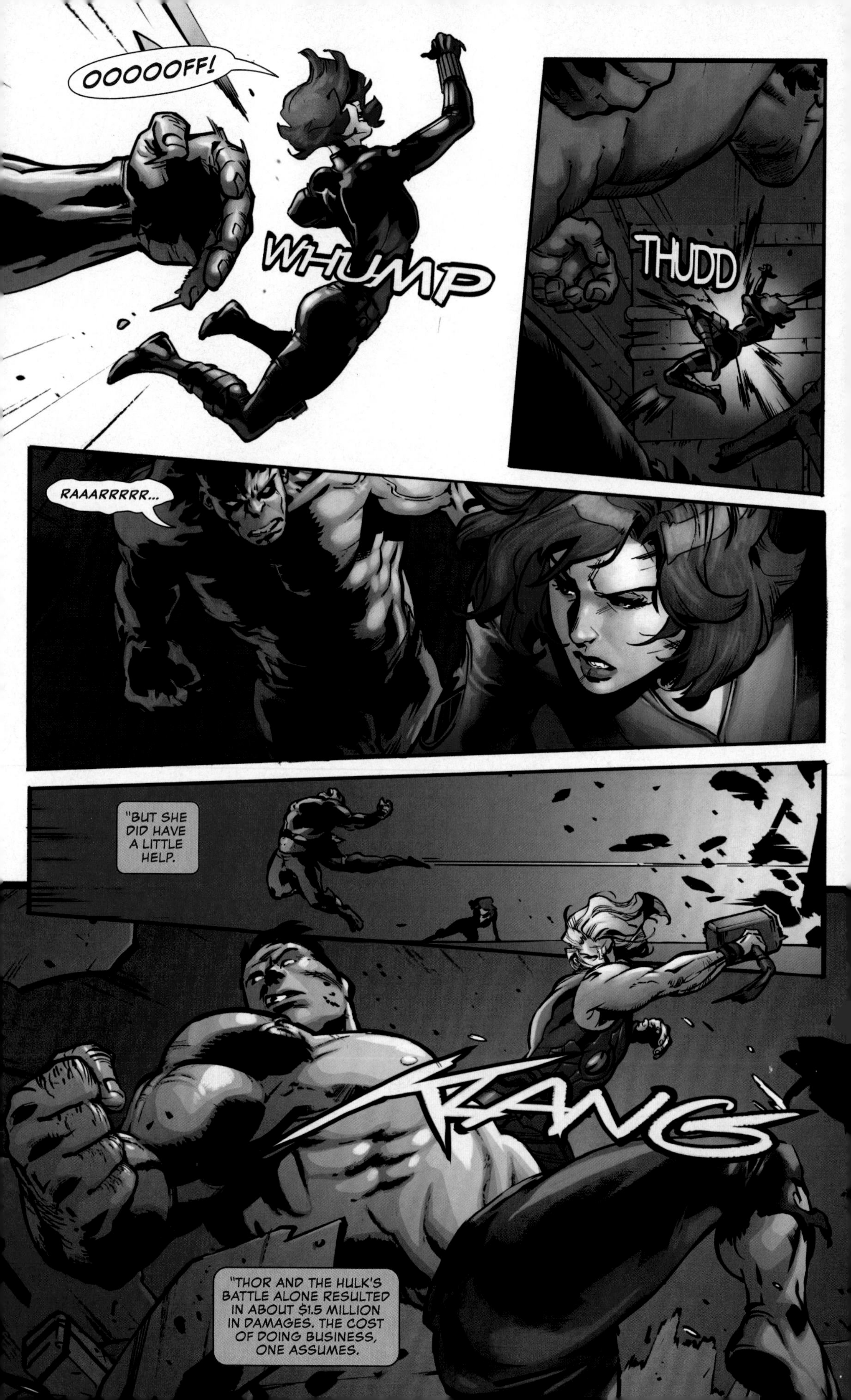
OOOOOFF!
WHUMP
THUDD
RAAARRRRR...
"BUT SHE DID HAVE A LITTLE HELP.
KRANG
"THOR AND THE HULK'S BATTLE ALONE RESULTED IN ABOUT $1.5 MILLION IN DAMAGES. THE COST OF DOING BUSINESS, ONE ASSUMES.

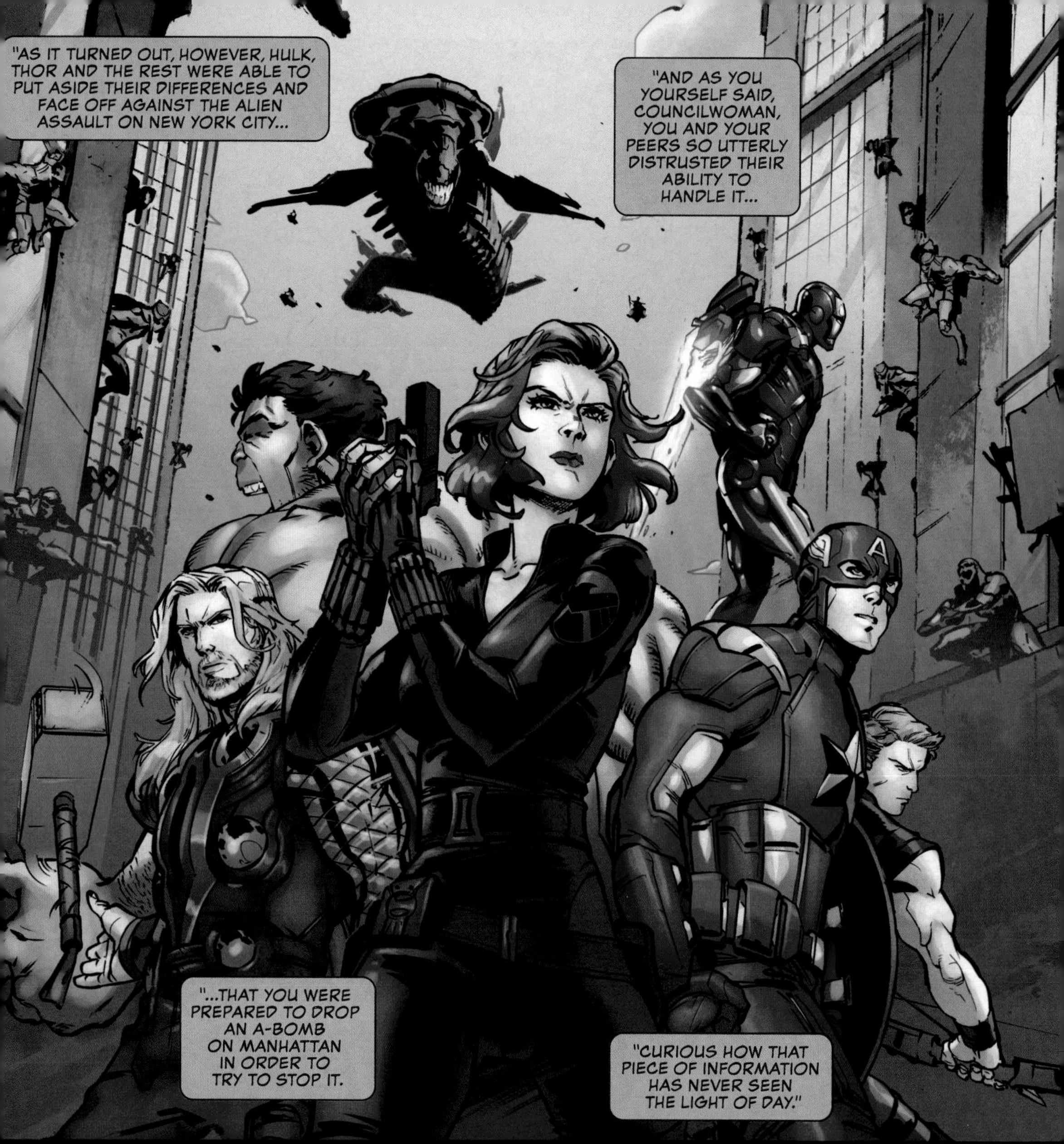
"AS IT TURNED OUT, HOWEVER, HULK, THOR AND THE REST WERE ABLE TO PUT ASIDE THEIR DIFFERENCES AND FACE OFF AGAINST THE ALIEN ASSAULT ON NEW YORK CITY...
"AND AS YOU YOURSELF SAID, COUNCILWOMAN, YOU AND YOUR PEERS SO UTTERLY DISTRUSTED THEIR ABILITY TO HANDLE IT...
"...THAT YOU WERE PREPARED TO DROP AN A-BOMB ON MANHATTAN IN ORDER TO TRY TO STOP IT.
"CURIOUS HOW THAT PIECE OF INFORMATION HAS NEVER SEEN THE LIGHT OF DAY."

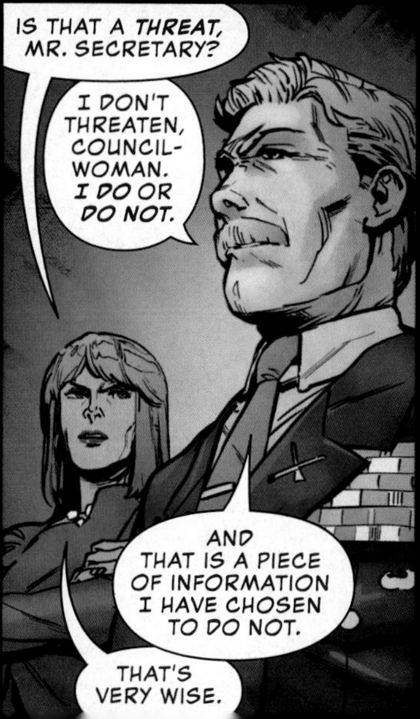
IS THAT A *THREAT*, MR. SECRETARY?
I DON'T THREATEN, COUNCIL-WOMAN. *I DO* OR *DO NOT*.
AND THAT IS A PIECE OF INFORMATION I HAVE CHOSEN TO DO NOT.
THAT'S VERY WISE.

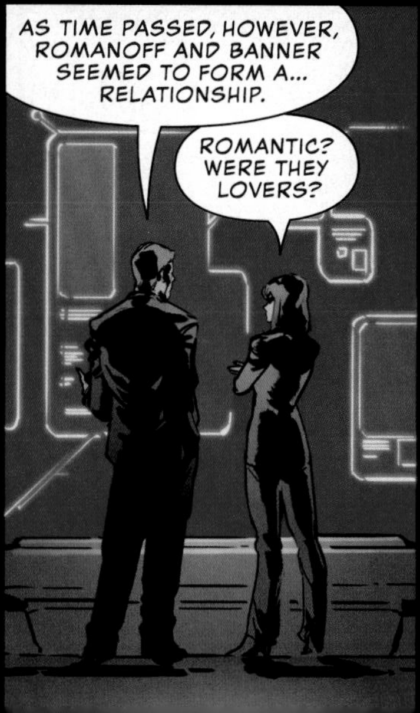
AS TIME PASSED, HOWEVER, ROMANOFF AND BANNER SEEMED TO FORM A... RELATIONSHIP.
ROMANTIC? WERE THEY LOVERS?

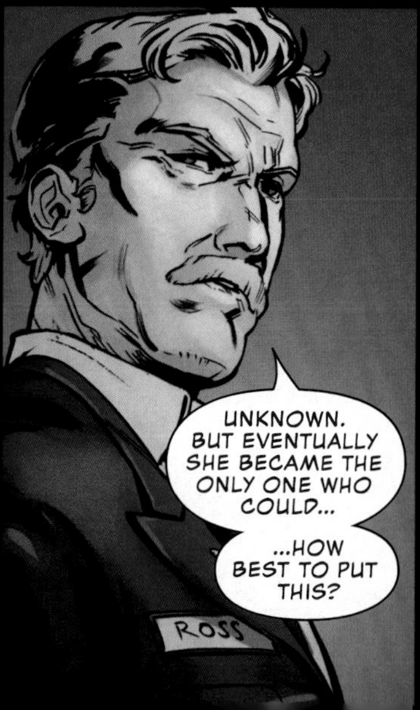
UNKNOWN. BUT EVENTUALLY SHE BECAME THE ONLY ONE WHO COULD...
...HOW BEST TO PUT THIS?
ROSS

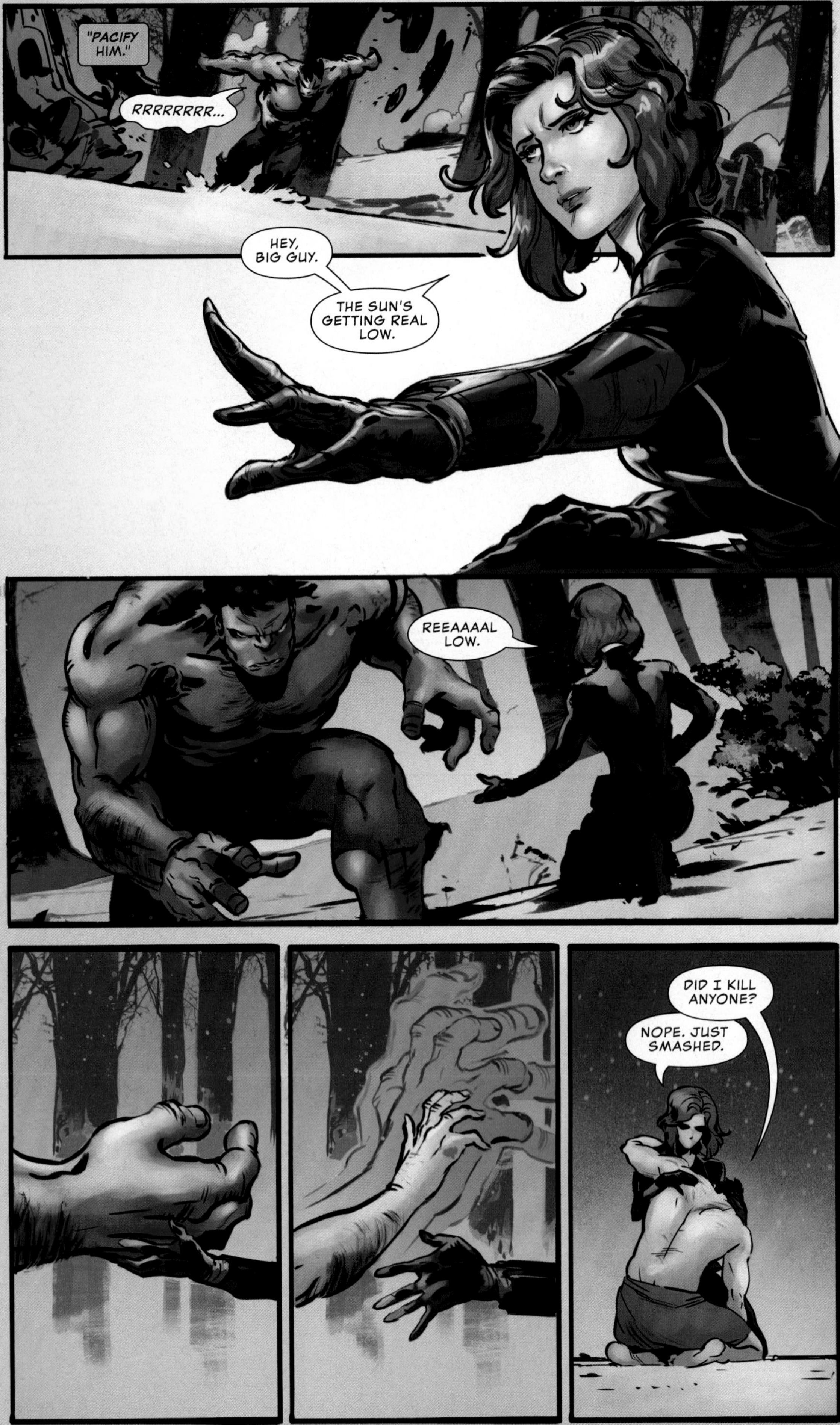
"PACIFY HIM."
RRRRRRRR...
HEY, BIG GUY.
THE SUN'S GETTING REAL LOW.
REEAAAAL LOW.
DID I KILL ANYONE?
NOPE. JUST SMASHED.

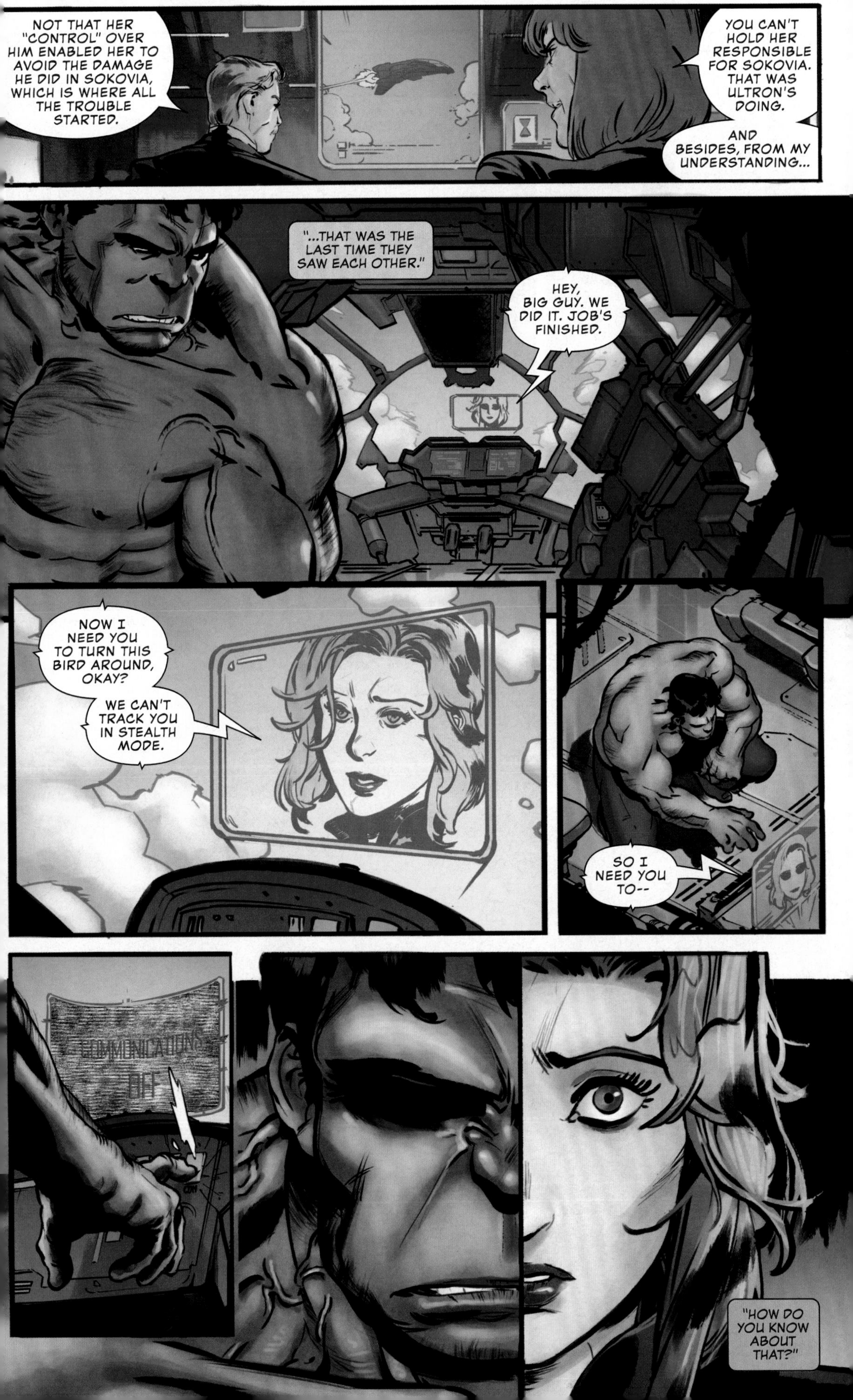
NOT THAT HER "CONTROL" OVER HIM ENABLED HER TO AVOID THE DAMAGE HE DID IN SOKOVIA, WHICH IS WHERE ALL THE TROUBLE STARTED.
YOU CAN'T HOLD HER RESPONSIBLE FOR SOKOVIA. THAT WAS ULTRON'S DOING.
AND BESIDES, FROM MY UNDERSTANDING...
"...THAT WAS THE LAST TIME THEY SAW EACH OTHER."
HEY, BIG GUY. WE DID IT. JOB'S FINISHED.
NOW I NEED YOU TO TURN THIS BIRD AROUND, OKAY?
WE CAN'T TRACK YOU IN STEALTH MODE.
SO I NEED YOU TO--
COMMUNICATIONS OFF
"HOW DO YOU KNOW ABOUT THAT?"

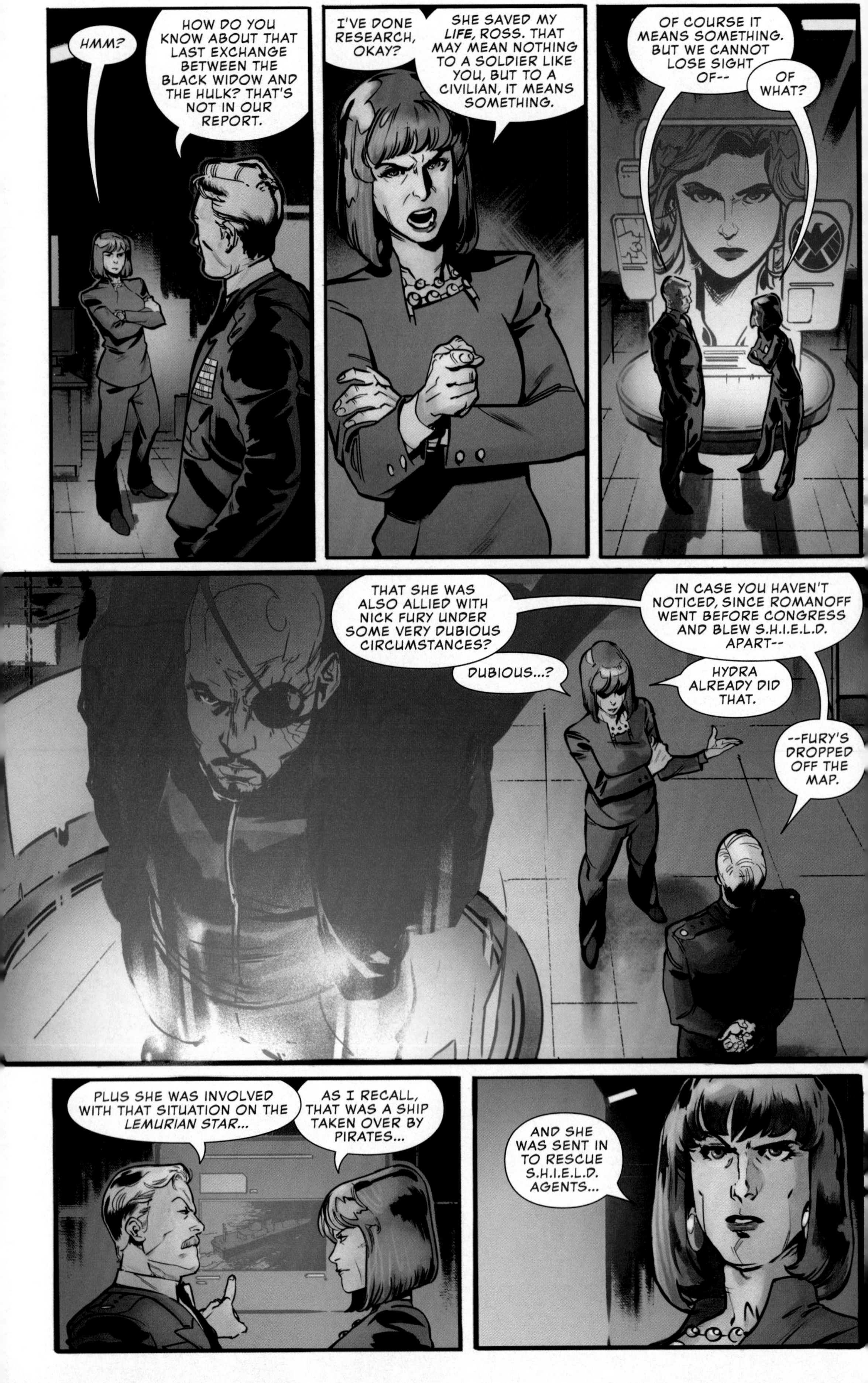
HMM?
HOW DO YOU KNOW ABOUT THAT LAST EXCHANGE BETWEEN THE BLACK WIDOW AND THE HULK? THAT'S NOT IN OUR REPORT.
I'VE DONE RESEARCH, OKAY?
SHE SAVED MY *LIFE*, ROSS. THAT MAY MEAN NOTHING TO A SOLDIER LIKE YOU, BUT TO A CIVILIAN, IT MEANS SOMETHING.
OF COURSE IT MEANS SOMETHING. BUT WE CANNOT LOSE SIGHT OF--
OF WHAT?
THAT SHE WAS ALSO ALLIED WITH NICK FURY UNDER SOME VERY DUBIOUS CIRCUMSTANCES?
DUBIOUS...?
IN CASE YOU HAVEN'T NOTICED, SINCE ROMANOFF WENT BEFORE CONGRESS AND BLEW S.H.I.E.L.D. APART--
HYDRA ALREADY DID THAT.
--FURY'S DROPPED OFF THE MAP.
PLUS SHE WAS INVOLVED WITH THAT SITUATION ON THE *LEMURIAN STAR*...
AS I RECALL, THAT WAS A SHIP TAKEN OVER BY PIRATES...
AND SHE WAS SENT IN TO RESCUE S.H.I.E.L.D. AGENTS...

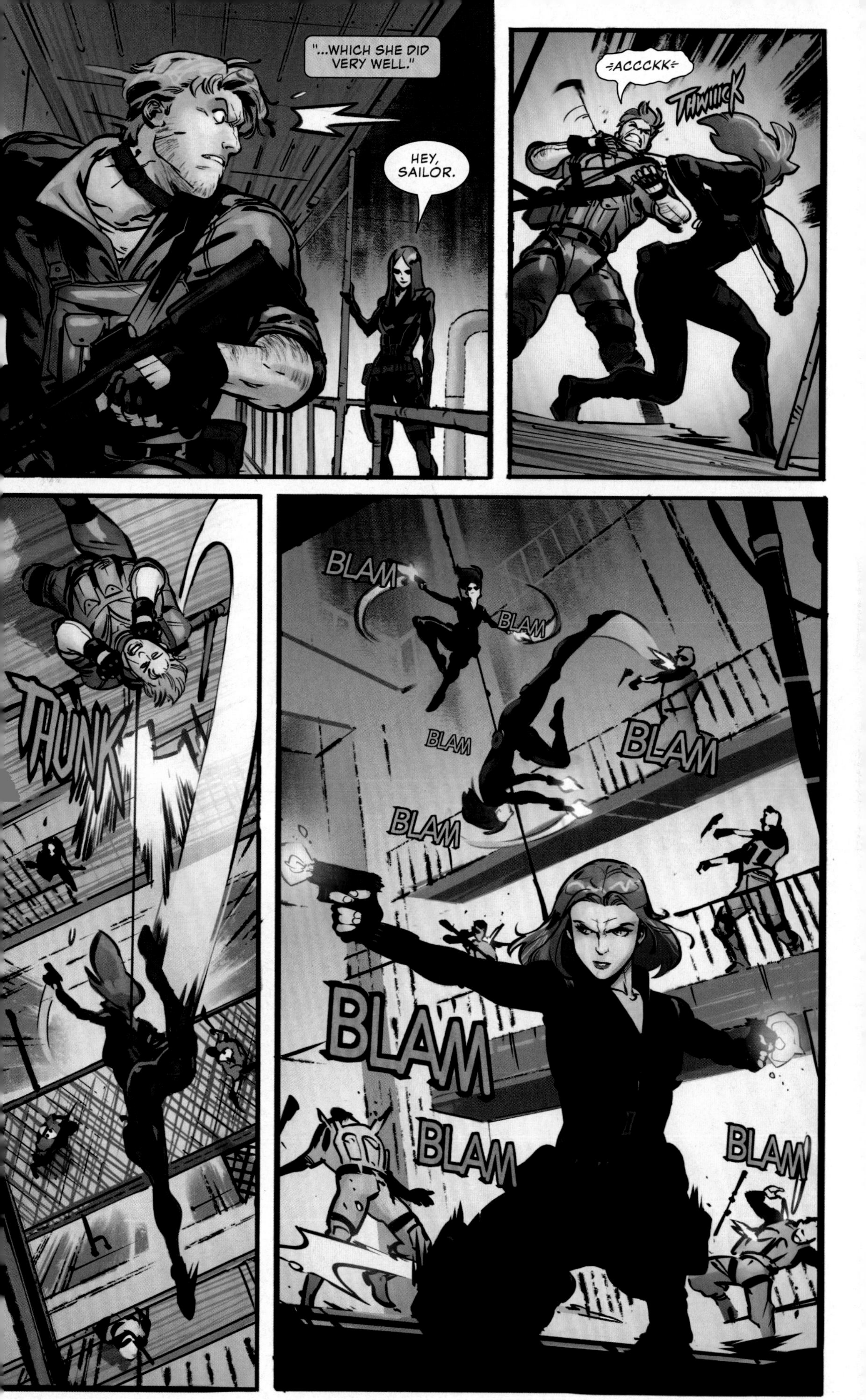
"...WHICH SHE DID VERY WELL."
HEY, SAILOR.
ACCCKK
THWIIICK
THUNK
BLAM
BLAM
BLAM
BLAM
BLAM
BLAM
BLAM
BLAM
BLAM

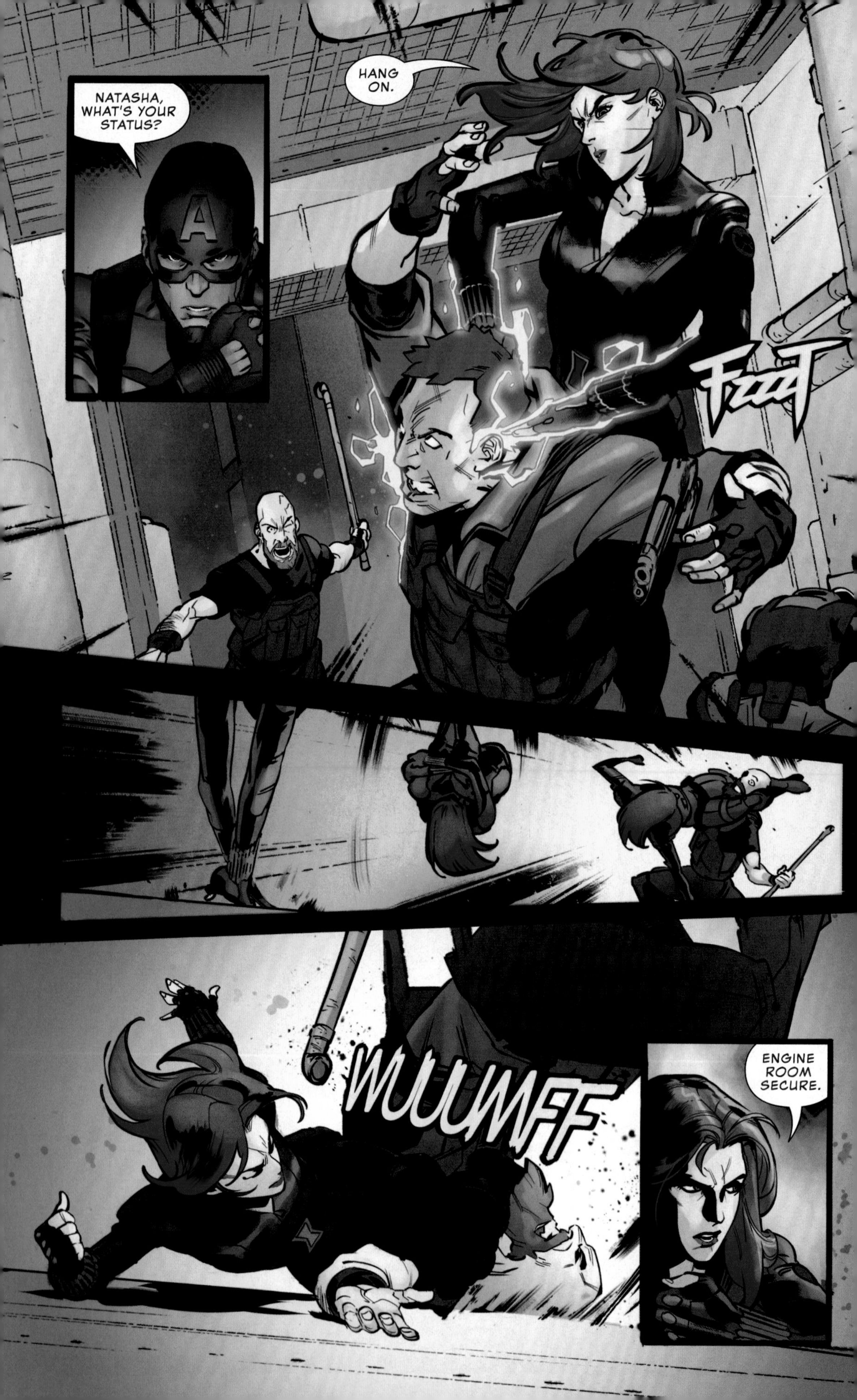
NATASHA, WHAT'S YOUR STATUS?
HANG ON.
FZZZT
WUUUMFF
ENGINE ROOM SECURE.

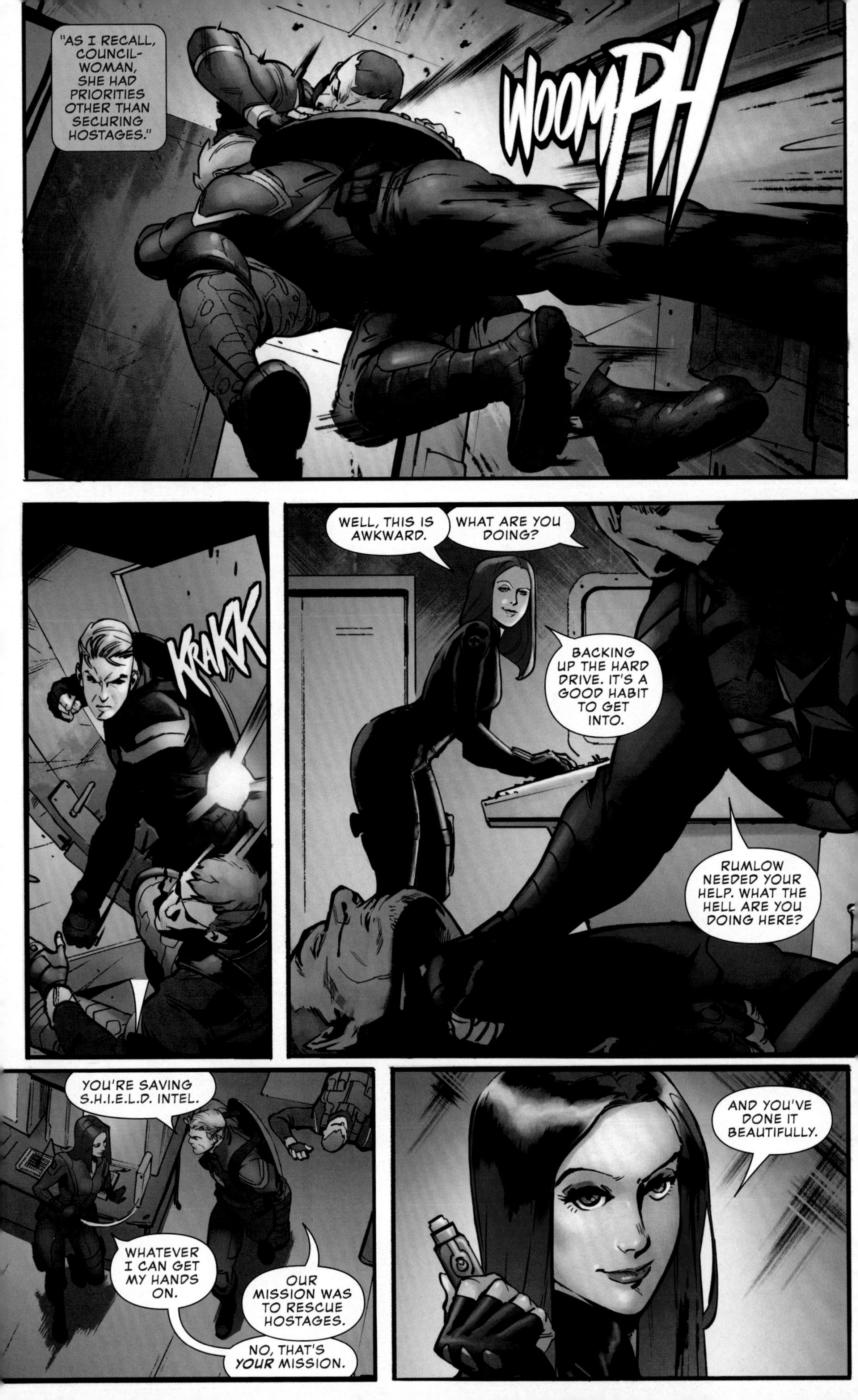
"AS I RECALL, COUNCIL-WOMAN, SHE HAD PRIORITIES OTHER THAN SECURING HOSTAGES."
WOOMPH
KRAKK
WELL, THIS IS AWKWARD.
WHAT ARE YOU DOING?
BACKING UP THE HARD DRIVE. IT'S A GOOD HABIT TO GET INTO.
RUMLOW NEEDED YOUR HELP. WHAT THE HELL ARE YOU DOING HERE?
YOU'RE SAVING S.H.I.E.L.D. INTEL.
WHATEVER I CAN GET MY HANDS ON.
OUR MISSION WAS TO RESCUE HOSTAGES.
NO, THAT'S *YOUR* MISSION.
AND YOU'VE DONE IT BEAUTIFULLY.

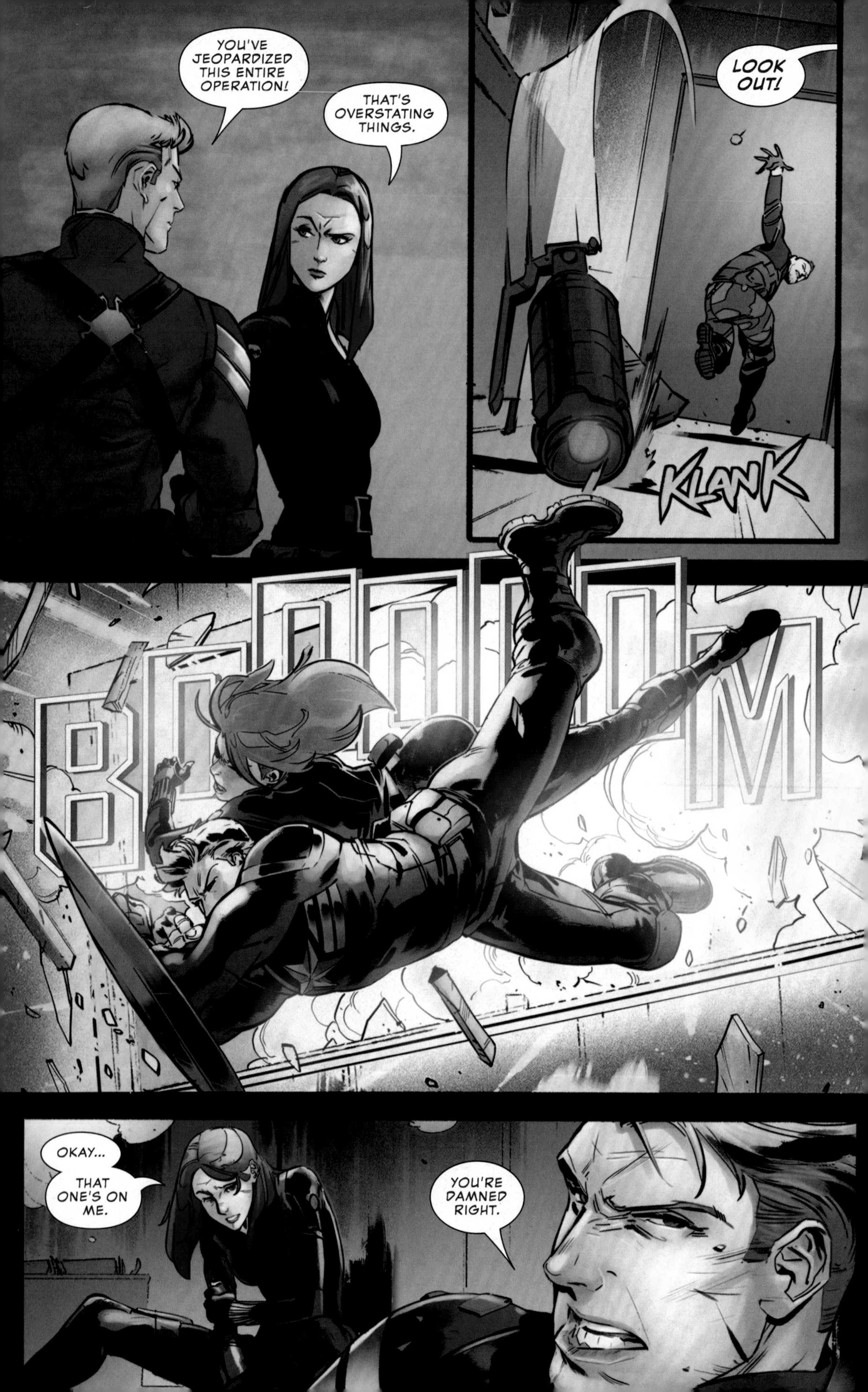
YOU'VE JEOPARDIZED THIS ENTIRE OPERATION!
THAT'S OVERSTATING THINGS.
LOOK OUT!
KLANK
BOOOOOM
OKAY... THAT ONE'S ON ME.
YOU'RE DAMNED RIGHT.

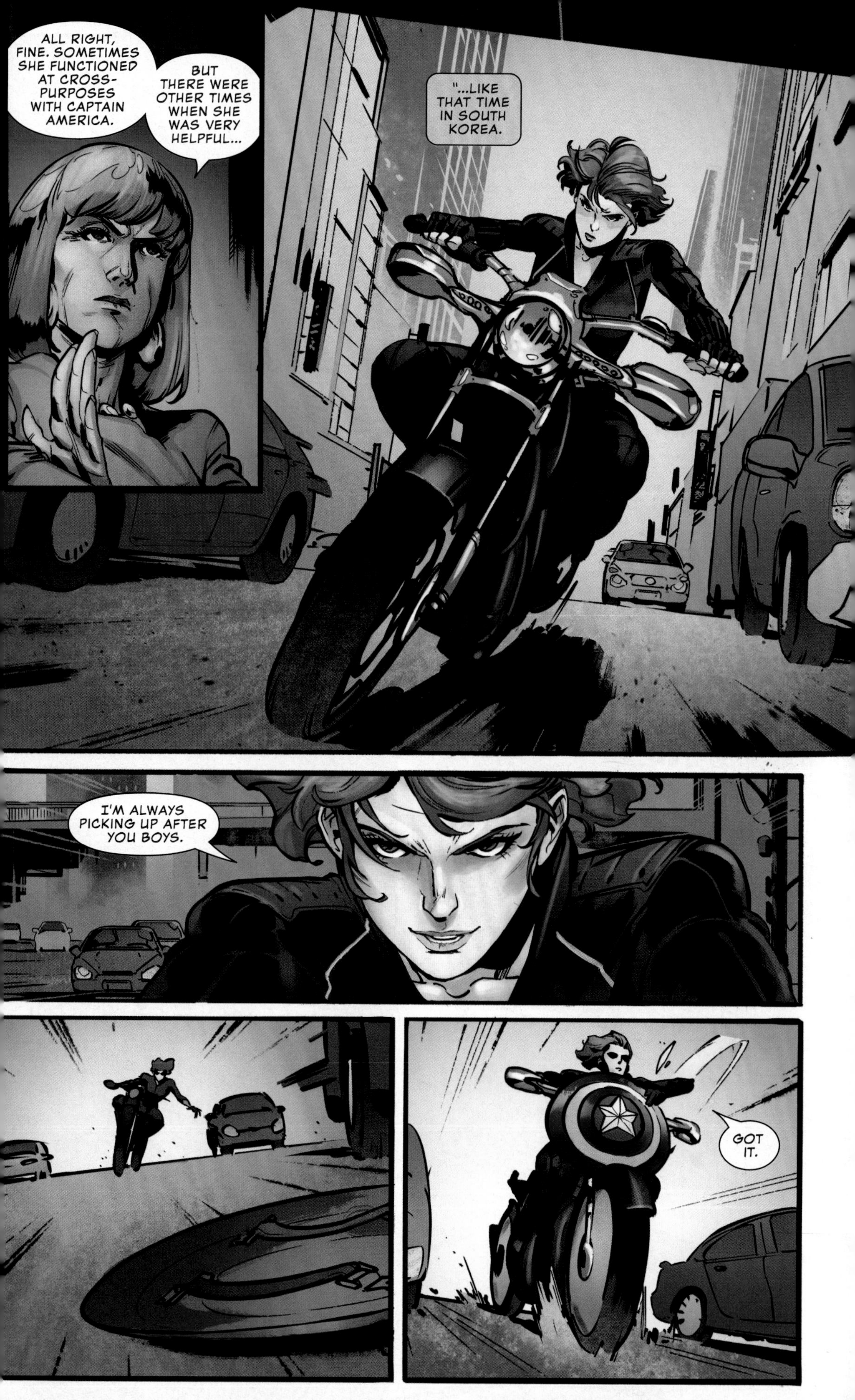
ALL RIGHT, FINE. SOMETIMES SHE FUNCTIONED AT CROSS-PURPOSES WITH CAPTAIN AMERICA.
BUT THERE WERE OTHER TIMES WHEN SHE WAS VERY HELPFUL...
"...LIKE THAT TIME IN SOUTH KOREA.
I'M ALWAYS PICKING UP AFTER YOU BOYS.
GOT IT.

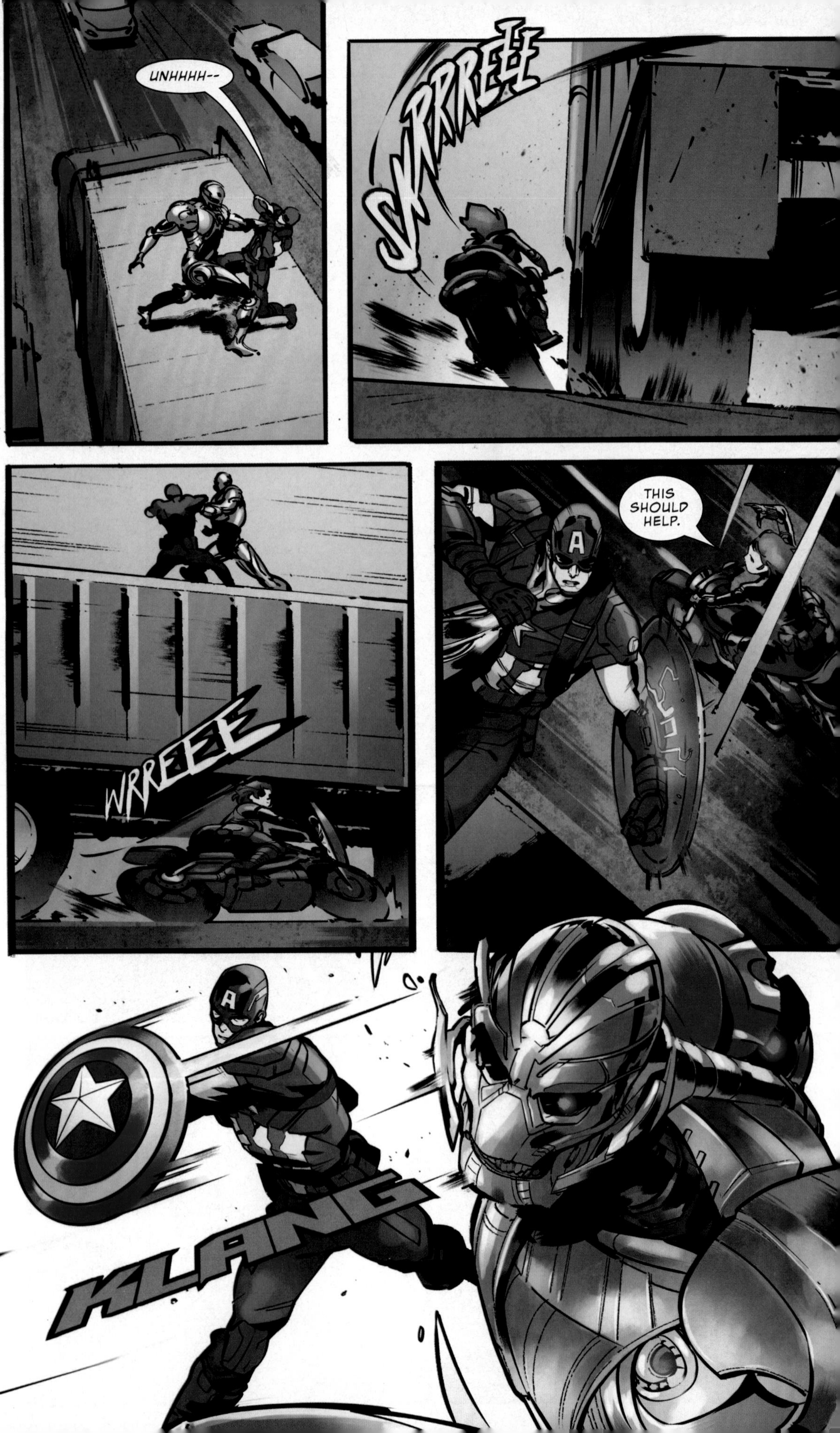
UNHHHH--
SKRRREEE
WRREEE
THIS SHOULD HELP.
KLANG

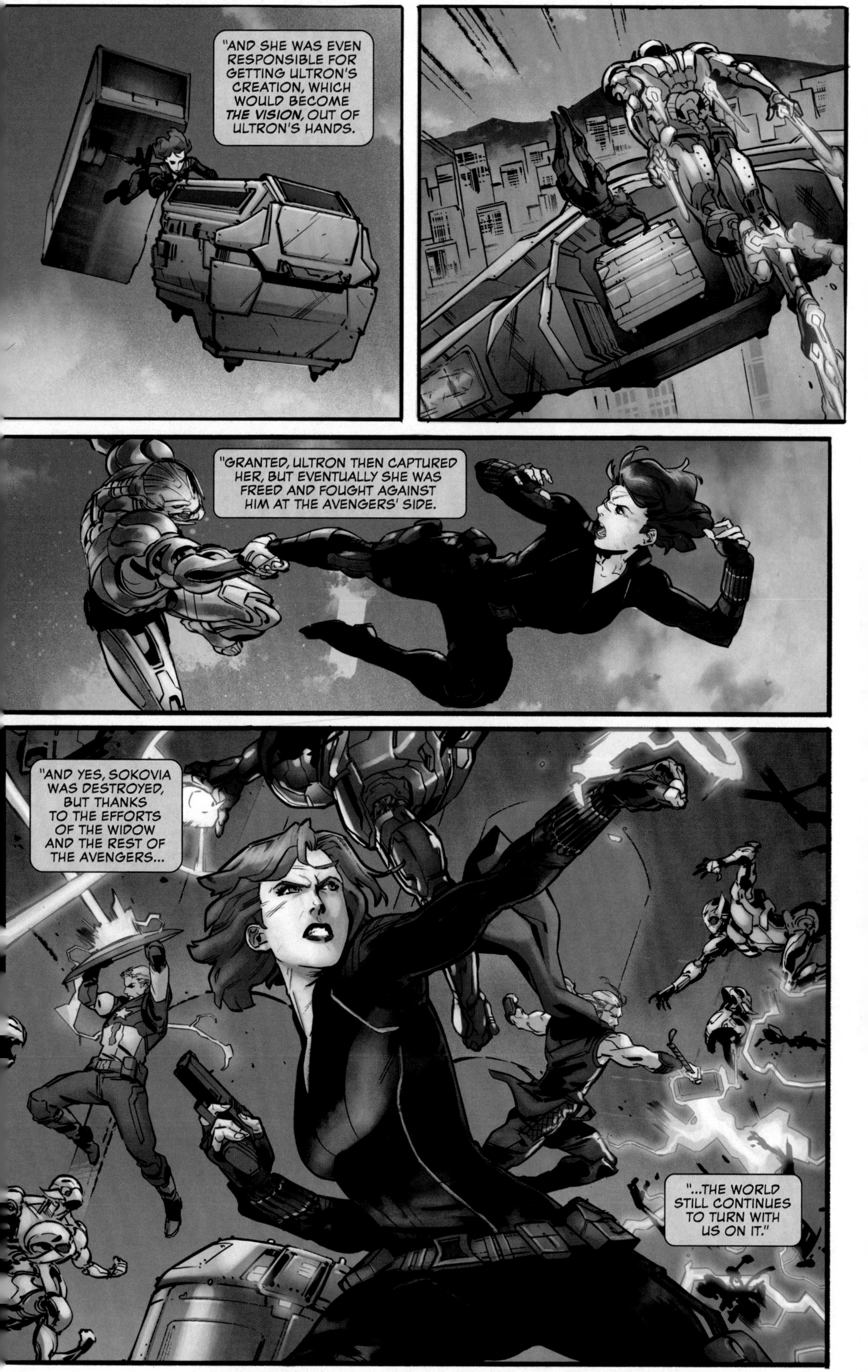
"AND SHE WAS EVEN RESPONSIBLE FOR GETTING ULTRON'S CREATION, WHICH WOULD BECOME THE VISION, OUT OF ULTRON'S HANDS.
"GRANTED, ULTRON THEN CAPTURED HER, BUT EVENTUALLY SHE WAS FREED AND FOUGHT AGAINST HIM AT THE AVENGERS' SIDE.
"AND YES, SOKOVIA WAS DESTROYED, BUT THANKS TO THE EFFORTS OF THE WIDOW AND THE REST OF THE AVENGERS...
"...THE WORLD STILL CONTINUES TO TURN WITH US ON IT."

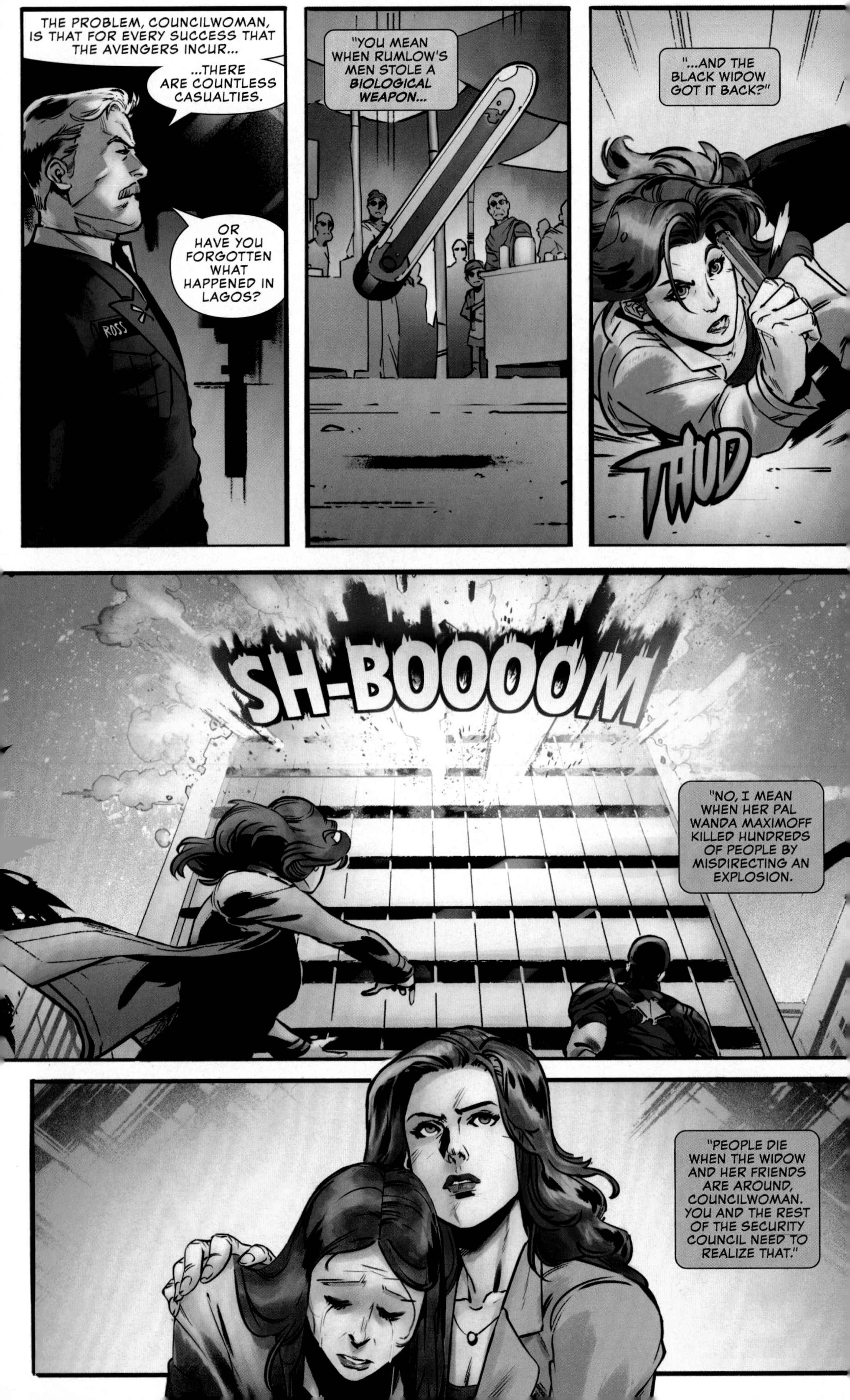
THE PROBLEM, COUNCILWOMAN, IS THAT FOR EVERY SUCCESS THAT THE AVENGERS INCUR...
...THERE ARE COUNTLESS CASUALTIES.
OR HAVE YOU FORGOTTEN WHAT HAPPENED IN LAGOS?
ROSS
"YOU MEAN WHEN RUMLOW'S MEN STOLE A *BIOLOGICAL WEAPON*...
"...AND THE BLACK WIDOW GOT IT BACK?"
THUD
SH-BOOOOOM
"NO, I MEAN WHEN HER PAL WANDA MAXIMOFF KILLED HUNDREDS OF PEOPLE BY MISDIRECTING AN EXPLOSION.
"PEOPLE DIE WHEN THE WIDOW AND HER FRIENDS ARE AROUND, COUNCILWOMAN. YOU AND THE REST OF THE SECURITY COUNCIL NEED TO REALIZE THAT."

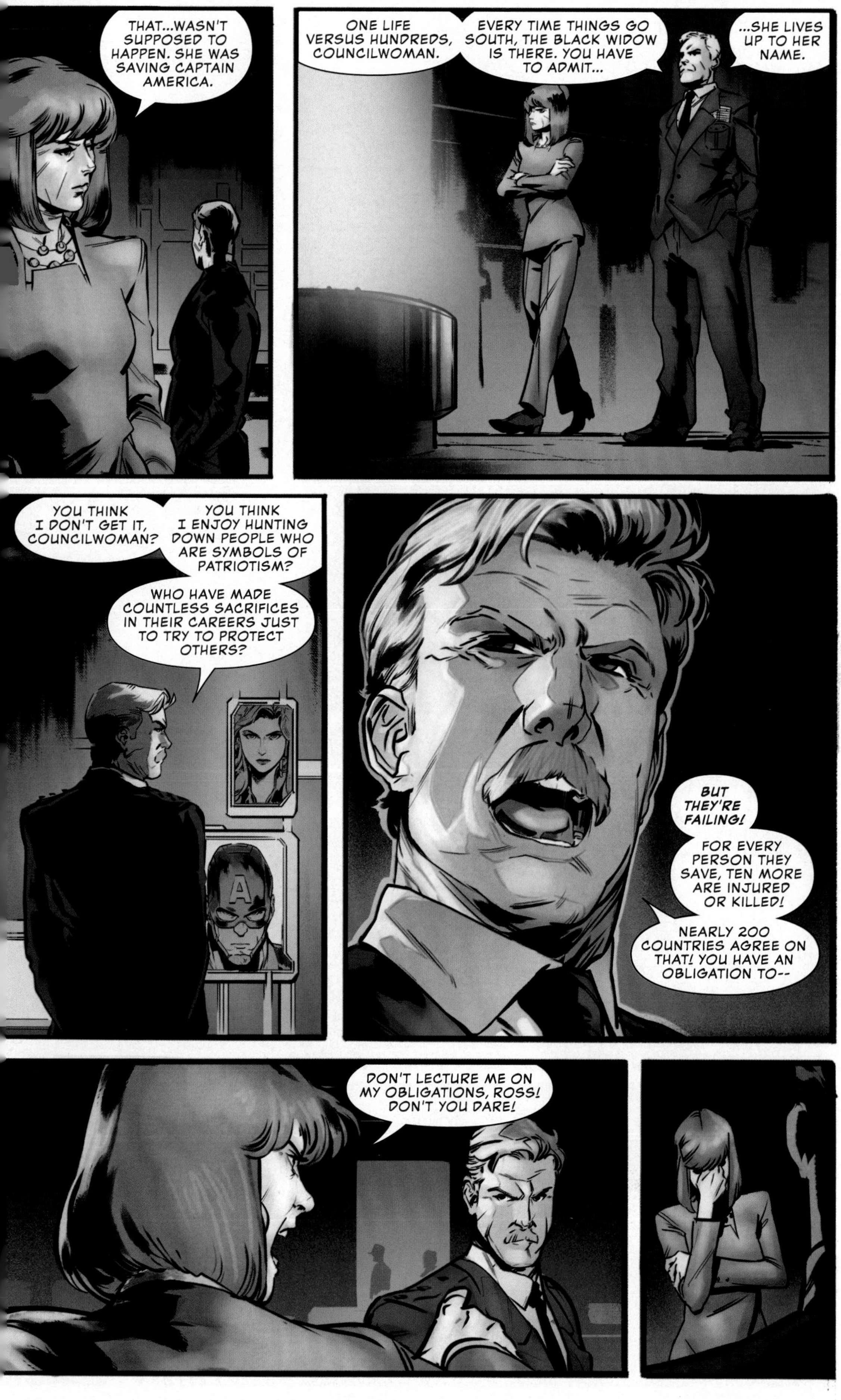
THAT...WASN'T SUPPOSED TO HAPPEN. SHE WAS SAVING CAPTAIN AMERICA.
ONE LIFE VERSUS HUNDREDS, COUNCILWOMAN.
EVERY TIME THINGS GO SOUTH, THE BLACK WIDOW IS THERE. YOU HAVE TO ADMIT...
...SHE LIVES UP TO HER NAME.
YOU THINK I DON'T GET IT, COUNCILWOMAN?
YOU THINK I ENJOY HUNTING DOWN PEOPLE WHO ARE SYMBOLS OF PATRIOTISM?
WHO HAVE MADE COUNTLESS SACRIFICES IN THEIR CAREERS JUST TO TRY TO PROTECT OTHERS?
BUT THEY'RE FAILING!
FOR EVERY PERSON THEY SAVE, TEN MORE ARE INJURED OR KILLED!
NEARLY 200 COUNTRIES AGREE ON THAT! YOU HAVE AN OBLIGATION TO--
DON'T LECTURE ME ON MY OBLIGATIONS, ROSS! DON'T YOU DARE!

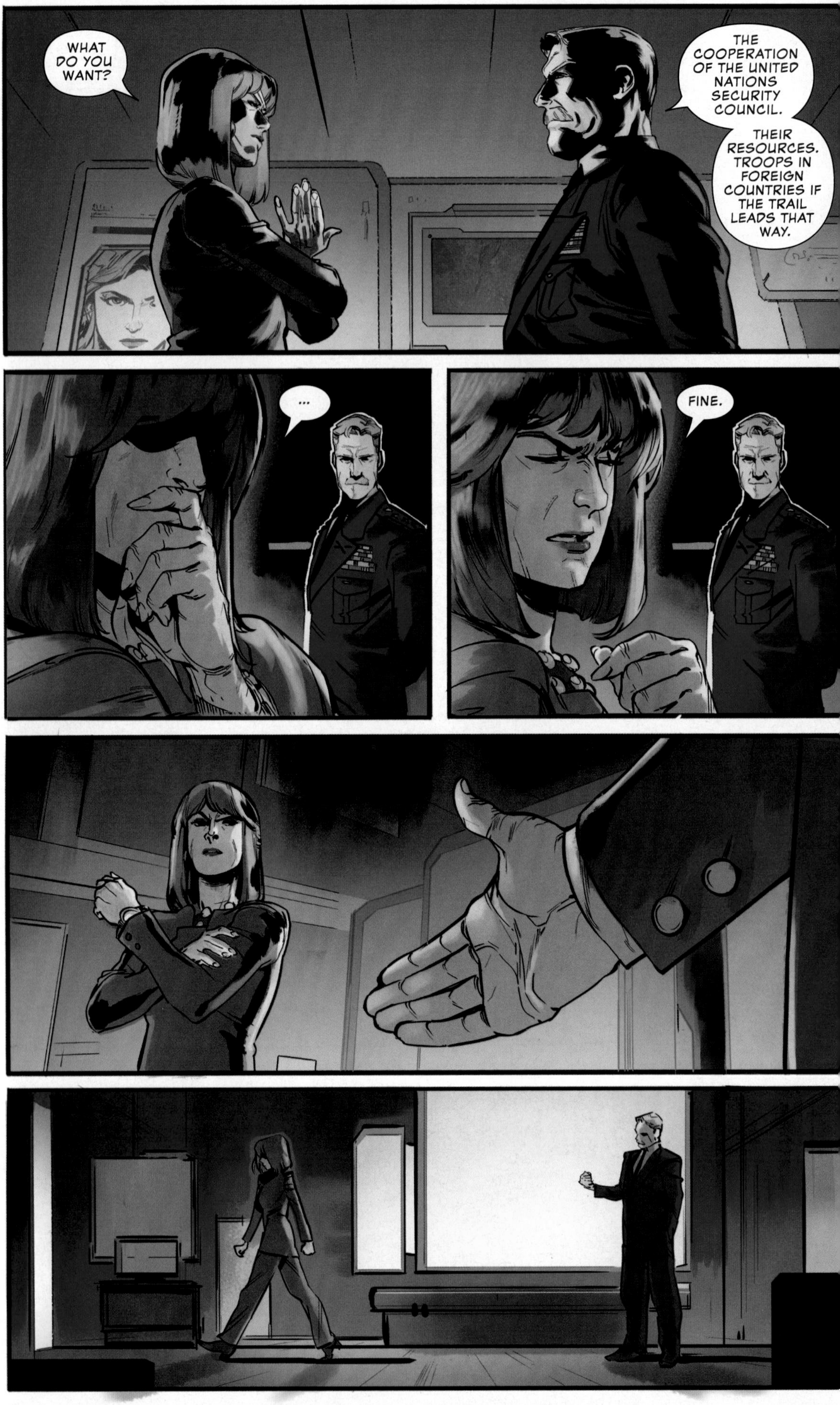
WHAT DO YOU WANT?
THE COOPERATION OF THE UNITED NATIONS SECURITY COUNCIL.
THEIR RESOURCES. TROOPS IN FOREIGN COUNTRIES IF THE TRAIL LEADS THAT WAY.
...
FINE.

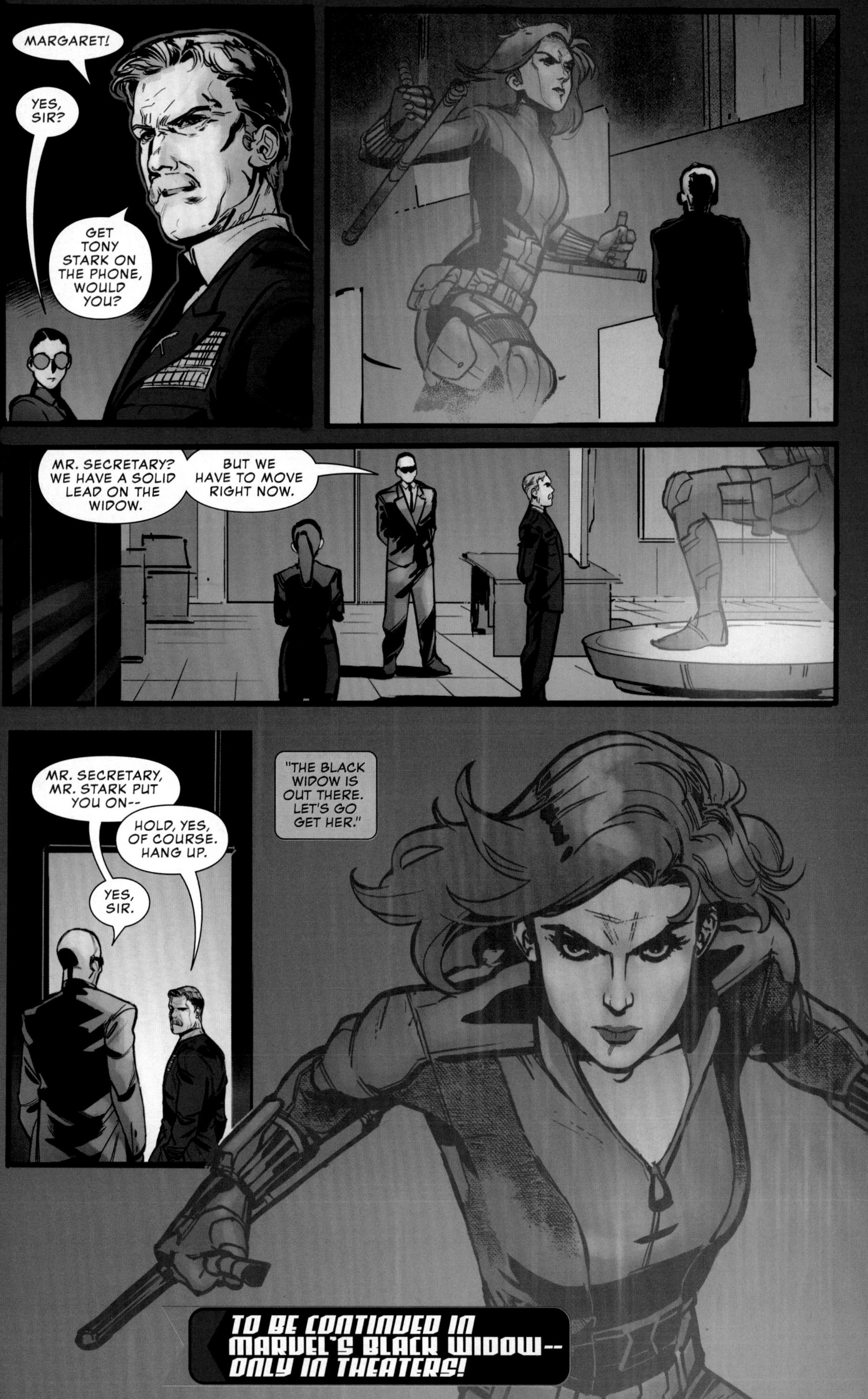

MARGARET!
YES, SIR?
GET TONY STARK ON THE PHONE, WOULD YOU?
MR. SECRETARY? WE HAVE A SOLID LEAD ON THE WIDOW.
BUT WE HAVE TO MOVE RIGHT NOW.
MR. SECRETARY, MR. STARK PUT YOU ON--
HOLD, YES, OF COURSE. HANG UP.
YES, SIR.
"THE BLACK WIDOW IS OUT THERE. LET'S GO GET HER."
TO BE CONTINUED IN MARVEL'S BLACK WIDOW-- ONLY IN THEATERS!

NATASHA ROMANOFF IS RUSSIA'S GREATEST SPY, BUT AN ENCOUNTER WITH IRON MAN PUTS HER ON THE RUN AND SEEKING REDEMPTION.

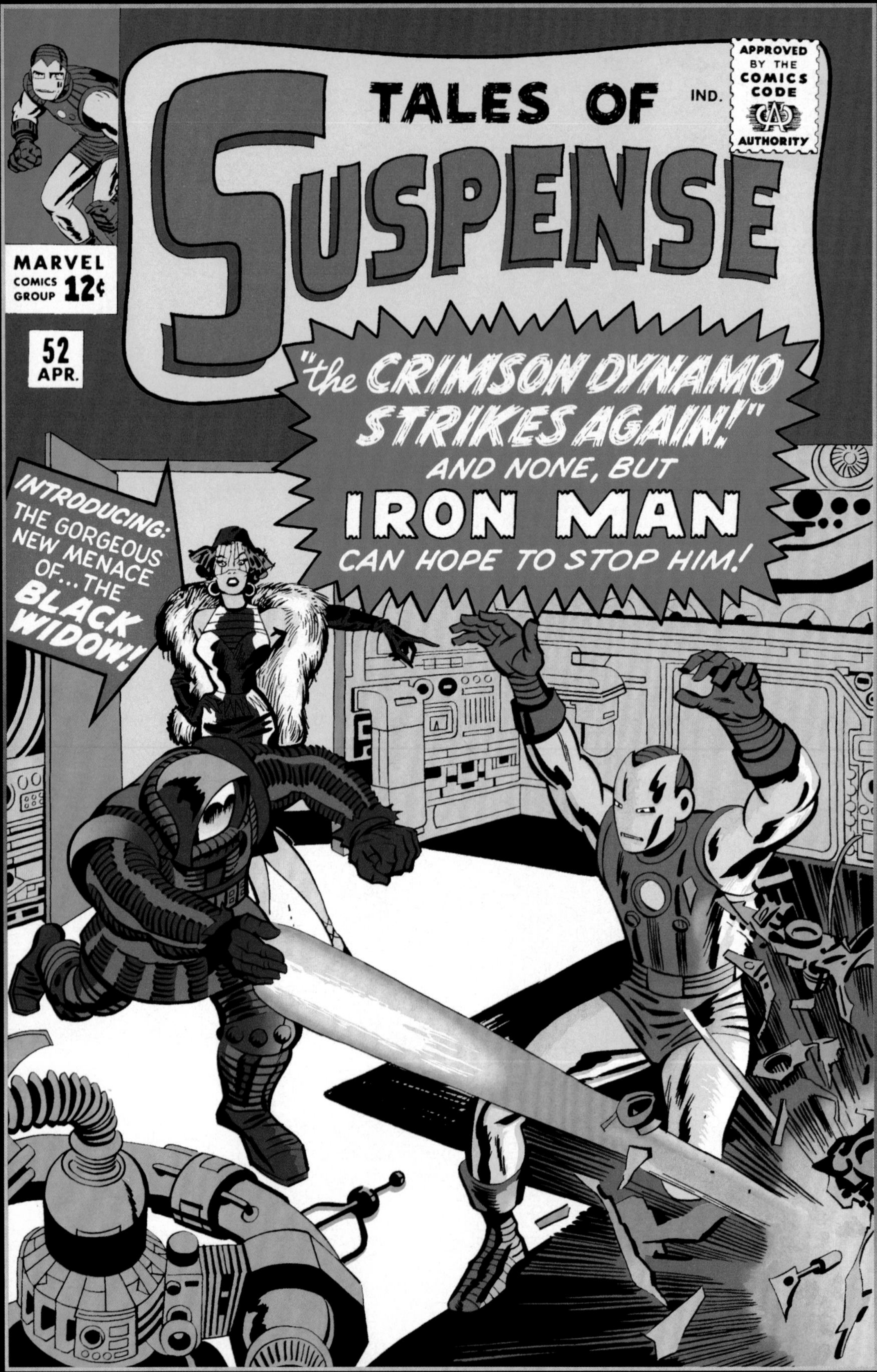

TALES OF SUSPENSE
IND.
APPROVED BY THE COMICS CODE AUTHORITY
MARVEL COMICS GROUP 12¢
52 APR.
"the CRIMSON DYNAMO STRIKES AGAIN!" AND NONE, BUT IRON MAN CAN HOPE TO STOP HIM!
INTRODUCING: THE GORGEOUS NEW MENACE OF... THE BLACK WIDOW!

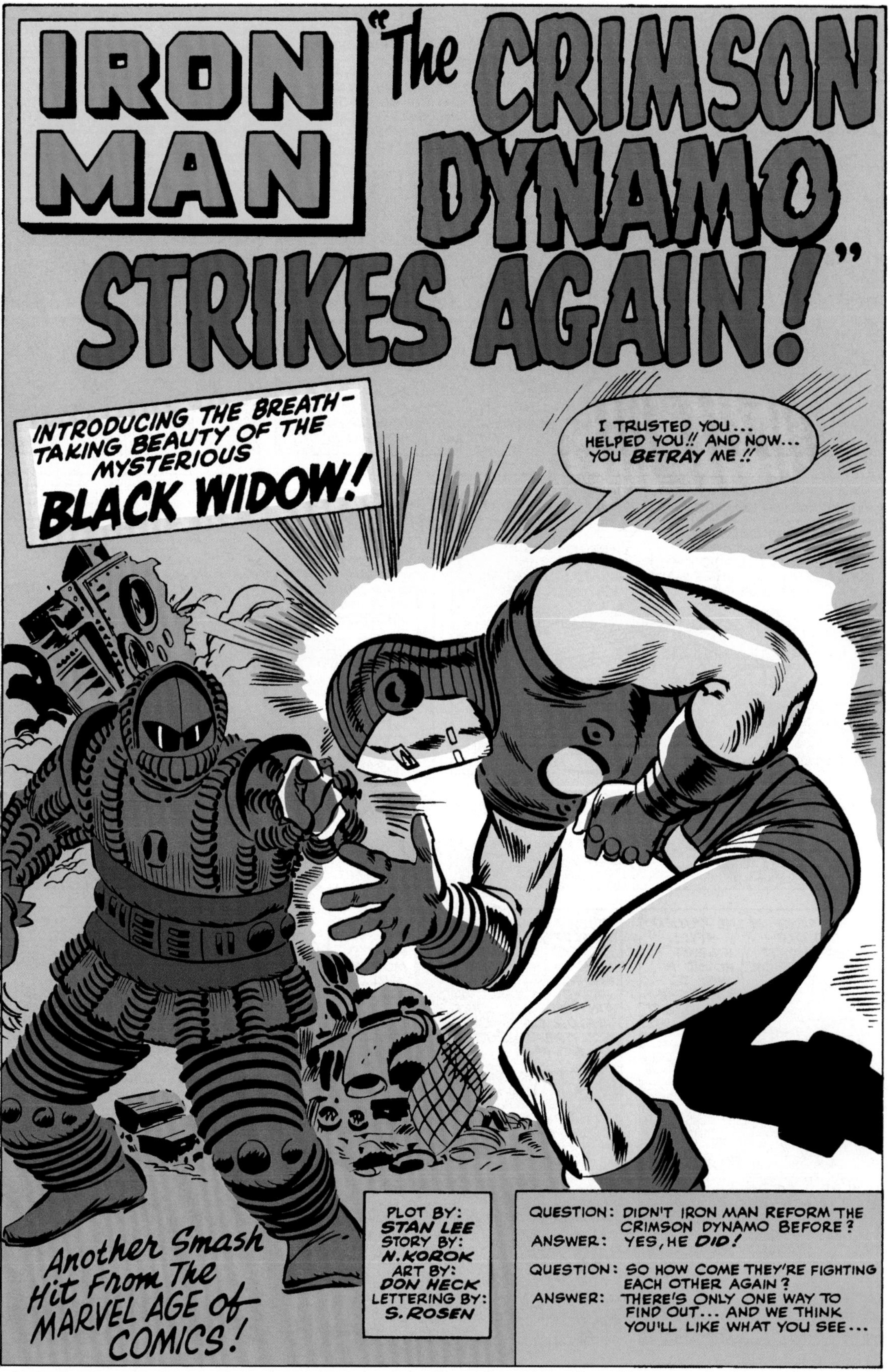
IRON MAN
"The CRIMSON DYNAMO STRIKES AGAIN!"
INTRODUCING THE BREATH-TAKING BEAUTY OF THE MYSTERIOUS BLACK WIDOW!
I TRUSTED YOU... HELPED YOU!! AND NOW... YOU BETRAY ME!!
Another Smash Hit From The MARVEL AGE of COMICS!
PLOT BY: STAN LEE
STORY BY: N. KOROK
ART BY: DON HECK
LETTERING BY: S. ROSEN
QUESTION: DIDN'T IRON MAN REFORM THE CRIMSON DYNAMO BEFORE?
ANSWER: YES, HE DID!
QUESTION: SO HOW COME THEY'RE FIGHTING EACH OTHER AGAIN?
ANSWER: THERE'S ONLY ONE WAY TO FIND OUT... AND WE THINK YOU'LL LIKE WHAT YOU SEE...

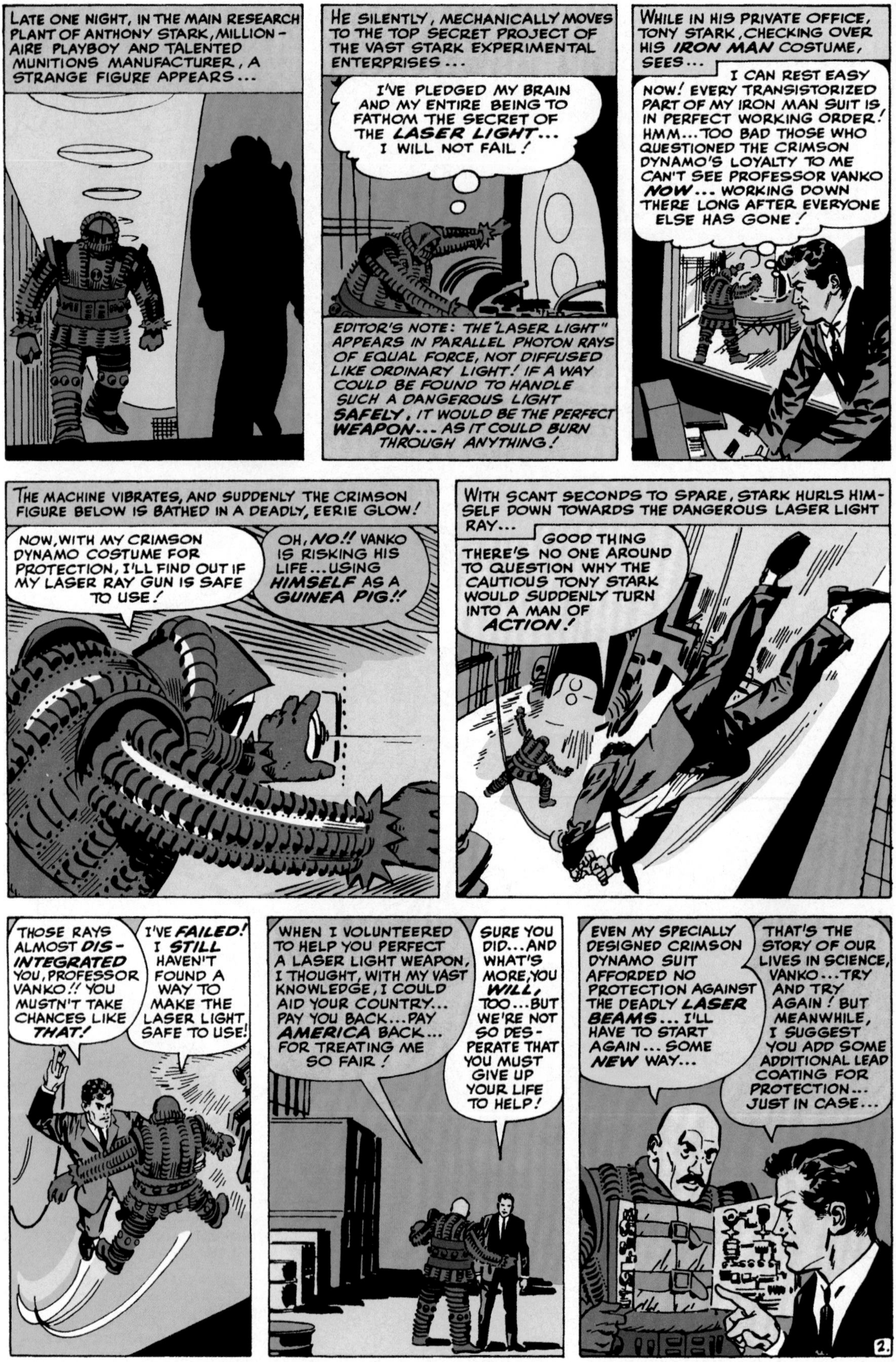

LATE ONE NIGHT, IN THE MAIN RESEARCH PLANT OF ANTHONY STARK, MILLION-AIRE PLAYBOY AND TALENTED MUNITIONS MANUFACTURER, A STRANGE FIGURE APPEARS...
HE SILENTLY, MECHANICALLY MOVES TO THE TOP SECRET PROJECT OF THE VAST STARK EXPERIMENTAL ENTERPRISES...
I'VE PLEDGED MY BRAIN AND MY ENTIRE BEING TO FATHOM THE SECRET OF THE LASER LIGHT... I WILL NOT FAIL!
EDITOR'S NOTE: THE "LASER LIGHT" APPEARS IN PARALLEL PHOTON RAYS OF EQUAL FORCE, NOT DIFFUSED LIKE ORDINARY LIGHT! IF A WAY COULD BE FOUND TO HANDLE SUCH A DANGEROUS LIGHT SAFELY, IT WOULD BE THE PERFECT WEAPON... AS IT COULD BURN THROUGH ANYTHING!
WHILE IN HIS PRIVATE OFFICE, TONY STARK, CHECKING OVER HIS IRON MAN COSTUME, SEES...
I CAN REST EASY NOW! EVERY TRANSISTORIZED PART OF MY IRON MAN SUIT IS IN PERFECT WORKING ORDER! HMM... TOO BAD THOSE WHO QUESTIONED THE CRIMSON DYNAMO'S LOYALTY TO ME CAN'T SEE PROFESSOR VANKO NOW... WORKING DOWN THERE LONG AFTER EVERYONE ELSE HAS GONE!
THE MACHINE VIBRATES, AND SUDDENLY THE CRIMSON FIGURE BELOW IS BATHED IN A DEADLY, EERIE GLOW!
NOW, WITH MY CRIMSON DYNAMO COSTUME FOR PROTECTION, I'LL FIND OUT IF MY LASER RAY GUN IS SAFE TO USE!
OH, NO!! VANKO IS RISKING HIS LIFE... USING HIMSELF AS A GUINEA PIG!!
WITH SCANT SECONDS TO SPARE, STARK HURLS HIMSELF DOWN TOWARDS THE DANGEROUS LASER LIGHT RAY...
GOOD THING THERE'S NO ONE AROUND TO QUESTION WHY THE CAUTIOUS TONY STARK WOULD SUDDENLY TURN INTO A MAN OF ACTION!
THOSE RAYS ALMOST DIS-INTEGRATED YOU, PROFESSOR VANKO!! YOU MUSTN'T TAKE CHANCES LIKE THAT!
I'VE FAILED! I STILL HAVEN'T FOUND A WAY TO MAKE THE LASER LIGHT SAFE TO USE!
WHEN I VOLUNTEERED TO HELP YOU PERFECT A LASER LIGHT WEAPON, I THOUGHT, WITH MY VAST KNOWLEDGE, I COULD AID YOUR COUNTRY... PAY YOU BACK... PAY AMERICA BACK... FOR TREATING ME SO FAIR!
SURE YOU DID... AND WHAT'S MORE, YOU WILL, TOO... BUT WE'RE NOT SO DES-PERATE THAT YOU MUST GIVE UP YOUR LIFE TO HELP!
EVEN MY SPECIALLY DESIGNED CRIMSON DYNAMO SUIT AFFORDED NO PROTECTION AGAINST THE DEADLY LASER BEAMS... I'LL HAVE TO START AGAIN... SOME NEW WAY...
THAT'S THE STORY OF OUR LIVES IN SCIENCE, VANKO... TRY AND TRY AGAIN! BUT MEANWHILE, I SUGGEST YOU ADD SOME ADDITIONAL LEAD COATING FOR PROTECTION... JUST IN CASE...
2.

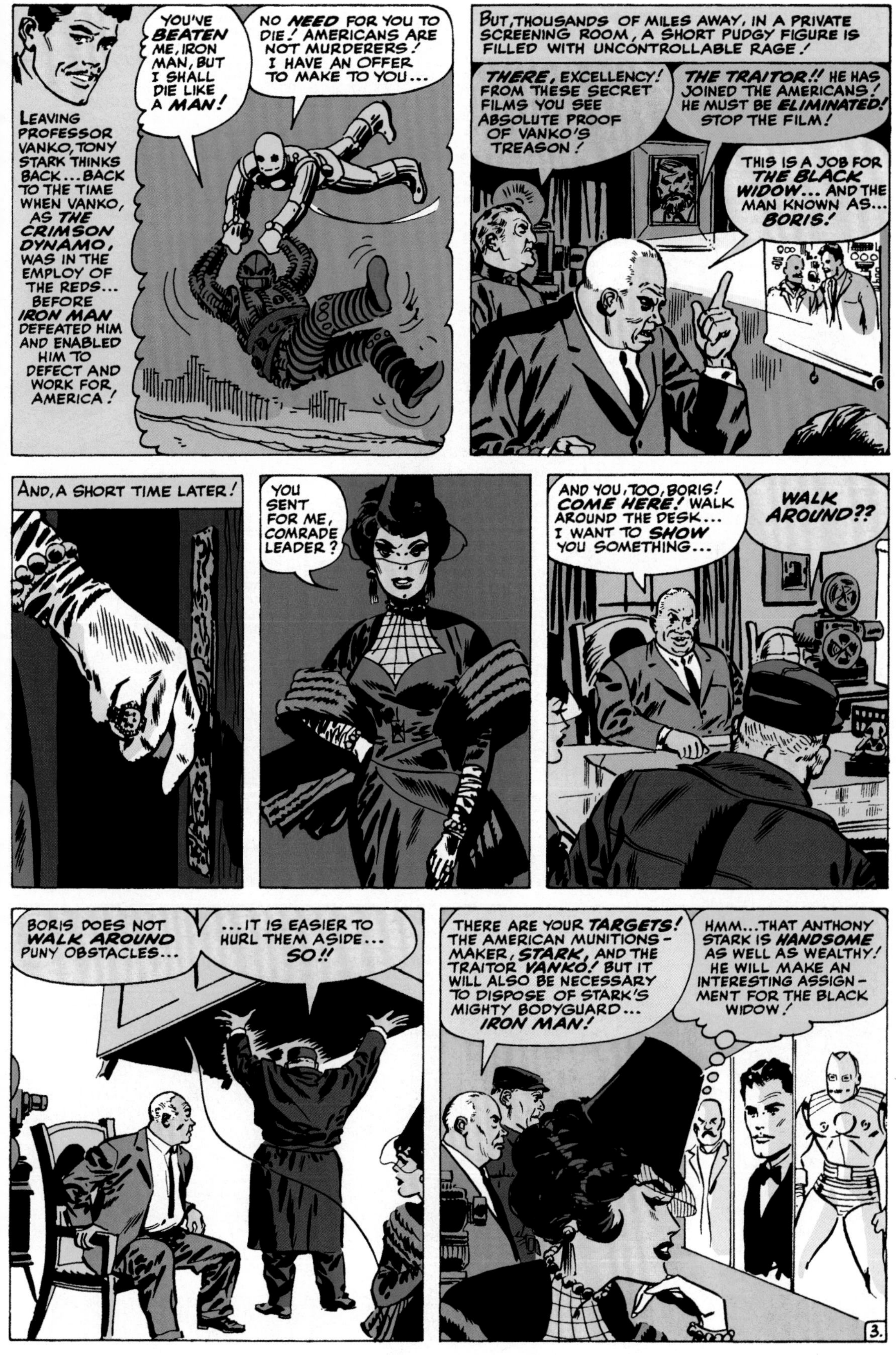
LEAVING PROFESSOR VANKO, TONY STARK THINKS BACK... BACK TO THE TIME WHEN VANKO, AS THE CRIMSON DYNAMO, WAS IN THE EMPLOY OF THE REDS... BEFORE IRON MAN DEFEATED HIM AND ENABLED HIM TO DEFECT AND WORK FOR AMERICA!
YOU'VE BEATEN ME, IRON MAN, BUT I SHALL DIE LIKE A MAN!
NO NEED FOR YOU TO DIE! AMERICANS ARE NOT MURDERERS! I HAVE AN OFFER TO MAKE TO YOU...
BUT, THOUSANDS OF MILES AWAY, IN A PRIVATE SCREENING ROOM, A SHORT PUDGY FIGURE IS FILLED WITH UNCONTROLLABLE RAGE!
THERE, EXCELLENCY! FROM THESE SECRET FILMS YOU SEE ABSOLUTE PROOF OF VANKO'S TREASON!
THE TRAITOR!! HE HAS JOINED THE AMERICANS! HE MUST BE ELIMINATED! STOP THE FILM!
THIS IS A JOB FOR THE BLACK WIDOW... AND THE MAN KNOWN AS... BORIS!
AND, A SHORT TIME LATER!
YOU SENT FOR ME, COMRADE LEADER?
AND YOU, TOO, BORIS! COME HERE! WALK AROUND THE DESK... I WANT TO SHOW YOU SOMETHING...
WALK AROUND??
BORIS DOES NOT WALK AROUND PUNY OBSTACLES...
...IT IS EASIER TO HURL THEM ASIDE... SO!!
THERE ARE YOUR TARGETS! THE AMERICAN MUNITIONS-MAKER, STARK, AND THE TRAITOR VANKO! BUT IT WILL ALSO BE NECESSARY TO DISPOSE OF STARK'S MIGHTY BODYGUARD... IRON MAN!
HMM... THAT ANTHONY STARK IS HANDSOME AS WELL AS WEALTHY! HE WILL MAKE AN INTERESTING ASSIGNMENT FOR THE BLACK WIDOW!
3.

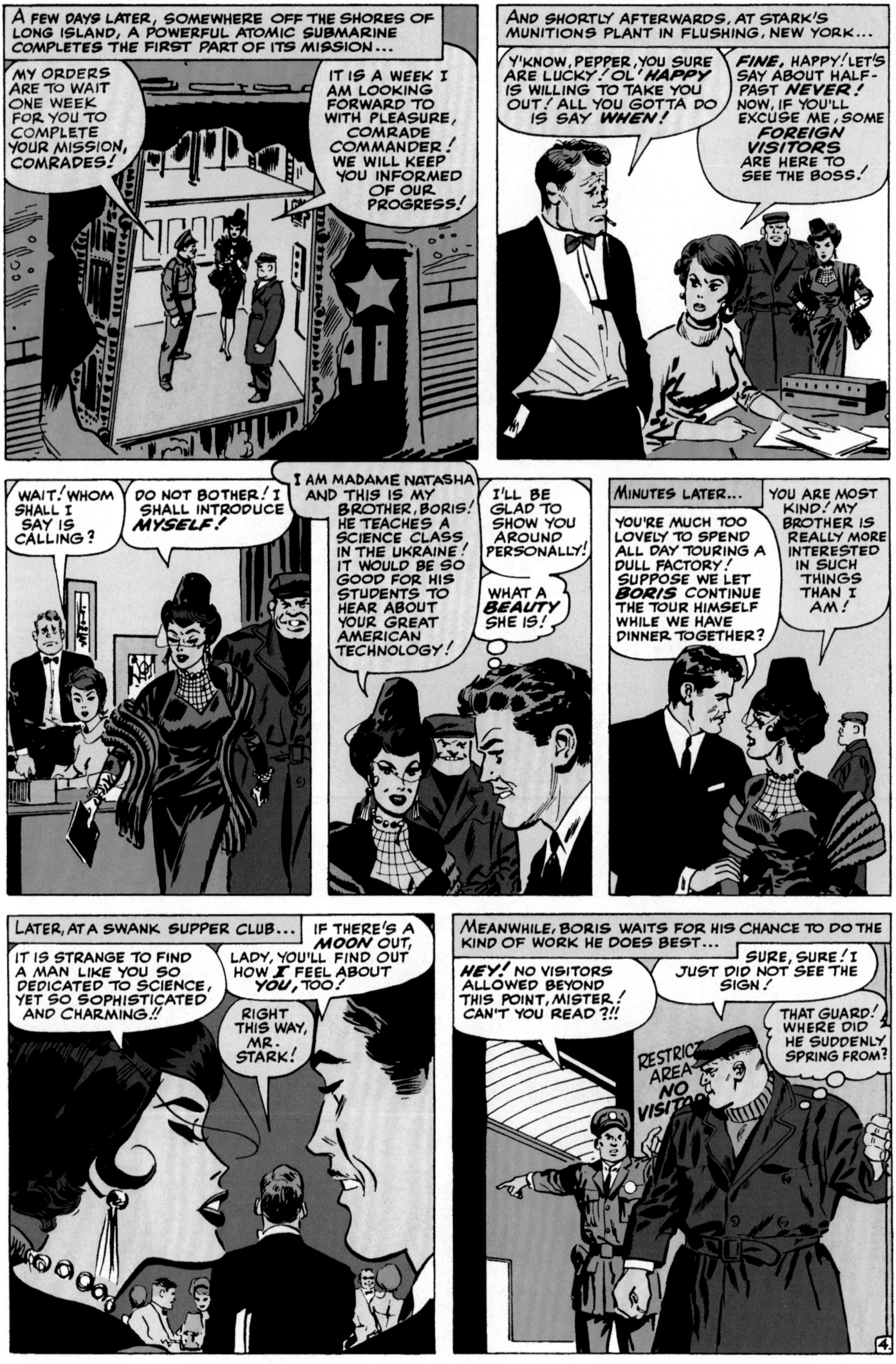

A FEW DAYS LATER, SOMEWHERE OFF THE SHORES OF LONG ISLAND, A POWERFUL ATOMIC SUBMARINE COMPLETES THE FIRST PART OF ITS MISSION...
MY ORDERS ARE TO WAIT ONE WEEK FOR YOU TO COMPLETE YOUR MISSION, COMRADES!
IT IS A WEEK I AM LOOKING FORWARD TO WITH PLEASURE, COMRADE COMMANDER! WE WILL KEEP YOU INFORMED OF OUR PROGRESS!
AND SHORTLY AFTERWARDS, AT STARK'S MUNITIONS PLANT IN FLUSHING, NEW YORK...
Y'KNOW, PEPPER, YOU SURE ARE LUCKY! OL' HAPPY IS WILLING TO TAKE YOU OUT! ALL YOU GOTTA DO IS SAY WHEN!
FINE, HAPPY! LET'S SAY ABOUT HALF-PAST NEVER! NOW, IF YOU'LL EXCUSE ME, SOME FOREIGN VISITORS ARE HERE TO SEE THE BOSS!
WAIT! WHOM SHALL I SAY IS CALLING?
DO NOT BOTHER! I SHALL INTRODUCE MYSELF!
I AM MADAME NATASHA AND THIS IS MY BROTHER, BORIS! HE TEACHES A SCIENCE CLASS IN THE UKRAINE! IT WOULD BE SO GOOD FOR HIS STUDENTS TO HEAR ABOUT YOUR GREAT AMERICAN TECHNOLOGY!
I'LL BE GLAD TO SHOW YOU AROUND PERSONALLY!
WHAT A BEAUTY SHE IS!
MINUTES LATER...
YOU'RE MUCH TOO LOVELY TO SPEND ALL DAY TOURING A DULL FACTORY! SUPPOSE WE LET BORIS CONTINUE THE TOUR HIMSELF WHILE WE HAVE DINNER TOGETHER?
YOU ARE MOST KIND! MY BROTHER IS REALLY MORE INTERESTED IN SUCH THINGS THAN I AM!
LATER, AT A SWANK SUPPER CLUB...
IT IS STRANGE TO FIND A MAN LIKE YOU SO DEDICATED TO SCIENCE, YET SO SOPHISTICATED AND CHARMING!!
IF THERE'S A MOON OUT, LADY, YOU'LL FIND OUT HOW I FEEL ABOUT YOU, TOO!
RIGHT THIS WAY, MR. STARK!
MEANWHILE, BORIS WAITS FOR HIS CHANCE TO DO THE KIND OF WORK HE DOES BEST...
HEY! NO VISITORS ALLOWED BEYOND THIS POINT, MISTER! CAN'T YOU READ?!!
SURE, SURE! I JUST DID NOT SEE THE SIGN!
THAT GUARD! WHERE DID HE SUDDENLY SPRING FROM?
4

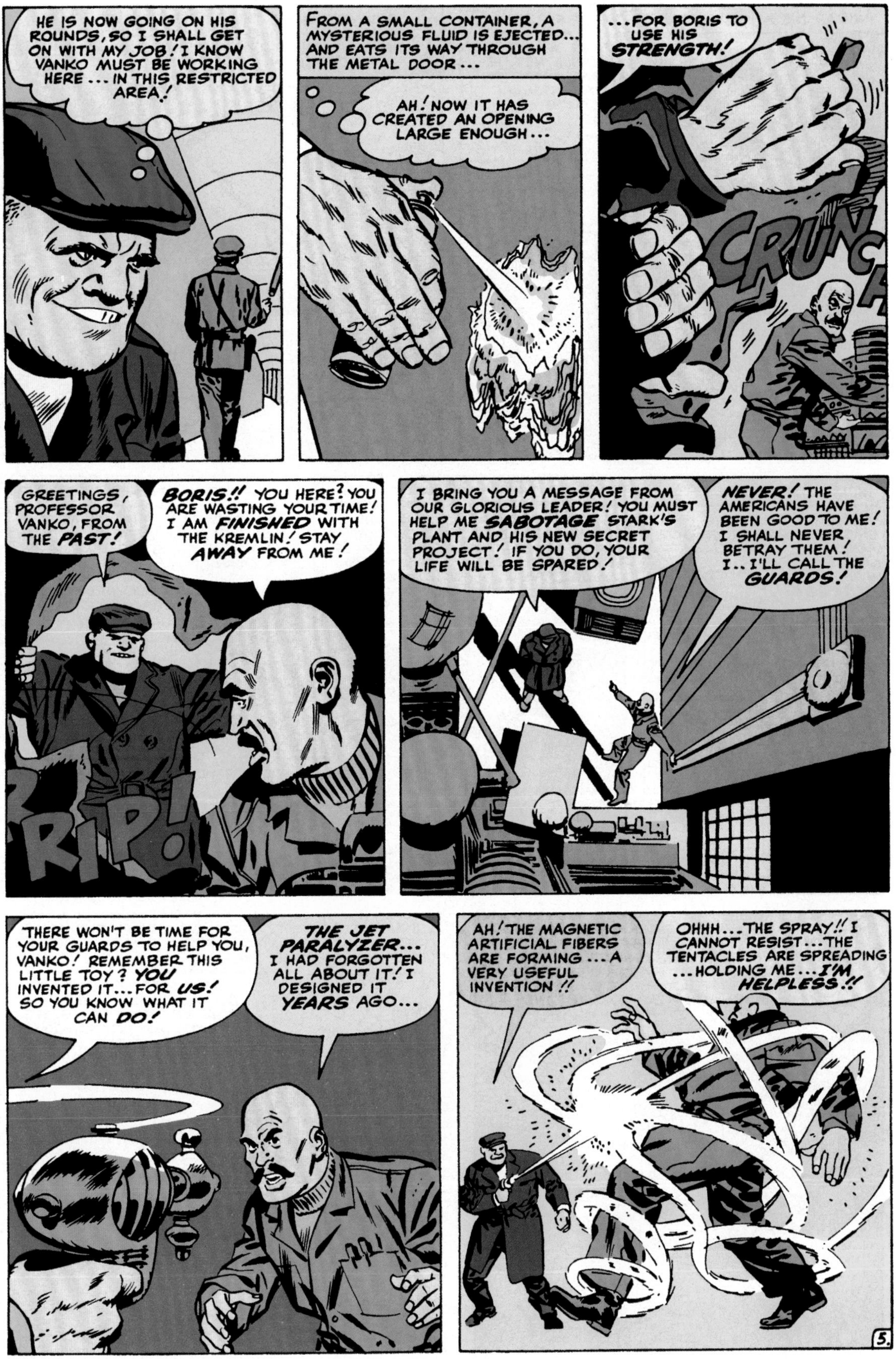
HE IS NOW GOING ON HIS ROUNDS, SO I SHALL GET ON WITH MY JOB! I KNOW VANKO MUST BE WORKING HERE ... IN THIS RESTRICTED AREA!
FROM A SMALL CONTAINER, A MYSTERIOUS FLUID IS EJECTED... AND EATS ITS WAY THROUGH THE METAL DOOR ...
AH! NOW IT HAS CREATED AN OPENING LARGE ENOUGH ...
...FOR BORIS TO USE HIS STRENGTH!
CRUNCH
GREETINGS, PROFESSOR VANKO, FROM THE PAST!
BORIS!! YOU HERE? YOU ARE WASTING YOUR TIME! I AM FINISHED WITH THE KREMLIN! STAY AWAY FROM ME!
RIP!
I BRING YOU A MESSAGE FROM OUR GLORIOUS LEADER! YOU MUST HELP ME SABOTAGE STARK'S PLANT AND HIS NEW SECRET PROJECT! IF YOU DO, YOUR LIFE WILL BE SPARED!
NEVER! THE AMERICANS HAVE BEEN GOOD TO ME! I SHALL NEVER BETRAY THEM! I.. I'LL CALL THE GUARDS!
THERE WON'T BE TIME FOR YOUR GUARDS TO HELP YOU, VANKO! REMEMBER THIS LITTLE TOY? YOU INVENTED IT... FOR US! SO YOU KNOW WHAT IT CAN DO!
THE JET PARALYZER... I HAD FORGOTTEN ALL ABOUT IT! I DESIGNED IT YEARS AGO...
AH! THE MAGNETIC ARTIFICIAL FIBERS ARE FORMING ... A VERY USEFUL INVENTION !!
OHHH ... THE SPRAY!! I CANNOT RESIST ... THE TENTACLES ARE SPREADING ... HOLDING ME ... I'M HELPLESS!!
5.

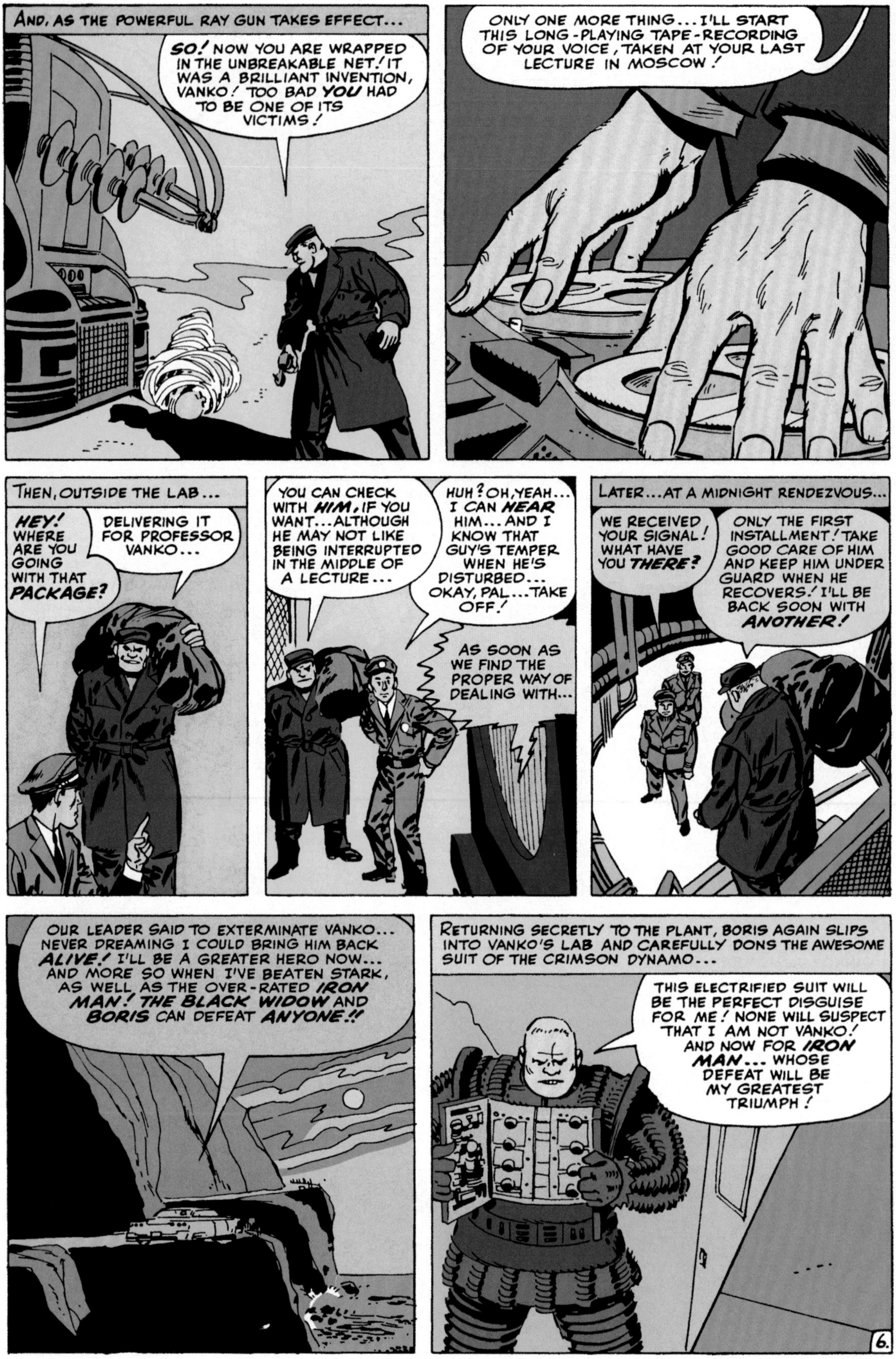
AND, AS THE POWERFUL RAY GUN TAKES EFFECT...
SO! NOW YOU ARE WRAPPED IN THE UNBREAKABLE NET! IT WAS A BRILLIANT INVENTION, VANKO! TOO BAD YOU HAD TO BE ONE OF ITS VICTIMS!
ONLY ONE MORE THING... I'LL START THIS LONG-PLAYING TAPE-RECORDING OF YOUR VOICE, TAKEN AT YOUR LAST LECTURE IN MOSCOW!
THEN, OUTSIDE THE LAB...
HEY! WHERE ARE YOU GOING WITH THAT PACKAGE?
DELIVERING IT FOR PROFESSOR VANKO...
YOU CAN CHECK WITH HIM, IF YOU WANT... ALTHOUGH HE MAY NOT LIKE BEING INTERRUPTED IN THE MIDDLE OF A LECTURE...
HUH? OH, YEAH... I CAN HEAR HIM... AND I KNOW THAT GUY'S TEMPER WHEN HE'S DISTURBED... OKAY, PAL... TAKE OFF!
AS SOON AS WE FIND THE PROPER WAY OF DEALING WITH...
LATER... AT A MIDNIGHT RENDEZVOUS...
WE RECEIVED YOUR SIGNAL! WHAT HAVE YOU THERE?
ONLY THE FIRST INSTALLMENT! TAKE GOOD CARE OF HIM AND KEEP HIM UNDER GUARD WHEN HE RECOVERS! I'LL BE BACK SOON WITH ANOTHER!
OUR LEADER SAID TO EXTERMINATE VANKO... NEVER DREAMING I COULD BRING HIM BACK ALIVE! I'LL BE A GREATER HERO NOW... AND MORE SO WHEN I'VE BEATEN STARK, AS WELL AS THE OVER-RATED IRON MAN! THE BLACK WIDOW AND BORIS CAN DEFEAT ANYONE!!
RETURNING SECRETLY TO THE PLANT, BORIS AGAIN SLIPS INTO VANKO'S LAB AND CAREFULLY DONS THE AWESOME SUIT OF THE CRIMSON DYNAMO...
THIS ELECTRIFIED SUIT WILL BE THE PERFECT DISGUISE FOR ME! NONE WILL SUSPECT THAT I AM NOT VANKO! AND NOW FOR IRON MAN... WHOSE DEFEAT WILL BE MY GREATEST TRIUMPH!
6.

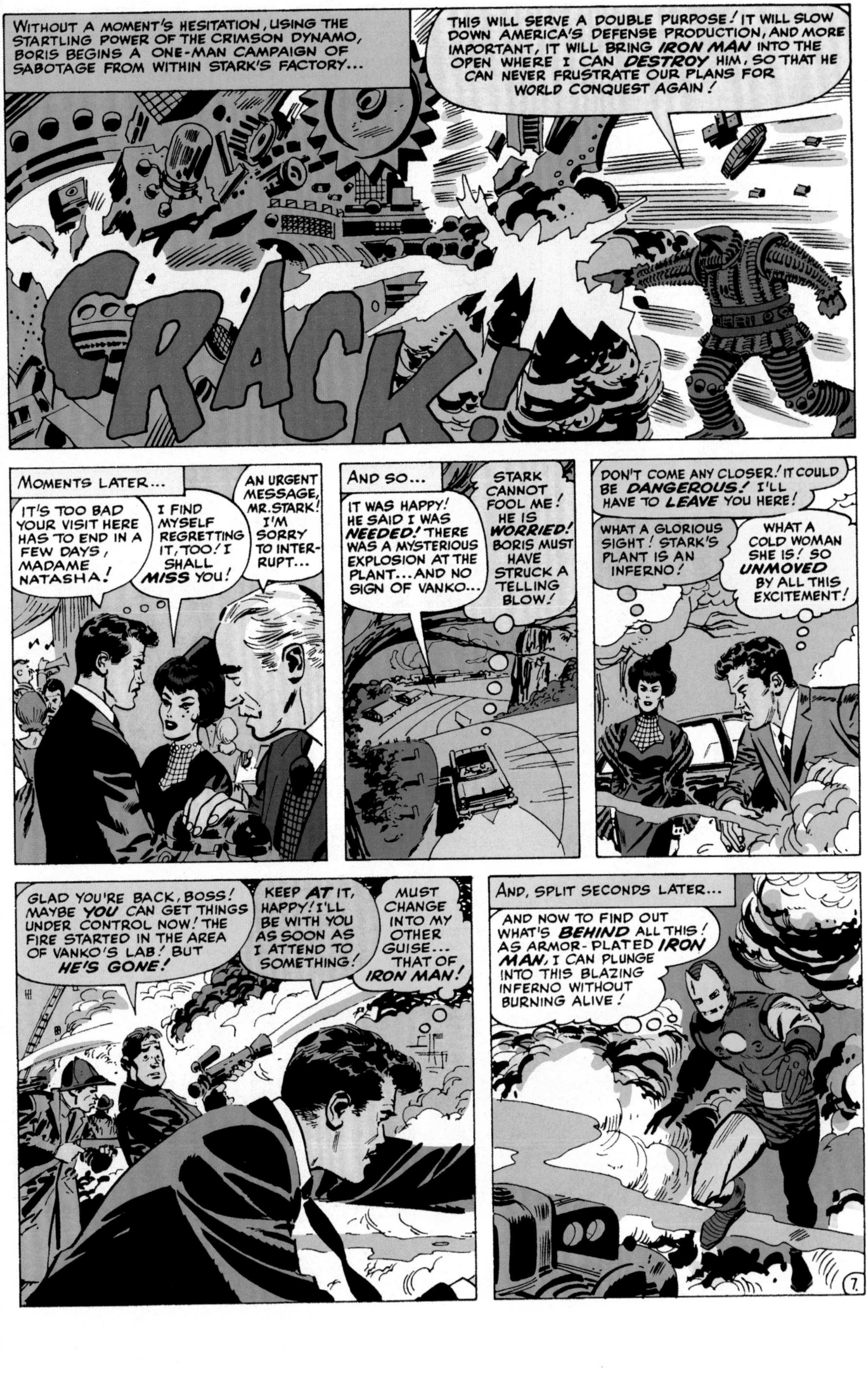

WITHOUT A MOMENT'S HESITATION, USING THE STARTLING POWER OF THE CRIMSON DYNAMO, BORIS BEGINS A ONE-MAN CAMPAIGN OF SABOTAGE FROM WITHIN STARK'S FACTORY...
THIS WILL SERVE A DOUBLE PURPOSE! IT WILL SLOW DOWN AMERICA'S DEFENSE PRODUCTION, AND MORE IMPORTANT, IT WILL BRING IRON MAN INTO THE OPEN WHERE I CAN DESTROY HIM, SO THAT HE CAN NEVER FRUSTRATE OUR PLANS FOR WORLD CONQUEST AGAIN!
CRACK!
MOMENTS LATER...
IT'S TOO BAD YOUR VISIT HERE HAS TO END IN A FEW DAYS, MADAME NATASHA!
I FIND MYSELF REGRETTING IT, TOO! I SHALL MISS YOU!
AN URGENT MESSAGE, MR. STARK! I'M SORRY TO INTERRUPT...
AND SO...
IT WAS HAPPY! HE SAID I WAS NEEDED! THERE WAS A MYSTERIOUS EXPLOSION AT THE PLANT... AND NO SIGN OF VANKO...
STARK CANNOT FOOL ME! HE IS WORRIED! BORIS MUST HAVE STRUCK A TELLING BLOW!
DON'T COME ANY CLOSER! IT COULD BE DANGEROUS! I'LL HAVE TO LEAVE YOU HERE!
WHAT A GLORIOUS SIGHT! STARK'S PLANT IS AN INFERNO!
WHAT A COLD WOMAN SHE IS! SO UNMOVED BY ALL THIS EXCITEMENT!
GLAD YOU'RE BACK, BOSS! MAYBE YOU CAN GET THINGS UNDER CONTROL NOW! THE FIRE STARTED IN THE AREA OF VANKO'S LAB! BUT HE'S GONE!
KEEP AT IT, HAPPY! I'LL BE WITH YOU AS SOON AS I ATTEND TO SOMETHING!
MUST CHANGE INTO MY OTHER GUISE... THAT OF IRON MAN!
AND, SPLIT SECONDS LATER...
AND NOW TO FIND OUT WHAT'S BEHIND ALL THIS! AS ARMOR-PLATED IRON MAN, I CAN PLUNGE INTO THIS BLAZING INFERNO WITHOUT BURNING ALIVE!
7.

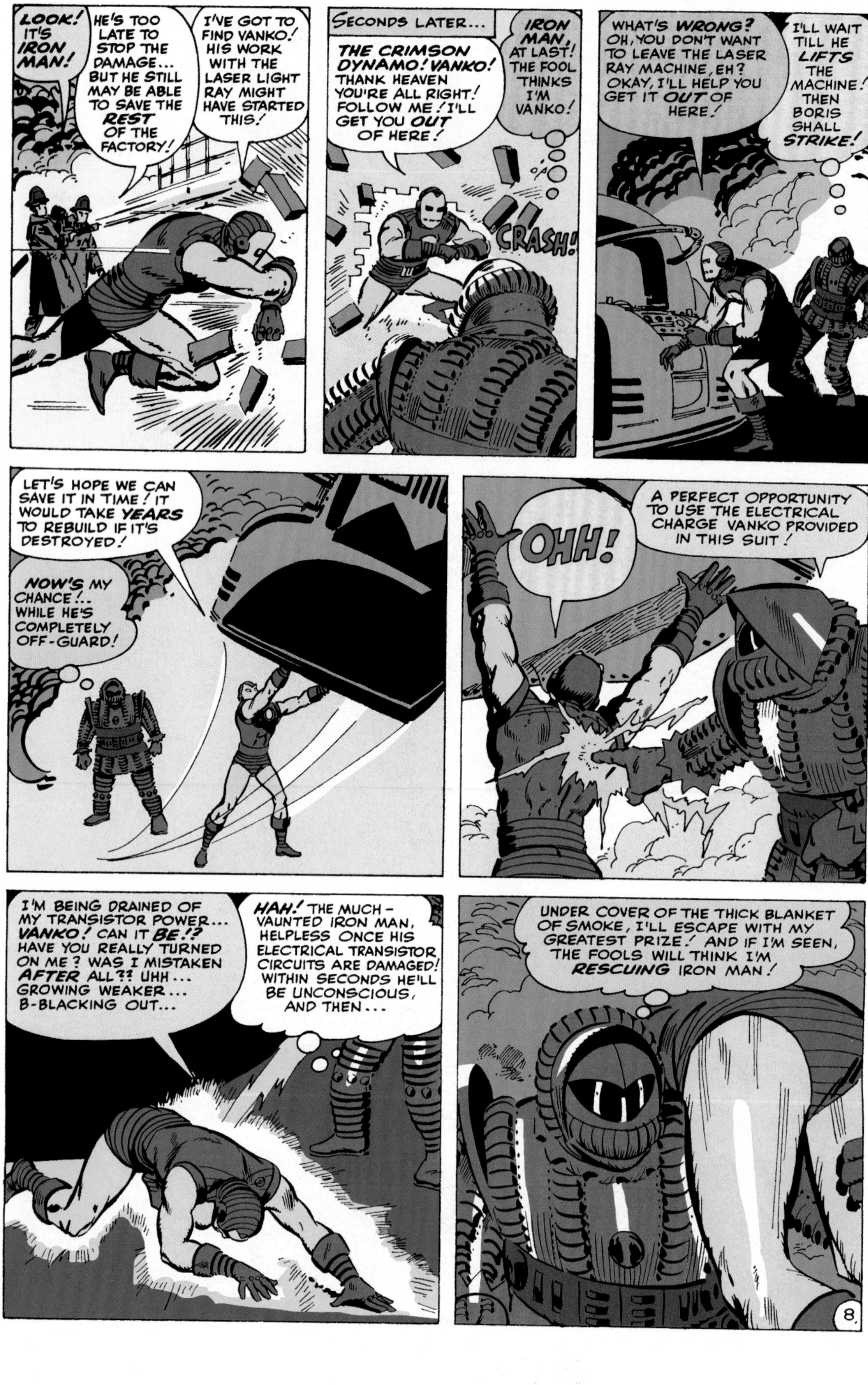
LOOK! IT'S IRON MAN!
HE'S TOO LATE TO STOP THE DAMAGE... BUT HE STILL MAY BE ABLE TO SAVE THE REST OF THE FACTORY!
I'VE GOT TO FIND VANKO! HIS WORK WITH THE LASER LIGHT RAY MIGHT HAVE STARTED THIS!
SECONDS LATER...
THE CRIMSON DYNAMO! VANKO! THANK HEAVEN YOU'RE ALL RIGHT! FOLLOW ME! I'LL GET YOU OUT OF HERE!
IRON MAN, AT LAST! THE FOOL THINKS I'M VANKO!
CRASH!
WHAT'S WRONG? OH, YOU DON'T WANT TO LEAVE THE LASER RAY MACHINE, EH? OKAY, I'LL HELP YOU GET IT OUT OF HERE!
I'LL WAIT TILL HE LIFTS THE MACHINE! THEN BORIS SHALL STRIKE!
LET'S HOPE WE CAN SAVE IT IN TIME! IT WOULD TAKE YEARS TO REBUILD IF IT'S DESTROYED!
NOW'S MY CHANCE!.. WHILE HE'S COMPLETELY OFF-GUARD!
A PERFECT OPPORTUNITY TO USE THE ELECTRICAL CHARGE VANKO PROVIDED IN THIS SUIT!
OHH!
I'M BEING DRAINED OF MY TRANSISTOR POWER... VANKO! CAN IT BE!? HAVE YOU REALLY TURNED ON ME? WAS I MISTAKEN AFTER ALL?? UHH... GROWING WEAKER... B-BLACKING OUT...
HAH! THE MUCH-VAUNTED IRON MAN, HELPLESS ONCE HIS ELECTRICAL TRANSISTOR CIRCUITS ARE DAMAGED! WITHIN SECONDS HE'LL BE UNCONSCIOUS, AND THEN...
UNDER COVER OF THE THICK BLANKET OF SMOKE, I'LL ESCAPE WITH MY GREATEST PRIZE! AND IF I'M SEEN, THE FOOLS WILL THINK I'M RESCUING IRON MAN!
8.

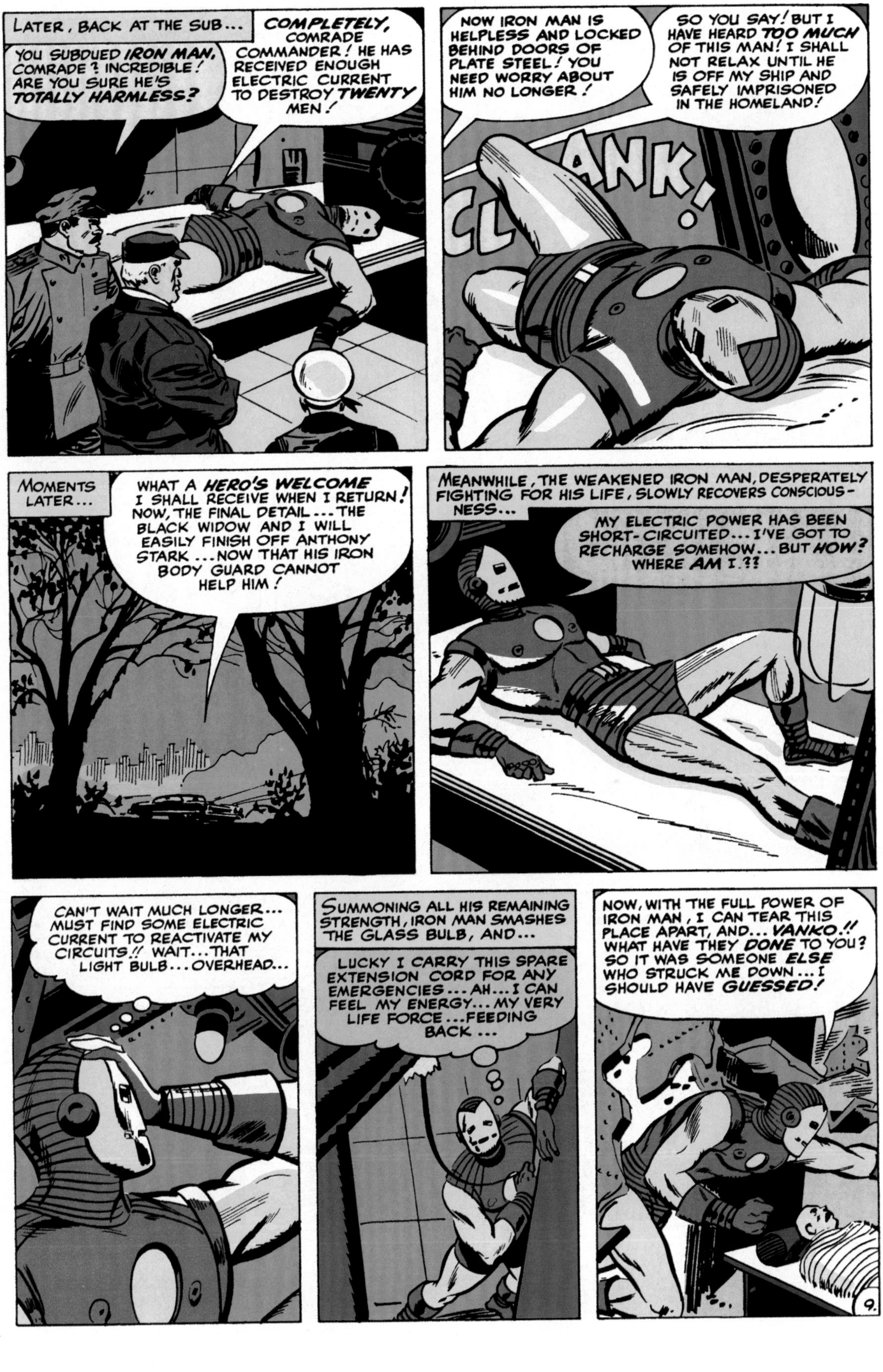
LATER, BACK AT THE SUB...
YOU SUBDUED IRON MAN, COMRADE? INCREDIBLE! ARE YOU SURE HE'S TOTALLY HARMLESS?
COMPLETELY, COMRADE COMMANDER! HE HAS RECEIVED ENOUGH ELECTRIC CURRENT TO DESTROY TWENTY MEN!
NOW IRON MAN IS HELPLESS AND LOCKED BEHIND DOORS OF PLATE STEEL! YOU NEED WORRY ABOUT HIM NO LONGER!
SO YOU SAY! BUT I HAVE HEARD TOO MUCH OF THIS MAN! I SHALL NOT RELAX UNTIL HE IS OFF MY SHIP AND SAFELY IMPRISONED IN THE HOMELAND!
CLANK!
MOMENTS LATER...
WHAT A HERO'S WELCOME I SHALL RECEIVE WHEN I RETURN! NOW, THE FINAL DETAIL... THE BLACK WIDOW AND I WILL EASILY FINISH OFF ANTHONY STARK... NOW THAT HIS IRON BODY GUARD CANNOT HELP HIM!
MEANWHILE, THE WEAKENED IRON MAN, DESPERATELY FIGHTING FOR HIS LIFE, SLOWLY RECOVERS CONSCIOUSNESS...
MY ELECTRIC POWER HAS BEEN SHORT-CIRCUITED... I'VE GOT TO RECHARGE SOMEHOW... BUT HOW? WHERE AM I.??
CAN'T WAIT MUCH LONGER... MUST FIND SOME ELECTRIC CURRENT TO REACTIVATE MY CIRCUITS!! WAIT... THAT LIGHT BULB... OVERHEAD...
SUMMONING ALL HIS REMAINING STRENGTH, IRON MAN SMASHES THE GLASS BULB, AND...
LUCKY I CARRY THIS SPARE EXTENSION CORD FOR ANY EMERGENCIES... AH... I CAN FEEL MY ENERGY... MY VERY LIFE FORCE... FEEDING BACK...
NOW, WITH THE FULL POWER OF IRON MAN, I CAN TEAR THIS PLACE APART, AND... VANKO.!! WHAT HAVE THEY DONE TO YOU? SO IT WAS SOMEONE ELSE WHO STRUCK ME DOWN... I SHOULD HAVE GUESSED!
9.

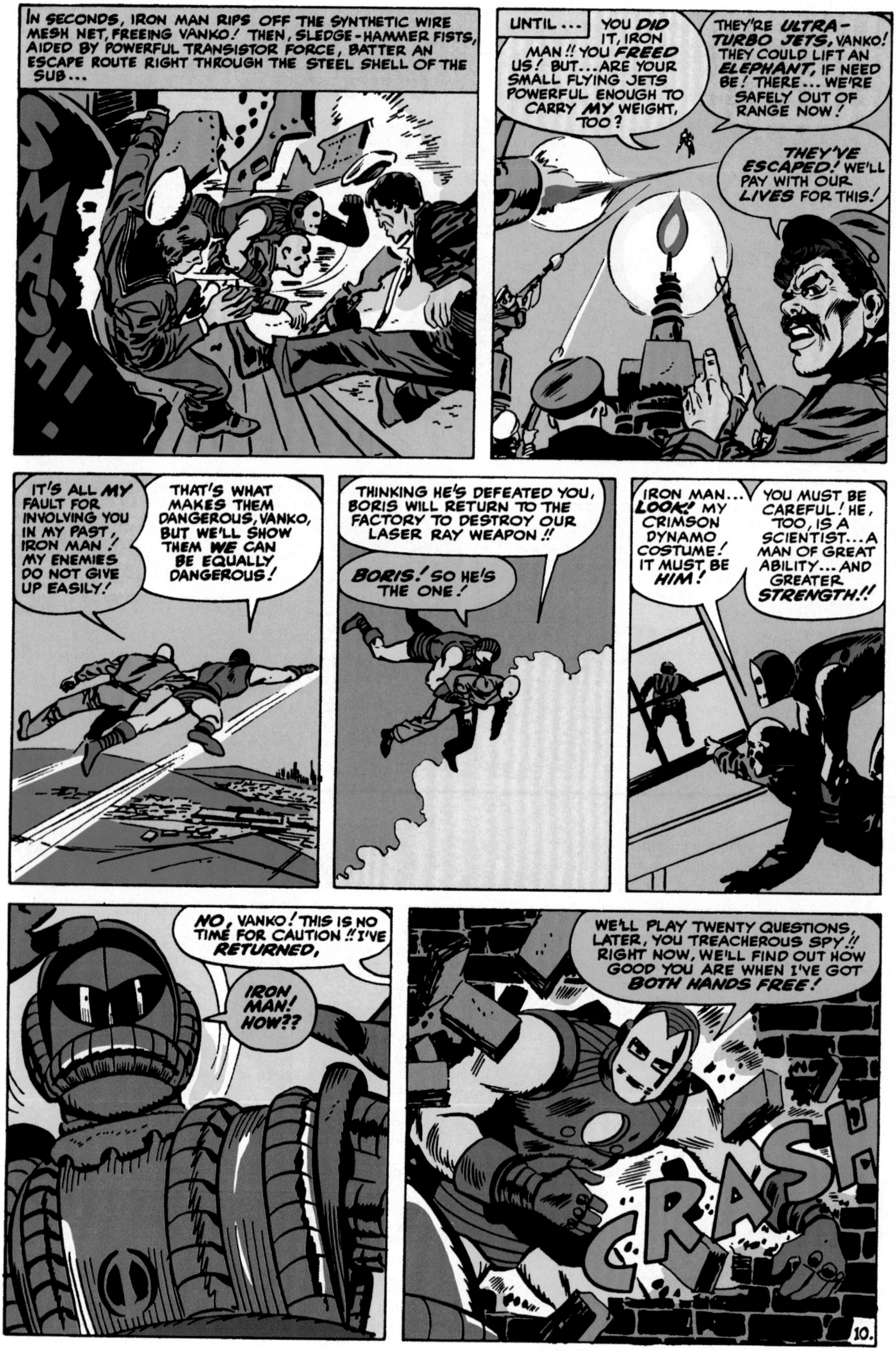

IN SECONDS, IRON MAN RIPS OFF THE SYNTHETIC WIRE MESH NET, FREEING VANKO! THEN, SLEDGE-HAMMER FISTS, AIDED BY POWERFUL TRANSISTOR FORCE, BATTER AN ESCAPE ROUTE RIGHT THROUGH THE STEEL SHELL OF THE SUB...
SMASH!
UNTIL...
YOU DID IT, IRON MAN!! YOU FREED US! BUT...ARE YOUR SMALL FLYING JETS POWERFUL ENOUGH TO CARRY MY WEIGHT, TOO?
THEY'RE ULTRA-TURBO JETS, VANKO! THEY COULD LIFT AN ELEPHANT, IF NEED BE! THERE...WE'RE SAFELY OUT OF RANGE NOW!
THEY'VE ESCAPED! WE'LL PAY WITH OUR LIVES FOR THIS!
IT'S ALL MY FAULT FOR INVOLVING YOU IN MY PAST, IRON MAN! MY ENEMIES DO NOT GIVE UP EASILY!
THAT'S WHAT MAKES THEM DANGEROUS, VANKO, BUT WE'LL SHOW THEM WE CAN BE EQUALLY DANGEROUS!
THINKING HE'S DEFEATED YOU, BORIS WILL RETURN TO THE FACTORY TO DESTROY OUR LASER RAY WEAPON!!
BORIS! SO HE'S THE ONE!
IRON MAN...LOOK! MY CRIMSON DYNAMO COSTUME! IT MUST BE HIM!
YOU MUST BE CAREFUL! HE, TOO, IS A SCIENTIST...A MAN OF GREAT ABILITY...AND GREATER STRENGTH!!
NO, VANKO! THIS IS NO TIME FOR CAUTION!! I'VE RETURNED,
IRON MAN! HOW??
WE'LL PLAY TWENTY QUESTIONS LATER, YOU TREACHEROUS SPY!! RIGHT NOW, WE'LL FIND OUT HOW GOOD YOU ARE WHEN I'VE GOT BOTH HANDS FREE!
CRASH

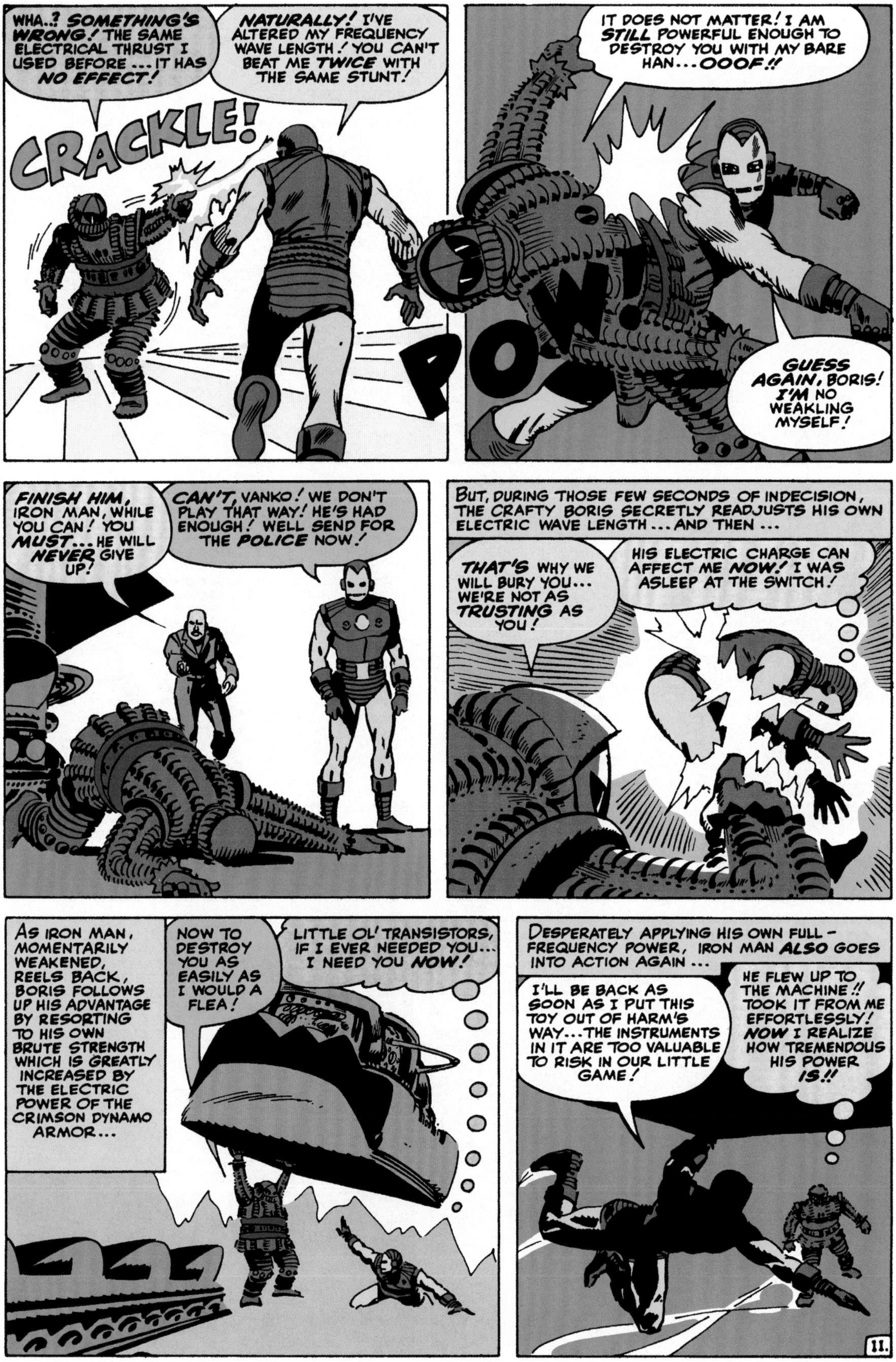

WHA..? SOMETHING'S WRONG! THE SAME ELECTRICAL THRUST I USED BEFORE ... IT HAS NO EFFECT!
NATURALLY! I'VE ALTERED MY FREQUENCY WAVE LENGTH! YOU CAN'T BEAT ME TWICE WITH THE SAME STUNT!
CRACKLE!
IT DOES NOT MATTER! I AM STILL POWERFUL ENOUGH TO DESTROY YOU WITH MY BARE HAN... OOOF!!
POW!
GUESS AGAIN, BORIS! I'M NO WEAKLING MYSELF!
FINISH HIM, IRON MAN, WHILE YOU CAN! YOU MUST... HE WILL NEVER GIVE UP!
CAN'T, VANKO! WE DON'T PLAY THAT WAY! HE'S HAD ENOUGH! WELL SEND FOR THE POLICE NOW!
BUT, DURING THOSE FEW SECONDS OF INDECISION, THE CRAFTY BORIS SECRETLY READJUSTS HIS OWN ELECTRIC WAVE LENGTH ... AND THEN ...
THAT'S WHY WE WILL BURY YOU... WE'RE NOT AS TRUSTING AS YOU!
HIS ELECTRIC CHARGE CAN AFFECT ME NOW! I WAS ASLEEP AT THE SWITCH!
AS IRON MAN, MOMENTARILY WEAKENED, REELS BACK, BORIS FOLLOWS UP HIS ADVANTAGE BY RESORTING TO HIS OWN BRUTE STRENGTH WHICH IS GREATLY INCREASED BY THE ELECTRIC POWER OF THE CRIMSON DYNAMO ARMOR...
NOW TO DESTROY YOU AS EASILY AS I WOULD A FLEA!
LITTLE OL' TRANSISTORS, IF I EVER NEEDED YOU... I NEED YOU NOW!
DESPERATELY APPLYING HIS OWN FULL-FREQUENCY POWER, IRON MAN ALSO GOES INTO ACTION AGAIN ...
I'LL BE BACK AS SOON AS I PUT THIS TOY OUT OF HARM'S WAY... THE INSTRUMENTS IN IT ARE TOO VALUABLE TO RISK IN OUR LITTLE GAME!
HE FLEW UP TO THE MACHINE!! TOOK IT FROM ME EFFORTLESSLY! NOW I REALIZE HOW TREMENDOUS HIS POWER IS!!
11.

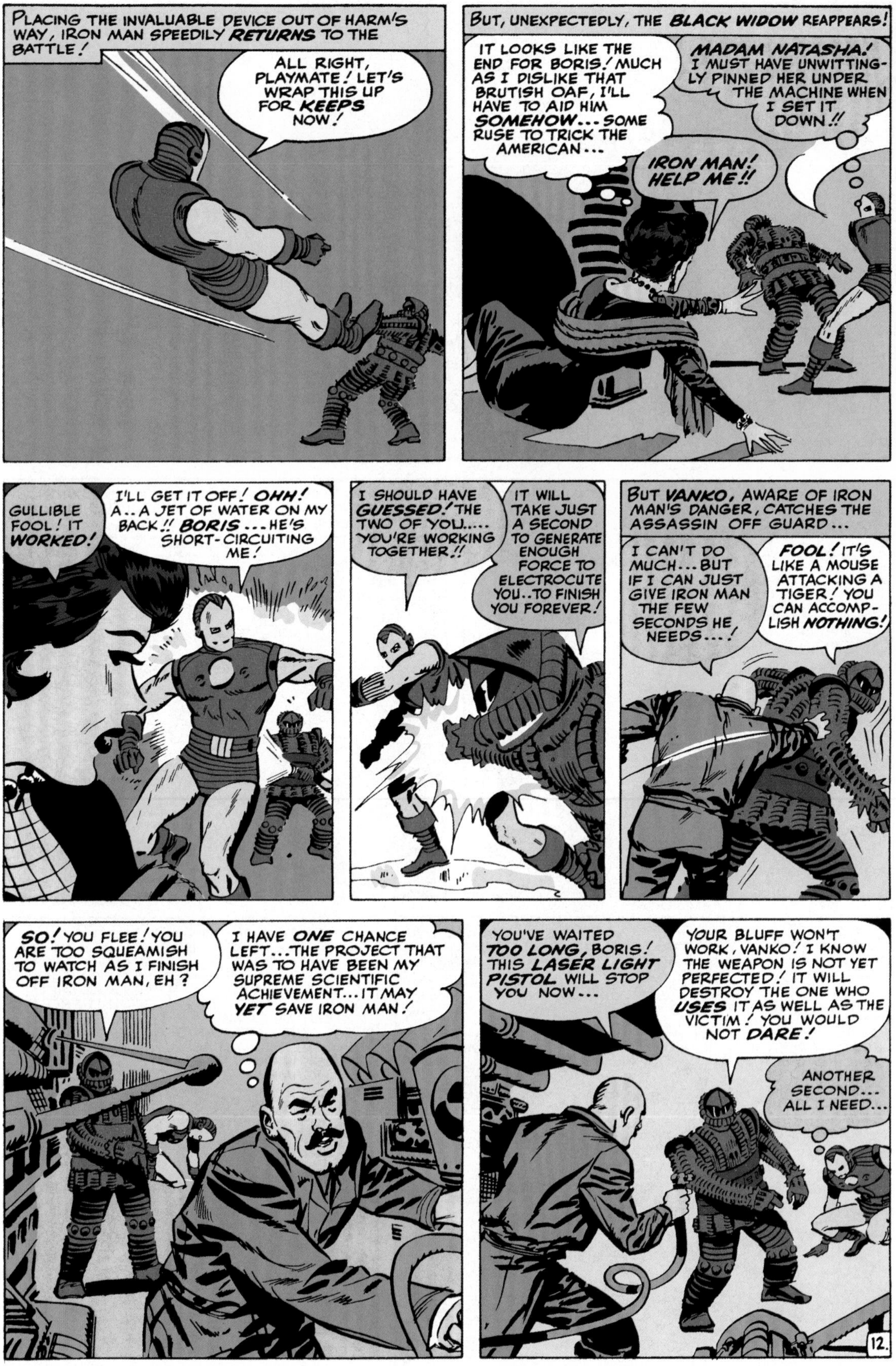

PLACING THE INVALUABLE DEVICE OUT OF HARM'S WAY, IRON MAN SPEEDILY RETURNS TO THE BATTLE!
ALL RIGHT, PLAYMATE! LET'S WRAP THIS UP FOR KEEPS NOW!
BUT, UNEXPECTEDLY, THE BLACK WIDOW REAPPEARS!
IT LOOKS LIKE THE END FOR BORIS! MUCH AS I DISLIKE THAT BRUTISH OAF, I'LL HAVE TO AID HIM SOMEHOW... SOME RUSE TO TRICK THE AMERICAN...
MADAM NATASHA! I MUST HAVE UNWITTINGLY PINNED HER UNDER THE MACHINE WHEN I SET IT DOWN!!
IRON MAN! HELP ME!!
GULLIBLE FOOL! IT WORKED!
I'LL GET IT OFF! OHH! A.. A JET OF WATER ON MY BACK!! BORIS... HE'S SHORT-CIRCUITING ME!
I SHOULD HAVE GUESSED! THE TWO OF YOU..... YOU'RE WORKING TOGETHER!!
IT WILL TAKE JUST A SECOND TO GENERATE ENOUGH FORCE TO ELECTROCUTE YOU.. TO FINISH YOU FOREVER!
BUT VANKO, AWARE OF IRON MAN'S DANGER, CATCHES THE ASSASSIN OFF GUARD...
I CAN'T DO MUCH... BUT IF I CAN JUST GIVE IRON MAN THE FEW SECONDS HE NEEDS...!
FOOL! IT'S LIKE A MOUSE ATTACKING A TIGER! YOU CAN ACCOMPLISH NOTHING!
SO! YOU FLEE! YOU ARE TOO SQUEAMISH TO WATCH AS I FINISH OFF IRON MAN, EH?
I HAVE ONE CHANCE LEFT... THE PROJECT THAT WAS TO HAVE BEEN MY SUPREME SCIENTIFIC ACHIEVEMENT... IT MAY YET SAVE IRON MAN!
YOU'VE WAITED TOO LONG, BORIS! THIS LASER LIGHT PISTOL WILL STOP YOU NOW...
YOUR BLUFF WON'T WORK, VANKO! I KNOW THE WEAPON IS NOT YET PERFECTED! IT WILL DESTROY THE ONE WHO USES IT AS WELL AS THE VICTIM! YOU WOULD NOT DARE!
ANOTHER SECOND... ALL I NEED...
12.

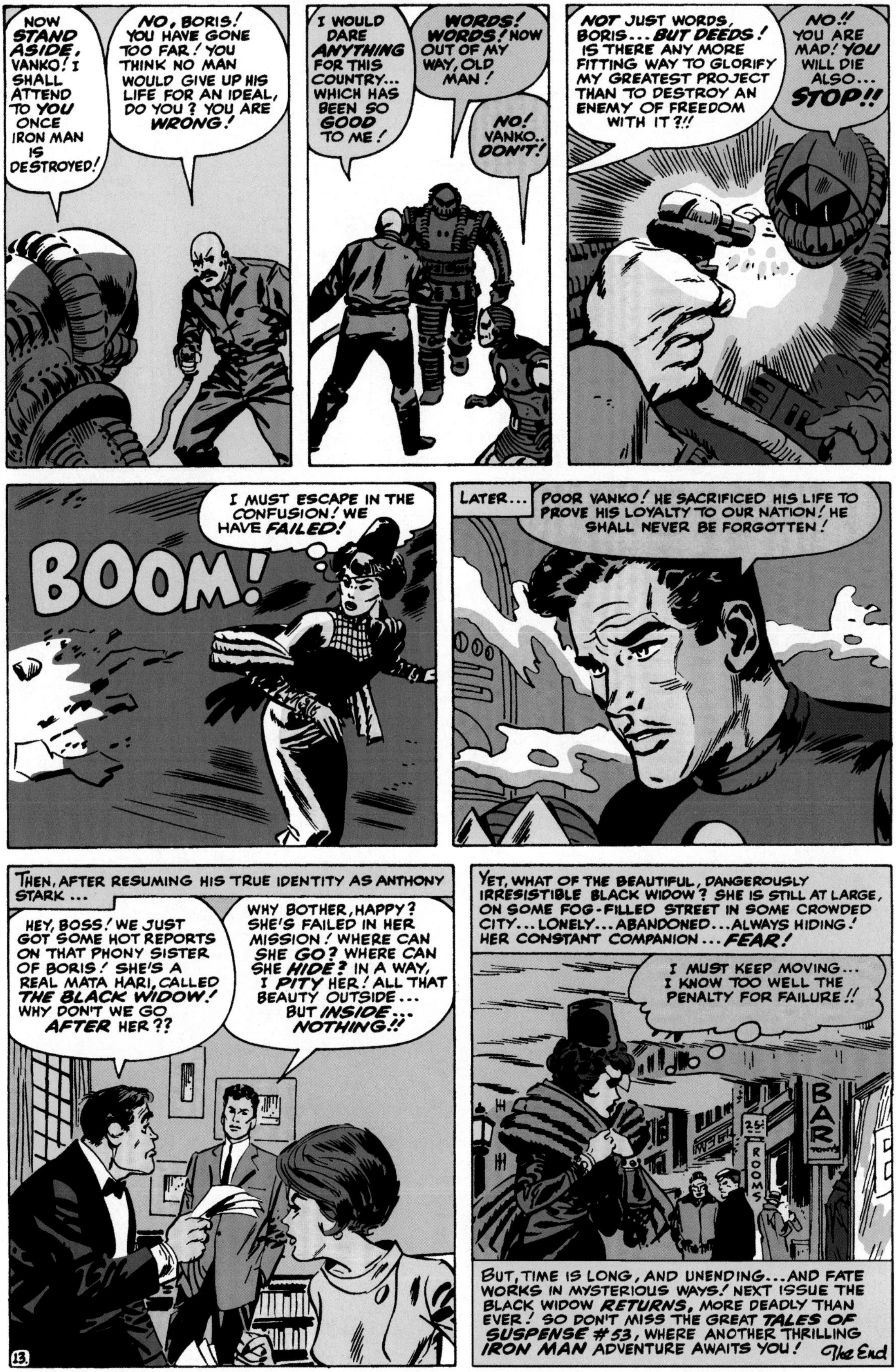
NOW STAND ASIDE, VANKO! I SHALL ATTEND TO YOU ONCE IRON MAN IS DESTROYED!
NO, BORIS! YOU HAVE GONE TOO FAR! YOU THINK NO MAN WOULD GIVE UP HIS LIFE FOR AN IDEAL, DO YOU? YOU ARE WRONG!
I WOULD DARE ANYTHING FOR THIS COUNTRY... WHICH HAS BEEN SO GOOD TO ME!
WORDS! WORDS! NOW OUT OF MY WAY, OLD MAN!
NO! VANKO.. DON'T!
NOT JUST WORDS, BORIS... BUT DEEDS! IS THERE ANY MORE FITTING WAY TO GLORIFY MY GREATEST PROJECT THAN TO DESTROY AN ENEMY OF FREEDOM WITH IT?!!
NO!! YOU ARE MAD! YOU WILL DIE ALSO... STOP!!
I MUST ESCAPE IN THE CONFUSION! WE HAVE FAILED!
BOOM!
LATER...
POOR VANKO! HE SACRIFICED HIS LIFE TO PROVE HIS LOYALTY TO OUR NATION! HE SHALL NEVER BE FORGOTTEN!
THEN, AFTER RESUMING HIS TRUE IDENTITY AS ANTHONY STARK...
HEY, BOSS! WE JUST GOT SOME HOT REPORTS ON THAT PHONY SISTER OF BORIS! SHE'S A REAL MATA HARI, CALLED THE BLACK WIDOW! WHY DON'T WE GO AFTER HER??
WHY BOTHER, HAPPY? SHE'S FAILED IN HER MISSION! WHERE CAN SHE GO? WHERE CAN SHE HIDE? IN A WAY, I PITY HER! ALL THAT BEAUTY OUTSIDE... BUT INSIDE... NOTHING!!
13.
YET, WHAT OF THE BEAUTIFUL, DANGEROUSLY IRRESISTIBLE BLACK WIDOW? SHE IS STILL AT LARGE, ON SOME FOG-FILLED STREET IN SOME CROWDED CITY... LONELY... ABANDONED... ALWAYS HIDING! HER CONSTANT COMPANION... FEAR!
I MUST KEEP MOVING... I KNOW TOO WELL THE PENALTY FOR FAILURE!!
BAR
25¢
ROOMS
BUT, TIME IS LONG, AND UNENDING... AND FATE WORKS IN MYSTERIOUS WAYS! NEXT ISSUE THE BLACK WIDOW RETURNS, MORE DEADLY THAN EVER! SO DON'T MISS THE GREAT TALES OF SUSPENSE #53, WHERE ANOTHER THRILLING IRON MAN ADVENTURE AWAITS YOU!
The End

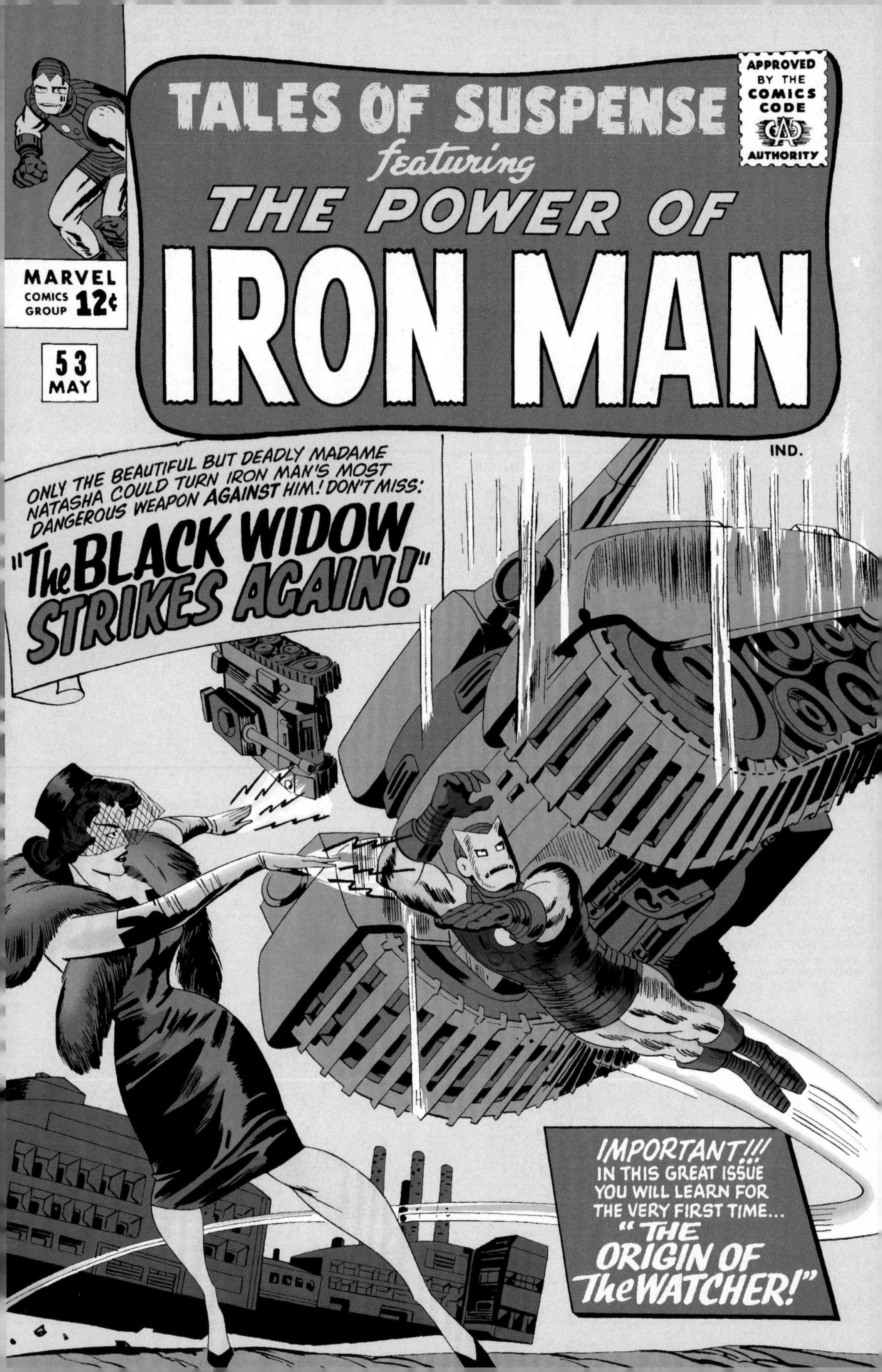

TALES OF SUSPENSE
featuring
THE POWER OF
IRON MAN
APPROVED BY THE COMICS CODE AUTHORITY
MARVEL COMICS GROUP 12¢
53 MAY
IND.
ONLY THE BEAUTIFUL BUT DEADLY MADAME NATASHA COULD TURN IRON MAN'S MOST DANGEROUS WEAPON AGAINST HIM! DON'T MISS:
"The BLACK WIDOW STRIKES AGAIN!"
IMPORTANT!!! IN THIS GREAT ISSUE YOU WILL LEARN FOR THE VERY FIRST TIME...
"THE ORIGIN OF The WATCHER!"

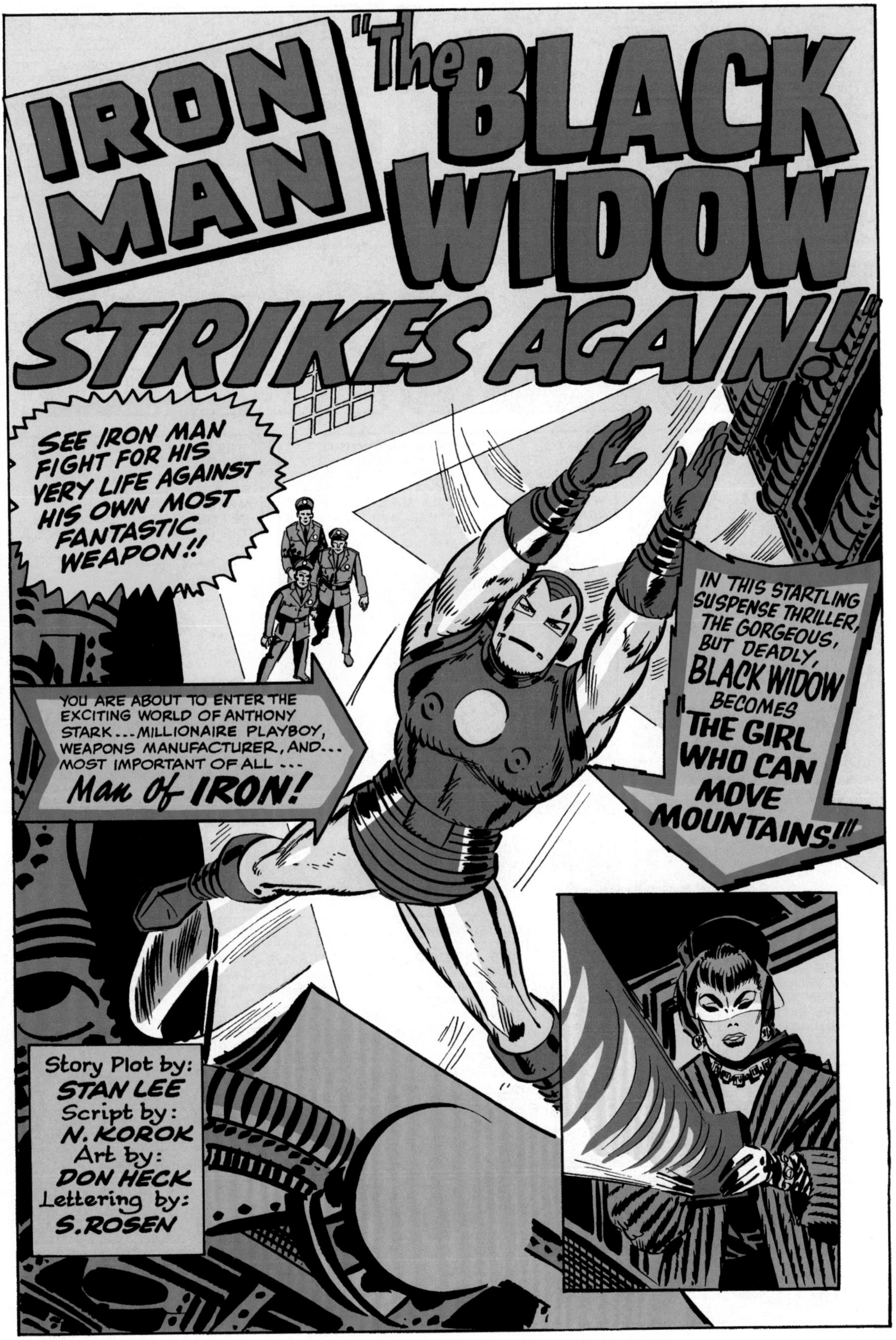
IRON MAN
"The BLACK WIDOW STRIKES AGAIN!"
SEE IRON MAN FIGHT FOR HIS VERY LIFE AGAINST HIS OWN MOST FANTASTIC WEAPON!!
YOU ARE ABOUT TO ENTER THE EXCITING WORLD OF ANTHONY STARK...MILLIONAIRE PLAYBOY, WEAPONS MANUFACTURER, AND... MOST IMPORTANT OF ALL... Man of IRON!
IN THIS STARTLING SUSPENSE THRILLER, THE GORGEOUS, BUT DEADLY, BLACK WIDOW BECOMES THE GIRL WHO CAN MOVE MOUNTAINS!!
Story Plot by: STAN LEE
Script by: N. KOROK
Art by: DON HECK
Lettering by: S. ROSEN

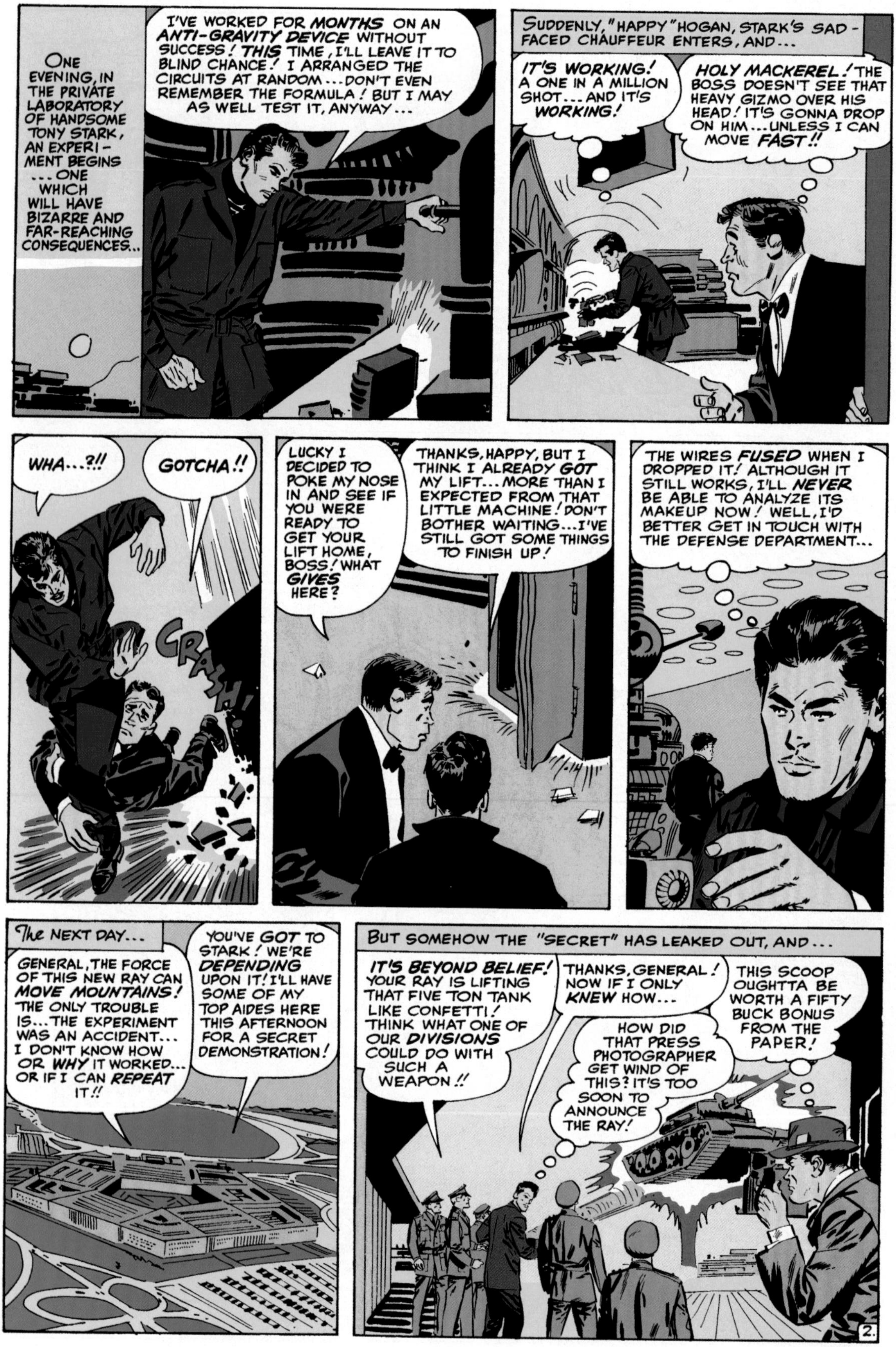
ONE EVENING, IN THE PRIVATE LABORATORY OF HANDSOME TONY STARK, AN EXPERIMENT BEGINS ...ONE WHICH WILL HAVE BIZARRE AND FAR-REACHING CONSEQUENCES...
I'VE WORKED FOR MONTHS ON AN ANTI-GRAVITY DEVICE WITHOUT SUCCESS! THIS TIME, I'LL LEAVE IT TO BLIND CHANCE! I ARRANGED THE CIRCUITS AT RANDOM...DON'T EVEN REMEMBER THE FORMULA! BUT I MAY AS WELL TEST IT, ANYWAY...
SUDDENLY, "HAPPY" HOGAN, STARK'S SAD-FACED CHAUFFEUR ENTERS, AND...
IT'S WORKING! A ONE IN A MILLION SHOT...AND IT'S WORKING!
HOLY MACKEREL! THE BOSS DOESN'T SEE THAT HEAVY GIZMO OVER HIS HEAD! IT'S GONNA DROP ON HIM...UNLESS I CAN MOVE FAST!!
WHA...?!!
GOTCHA!!
CRASH!
LUCKY I DECIDED TO POKE MY NOSE IN AND SEE IF YOU WERE READY TO GET YOUR LIFT HOME, BOSS! WHAT GIVES HERE?
THANKS, HAPPY, BUT I THINK I ALREADY GOT MY LIFT...MORE THAN I EXPECTED FROM THAT LITTLE MACHINE! DON'T BOTHER WAITING...I'VE STILL GOT SOME THINGS TO FINISH UP!
THE WIRES FUSED WHEN I DROPPED IT! ALTHOUGH IT STILL WORKS, I'LL NEVER BE ABLE TO ANALYZE ITS MAKEUP NOW! WELL, I'D BETTER GET IN TOUCH WITH THE DEFENSE DEPARTMENT...
The NEXT DAY...
GENERAL, THE FORCE OF THIS NEW RAY CAN MOVE MOUNTAINS! THE ONLY TROUBLE IS...THE EXPERIMENT WAS AN ACCIDENT... I DON'T KNOW HOW OR WHY IT WORKED... OR IF I CAN REPEAT IT!!
YOU'VE GOT TO STARK! WE'RE DEPENDING UPON IT! I'LL HAVE SOME OF MY TOP AIDES HERE THIS AFTERNOON FOR A SECRET DEMONSTRATION!
BUT SOMEHOW THE "SECRET" HAS LEAKED OUT, AND...
IT'S BEYOND BELIEF! YOUR RAY IS LIFTING THAT FIVE TON TANK LIKE CONFETTI! THINK WHAT ONE OF OUR DIVISIONS COULD DO WITH SUCH A WEAPON!!
THANKS, GENERAL! NOW IF I ONLY KNEW HOW...
HOW DID THAT PRESS PHOTOGRAPHER GET WIND OF THIS? IT'S TOO SOON TO ANNOUNCE THE RAY!
THIS SCOOP OUGHTTA BE WORTH A FIFTY BUCK BONUS FROM THE PAPER!
2.

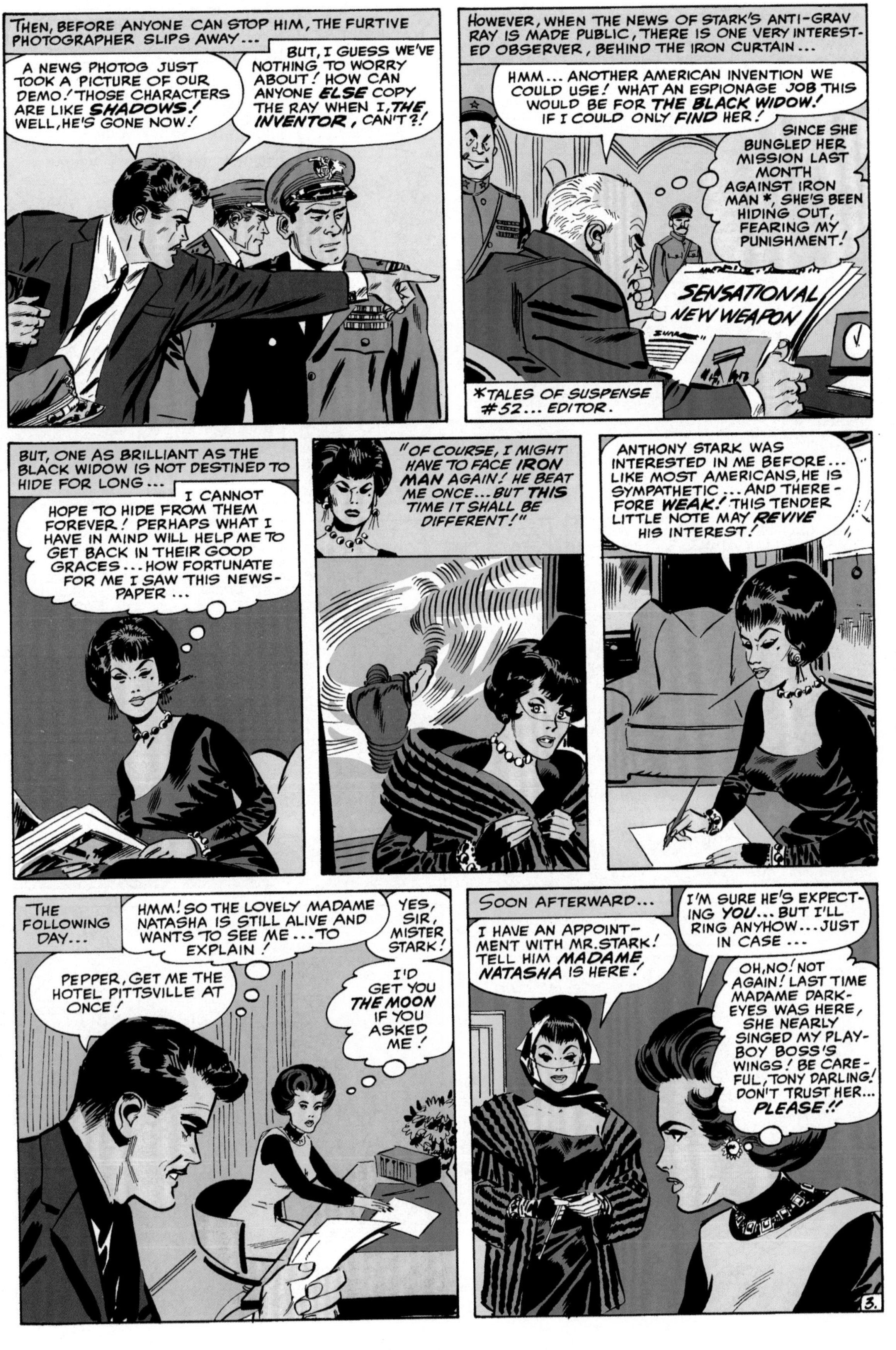
THEN, BEFORE ANYONE CAN STOP HIM, THE FURTIVE PHOTOGRAPHER SLIPS AWAY...
A NEWS PHOTOG JUST TOOK A PICTURE OF OUR DEMO! THOSE CHARACTERS ARE LIKE SHADOWS! WELL, HE'S GONE NOW!
BUT, I GUESS WE'VE NOTHING TO WORRY ABOUT! HOW CAN ANYONE ELSE COPY THE RAY WHEN I, THE INVENTOR, CAN'T?!
HOWEVER, WHEN THE NEWS OF STARK'S ANTI-GRAV RAY IS MADE PUBLIC, THERE IS ONE VERY INTERESTED OBSERVER, BEHIND THE IRON CURTAIN...
HMM... ANOTHER AMERICAN INVENTION WE COULD USE! WHAT AN ESPIONAGE JOB THIS WOULD BE FOR THE BLACK WIDOW! IF I COULD ONLY FIND HER!
SINCE SHE BUNGLED HER MISSION LAST MONTH AGAINST IRON MAN *, SHE'S BEEN HIDING OUT, FEARING MY PUNISHMENT!
SENSATIONAL NEW WEAPON
*TALES OF SUSPENSE #52... EDITOR.
BUT, ONE AS BRILLIANT AS THE BLACK WIDOW IS NOT DESTINED TO HIDE FOR LONG...
I CANNOT HOPE TO HIDE FROM THEM FOREVER! PERHAPS WHAT I HAVE IN MIND WILL HELP ME TO GET BACK IN THEIR GOOD GRACES... HOW FORTUNATE FOR ME I SAW THIS NEWSPAPER...
"OF COURSE, I MIGHT HAVE TO FACE IRON MAN AGAIN! HE BEAT ME ONCE... BUT THIS TIME IT SHALL BE DIFFERENT!"
ANTHONY STARK WAS INTERESTED IN ME BEFORE... LIKE MOST AMERICANS, HE IS SYMPATHETIC... AND THEREFORE WEAK! THIS TENDER LITTLE NOTE MAY REVIVE HIS INTEREST!
THE FOLLOWING DAY...
HMM! SO THE LOVELY MADAME NATASHA IS STILL ALIVE AND WANTS TO SEE ME... TO EXPLAIN!
YES, SIR, MISTER STARK!
PEPPER, GET ME THE HOTEL PITTSVILLE AT ONCE!
I'D GET YOU THE MOON IF YOU ASKED ME!
SOON AFTERWARD...
I HAVE AN APPOINTMENT WITH MR. STARK! TELL HIM MADAME NATASHA IS HERE!
I'M SURE HE'S EXPECTING YOU... BUT I'LL RING ANYHOW... JUST IN CASE...
OH, NO! NOT AGAIN! LAST TIME MADAME DARK-EYES WAS HERE, SHE NEARLY SINGED MY PLAYBOY BOSS'S WINGS! BE CAREFUL, TONY DARLING! DON'T TRUST HER... PLEASE!!
3.

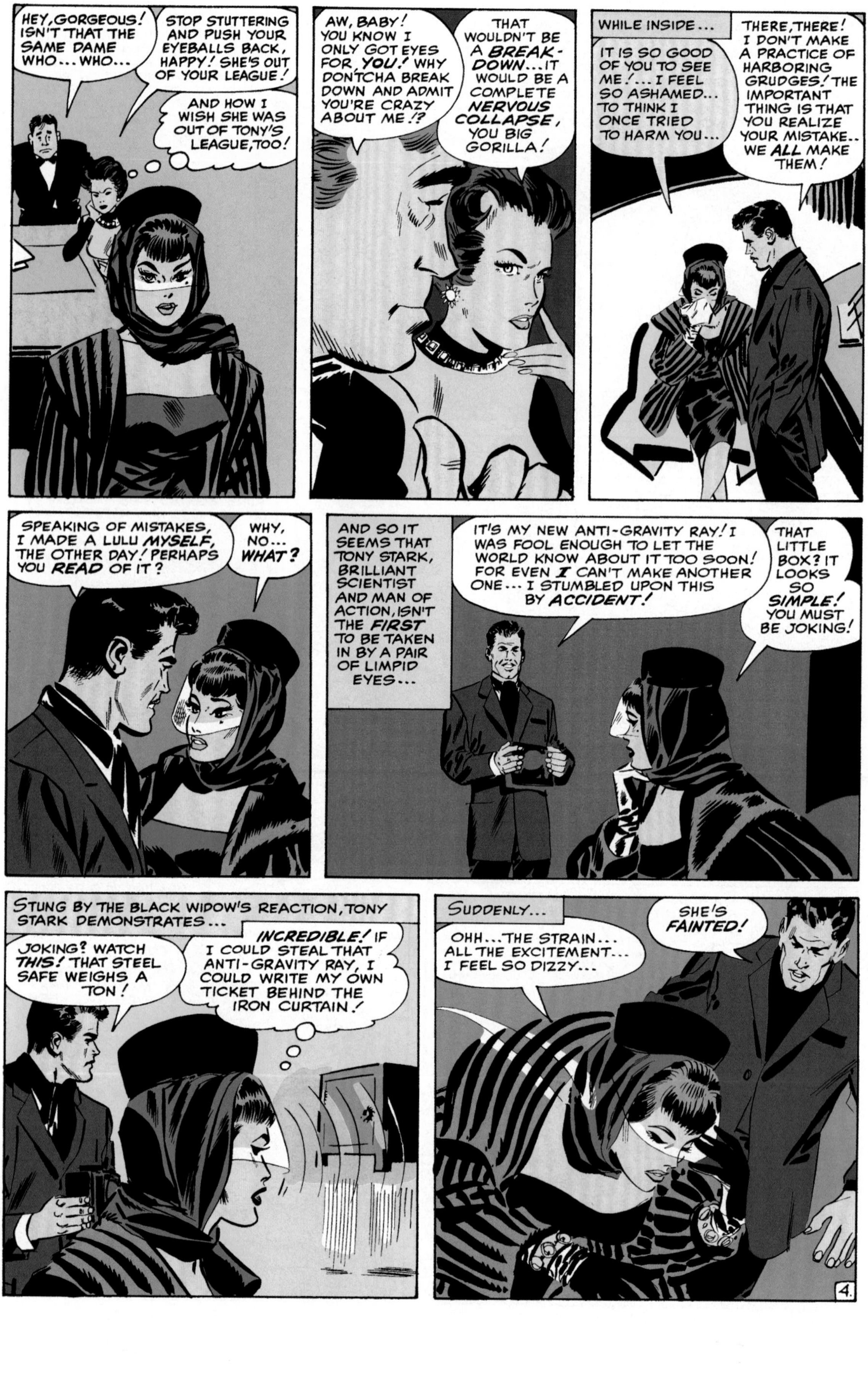
HEY, GORGEOUS! ISN'T THAT THE SAME DAME WHO... WHO...
STOP STUTTERING AND PUSH YOUR EYEBALLS BACK, HAPPY! SHE'S OUT OF YOUR LEAGUE!
AND HOW I WISH SHE WAS OUT OF TONY'S LEAGUE, TOO!
AW, BABY! YOU KNOW I ONLY GOT EYES FOR YOU! WHY DON'TCHA BREAK DOWN AND ADMIT YOU'RE CRAZY ABOUT ME!?
THAT WOULDN'T BE A BREAK-DOWN... IT WOULD BE A COMPLETE NERVOUS COLLAPSE, YOU BIG GORILLA!
WHILE INSIDE...
IT IS SO GOOD OF YOU TO SEE ME!... I FEEL SO ASHAMED... TO THINK I ONCE TRIED TO HARM YOU...
THERE, THERE! I DON'T MAKE A PRACTICE OF HARBORING GRUDGES! THE IMPORTANT THING IS THAT YOU REALIZE YOUR MISTAKE.. WE ALL MAKE THEM!
SPEAKING OF MISTAKES, I MADE A LULU MYSELF, THE OTHER DAY! PERHAPS YOU READ OF IT?
WHY, NO... WHAT?
AND SO IT SEEMS THAT TONY STARK, BRILLIANT SCIENTIST AND MAN OF ACTION, ISN'T THE FIRST TO BE TAKEN IN BY A PAIR OF LIMPID EYES...
IT'S MY NEW ANTI-GRAVITY RAY! I WAS FOOL ENOUGH TO LET THE WORLD KNOW ABOUT IT TOO SOON! FOR EVEN I CAN'T MAKE ANOTHER ONE... I STUMBLED UPON THIS BY ACCIDENT!
THAT LITTLE BOX? IT LOOKS SO SIMPLE! YOU MUST BE JOKING!
STUNG BY THE BLACK WIDOW'S REACTION, TONY STARK DEMONSTRATES...
JOKING? WATCH THIS! THAT STEEL SAFE WEIGHS A TON!
INCREDIBLE! IF I COULD STEAL THAT ANTI-GRAVITY RAY, I COULD WRITE MY OWN TICKET BEHIND THE IRON CURTAIN!
SUDDENLY...
OHH... THE STRAIN... ALL THE EXCITEMENT... I FEEL SO DIZZY...
SHE'S FAINTED!
4.

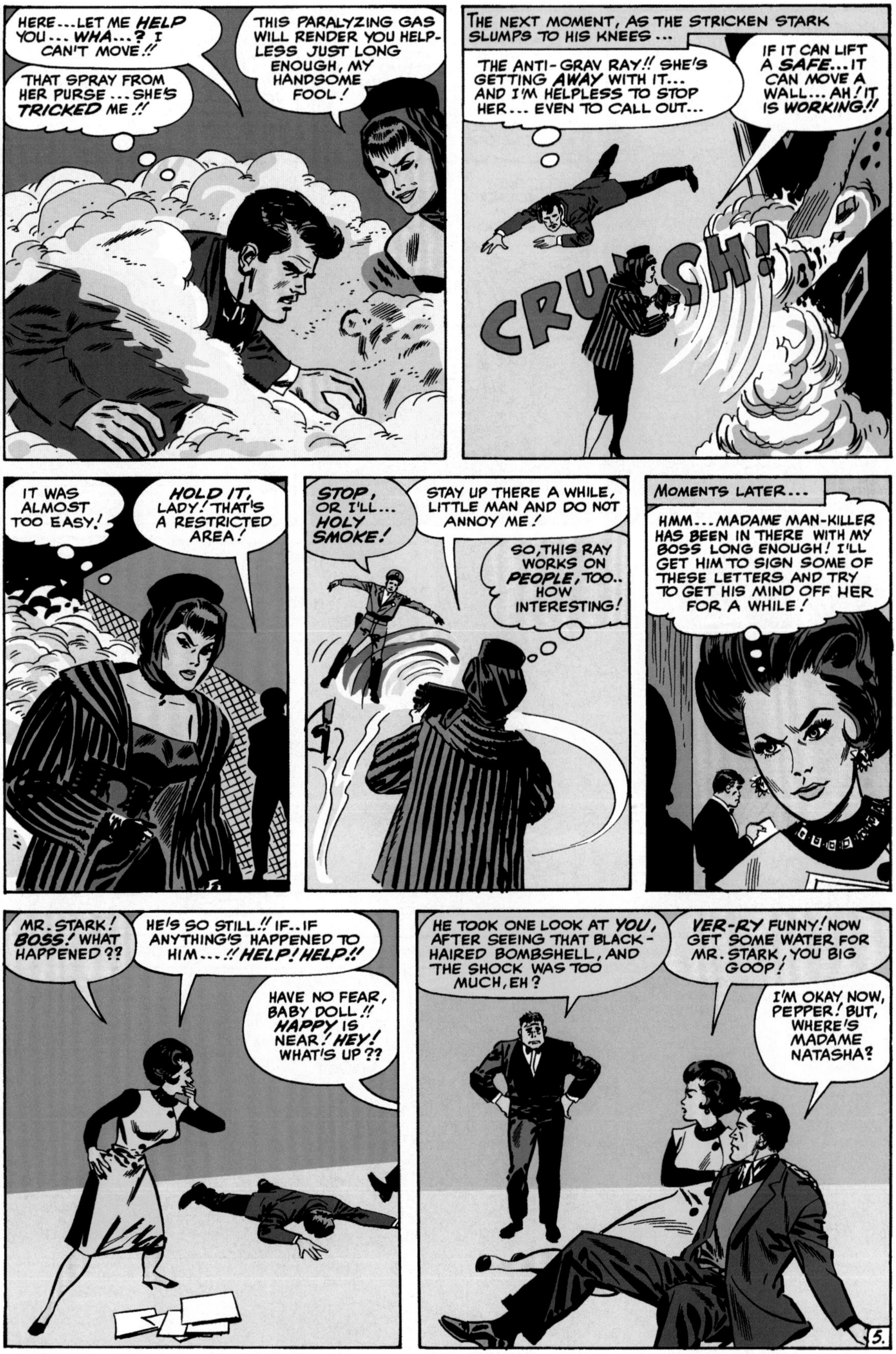
HERE...LET ME HELP YOU... WHA...? I CAN'T MOVE!!
THAT SPRAY FROM HER PURSE ... SHE'S TRICKED ME !!
THIS PARALYZING GAS WILL RENDER YOU HELPLESS JUST LONG ENOUGH, MY HANDSOME FOOL!
THE NEXT MOMENT, AS THE STRICKEN STARK SLUMPS TO HIS KNEES ...
THE ANTI-GRAV RAY!! SHE'S GETTING AWAY WITH IT... AND I'M HELPLESS TO STOP HER... EVEN TO CALL OUT...
IF IT CAN LIFT A SAFE... IT CAN MOVE A WALL... AH! IT IS WORKING!!
CRUSH!
IT WAS ALMOST TOO EASY!
HOLD IT, LADY! THAT'S A RESTRICTED AREA!
STOP, OR I'LL... HOLY SMOKE!
STAY UP THERE A WHILE, LITTLE MAN AND DO NOT ANNOY ME!
SO, THIS RAY WORKS ON PEOPLE, TOO.. HOW INTERESTING!
MOMENTS LATER...
HMM... MADAME MAN-KILLER HAS BEEN IN THERE WITH MY BOSS LONG ENOUGH! I'LL GET HIM TO SIGN SOME OF THESE LETTERS AND TRY TO GET HIS MIND OFF HER FOR A WHILE!
MR. STARK! BOSS! WHAT HAPPENED??
HE'S SO STILL!! IF..IF ANYTHING'S HAPPENED TO HIM...!! HELP! HELP!!
HAVE NO FEAR, BABY DOLL!! HAPPY IS NEAR! HEY! WHAT'S UP??
HE TOOK ONE LOOK AT YOU, AFTER SEEING THAT BLACK-HAIRED BOMBSHELL, AND THE SHOCK WAS TOO MUCH, EH?
VER-RY FUNNY! NOW GET SOME WATER FOR MR. STARK, YOU BIG GOOP!
I'M OKAY, NOW, PEPPER! BUT, WHERE'S MADAME NATASHA?
5.

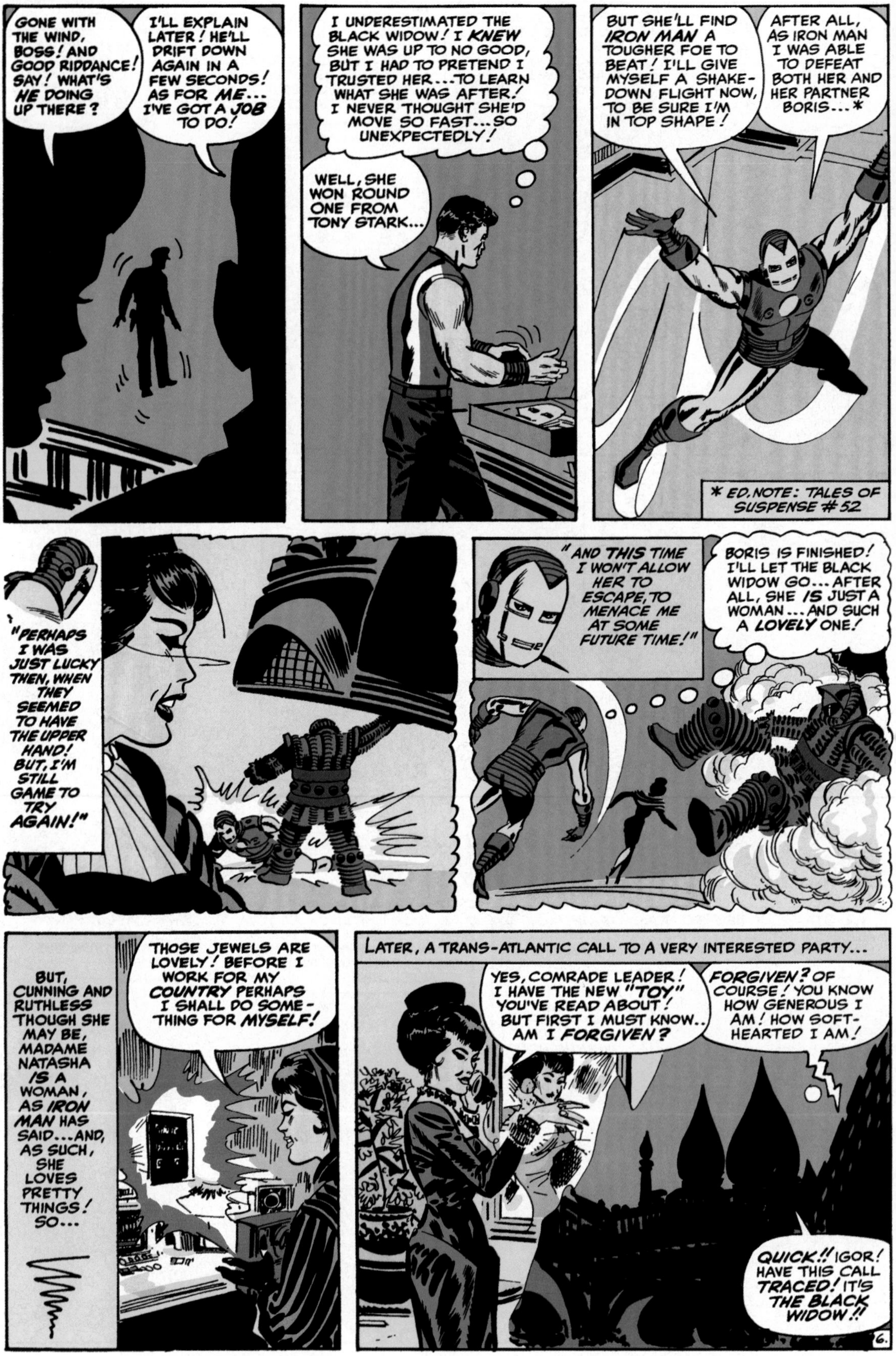
GONE WITH THE WIND, BOSS! AND GOOD RIDDANCE! SAY! WHAT'S HE DOING UP THERE?
I'LL EXPLAIN LATER! HE'LL DRIFT DOWN AGAIN IN A FEW SECONDS! AS FOR ME... I'VE GOT A JOB TO DO!
I UNDERESTIMATED THE BLACK WIDOW! I KNEW SHE WAS UP TO NO GOOD, BUT I HAD TO PRETEND I TRUSTED HER...TO LEARN WHAT SHE WAS AFTER! I NEVER THOUGHT SHE'D MOVE SO FAST...SO UNEXPECTEDLY!
WELL, SHE WON ROUND ONE FROM TONY STARK...
BUT SHE'LL FIND IRON MAN A TOUGHER FOE TO BEAT! I'LL GIVE MYSELF A SHAKE-DOWN FLIGHT NOW, TO BE SURE I'M IN TOP SHAPE!
AFTER ALL, AS IRON MAN I WAS ABLE TO DEFEAT BOTH HER AND HER PARTNER BORIS...*
* ED. NOTE: TALES OF SUSPENSE #52
"PERHAPS I WAS JUST LUCKY THEN, WHEN THEY SEEMED TO HAVE THE UPPER HAND! BUT, I'M STILL GAME TO TRY AGAIN!"
"AND THIS TIME I WON'T ALLOW HER TO ESCAPE, TO MENACE ME AT SOME FUTURE TIME!"
BORIS IS FINISHED! I'LL LET THE BLACK WIDOW GO... AFTER ALL, SHE IS JUST A WOMAN... AND SUCH A LOVELY ONE!
BUT, CUNNING AND RUTHLESS THOUGH SHE MAY BE, MADAME NATASHA IS A WOMAN, AS IRON MAN HAS SAID...AND, AS SUCH, SHE LOVES PRETTY THINGS! SO...
THOSE JEWELS ARE LOVELY! BEFORE I WORK FOR MY COUNTRY PERHAPS I SHALL DO SOME-THING FOR MYSELF!
LATER, A TRANS-ATLANTIC CALL TO A VERY INTERESTED PARTY...
YES, COMRADE LEADER! I HAVE THE NEW "TOY" YOU'VE READ ABOUT! BUT FIRST I MUST KNOW.. AM I FORGIVEN?
FORGIVEN? OF COURSE! YOU KNOW HOW GENEROUS I AM! HOW SOFT-HEARTED I AM!
QUICK!! IGOR! HAVE THIS CALL TRACED! IT'S THE BLACK WIDOW!!
6.

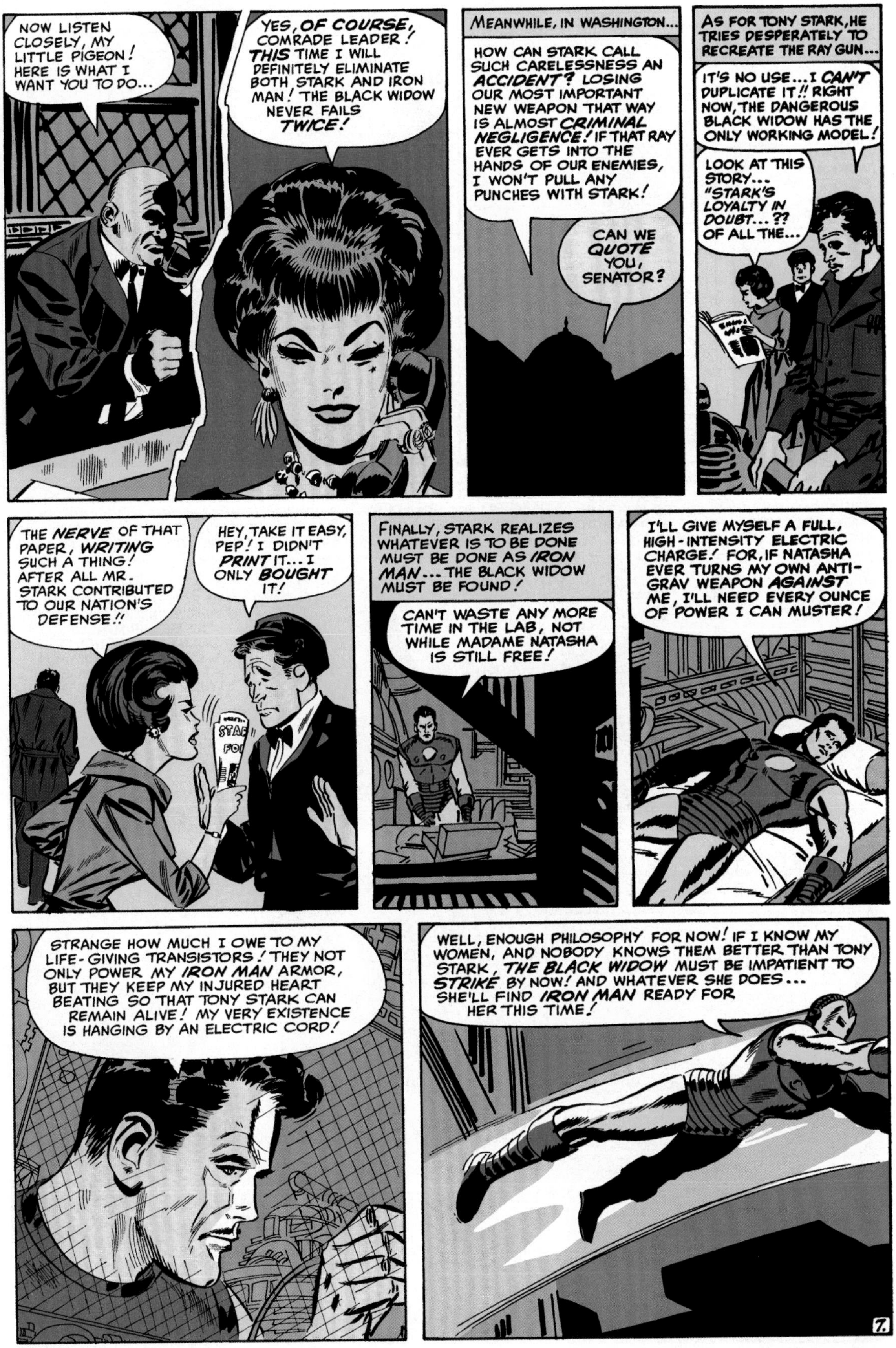

NOW LISTEN CLOSELY, MY LITTLE PIGEON! HERE IS WHAT I WANT YOU TO DO...
YES, OF COURSE, COMRADE LEADER! THIS TIME I WILL DEFINITELY ELIMINATE BOTH STARK AND IRON MAN! THE BLACK WIDOW NEVER FAILS TWICE!
MEANWHILE, IN WASHINGTON...
HOW CAN STARK CALL SUCH CARELESSNESS AN ACCIDENT? LOSING OUR MOST IMPORTANT NEW WEAPON THAT WAY IS ALMOST CRIMINAL NEGLIGENCE! IF THAT RAY EVER GETS INTO THE HANDS OF OUR ENEMIES, I WON'T PULL ANY PUNCHES WITH STARK!
CAN WE QUOTE YOU, SENATOR?
AS FOR TONY STARK, HE TRIES DESPERATELY TO RECREATE THE RAY GUN...
IT'S NO USE... I CAN'T DUPLICATE IT!! RIGHT NOW, THE DANGEROUS BLACK WIDOW HAS THE ONLY WORKING MODEL!
LOOK AT THIS STORY... "STARK'S LOYALTY IN DOUBT...?? OF ALL THE...
THE NERVE OF THAT PAPER, WRITING SUCH A THING! AFTER ALL MR. STARK CONTRIBUTED TO OUR NATION'S DEFENSE!!
HEY, TAKE IT EASY, PEP! I DIDN'T PRINT IT... I ONLY BOUGHT IT!
FINALLY, STARK REALIZES WHATEVER IS TO BE DONE MUST BE DONE AS IRON MAN... THE BLACK WIDOW MUST BE FOUND!
CAN'T WASTE ANY MORE TIME IN THE LAB, NOT WHILE MADAME NATASHA IS STILL FREE!
I'LL GIVE MYSELF A FULL, HIGH-INTENSITY ELECTRIC CHARGE! FOR, IF NATASHA EVER TURNS MY OWN ANTI-GRAV WEAPON AGAINST ME, I'LL NEED EVERY OUNCE OF POWER I CAN MUSTER!
STRANGE HOW MUCH I OWE TO MY LIFE-GIVING TRANSISTORS! THEY NOT ONLY POWER MY IRON MAN ARMOR, BUT THEY KEEP MY INJURED HEART BEATING SO THAT TONY STARK CAN REMAIN ALIVE! MY VERY EXISTENCE IS HANGING BY AN ELECTRIC CORD!
WELL, ENOUGH PHILOSOPHY FOR NOW! IF I KNOW MY WOMEN, AND NOBODY KNOWS THEM BETTER THAN TONY STARK, THE BLACK WIDOW MUST BE IMPATIENT TO STRIKE BY NOW! AND WHATEVER SHE DOES... SHE'LL FIND IRON MAN READY FOR HER THIS TIME!
7.

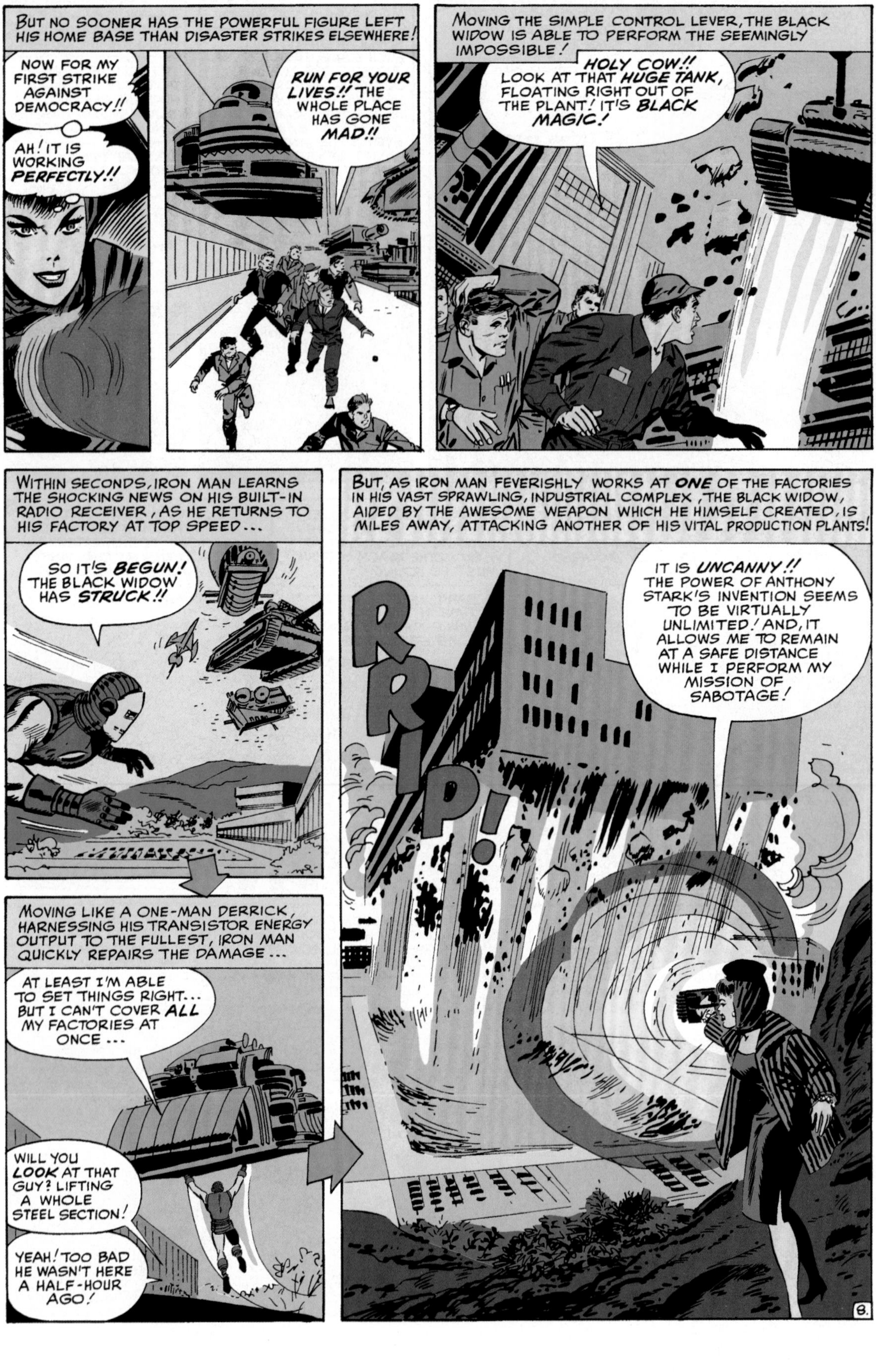

BUT NO SOONER HAS THE POWERFUL FIGURE LEFT HIS HOME BASE THAN DISASTER STRIKES ELSEWHERE!
NOW FOR MY FIRST STRIKE AGAINST DEMOCRACY!!
AH! IT IS WORKING PERFECTLY!!
RUN FOR YOUR LIVES!! THE WHOLE PLACE HAS GONE MAD!!
MOVING THE SIMPLE CONTROL LEVER, THE BLACK WIDOW IS ABLE TO PERFORM THE SEEMINGLY IMPOSSIBLE!
HOLY COW!! LOOK AT THAT HUGE TANK, FLOATING RIGHT OUT OF THE PLANT! IT'S BLACK MAGIC!
WITHIN SECONDS, IRON MAN LEARNS THE SHOCKING NEWS ON HIS BUILT-IN RADIO RECEIVER, AS HE RETURNS TO HIS FACTORY AT TOP SPEED...
SO IT'S BEGUN! THE BLACK WIDOW HAS STRUCK!!
MOVING LIKE A ONE-MAN DERRICK, HARNESSING HIS TRANSISTOR ENERGY OUTPUT TO THE FULLEST, IRON MAN QUICKLY REPAIRS THE DAMAGE...
AT LEAST I'M ABLE TO SET THINGS RIGHT... BUT I CAN'T COVER ALL MY FACTORIES AT ONCE...
WILL YOU LOOK AT THAT GUY? LIFTING A WHOLE STEEL SECTION!
YEAH! TOO BAD HE WASN'T HERE A HALF-HOUR AGO!
BUT, AS IRON MAN FEVERISHLY WORKS AT ONE OF THE FACTORIES IN HIS VAST SPRAWLING, INDUSTRIAL COMPLEX, THE BLACK WIDOW, AIDED BY THE AWESOME WEAPON WHICH HE HIMSELF CREATED, IS MILES AWAY, ATTACKING ANOTHER OF HIS VITAL PRODUCTION PLANTS!
RRIP!
IT IS UNCANNY!! THE POWER OF ANTHONY STARK'S INVENTION SEEMS TO BE VIRTUALLY UNLIMITED! AND, IT ALLOWS ME TO REMAIN AT A SAFE DISTANCE WHILE I PERFORM MY MISSION OF SABOTAGE!
8.

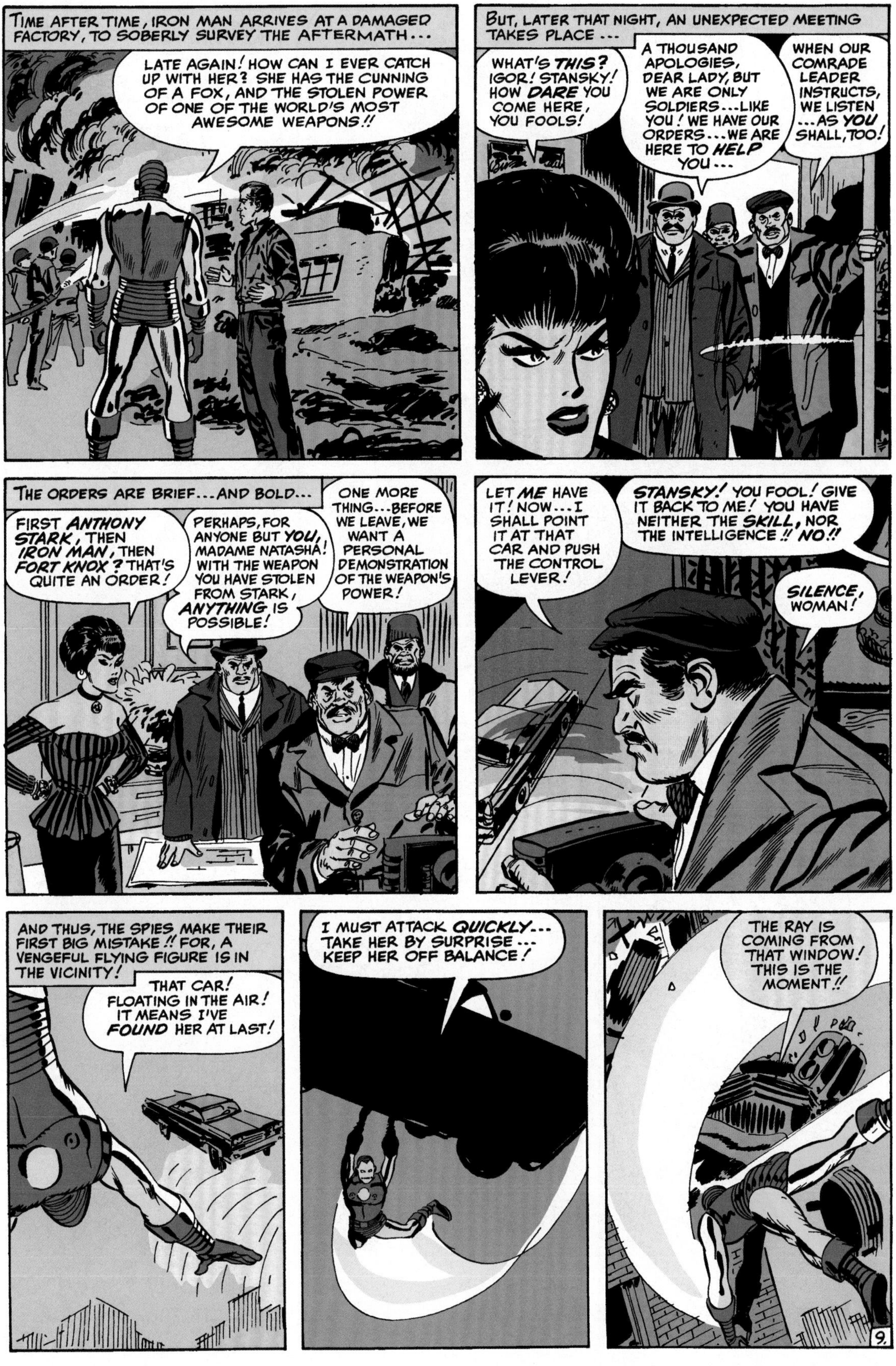
TIME AFTER TIME, IRON MAN ARRIVES AT A DAMAGED FACTORY, TO SOBERLY SURVEY THE AFTERMATH...
LATE AGAIN! HOW CAN I EVER CATCH UP WITH HER? SHE HAS THE CUNNING OF A FOX, AND THE STOLEN POWER OF ONE OF THE WORLD'S MOST AWESOME WEAPONS!!
BUT, LATER THAT NIGHT, AN UNEXPECTED MEETING TAKES PLACE...
WHAT'S THIS? IGOR! STANSKY! HOW DARE YOU COME HERE, YOU FOOLS!
A THOUSAND APOLOGIES, DEAR LADY, BUT WE ARE ONLY SOLDIERS...LIKE YOU! WE HAVE OUR ORDERS...WE ARE HERE TO HELP YOU...
WHEN OUR COMRADE LEADER INSTRUCTS, WE LISTEN ...AS YOU SHALL, TOO!
THE ORDERS ARE BRIEF...AND BOLD...
FIRST ANTHONY STARK, THEN IRON MAN, THEN FORT KNOX? THAT'S QUITE AN ORDER!
PERHAPS, FOR ANYONE BUT YOU, MADAME NATASHA! WITH THE WEAPON YOU HAVE STOLEN FROM STARK, ANYTHING IS POSSIBLE!
ONE MORE THING...BEFORE WE LEAVE, WE WANT A PERSONAL DEMONSTRATION OF THE WEAPON'S POWER!
LET ME HAVE IT! NOW...I SHALL POINT IT AT THAT CAR AND PUSH THE CONTROL LEVER!
STANSKY! YOU FOOL! GIVE IT BACK TO ME! YOU HAVE NEITHER THE SKILL, NOR THE INTELLIGENCE!! NO!!
SILENCE, WOMAN!
AND THUS, THE SPIES MAKE THEIR FIRST BIG MISTAKE!! FOR, A VENGEFUL FLYING FIGURE IS IN THE VICINITY!
THAT CAR! FLOATING IN THE AIR! IT MEANS I'VE FOUND HER AT LAST!
I MUST ATTACK QUICKLY... TAKE HER BY SURPRISE... KEEP HER OFF BALANCE!
THE RAY IS COMING FROM THAT WINDOW! THIS IS THE MOMENT!!
9.

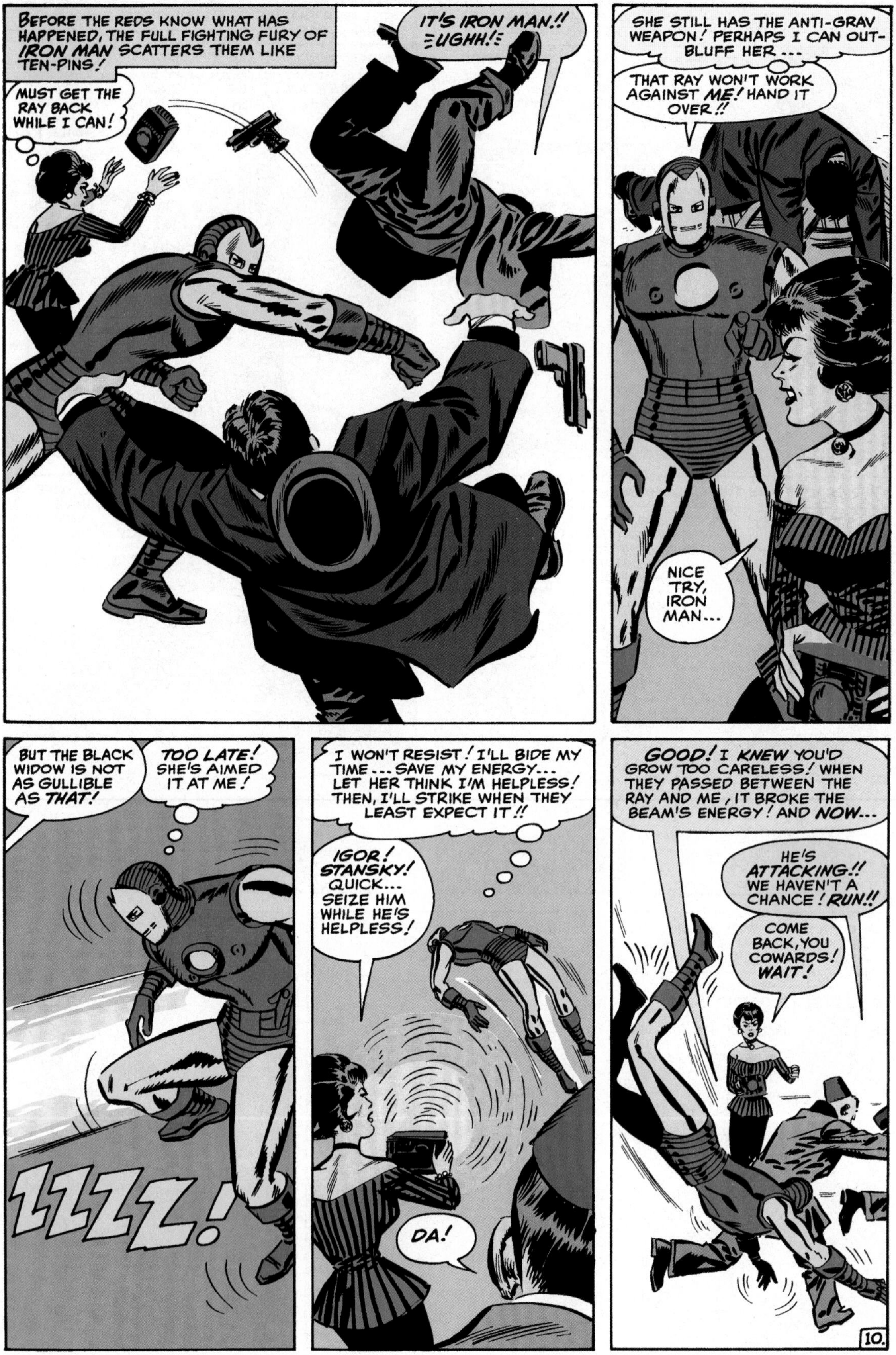

BEFORE THE REDS KNOW WHAT HAS HAPPENED, THE FULL FIGHTING FURY OF IRON MAN SCATTERS THEM LIKE TEN-PINS!
IT'S IRON MAN!! UGHH!
MUST GET THE RAY BACK WHILE I CAN!
SHE STILL HAS THE ANTI-GRAV WEAPON! PERHAPS I CAN OUT-BLUFF HER...
THAT RAY WON'T WORK AGAINST ME! HAND IT OVER!!
NICE TRY, IRON MAN...
BUT THE BLACK WIDOW IS NOT AS GULLIBLE AS THAT!
TOO LATE! SHE'S AIMED IT AT ME!
ZZZZ!
I WON'T RESIST! I'LL BIDE MY TIME... SAVE MY ENERGY... LET HER THINK I'M HELPLESS! THEN, I'LL STRIKE WHEN THEY LEAST EXPECT IT!!
IGOR! STANSKY! QUICK... SEIZE HIM WHILE HE'S HELPLESS!
DA!
GOOD! I KNEW YOU'D GROW TOO CARELESS! WHEN THEY PASSED BETWEEN THE RAY AND ME, IT BROKE THE BEAM'S ENERGY! AND NOW...
HE'S ATTACKING!! WE HAVEN'T A CHANCE! RUN!!
COME BACK, YOU COWARDS! WAIT!
10.

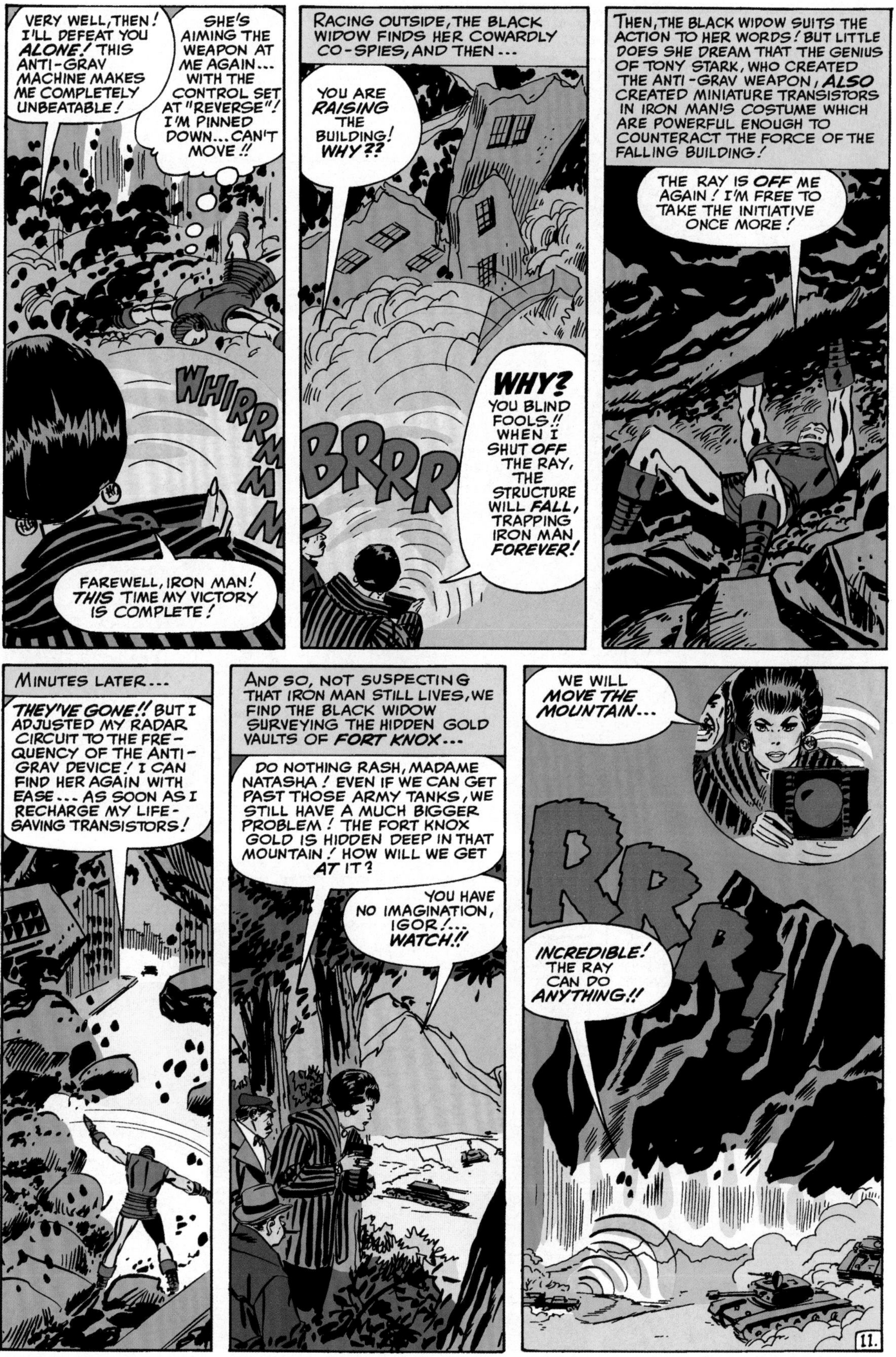
VERY WELL, THEN! I'LL DEFEAT YOU ALONE! THIS ANTI-GRAV MACHINE MAKES ME COMPLETELY UNBEATABLE!
SHE'S AIMING THE WEAPON AT ME AGAIN... WITH THE CONTROL SET AT "REVERSE"! I'M PINNED DOWN... CAN'T MOVE!!
WHIRRMMM
FAREWELL, IRON MAN! THIS TIME MY VICTORY IS COMPLETE!
RACING OUTSIDE, THE BLACK WIDOW FINDS HER COWARDLY CO-SPIES, AND THEN...
YOU ARE RAISING THE BUILDING! WHY??
BRRRR
WHY? YOU BLIND FOOLS!! WHEN I SHUT OFF THE RAY, THE STRUCTURE WILL FALL, TRAPPING IRON MAN FOREVER!
THEN, THE BLACK WIDOW SUITS THE ACTION TO HER WORDS! BUT LITTLE DOES SHE DREAM THAT THE GENIUS OF TONY STARK, WHO CREATED THE ANTI-GRAV WEAPON, ALSO CREATED MINIATURE TRANSISTORS IN IRON MAN'S COSTUME WHICH ARE POWERFUL ENOUGH TO COUNTERACT THE FORCE OF THE FALLING BUILDING!
THE RAY IS OFF ME AGAIN! I'M FREE TO TAKE THE INITIATIVE ONCE MORE!
MINUTES LATER...
THEY'VE GONE!! BUT I ADJUSTED MY RADAR CIRCUIT TO THE FREQUENCY OF THE ANTI-GRAV DEVICE! I CAN FIND HER AGAIN WITH EASE... AS SOON AS I RECHARGE MY LIFE-SAVING TRANSISTORS!
AND SO, NOT SUSPECTING THAT IRON MAN STILL LIVES, WE FIND THE BLACK WIDOW SURVEYING THE HIDDEN GOLD VAULTS OF FORT KNOX...
DO NOTHING RASH, MADAME NATASHA! EVEN IF WE CAN GET PAST THOSE ARMY TANKS, WE STILL HAVE A MUCH BIGGER PROBLEM! THE FORT KNOX GOLD IS HIDDEN DEEP IN THAT MOUNTAIN! HOW WILL WE GET AT IT?
YOU HAVE NO IMAGINATION, IGOR!... WATCH!!
WE WILL MOVE THE MOUNTAIN...
RRR!
INCREDIBLE! THE RAY CAN DO ANYTHING!!
11.

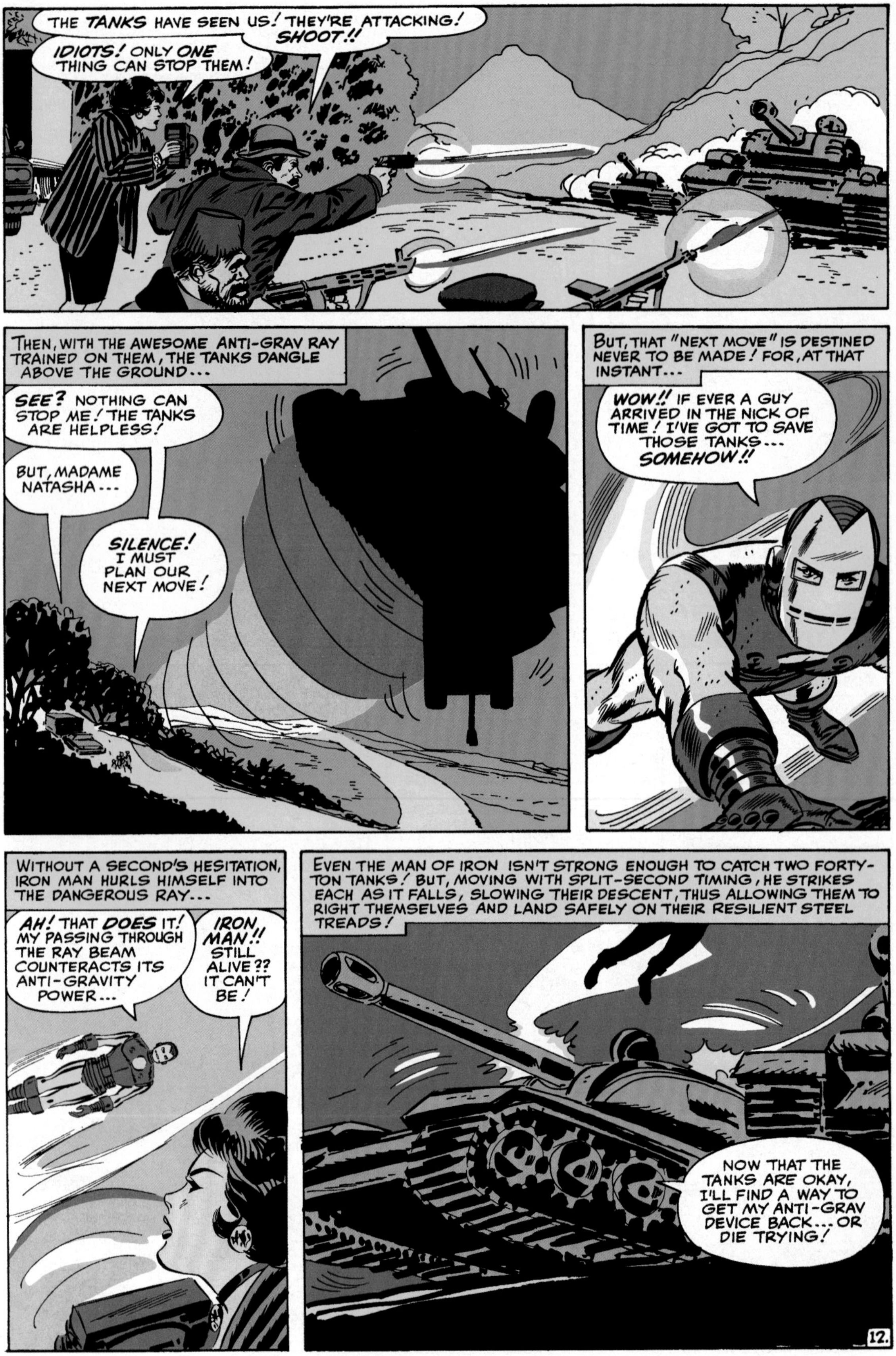
THE TANKS HAVE SEEN US! THEY'RE ATTACKING! SHOOT!!
IDIOTS! ONLY ONE THING CAN STOP THEM!
THEN, WITH THE AWESOME ANTI-GRAV RAY TRAINED ON THEM, THE TANKS DANGLE ABOVE THE GROUND...
SEE? NOTHING CAN STOP ME! THE TANKS ARE HELPLESS!
BUT, MADAME NATASHA...
SILENCE! I MUST PLAN OUR NEXT MOVE!
BUT, THAT "NEXT MOVE" IS DESTINED NEVER TO BE MADE! FOR, AT THAT INSTANT...
WOW!! IF EVER A GUY ARRIVED IN THE NICK OF TIME! I'VE GOT TO SAVE THOSE TANKS... SOMEHOW!!
WITHOUT A SECOND'S HESITATION, IRON MAN HURLS HIMSELF INTO THE DANGEROUS RAY...
AH! THAT DOES IT! MY PASSING THROUGH THE RAY BEAM COUNTERACTS ITS ANTI-GRAVITY POWER...
IRON MAN!! STILL ALIVE?? IT CAN'T BE!
EVEN THE MAN OF IRON ISN'T STRONG ENOUGH TO CATCH TWO FORTY-TON TANKS! BUT, MOVING WITH SPLIT-SECOND TIMING, HE STRIKES EACH AS IT FALLS, SLOWING THEIR DESCENT, THUS ALLOWING THEM TO RIGHT THEMSELVES AND LAND SAFELY ON THEIR RESILIENT STEEL TREADS!
NOW THAT THE TANKS ARE OKAY, I'LL FIND A WAY TO GET MY ANTI-GRAV DEVICE BACK... OR DIE TRYING!
12.

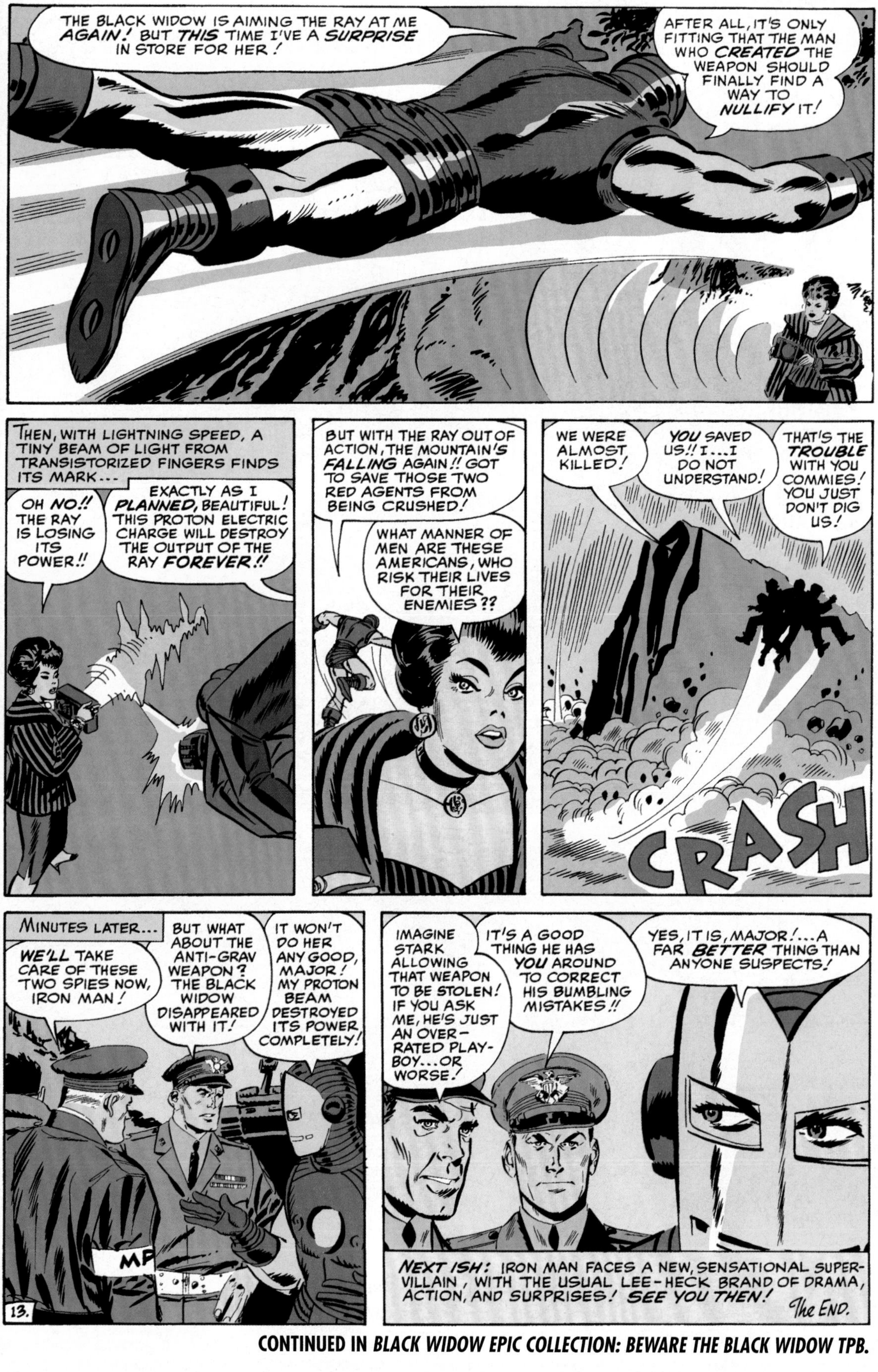
THE BLACK WIDOW IS AIMING THE RAY AT ME AGAIN! BUT THIS TIME I'VE A SURPRISE IN STORE FOR HER!
AFTER ALL, IT'S ONLY FITTING THAT THE MAN WHO CREATED THE WEAPON SHOULD FINALLY FIND A WAY TO NULLIFY IT!
THEN, WITH LIGHTNING SPEED, A TINY BEAM OF LIGHT FROM TRANSISTORIZED FINGERS FINDS ITS MARK...
OH NO!! THE RAY IS LOSING ITS POWER!!
EXACTLY AS I PLANNED, BEAUTIFUL! THIS PROTON ELECTRIC CHARGE WILL DESTROY THE OUTPUT OF THE RAY FOREVER!!
BUT WITH THE RAY OUT OF ACTION, THE MOUNTAIN'S FALLING AGAIN!! GOT TO SAVE THOSE TWO RED AGENTS FROM BEING CRUSHED!
WHAT MANNER OF MEN ARE THESE AMERICANS, WHO RISK THEIR LIVES FOR THEIR ENEMIES??
WE WERE ALMOST KILLED!
YOU SAVED US!! I...I DO NOT UNDERSTAND!
THAT'S THE TROUBLE WITH YOU COMMIES! YOU JUST DON'T DIG US!
CRASH
MINUTES LATER...
WE'LL TAKE CARE OF THESE TWO SPIES NOW, IRON MAN!
BUT WHAT ABOUT THE ANTI-GRAV WEAPON? THE BLACK WIDOW DISAPPEARED WITH IT!
IT WON'T DO HER ANY GOOD, MAJOR! MY PROTON BEAM DESTROYED ITS POWER COMPLETELY!
MP
13.
IMAGINE STARK ALLOWING THAT WEAPON TO BE STOLEN! IF YOU ASK ME, HE'S JUST AN OVER-RATED PLAY-BOY...OR WORSE!
IT'S A GOOD THING HE HAS YOU AROUND TO CORRECT HIS BUMBLING MISTAKES!!
YES, IT IS, MAJOR!...A FAR BETTER THING THAN ANYONE SUSPECTS!
NEXT ISH: IRON MAN FACES A NEW, SENSATIONAL SUPER-VILLAIN, WITH THE USUAL LEE-HECK BRAND OF DRAMA, ACTION, AND SURPRISES! SEE YOU THEN!
The END.

CONTINUED IN *BLACK WIDOW EPIC COLLECTION: BEWARE THE BLACK WIDOW* TPB.

AS THE AVENGERS TRACK DOWN A CAPTURED BLACK WIDOW, THEY WILL HAVE TO CONTEND WITH RUSSIA'S OWN SUPER-SOLDIER, THE RED GUARDIAN!

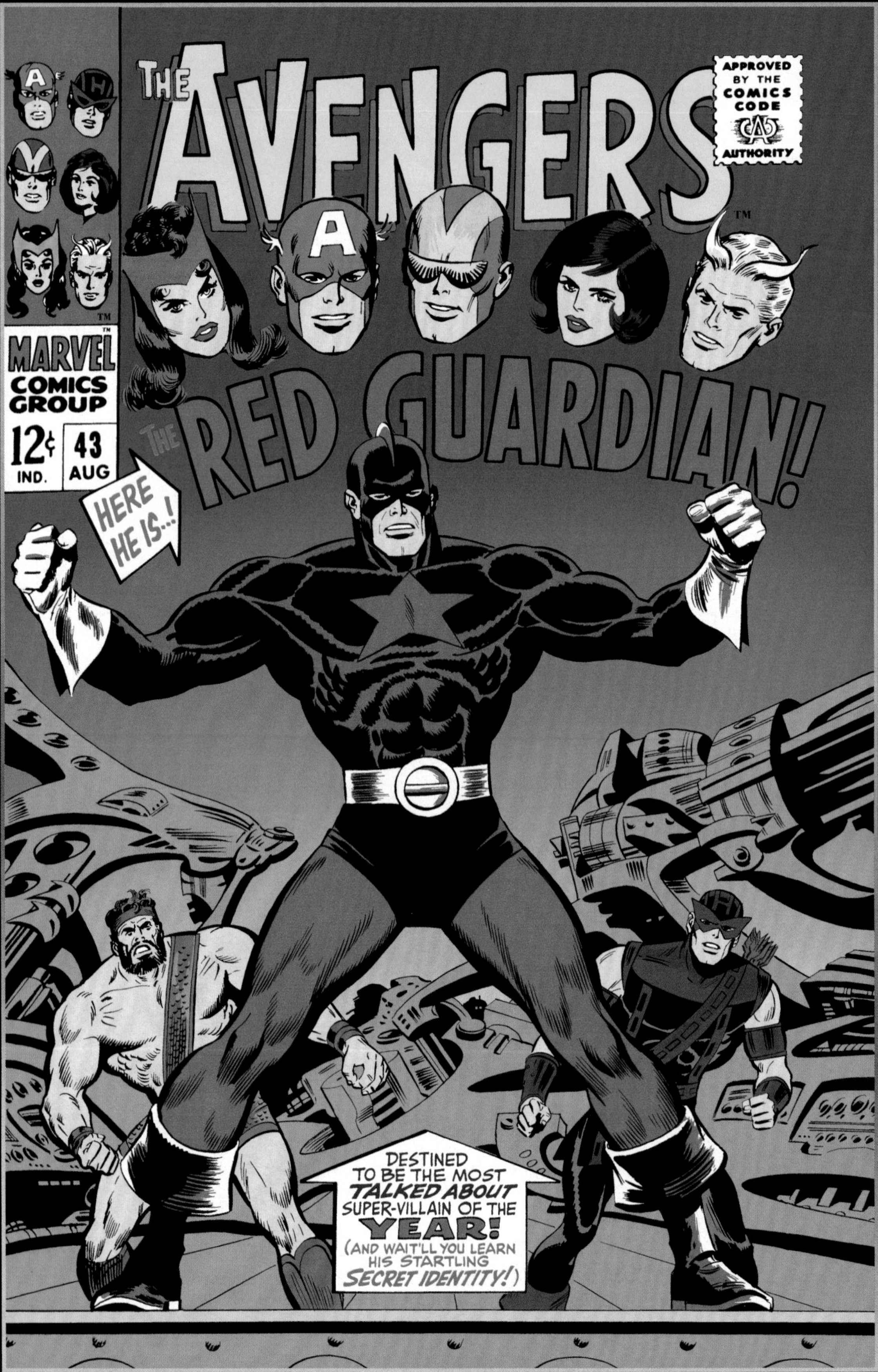

THE AVENGERS
APPROVED BY THE COMICS CODE AUTHORITY
MARVEL COMICS GROUP
12¢ IND.
43 AUG
THE RED GUARDIAN!
HERE HE IS..!
DESTINED TO BE THE MOST TALKED ABOUT SUPER-VILLAIN OF THE YEAR! (AND WAIT'LL YOU LEARN HIS STARTLING SECRET IDENTITY!)

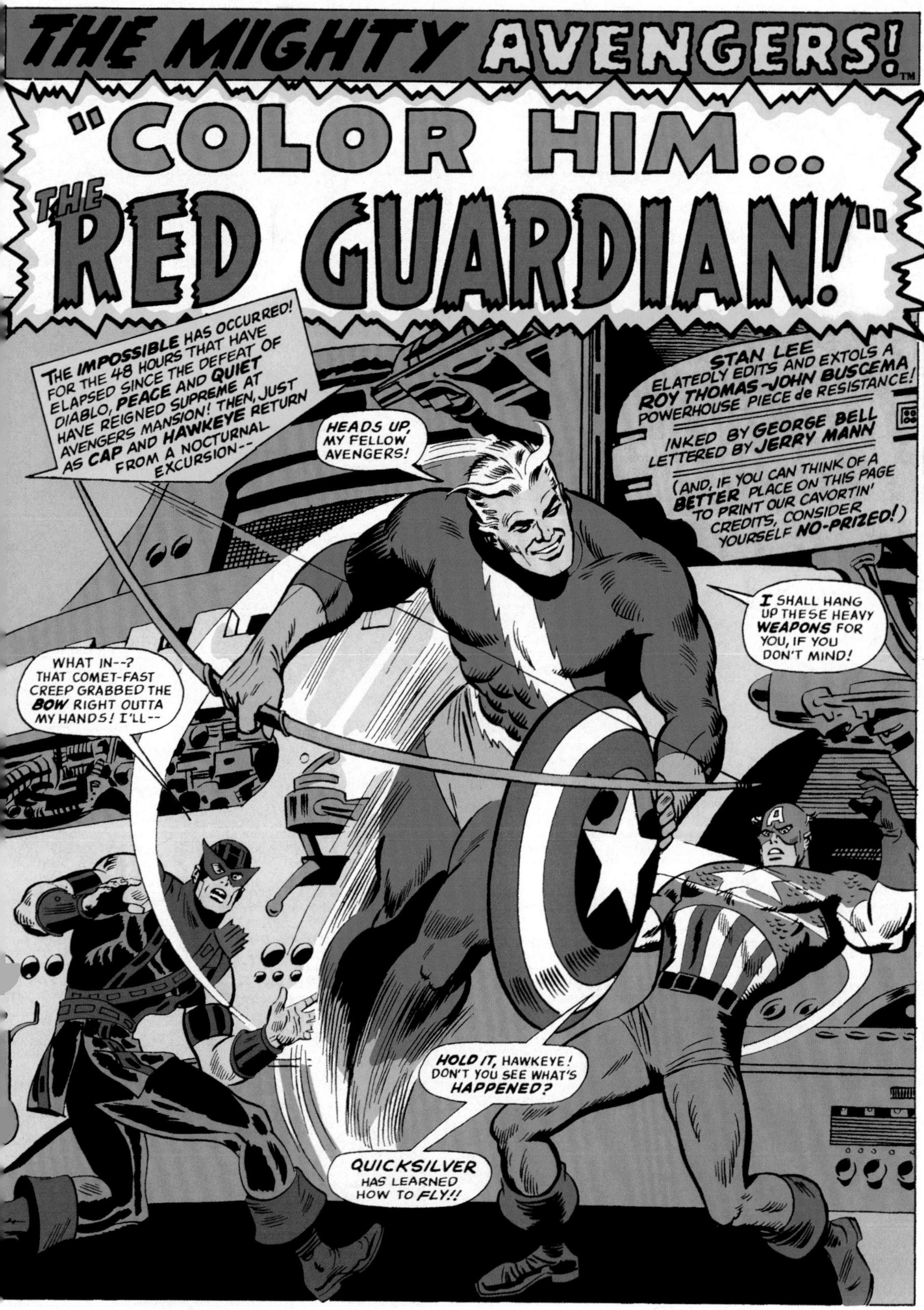
THE MIGHTY AVENGERS!
"COLOR HIM... THE RED GUARDIAN!"
THE IMPOSSIBLE HAS OCCURRED! FOR THE 48 HOURS THAT HAVE ELAPSED SINCE THE DEFEAT OF DIABLO, PEACE AND QUIET HAVE REIGNED SUPREME AT AVENGERS MANSION! THEN, JUST AS CAP AND HAWKEYE RETURN FROM A NOCTURNAL EXCURSION--
STAN LEE ELATEDLY EDITS AND EXTOLS A ROY THOMAS-JOHN BUSCEMA POWERHOUSE PIECE de RESISTANCE!
INKED BY GEORGE BELL LETTERED BY JERRY MANN
(AND, IF YOU CAN THINK OF A BETTER PLACE ON THIS PAGE TO PRINT OUR CAVORTIN' CREDITS, CONSIDER YOURSELF NO-PRIZED!)
HEADS UP, MY FELLOW AVENGERS!
I SHALL HANG UP THESE HEAVY WEAPONS FOR YOU, IF YOU DON'T MIND!
WHAT IN--? THAT COMET-FAST CREEP GRABBED THE BOW RIGHT OUTTA MY HANDS! I'LL--
HOLD IT, HAWKEYE! DON'T YOU SEE WHAT'S HAPPENED?
QUICKSILVER HAS LEARNED HOW TO FLY!!

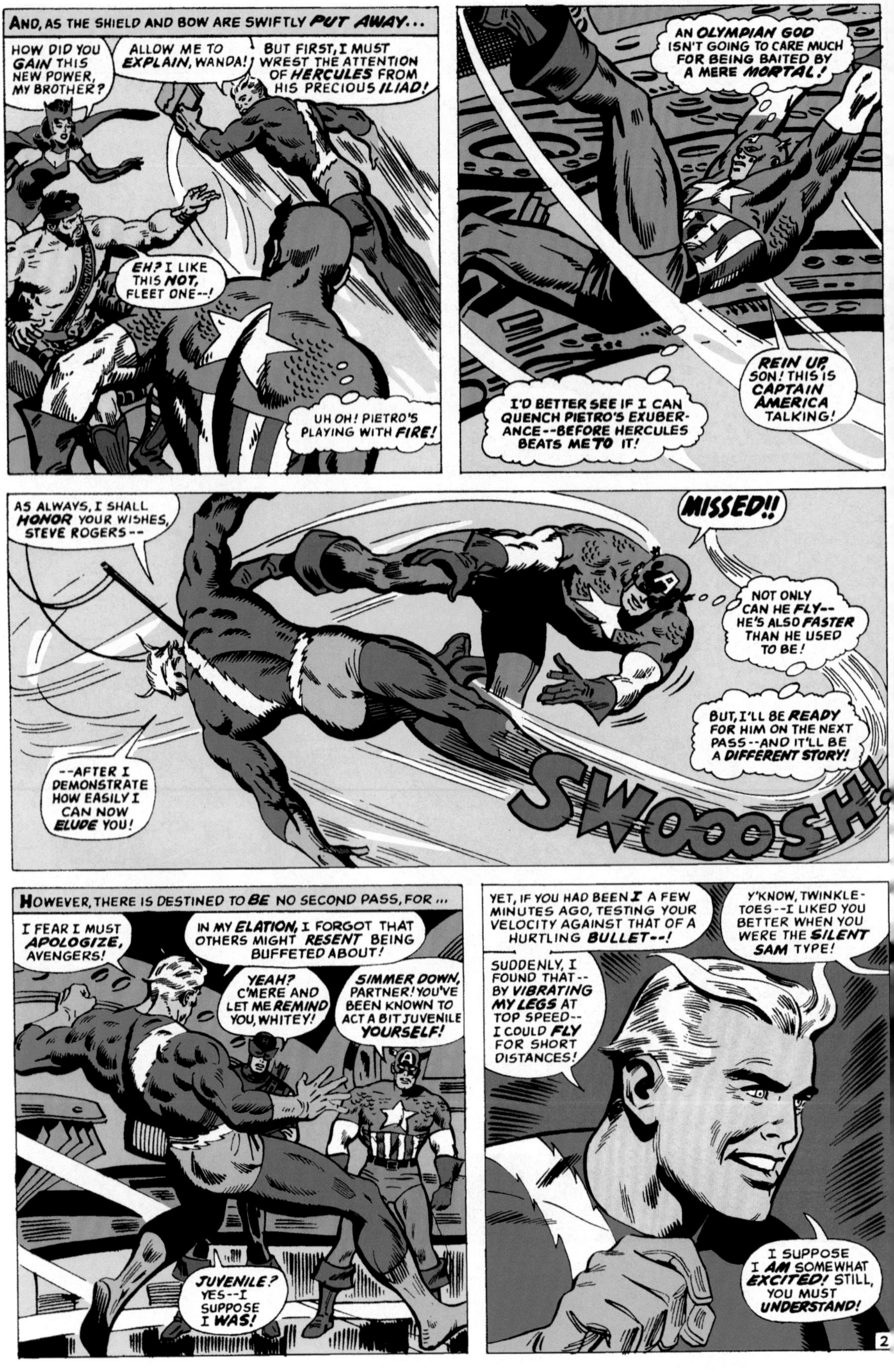
AND, AS THE SHIELD AND BOW ARE SWIFTLY PUT AWAY...
HOW DID YOU GAIN THIS NEW POWER, MY BROTHER?
ALLOW ME TO EXPLAIN, WANDA!
BUT FIRST, I MUST WREST THE ATTENTION OF HERCULES FROM HIS PRECIOUS ILIAD!
EH? I LIKE THIS NOT, FLEET ONE--!
UH OH! PIETRO'S PLAYING WITH FIRE!
AN OLYMPIAN GOD ISN'T GOING TO CARE MUCH FOR BEING BAITED BY A MERE MORTAL!
I'D BETTER SEE IF I CAN QUENCH PIETRO'S EXUBERANCE--BEFORE HERCULES BEATS ME TO IT!
REIN UP, SON! THIS IS CAPTAIN AMERICA TALKING!
AS ALWAYS, I SHALL HONOR YOUR WISHES, STEVE ROGERS--
--AFTER I DEMONSTRATE HOW EASILY I CAN NOW ELUDE YOU!
MISSED!!
NOT ONLY CAN HE FLY-- HE'S ALSO FASTER THAN HE USED TO BE!
BUT, I'LL BE READY FOR HIM ON THE NEXT PASS--AND IT'LL BE A DIFFERENT STORY!
SWOOOSH!
HOWEVER, THERE IS DESTINED TO BE NO SECOND PASS, FOR ...
I FEAR I MUST APOLOGIZE, AVENGERS!
IN MY ELATION, I FORGOT THAT OTHERS MIGHT RESENT BEING BUFFETED ABOUT!
YEAH? C'MERE AND LET ME REMIND YOU, WHITEY!
SIMMER DOWN, PARTNER! YOU'VE BEEN KNOWN TO ACT A BIT JUVENILE YOURSELF!
JUVENILE? YES--I SUPPOSE I WAS!
YET, IF YOU HAD BEEN I A FEW MINUTES AGO, TESTING YOUR VELOCITY AGAINST THAT OF A HURTLING BULLET--!
SUDDENLY, I FOUND THAT--BY VIBRATING MY LEGS AT TOP SPEED--I COULD FLY FOR SHORT DISTANCES!
Y'KNOW, TWINKLE-TOES--I LIKED YOU BETTER WHEN YOU WERE THE SILENT SAM TYPE!
I SUPPOSE I AM SOMEWHAT EXCITED! STILL, YOU MUST UNDERSTAND!

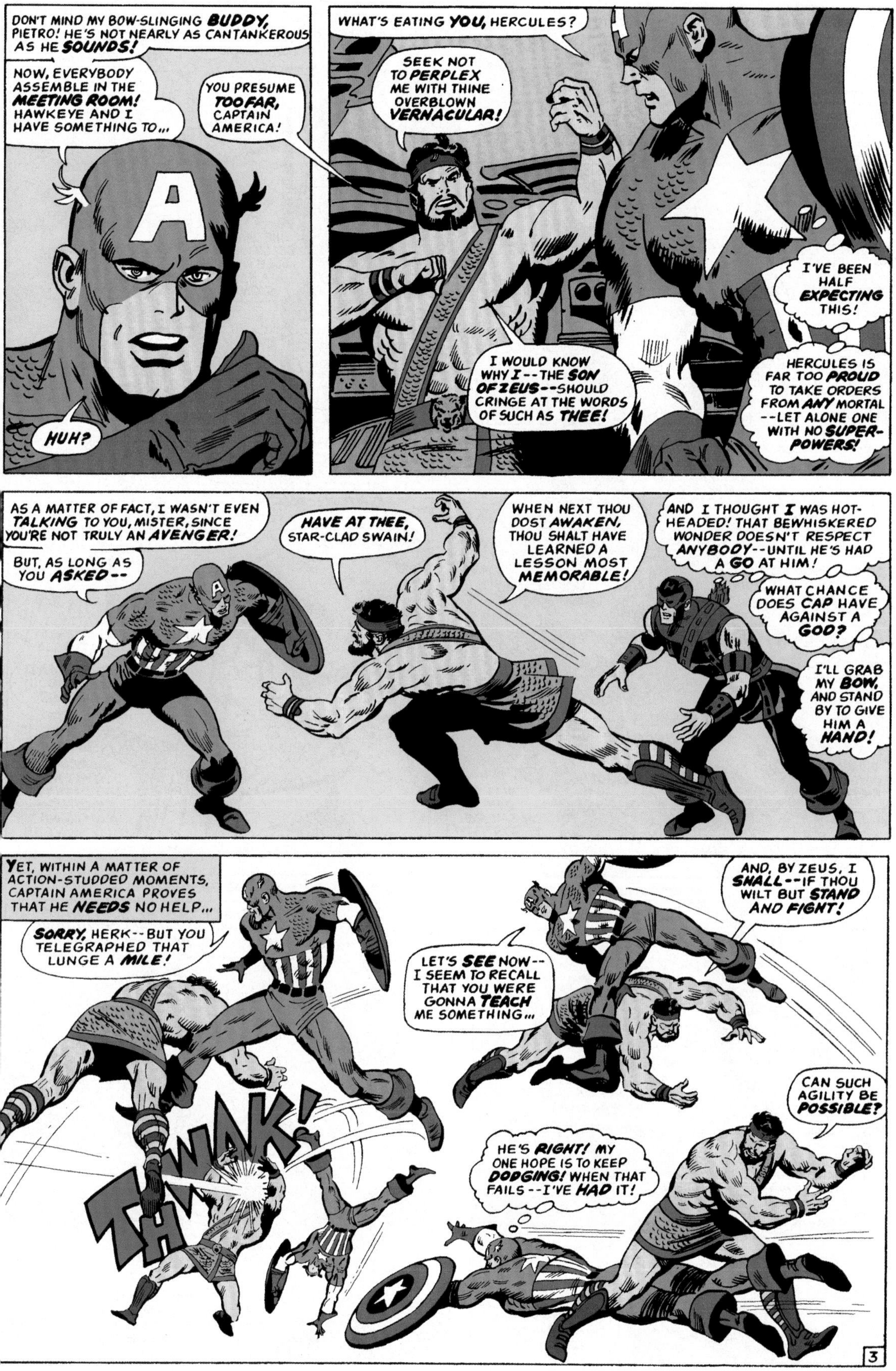
DON'T MIND MY BOW-SLINGING BUDDY, PIETRO! HE'S NOT NEARLY AS CANTANKEROUS AS HE SOUNDS!
NOW, EVERYBODY ASSEMBLE IN THE MEETING ROOM! HAWKEYE AND I HAVE SOMETHING TO...
YOU PRESUME TOO FAR, CAPTAIN AMERICA!
HUH?
WHAT'S EATING YOU, HERCULES?
SEEK NOT TO PERPLEX ME WITH THINE OVERBLOWN VERNACULAR!
I WOULD KNOW WHY I--THE SON OF ZEUS--SHOULD CRINGE AT THE WORDS OF SUCH AS THEE!
I'VE BEEN HALF EXPECTING THIS!
HERCULES IS FAR TOO PROUD TO TAKE ORDERS FROM ANY MORTAL --LET ALONE ONE WITH NO SUPER-POWERS!
AS A MATTER OF FACT, I WASN'T EVEN TALKING TO YOU, MISTER, SINCE YOU'RE NOT TRULY AN AVENGER!
BUT, AS LONG AS YOU ASKED--
HAVE AT THEE, STAR-CLAD SWAIN!
WHEN NEXT THOU DOST AWAKEN, THOU SHALT HAVE LEARNED A LESSON MOST MEMORABLE!
AND I THOUGHT I WAS HOT-HEADED! THAT BEWHISKERED WONDER DOESN'T RESPECT ANYBODY--UNTIL HE'S HAD A GO AT HIM!
WHAT CHANCE DOES CAP HAVE AGAINST A GOD?
I'LL GRAB MY BOW, AND STAND BY TO GIVE HIM A HAND!
YET, WITHIN A MATTER OF ACTION-STUDDED MOMENTS, CAPTAIN AMERICA PROVES THAT HE NEEDS NO HELP...
SORRY, HERK--BUT YOU TELEGRAPHED THAT LUNGE A MILE!
THWAK!
LET'S SEE NOW-- I SEEM TO RECALL THAT YOU WERE GONNA TEACH ME SOMETHING...
AND, BY ZEUS, I SHALL--IF THOU WILT BUT STAND AND FIGHT!
CAN SUCH AGILITY BE POSSIBLE?
HE'S RIGHT! MY ONE HOPE IS TO KEEP DODGING! WHEN THAT FAILS--I'VE HAD IT!
3

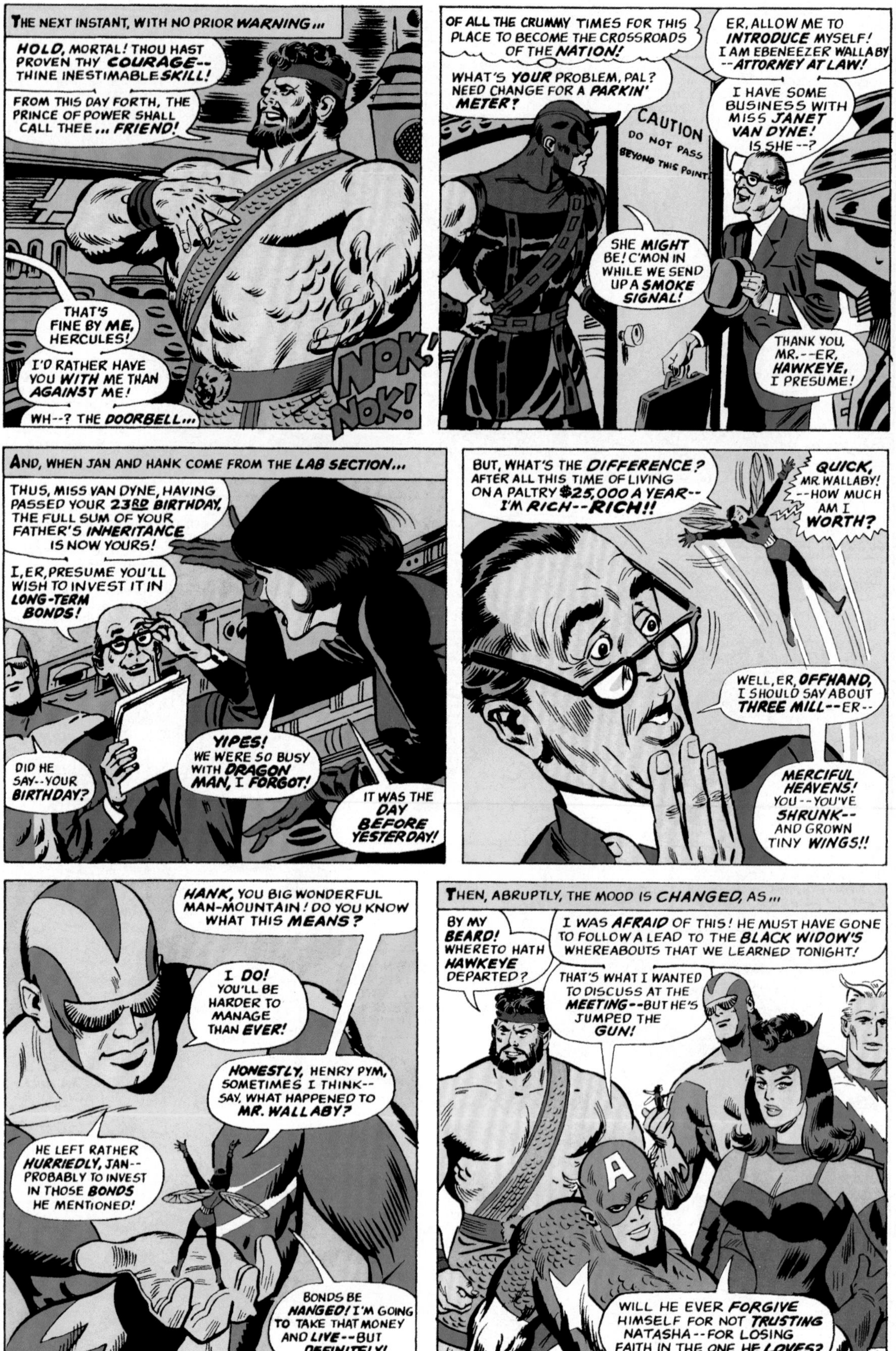

THE NEXT INSTANT, WITH NO PRIOR WARNING...
HOLD, MORTAL! THOU HAST PROVEN THY COURAGE-- THINE INESTIMABLE SKILL!
FROM THIS DAY FORTH, THE PRINCE OF POWER SHALL CALL THEE... FRIEND!
THAT'S FINE BY ME, HERCULES!
I'D RATHER HAVE YOU WITH ME THAN AGAINST ME!
WH--? THE DOORBELL...
NOK! NOK!
OF ALL THE CRUMMY TIMES FOR THIS PLACE TO BECOME THE CROSSROADS OF THE NATION!
WHAT'S YOUR PROBLEM, PAL? NEED CHANGE FOR A PARKIN' METER?
ER, ALLOW ME TO INTRODUCE MYSELF! I AM EBENEEZER WALLABY --ATTORNEY AT LAW!
I HAVE SOME BUSINESS WITH MISS JANET VAN DYNE! IS SHE--?
CAUTION DO NOT PASS BEYOND THIS POINT
SHE MIGHT BE! C'MON IN WHILE WE SEND UP A SMOKE SIGNAL!
THANK YOU, MR.--ER, HAWKEYE, I PRESUME!
AND, WHEN JAN AND HANK COME FROM THE LAB SECTION...
THUS, MISS VAN DYNE, HAVING PASSED YOUR 23RD BIRTHDAY, THE FULL SUM OF YOUR FATHER'S INHERITANCE IS NOW YOURS!
I, ER, PRESUME YOU'LL WISH TO INVEST IT IN LONG-TERM BONDS!
DID HE SAY--YOUR BIRTHDAY?
YIPES! WE WERE SO BUSY WITH DRAGON MAN, I FORGOT!
IT WAS THE DAY BEFORE YESTERDAY!
BUT, WHAT'S THE DIFFERENCE? AFTER ALL THIS TIME OF LIVING ON A PALTRY $25,000 A YEAR-- I'M RICH--RICH!!
QUICK, MR. WALLABY! --HOW MUCH AM I WORTH?
WELL, ER, OFFHAND, I SHOULD SAY ABOUT THREE MILL--ER--
MERCIFUL HEAVENS! YOU--YOU'VE SHRUNK-- AND GROWN TINY WINGS!!
HANK, YOU BIG WONDERFUL MAN-MOUNTAIN! DO YOU KNOW WHAT THIS MEANS?
I DO! YOU'LL BE HARDER TO MANAGE THAN EVER!
HONESTLY, HENRY PYM, SOMETIMES I THINK-- SAY, WHAT HAPPENED TO MR. WALLABY?
HE LEFT RATHER HURRIEDLY, JAN-- PROBABLY TO INVEST IN THOSE BONDS HE MENTIONED!
BONDS BE HANGED! I'M GOING TO TAKE THAT MONEY AND LIVE--BUT DEFINITELY!
THEN, ABRUPTLY, THE MOOD IS CHANGED, AS...
BY MY BEARD! WHERETO HATH HAWKEYE DEPARTED?
I WAS AFRAID OF THIS! HE MUST HAVE GONE TO FOLLOW A LEAD TO THE BLACK WIDOW'S WHEREABOUTS THAT WE LEARNED TONIGHT!
THAT'S WHAT I WANTED TO DISCUSS AT THE MEETING--BUT HE'S JUMPED THE GUN!
WILL HE EVER FORGIVE HIMSELF FOR NOT TRUSTING NATASHA--FOR LOSING FAITH IN THE ONE HE LOVES?

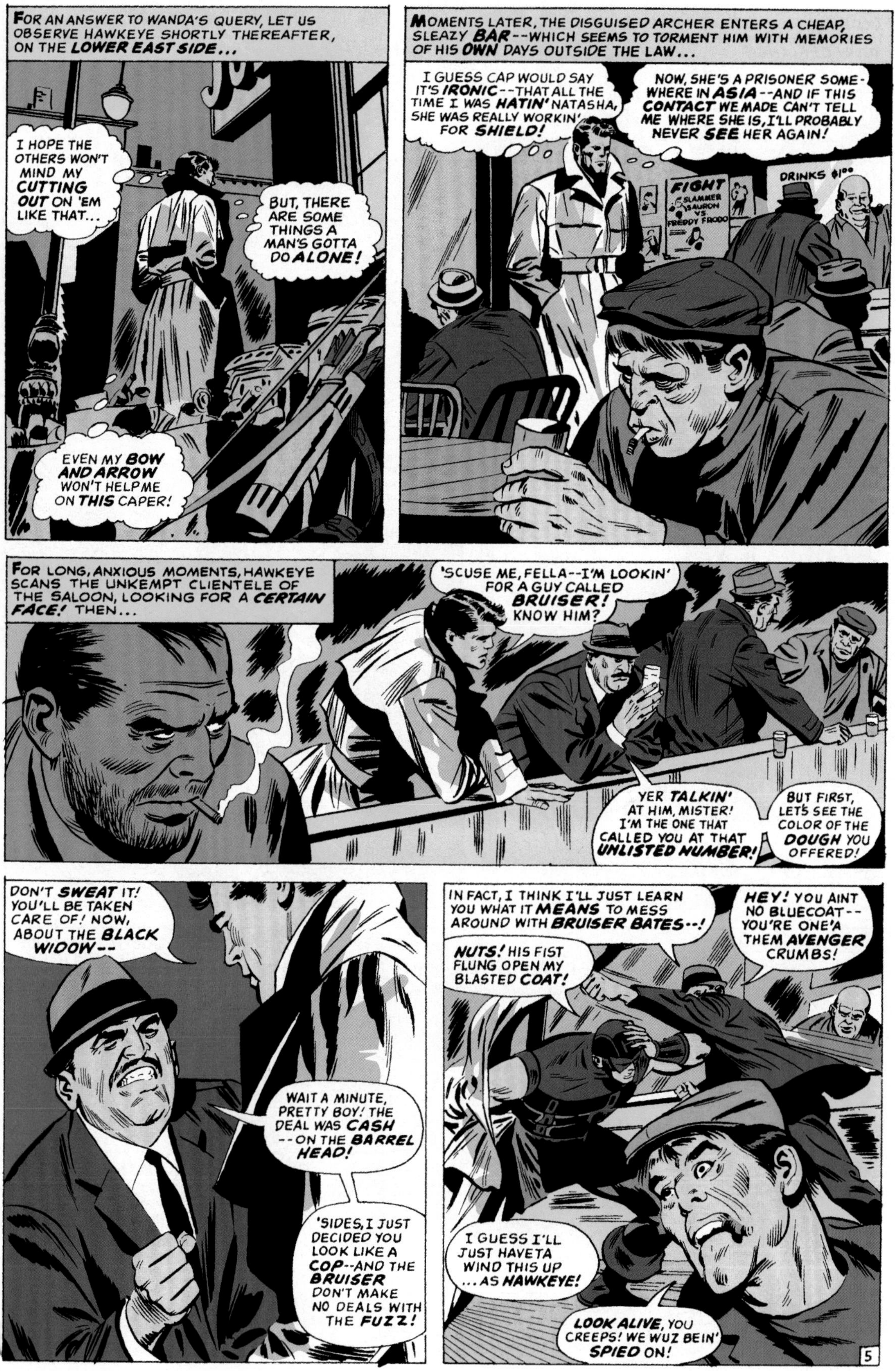

FOR AN ANSWER TO WANDA'S QUERY, LET US OBSERVE HAWKEYE SHORTLY THEREAFTER, ON THE LOWER EAST SIDE...
I HOPE THE OTHERS WON'T MIND MY CUTTING OUT ON 'EM LIKE THAT...
BUT, THERE ARE SOME THINGS A MAN'S GOTTA DO ALONE!
EVEN MY BOW AND ARROW WON'T HELP ME ON THIS CAPER!
MOMENTS LATER, THE DISGUISED ARCHER ENTERS A CHEAP, SLEAZY BAR--WHICH SEEMS TO TORMENT HIM WITH MEMORIES OF HIS OWN DAYS OUTSIDE THE LAW...
I GUESS CAP WOULD SAY IT'S IRONIC--THAT ALL THE TIME I WAS HATIN' NATASHA, SHE WAS REALLY WORKIN' FOR SHIELD!
NOW, SHE'S A PRISONER SOMEWHERE IN ASIA--AND IF THIS CONTACT WE MADE CAN'T TELL ME WHERE SHE IS, I'LL PROBABLY NEVER SEE HER AGAIN!
FIGHT
SLAMMER SAURON VS FREDDY FRODO
DRINKS $1.00
FOR LONG, ANXIOUS MOMENTS, HAWKEYE SCANS THE UNKEMPT CLIENTELE OF THE SALOON, LOOKING FOR A CERTAIN FACE! THEN...
'SCUSE ME, FELLA--I'M LOOKIN' FOR A GUY CALLED BRUISER! KNOW HIM?
YER TALKIN' AT HIM, MISTER! I'M THE ONE THAT CALLED YOU AT THAT UNLISTED NUMBER!
BUT FIRST, LET'S SEE THE COLOR OF THE DOUGH YOU OFFERED!
DON'T SWEAT IT! YOU'LL BE TAKEN CARE OF! NOW, ABOUT THE BLACK WIDOW--
WAIT A MINUTE, PRETTY BOY! THE DEAL WAS CASH--ON THE BARREL HEAD!
'SIDES, I JUST DECIDED YOU LOOK LIKE A COP--AND THE BRUISER DON'T MAKE NO DEALS WITH THE FUZZ!
IN FACT, I THINK I'LL JUST LEARN YOU WHAT IT MEANS TO MESS AROUND WITH BRUISER BATES--!
NUTS! HIS FIST FLUNG OPEN MY BLASTED COAT!
HEY! YOU AINT NO BLUECOAT--YOU'RE ONE'A THEM AVENGER CRUMBS!
I GUESS I'LL JUST HAVETA WIND THIS UP...AS HAWKEYE!
LOOK ALIVE, YOU CREEPS! WE WUZ BEIN' SPIED ON!

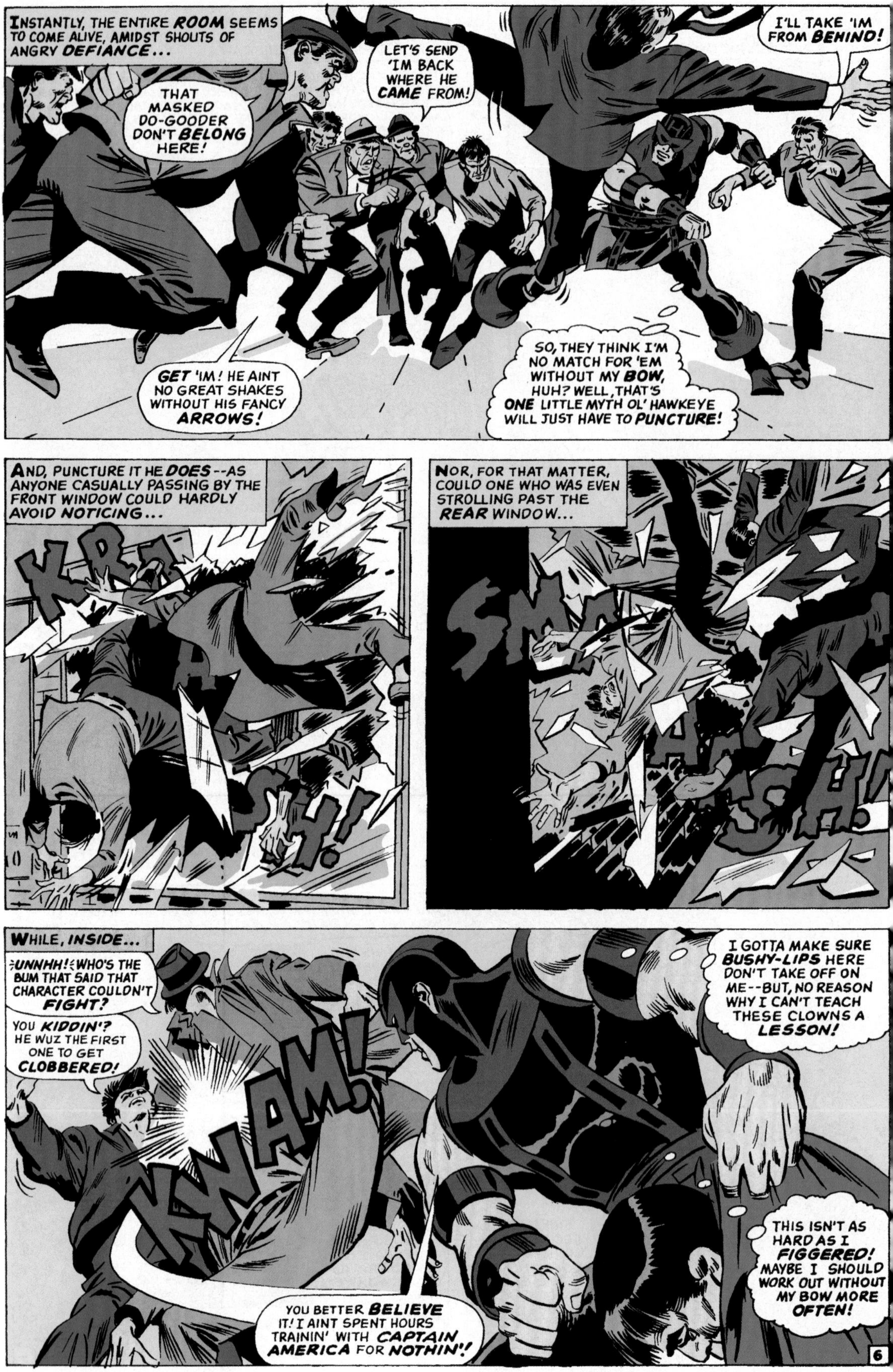
INSTANTLY, THE ENTIRE ROOM SEEMS TO COME ALIVE, AMIDST SHOUTS OF ANGRY DEFIANCE...
THAT MASKED DO-GOODER DON'T BELONG HERE!
LET'S SEND 'IM BACK WHERE HE CAME FROM!
I'LL TAKE 'IM FROM BEHIND!
GET 'IM! HE AINT NO GREAT SHAKES WITHOUT HIS FANCY ARROWS!
SO, THEY THINK I'M NO MATCH FOR 'EM WITHOUT MY BOW, HUH? WELL, THAT'S ONE LITTLE MYTH OL' HAWKEYE WILL JUST HAVE TO PUNCTURE!
AND, PUNCTURE IT HE DOES--AS ANYONE CASUALLY PASSING BY THE FRONT WINDOW COULD HARDLY AVOID NOTICING...
KRASH!
NOR, FOR THAT MATTER, COULD ONE WHO WAS EVEN STROLLING PAST THE REAR WINDOW...
SMASH!
WHILE, INSIDE...
UNNHH! WHO'S THE BUM THAT SAID THAT CHARACTER COULDN'T FIGHT?
YOU KIDDIN'? HE WUZ THE FIRST ONE TO GET CLOBBERED!
KWAM!
I GOTTA MAKE SURE BUSHY-LIPS HERE DON'T TAKE OFF ON ME--BUT, NO REASON WHY I CAN'T TEACH THESE CLOWNS A LESSON!
YOU BETTER BELIEVE IT! I AINT SPENT HOURS TRAININ' WITH CAPTAIN AMERICA FOR NOTHIN'!
THIS ISN'T AS HARD AS I FIGGERED! MAYBE I SHOULD WORK OUT WITHOUT MY BOW MORE OFTEN!
6

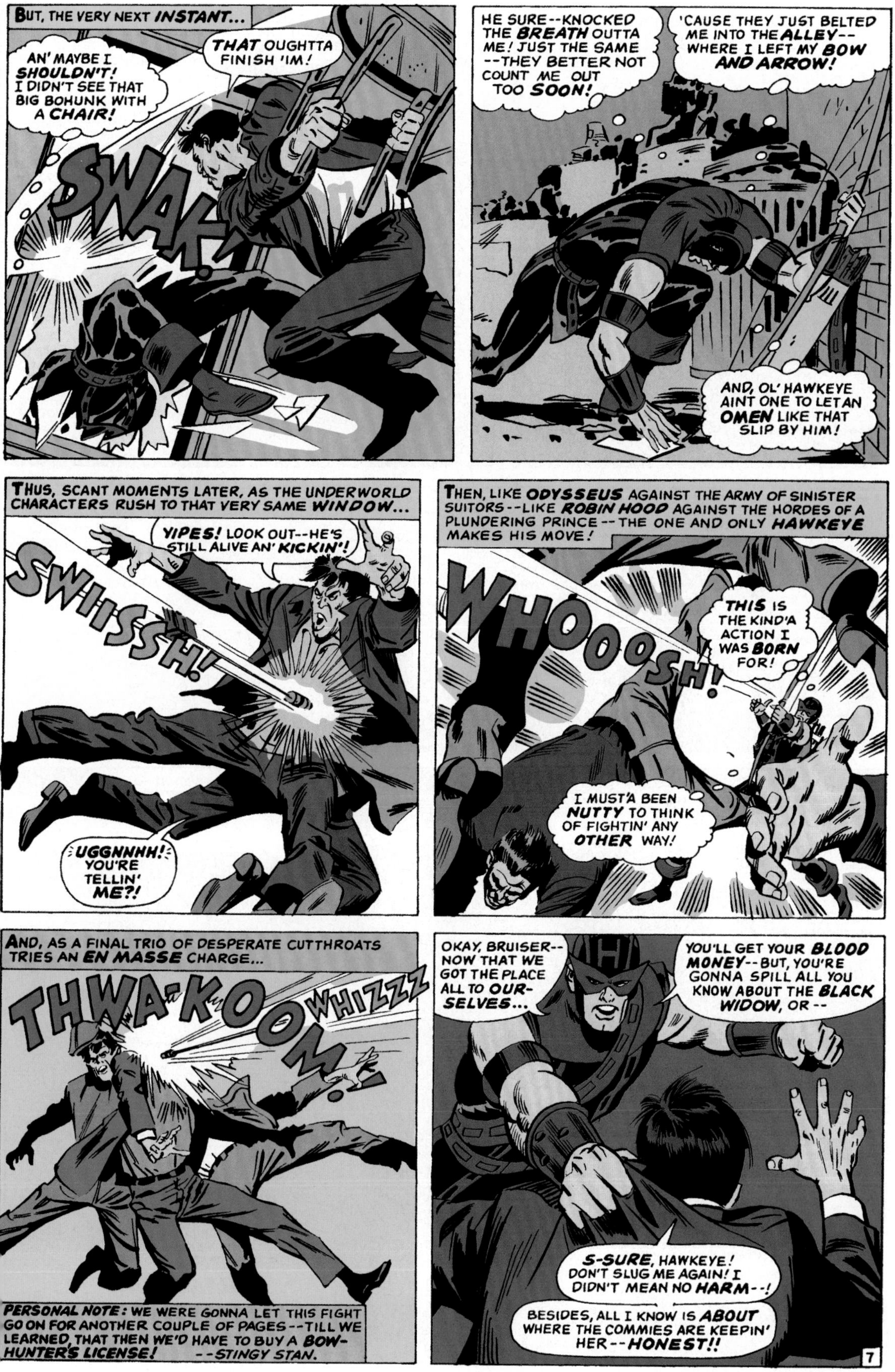

BUT, THE VERY NEXT INSTANT...
AN' MAYBE I SHOULDN'T! I DIDN'T SEE THAT BIG BOHUNK WITH A CHAIR!
THAT OUGHTTA FINISH 'IM!
SWAK!
HE SURE--KNOCKED THE BREATH OUTTA ME! JUST THE SAME --THEY BETTER NOT COUNT ME OUT TOO SOON!
'CAUSE THEY JUST BELTED ME INTO THE ALLEY-- WHERE I LEFT MY BOW AND ARROW!
AND, OL' HAWKEYE AINT ONE TO LET AN OMEN LIKE THAT SLIP BY HIM!
THUS, SCANT MOMENTS LATER, AS THE UNDERWORLD CHARACTERS RUSH TO THAT VERY SAME WINDOW...
YIPES! LOOK OUT--HE'S STILL ALIVE AN' KICKIN'!
SWIISSH!
UGGNNNH! YOU'RE TELLIN' ME?!
THEN, LIKE ODYSSEUS AGAINST THE ARMY OF SINISTER SUITORS--LIKE ROBIN HOOD AGAINST THE HORDES OF A PLUNDERING PRINCE -- THE ONE AND ONLY HAWKEYE MAKES HIS MOVE!
WHOOOOSH!
THIS IS THE KIND'A ACTION I WAS BORN FOR!
I MUST'A BEEN NUTTY TO THINK OF FIGHTIN' ANY OTHER WAY!
AND, AS A FINAL TRIO OF DESPERATE CUTTHROATS TRIES AN EN MASSE CHARGE...
THWA-KOOM!
WHIZZZ
PERSONAL NOTE: WE WERE GONNA LET THIS FIGHT GO ON FOR ANOTHER COUPLE OF PAGES--TILL WE LEARNED, THAT THEN WE'D HAVE TO BUY A BOW-HUNTER'S LICENSE! --STINGY STAN.
OKAY, BRUISER-- NOW THAT WE GOT THE PLACE ALL TO OUR-SELVES...
YOU'LL GET YOUR BLOOD MONEY--BUT, YOU'RE GONNA SPILL ALL YOU KNOW ABOUT THE BLACK WIDOW, OR --
S-SURE, HAWKEYE! DON'T SLUG ME AGAIN! I DIDN'T MEAN NO HARM--!
BESIDES, ALL I KNOW IS ABOUT WHERE THE COMMIES ARE KEEPIN' HER--HONEST!!
7

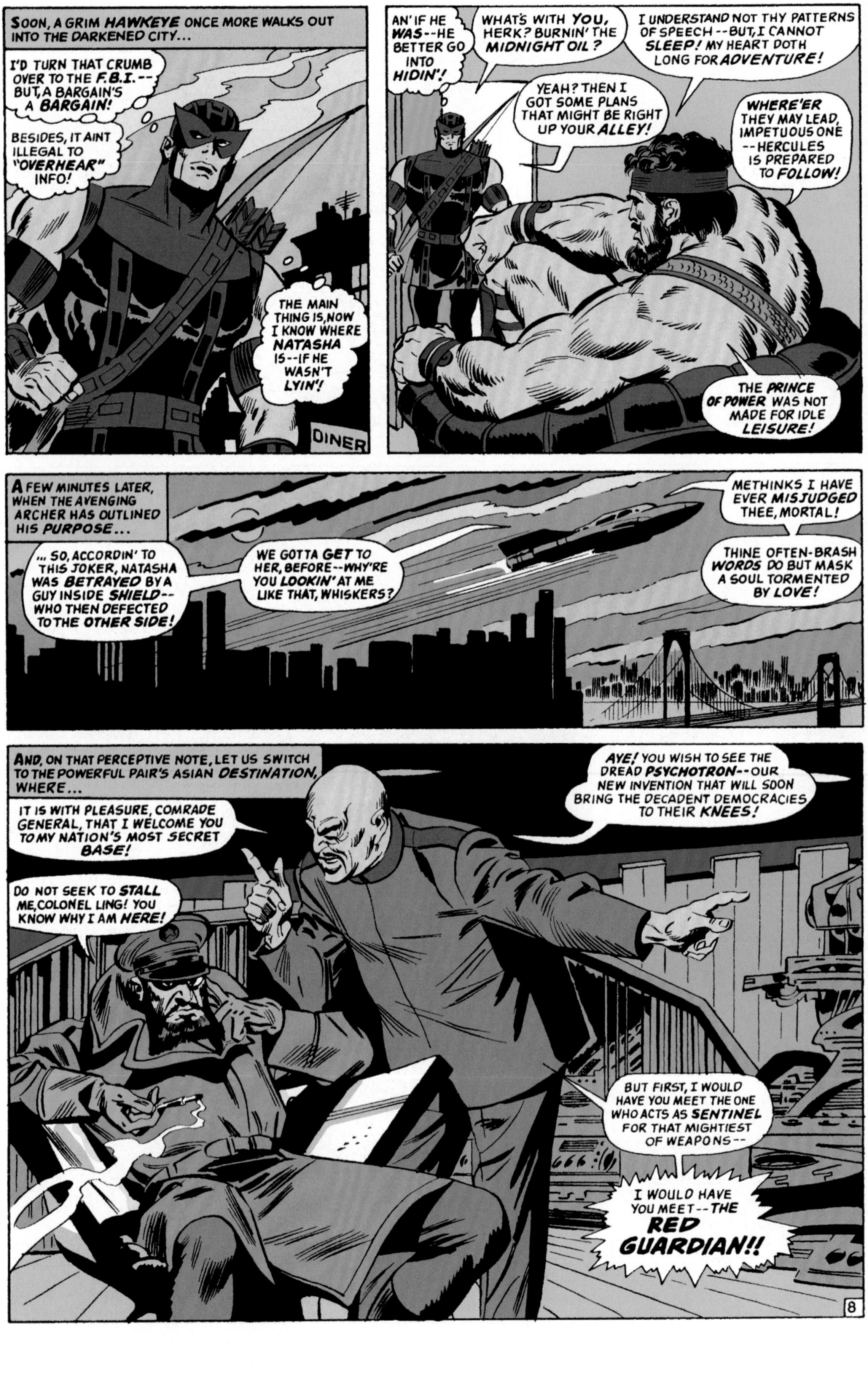
SOON, A GRIM HAWKEYE ONCE MORE WALKS OUT INTO THE DARKENED CITY...
I'D TURN THAT CRUMB OVER TO THE F.B.I.-- BUT, A BARGAIN'S A BARGAIN!
BESIDES, IT AINT ILLEGAL TO "OVERHEAR" INFO!
THE MAIN THING IS, NOW I KNOW WHERE NATASHA IS--IF HE WASN'T LYIN'!
DINER
AN' IF HE WAS--HE BETTER GO INTO HIDIN'!
WHAT'S WITH YOU, HERK? BURNIN' THE MIDNIGHT OIL?
I UNDERSTAND NOT THY PATTERNS OF SPEECH --BUT, I CANNOT SLEEP! MY HEART DOTH LONG FOR ADVENTURE!
YEAH? THEN I GOT SOME PLANS THAT MIGHT BE RIGHT UP YOUR ALLEY!
WHERE'ER THEY MAY LEAD, IMPETUOUS ONE --HERCULES IS PREPARED TO FOLLOW!
THE PRINCE OF POWER WAS NOT MADE FOR IDLE LEISURE!
A FEW MINUTES LATER, WHEN THE AVENGING ARCHER HAS OUTLINED HIS PURPOSE...
... SO, ACCORDIN' TO THIS JOKER, NATASHA WAS BETRAYED BY A GUY INSIDE SHIELD-- WHO THEN DEFECTED TO THE OTHER SIDE!
WE GOTTA GET TO HER, BEFORE--WHY'RE YOU LOOKIN' AT ME LIKE THAT, WHISKERS?
METHINKS I HAVE EVER MISJUDGED THEE, MORTAL!
THINE OFTEN-BRASH WORDS DO BUT MASK A SOUL TORMENTED BY LOVE!
AND, ON THAT PERCEPTIVE NOTE, LET US SWITCH TO THE POWERFUL PAIR'S ASIAN DESTINATION, WHERE...
IT IS WITH PLEASURE, COMRADE GENERAL, THAT I WELCOME YOU TO MY NATION'S MOST SECRET BASE!
DO NOT SEEK TO STALL ME, COLONEL LING! YOU KNOW WHY I AM HERE!
AYE! YOU WISH TO SEE THE DREAD PSYCHOTRON--OUR NEW INVENTION THAT WILL SOON BRING THE DECADENT DEMOCRACIES TO THEIR KNEES!
BUT FIRST, I WOULD HAVE YOU MEET THE ONE WHO ACTS AS SENTINEL FOR THAT MIGHTIEST OF WEAPONS--
I WOULD HAVE YOU MEET--THE RED GUARDIAN!!

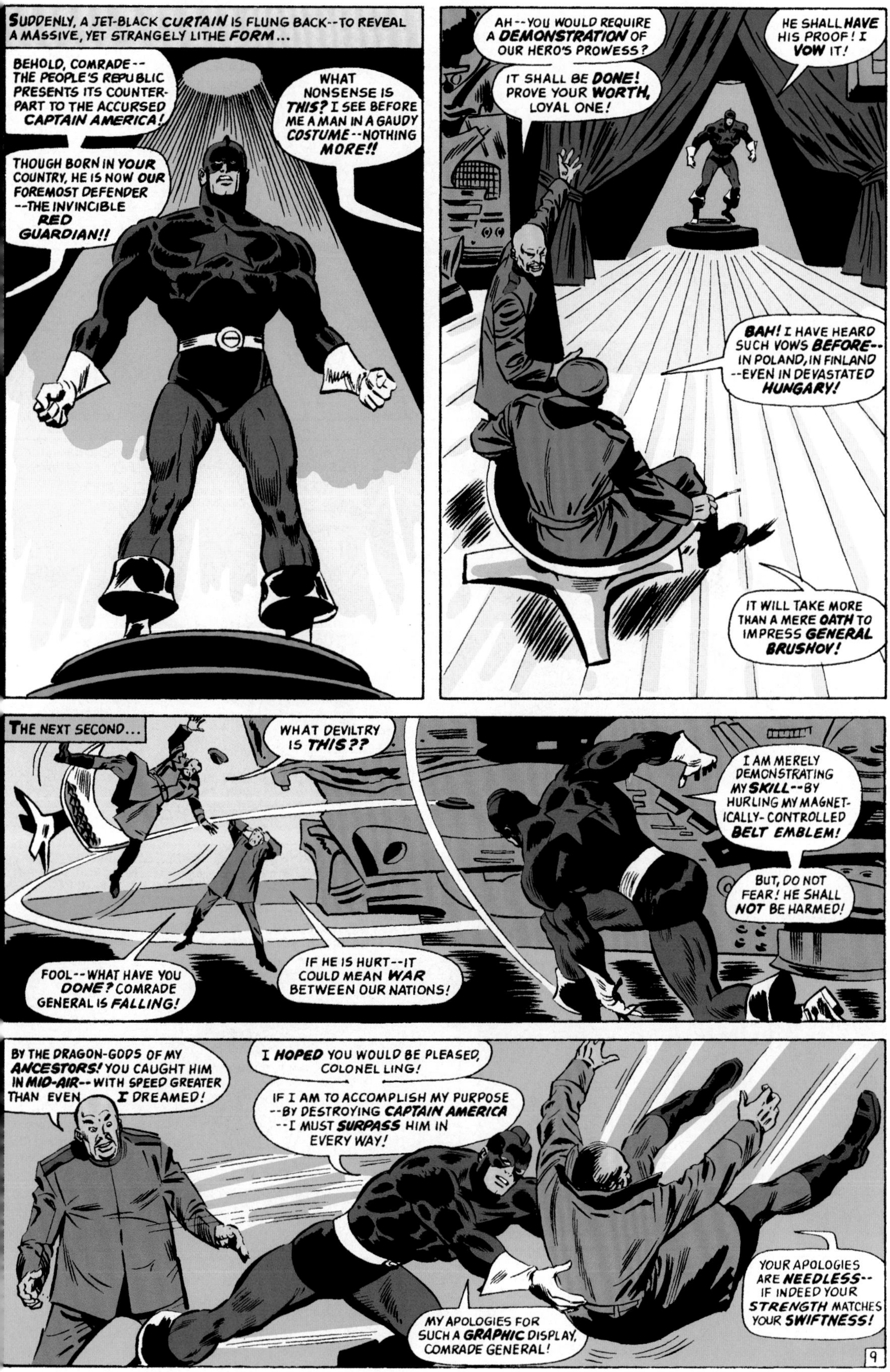
SUDDENLY, A JET-BLACK CURTAIN IS FLUNG BACK--TO REVEAL A MASSIVE, YET STRANGELY LITHE FORM...
BEHOLD, COMRADE-- THE PEOPLE'S REPUBLIC PRESENTS ITS COUNTERPART TO THE ACCURSED CAPTAIN AMERICA!
THOUGH BORN IN YOUR COUNTRY, HE IS NOW OUR FOREMOST DEFENDER --THE INVINCIBLE RED GUARDIAN!!
WHAT NONSENSE IS THIS? I SEE BEFORE ME A MAN IN A GAUDY COSTUME--NOTHING MORE!!
AH--YOU WOULD REQUIRE A DEMONSTRATION OF OUR HERO'S PROWESS?
IT SHALL BE DONE! PROVE YOUR WORTH, LOYAL ONE!
HE SHALL HAVE HIS PROOF! I VOW IT!
BAH! I HAVE HEARD SUCH VOWS BEFORE-- IN POLAND, IN FINLAND --EVEN IN DEVASTATED HUNGARY!
IT WILL TAKE MORE THAN A MERE OATH TO IMPRESS GENERAL BRUSHOV!
THE NEXT SECOND...
WHAT DEVILTRY IS THIS??
I AM MERELY DEMONSTRATING MY SKILL--BY HURLING MY MAGNETICALLY-CONTROLLED BELT EMBLEM!
BUT, DO NOT FEAR! HE SHALL NOT BE HARMED!
FOOL--WHAT HAVE YOU DONE? COMRADE GENERAL IS FALLING!
IF HE IS HURT--IT COULD MEAN WAR BETWEEN OUR NATIONS!
BY THE DRAGON-GODS OF MY ANCESTORS! YOU CAUGHT HIM IN MID-AIR--WITH SPEED GREATER THAN EVEN I DREAMED!
I HOPED YOU WOULD BE PLEASED, COLONEL LING!
IF I AM TO ACCOMPLISH MY PURPOSE --BY DESTROYING CAPTAIN AMERICA --I MUST SURPASS HIM IN EVERY WAY!
MY APOLOGIES FOR SUCH A GRAPHIC DISPLAY, COMRADE GENERAL!
YOUR APOLOGIES ARE NEEDLESS-- IF INDEED YOUR STRENGTH MATCHES YOUR SWIFTNESS!
9

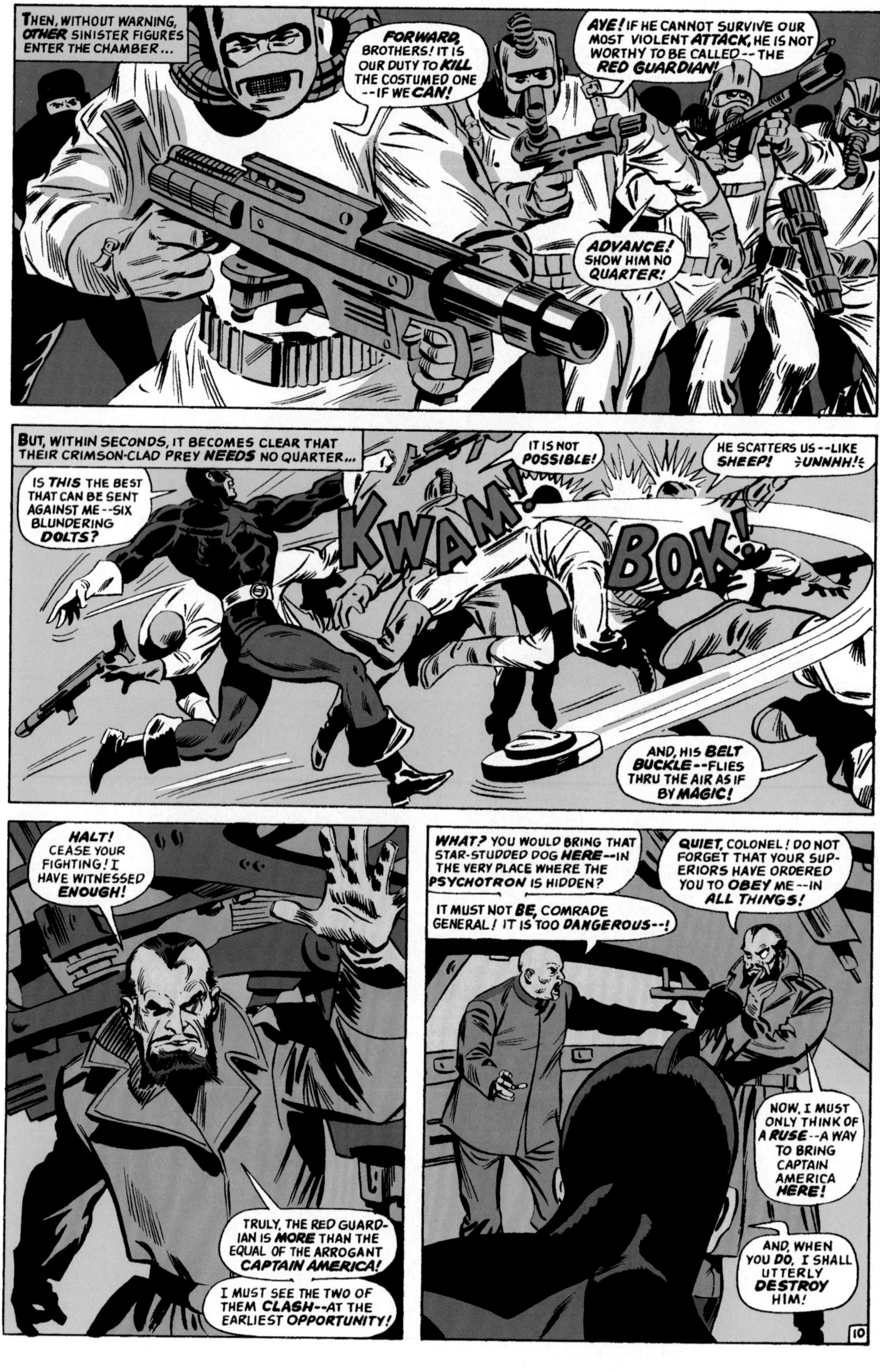
THEN, WITHOUT WARNING, OTHER SINISTER FIGURES ENTER THE CHAMBER...
FORWARD, BROTHERS! IT IS OUR DUTY TO KILL THE COSTUMED ONE --IF WE CAN!
AYE! IF HE CANNOT SURVIVE OUR MOST VIOLENT ATTACK, HE IS NOT WORTHY TO BE CALLED--THE RED GUARDIAN!
ADVANCE! SHOW HIM NO QUARTER!
BUT, WITHIN SECONDS, IT BECOMES CLEAR THAT THEIR CRIMSON-CLAD PREY NEEDS NO QUARTER...
IS THIS THE BEST THAT CAN BE SENT AGAINST ME--SIX BLUNDERING DOLTS?
IT IS NOT POSSIBLE!
HE SCATTERS US--LIKE SHEEP! UNNHH!
KWAM!
BOK!
AND, HIS BELT BUCKLE--FLIES THRU THE AIR AS IF BY MAGIC!
HALT! CEASE YOUR FIGHTING! I HAVE WITNESSED ENOUGH!
TRULY, THE RED GUARDIAN IS MORE THAN THE EQUAL OF THE ARROGANT CAPTAIN AMERICA!
I MUST SEE THE TWO OF THEM CLASH--AT THE EARLIEST OPPORTUNITY!
WHAT? YOU WOULD BRING THAT STAR-STUDDED DOG HERE--IN THE VERY PLACE WHERE THE PSYCHOTRON IS HIDDEN?
IT MUST NOT BE, COMRADE GENERAL! IT IS TOO DANGEROUS--!
QUIET, COLONEL! DO NOT FORGET THAT YOUR SUPERIORS HAVE ORDERED YOU TO OBEY ME--IN ALL THINGS!
NOW, I MUST ONLY THINK OF A RUSE--A WAY TO BRING CAPTAIN AMERICA HERE!
AND, WHEN YOU DO, I SHALL UTTERLY DESTROY HIM!
10

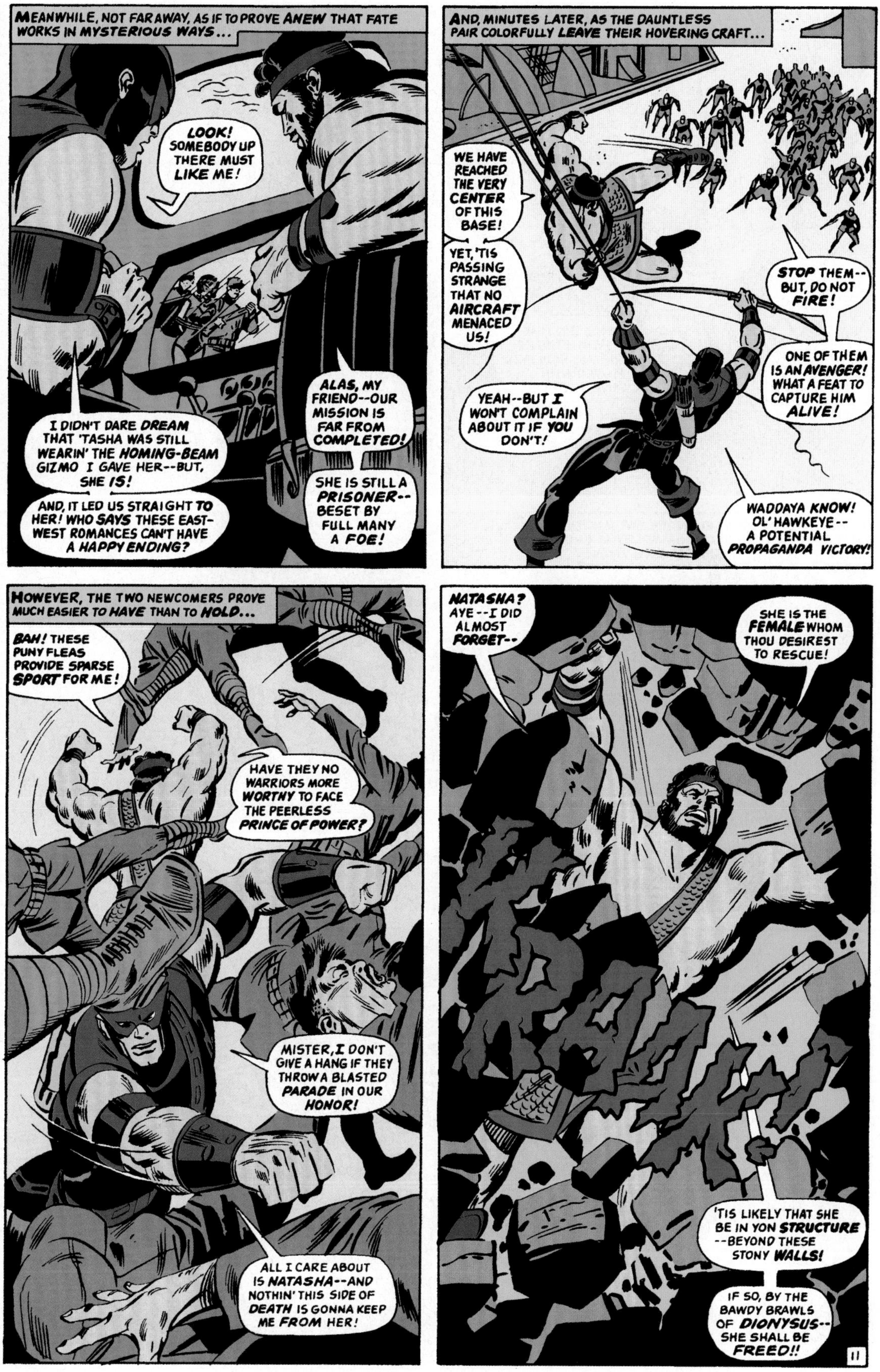

MEANWHILE, NOT FAR AWAY, AS IF TO PROVE ANEW THAT FATE WORKS IN MYSTERIOUS WAYS...
LOOK! SOMEBODY UP THERE MUST LIKE ME!
I DIDN'T DARE DREAM THAT 'TASHA WAS STILL WEARIN' THE HOMING-BEAM GIZMO I GAVE HER--BUT, SHE IS!
AND, IT LED US STRAIGHT TO HER! WHO SAYS THESE EAST-WEST ROMANCES CAN'T HAVE A HAPPY ENDING?
ALAS, MY FRIEND--OUR MISSION IS FAR FROM COMPLETED!
SHE IS STILL A PRISONER--BESET BY FULL MANY A FOE!
AND, MINUTES LATER, AS THE DAUNTLESS PAIR COLORFULLY LEAVE THEIR HOVERING CRAFT...
WE HAVE REACHED THE VERY CENTER OF THIS BASE!
YET, 'TIS PASSING STRANGE THAT NO AIRCRAFT MENACED US!
YEAH--BUT I WON'T COMPLAIN ABOUT IT IF YOU DON'T!
STOP THEM--BUT, DO NOT FIRE!
ONE OF THEM IS AN AVENGER! WHAT A FEAT TO CAPTURE HIM ALIVE!
WADDAYA KNOW! OL' HAWKEYE--A POTENTIAL PROPAGANDA VICTORY!
HOWEVER, THE TWO NEWCOMERS PROVE MUCH EASIER TO HAVE THAN TO HOLD...
BAH! THESE PUNY FLEAS PROVIDE SPARSE SPORT FOR ME!
HAVE THEY NO WARRIORS MORE WORTHY TO FACE THE PEERLESS PRINCE OF POWER?
MISTER, I DON'T GIVE A HANG IF THEY THROW A BLASTED PARADE IN OUR HONOR!
ALL I CARE ABOUT IS NATASHA--AND NOTHIN' THIS SIDE OF DEATH IS GONNA KEEP ME FROM HER!
NATASHA? AYE--I DID ALMOST FORGET--
SHE IS THE FEMALE WHOM THOU DESIREST TO RESCUE!
'TIS LIKELY THAT SHE BE IN YON STRUCTURE--BEYOND THESE STONY WALLS!
IF SO, BY THE BAWDY BRAWLS OF DIONYSUS--SHE SHALL BE FREED!!

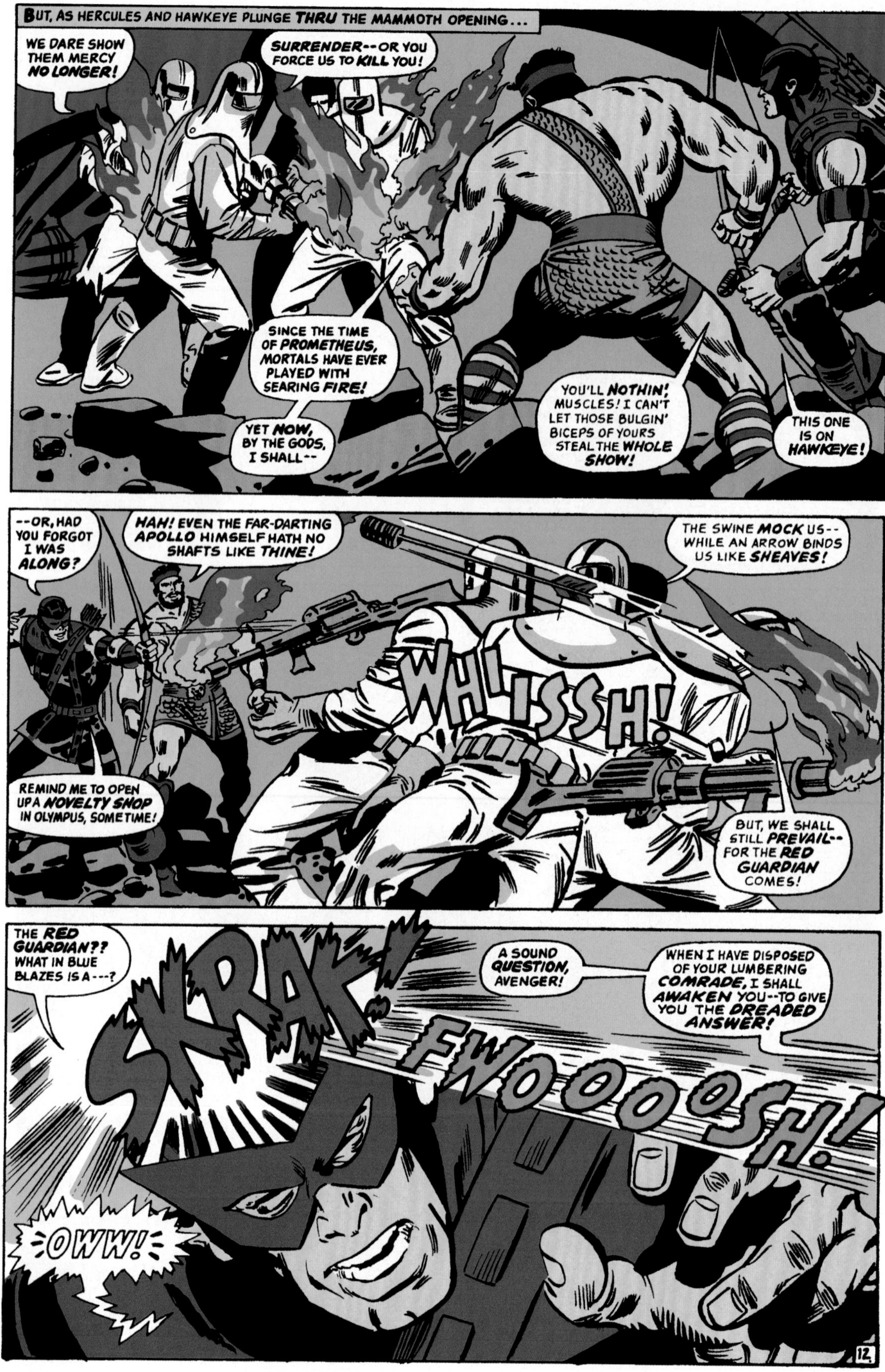

BUT, AS HERCULES AND HAWKEYE PLUNGE THRU THE MAMMOTH OPENING...
WE DARE SHOW THEM MERCY NO LONGER!
SURRENDER--OR YOU FORCE US TO KILL YOU!
SINCE THE TIME OF PROMETHEUS, MORTALS HAVE EVER PLAYED WITH SEARING FIRE!
YET NOW, BY THE GODS, I SHALL--
YOU'LL NOTHIN'! MUSCLES! I CAN'T LET THOSE BULGIN' BICEPS OF YOURS STEAL THE WHOLE SHOW!
THIS ONE IS ON HAWKEYE!
--OR, HAD YOU FORGOT I WAS ALONG?
HAH! EVEN THE FAR-DARTING APOLLO HIMSELF HATH NO SHAFTS LIKE THINE!
THE SWINE MOCK US--WHILE AN ARROW BINDS US LIKE SHEAVES!
WHIISSH!
REMIND ME TO OPEN UP A NOVELTY SHOP IN OLYMPUS, SOMETIME!
BUT, WE SHALL STILL PREVAIL--FOR THE RED GUARDIAN COMES!
THE RED GUARDIAN?? WHAT IN BLUE BLAZES IS A---?
SKRAK!
A SOUND QUESTION, AVENGER!
WHEN I HAVE DISPOSED OF YOUR LUMBERING COMRADE, I SHALL AWAKEN YOU--TO GIVE YOU THE DREADED ANSWER!
FWOOOOSH!
OWW!
12

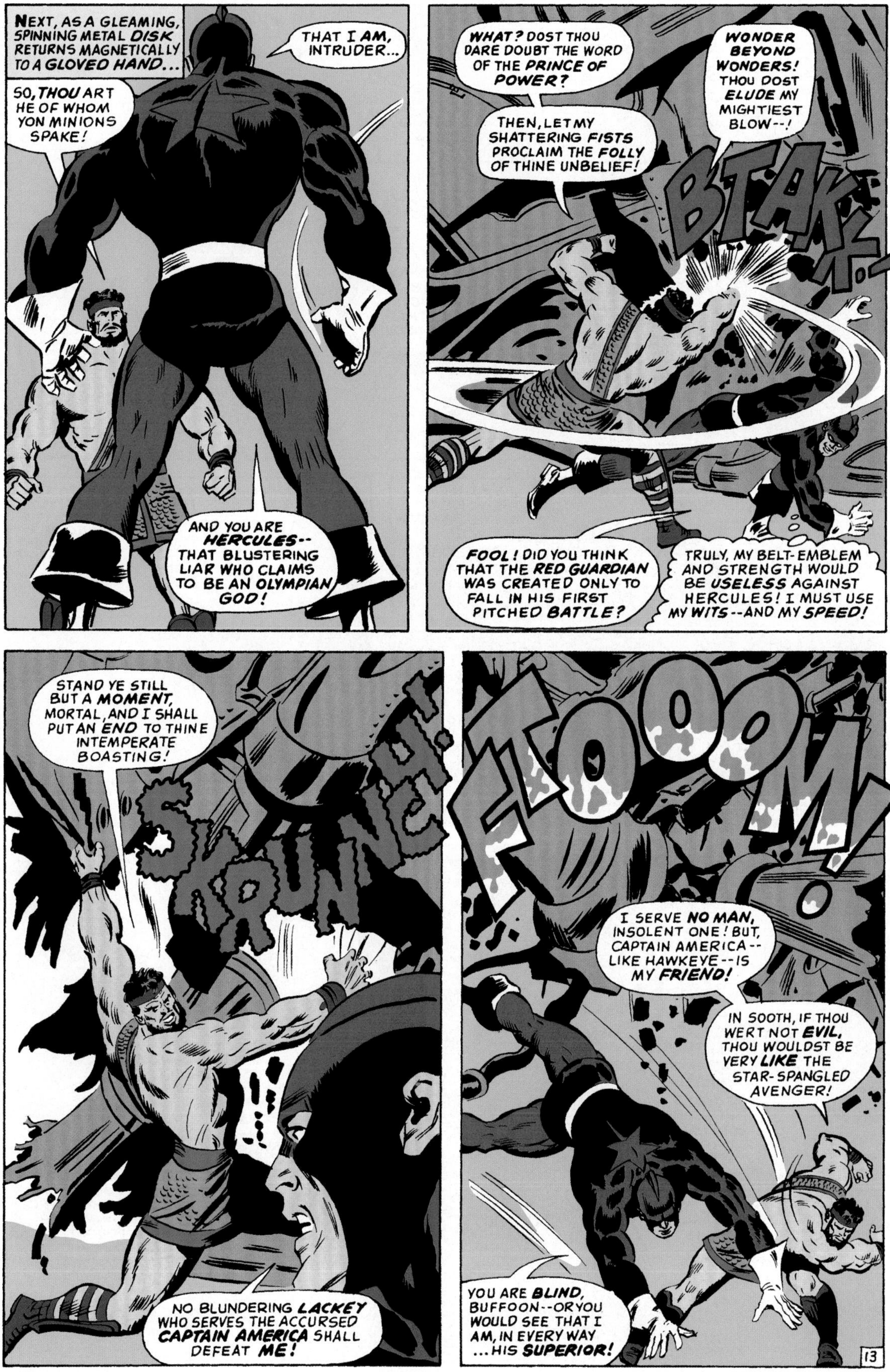
NEXT, AS A GLEAMING, SPINNING METAL DISK RETURNS MAGNETICALLY TO A GLOVED HAND...
SO, THOU ART HE OF WHOM YON MINIONS SPAKE!
THAT I AM, INTRUDER...
AND YOU ARE HERCULES-- THAT BLUSTERING LIAR WHO CLAIMS TO BE AN OLYMPIAN GOD!
WHAT? DOST THOU DARE DOUBT THE WORD OF THE PRINCE OF POWER?
THEN, LET MY SHATTERING FISTS PROCLAIM THE FOLLY OF THINE UNBELIEF!
WONDER BEYOND WONDERS! THOU DOST ELUDE MY MIGHTIEST BLOW--!
BTAKK-
FOOL! DID YOU THINK THAT THE RED GUARDIAN WAS CREATED ONLY TO FALL IN HIS FIRST PITCHED BATTLE?
TRULY, MY BELT-EMBLEM AND STRENGTH WOULD BE USELESS AGAINST HERCULES! I MUST USE MY WITS--AND MY SPEED!
STAND YE STILL BUT A MOMENT, MORTAL, AND I SHALL PUT AN END TO THINE INTEMPERATE BOASTING!
SKRUNNCH!
NO BLUNDERING LACKEY WHO SERVES THE ACCURSED CAPTAIN AMERICA SHALL DEFEAT ME!
FTOOOM!
I SERVE NO MAN, INSOLENT ONE! BUT, CAPTAIN AMERICA-- LIKE HAWKEYE--IS MY FRIEND!
IN SOOTH, IF THOU WERT NOT EVIL, THOU WOULDST BE VERY LIKE THE STAR-SPANGLED AVENGER!
YOU ARE BLIND, BUFFOON--OR YOU WOULD SEE THAT I AM, IN EVERY WAY ...HIS SUPERIOR!
13

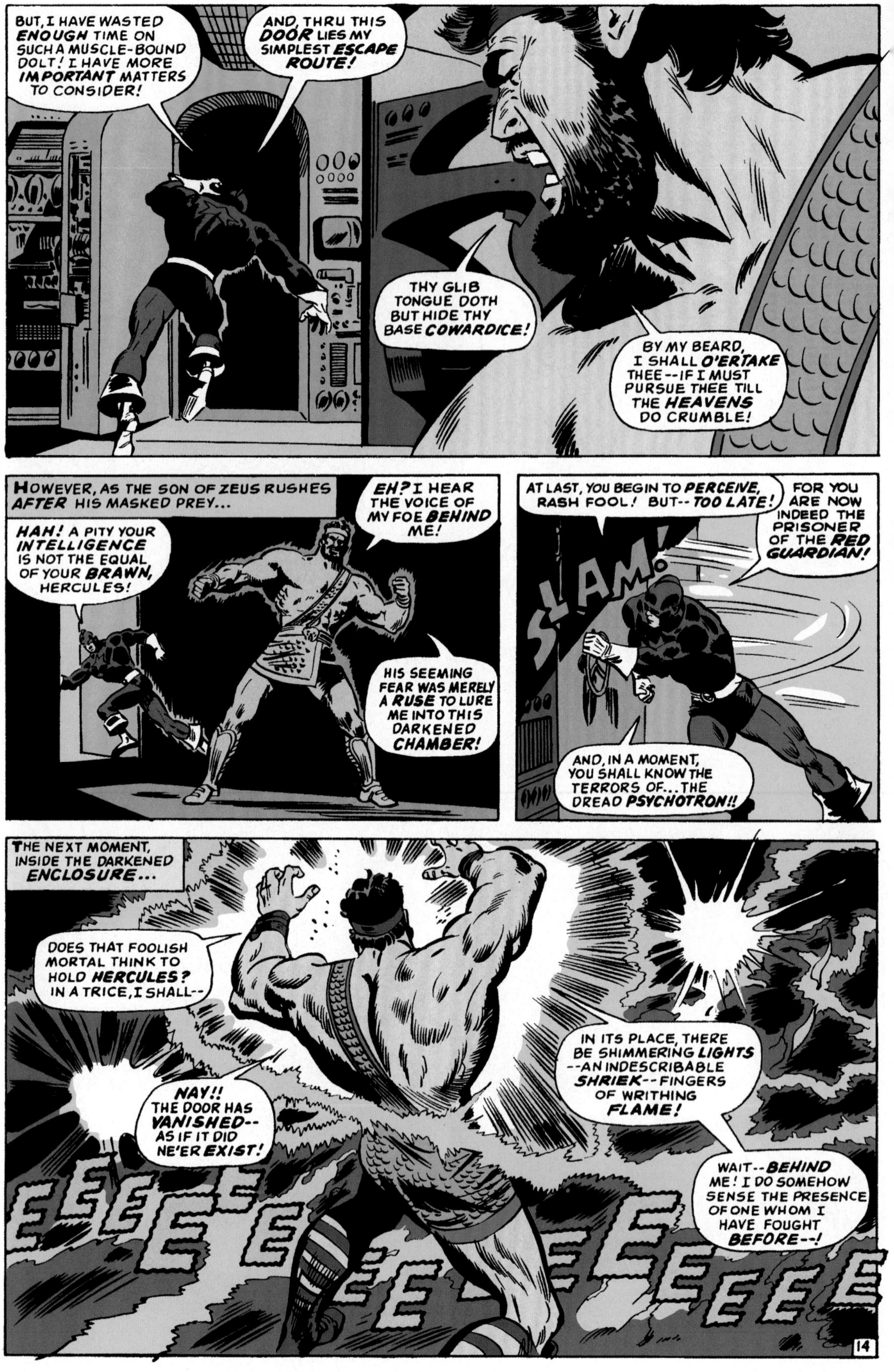

BUT, I HAVE WASTED ENOUGH TIME ON SUCH A MUSCLE-BOUND DOLT! I HAVE MORE IMPORTANT MATTERS TO CONSIDER!
AND, THRU THIS DOOR LIES MY SIMPLEST ESCAPE ROUTE!
THY GLIB TONGUE DOTH BUT HIDE THY BASE COWARDICE!
BY MY BEARD, I SHALL O'ERTAKE THEE--IF I MUST PURSUE THEE TILL THE HEAVENS DO CRUMBLE!
HOWEVER, AS THE SON OF ZEUS RUSHES AFTER HIS MASKED PREY...
HAH! A PITY YOUR INTELLIGENCE IS NOT THE EQUAL OF YOUR BRAWN, HERCULES!
EH? I HEAR THE VOICE OF MY FOE BEHIND ME!
HIS SEEMING FEAR WAS MERELY A RUSE TO LURE ME INTO THIS DARKENED CHAMBER!
AT LAST, YOU BEGIN TO PERCEIVE, RASH FOOL! BUT--TOO LATE!
FOR YOU ARE NOW INDEED THE PRISONER OF THE RED GUARDIAN!
SLAM!
AND, IN A MOMENT, YOU SHALL KNOW THE TERRORS OF... THE DREAD PSYCHOTRON!!
THE NEXT MOMENT, INSIDE THE DARKENED ENCLOSURE...
DOES THAT FOOLISH MORTAL THINK TO HOLD HERCULES? IN A TRICE, I SHALL--
NAY!! THE DOOR HAS VANISHED--AS IF IT DID NE'ER EXIST!
IN ITS PLACE, THERE BE SHIMMERING LIGHTS--AN INDESCRIBABLE SHRIEK--FINGERS OF WRITHING FLAME!
WAIT--BEHIND ME! I DO SOMEHOW SENSE THE PRESENCE OF ONE WHOM I HAVE FOUGHT BEFORE--!
EEEEEEEEEEEEEEEE

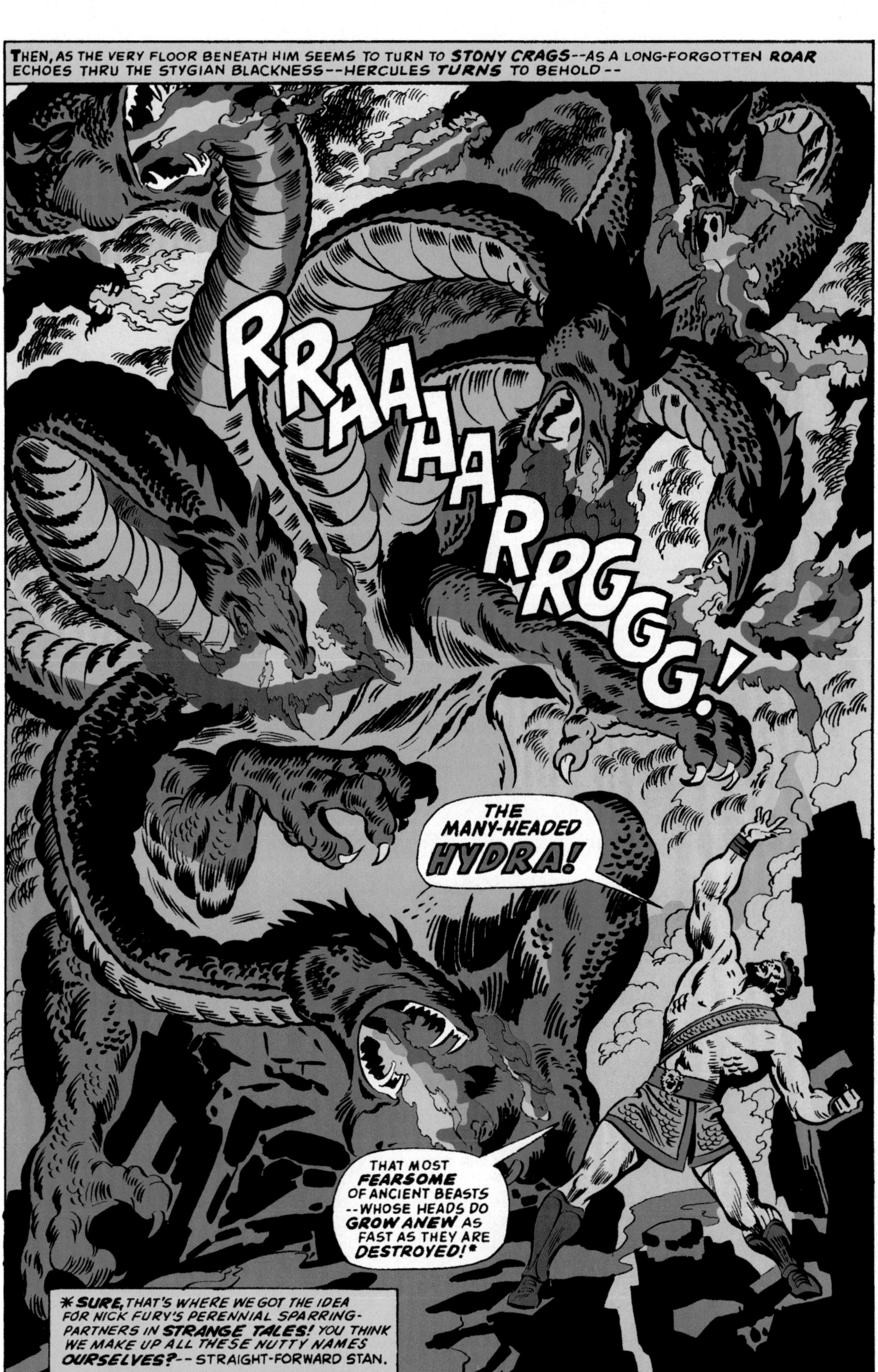

THEN, AS THE VERY FLOOR BENEATH HIM SEEMS TO TURN TO STONY CRAGS--AS A LONG-FORGOTTEN ROAR ECHOES THRU THE STYGIAN BLACKNESS--HERCULES TURNS TO BEHOLD--
RRAAAARRGGG!
THE MANY-HEADED HYDRA!
THAT MOST FEARSOME OF ANCIENT BEASTS --WHOSE HEADS DO GROW ANEW AS FAST AS THEY ARE DESTROYED!*
* SURE, THAT'S WHERE WE GOT THE IDEA FOR NICK FURY'S PERENNIAL SPARRING-PARTNERS IN STRANGE TALES! YOU THINK WE MAKE UP ALL THESE NUTTY NAMES OURSELVES?-- STRAIGHT-FORWARD STAN.

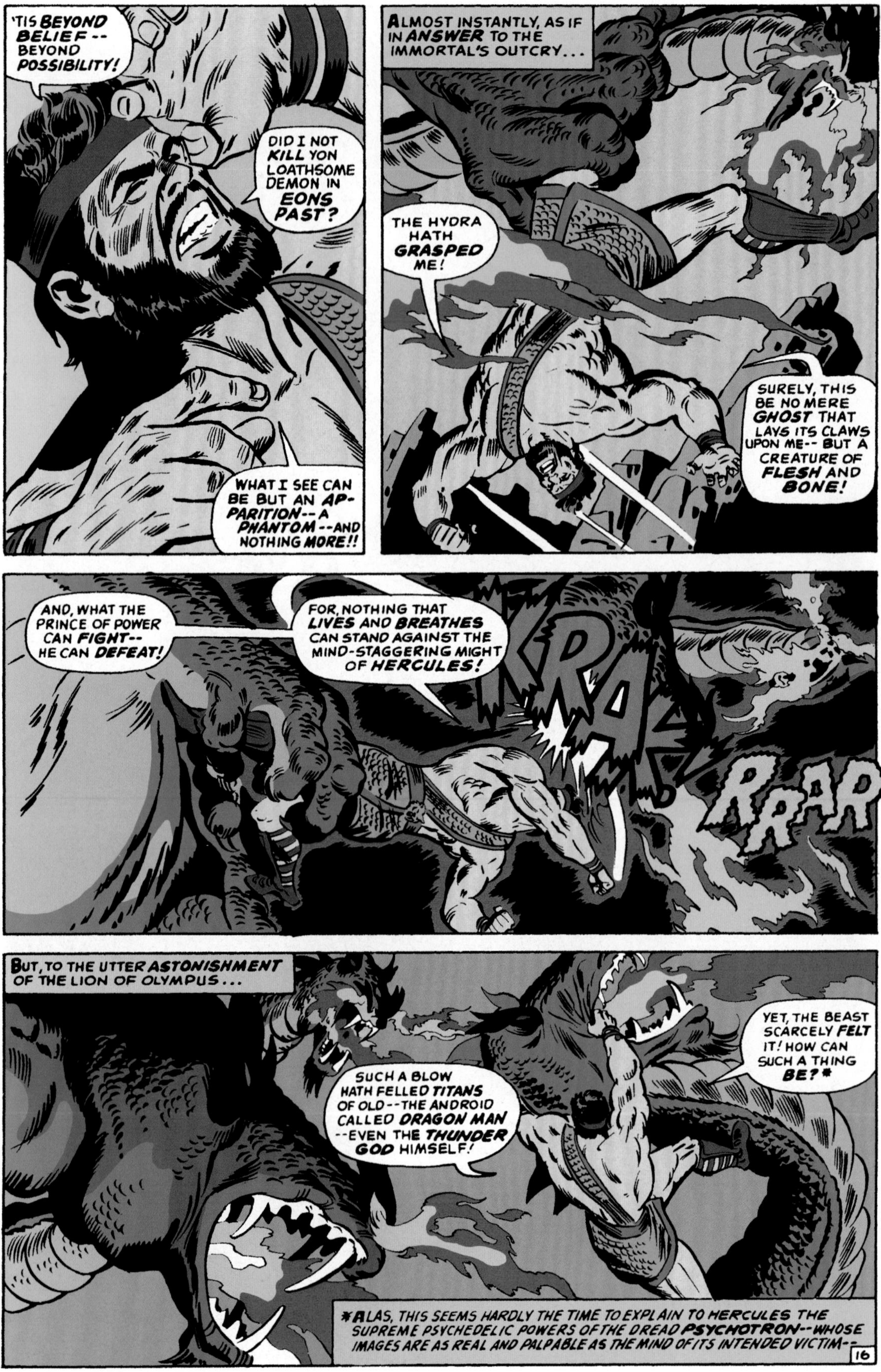
'TIS BEYOND BELIEF -- BEYOND POSSIBILITY!
DID I NOT KILL YON LOATHSOME DEMON IN EONS PAST?
WHAT I SEE CAN BE BUT AN AP-PARITION -- A PHANTOM -- AND NOTHING MORE!!
ALMOST INSTANTLY, AS IF IN ANSWER TO THE IMMORTAL'S OUTCRY...
THE HYDRA HATH GRASPED ME!
SURELY, THIS BE NO MERE GHOST THAT LAYS ITS CLAWS UPON ME -- BUT A CREATURE OF FLESH AND BONE!
AND, WHAT THE PRINCE OF POWER CAN FIGHT -- HE CAN DEFEAT!
FOR, NOTHING THAT LIVES AND BREATHES CAN STAND AGAINST THE MIND-STAGGERING MIGHT OF HERCULES!
KRA-
RRAR
BUT, TO THE UTTER ASTONISHMENT OF THE LION OF OLYMPUS...
SUCH A BLOW HATH FELLED TITANS OF OLD -- THE ANDROID CALLED DRAGON MAN -- EVEN THE THUNDER GOD HIMSELF!
YET, THE BEAST SCARCELY FELT IT! HOW CAN SUCH A THING BE?*
*ALAS, THIS SEEMS HARDLY THE TIME TO EXPLAIN TO HERCULES THE SUPREME PSYCHEDELIC POWERS OF THE DREAD PSYCHOTRON -- WHOSE IMAGES ARE AS REAL AND PALPABLE AS THE MIND OF ITS INTENDED VICTIM --

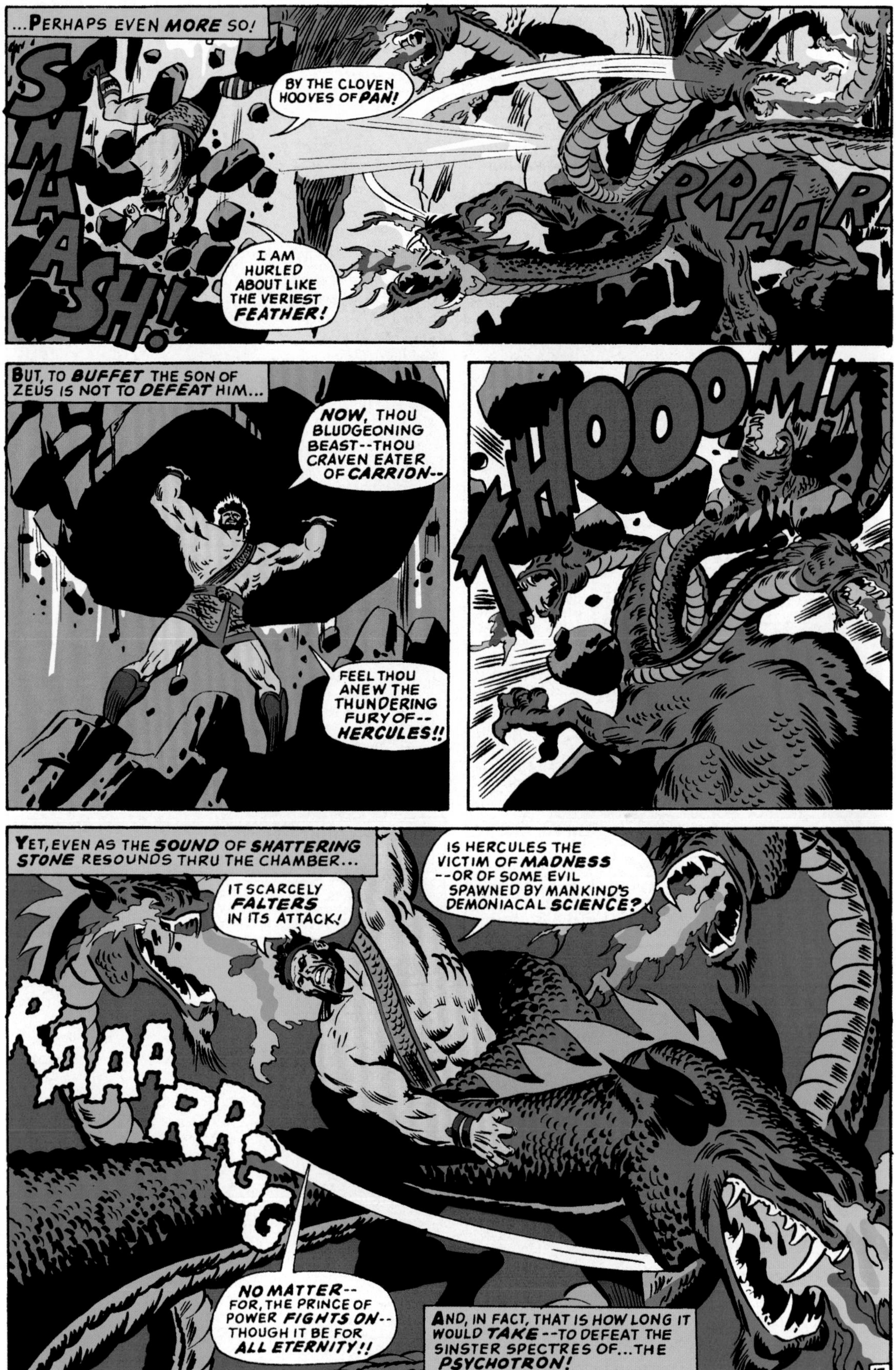
...PERHAPS EVEN MORE SO!
SMAAASH!
BY THE CLOVEN HOOVES OF PAN!
RRAAAR!
I AM HURLED ABOUT LIKE THE VERIEST FEATHER!
BUT, TO BUFFET THE SON OF ZEUS IS NOT TO DEFEAT HIM...
NOW, THOU BLUDGEONING BEAST--THOU CRAVEN EATER OF CARRION--
FEEL THOU ANEW THE THUNDERING FURY OF--HERCULES!!
KHOOOM!
YET, EVEN AS THE SOUND OF SHATTERING STONE RESOUNDS THRU THE CHAMBER...
IT SCARCELY FALTERS IN ITS ATTACK!
IS HERCULES THE VICTIM OF MADNESS --OR OF SOME EVIL SPAWNED BY MANKIND'S DEMONIACAL SCIENCE?
RAAARRGG
NO MATTER--FOR, THE PRINCE OF POWER FIGHTS ON--THOUGH IT BE FOR ALL ETERNITY!!
AND, IN FACT, THAT IS HOW LONG IT WOULD TAKE--TO DEFEAT THE SINSTER SPECTRES OF...THE PSYCHOTRON!
17

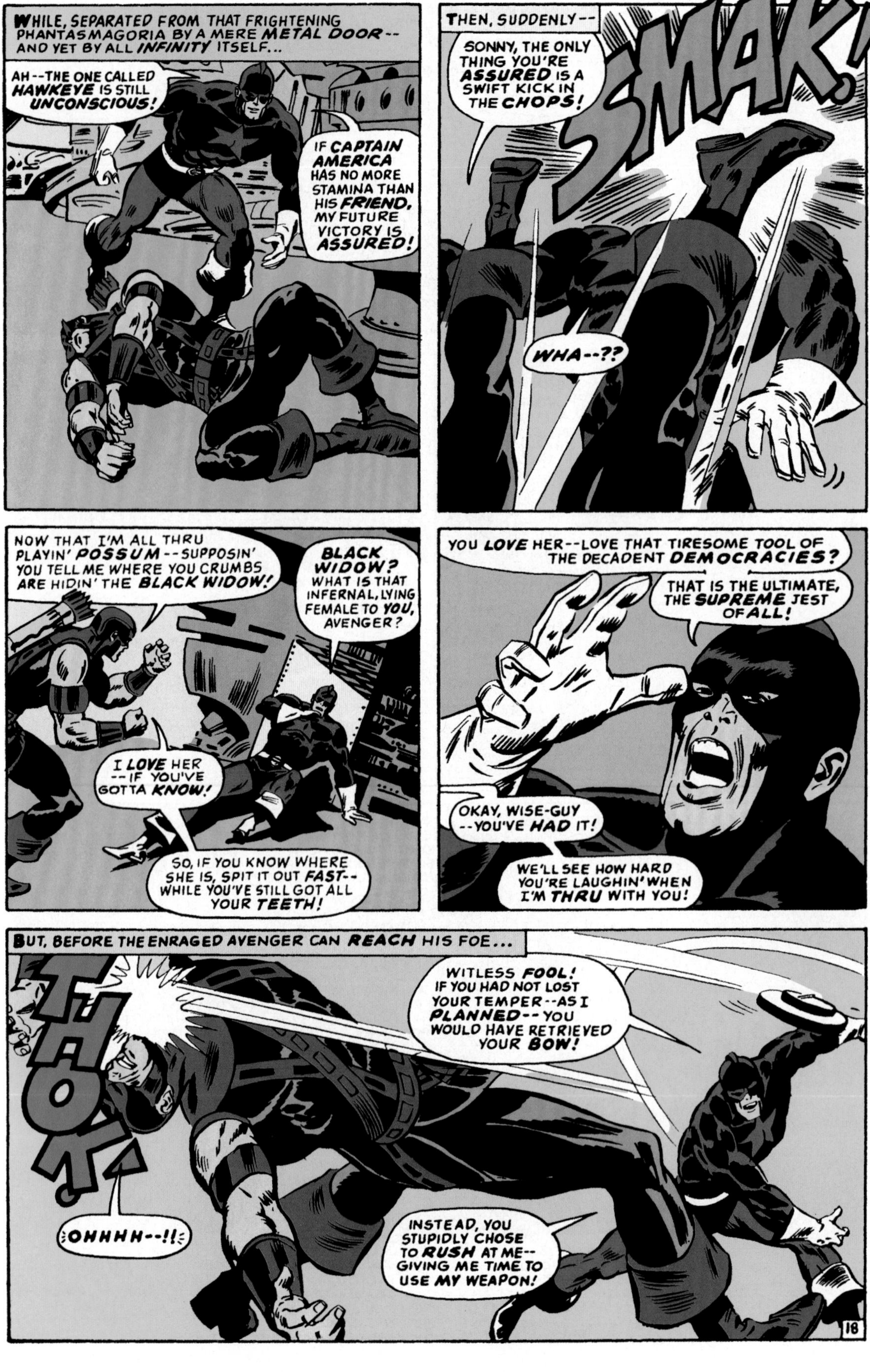
WHILE, SEPARATED FROM THAT FRIGHTENING PHANTASMAGORIA BY A MERE METAL DOOR -- AND YET BY ALL INFINITY ITSELF...
AH -- THE ONE CALLED HAWKEYE IS STILL UNCONSCIOUS!
IF CAPTAIN AMERICA HAS NO MORE STAMINA THAN HIS FRIEND, MY FUTURE VICTORY IS ASSURED!
THEN, SUDDENLY --
SONNY, THE ONLY THING YOU'RE ASSURED IS A SWIFT KICK IN THE CHOPS!
SMAK!
WHA--??
NOW THAT I'M ALL THRU PLAYIN' POSSUM -- SUPPOSIN' YOU TELL ME WHERE YOU CRUMBS ARE HIDIN' THE BLACK WIDOW!
BLACK WIDOW? WHAT IS THAT INFERNAL, LYING FEMALE TO YOU, AVENGER?
I LOVE HER -- IF YOU'VE GOTTA KNOW!
SO, IF YOU KNOW WHERE SHE IS, SPIT IT OUT FAST -- WHILE YOU'VE STILL GOT ALL YOUR TEETH!
YOU LOVE HER -- LOVE THAT TIRESOME TOOL OF THE DECADENT DEMOCRACIES?
THAT IS THE ULTIMATE, THE SUPREME JEST OF ALL!
OKAY, WISE-GUY -- YOU'VE HAD IT!
WE'LL SEE HOW HARD YOU'RE LAUGHIN' WHEN I'M THRU WITH YOU!
BUT, BEFORE THE ENRAGED AVENGER CAN REACH HIS FOE...
THOK
WITLESS FOOL! IF YOU HAD NOT LOST YOUR TEMPER -- AS I PLANNED -- YOU WOULD HAVE RETRIEVED YOUR BOW!
OHHHH--!!
INSTEAD, YOU STUPIDLY CHOSE TO RUSH AT ME -- GIVING ME TIME TO USE MY WEAPON!
18

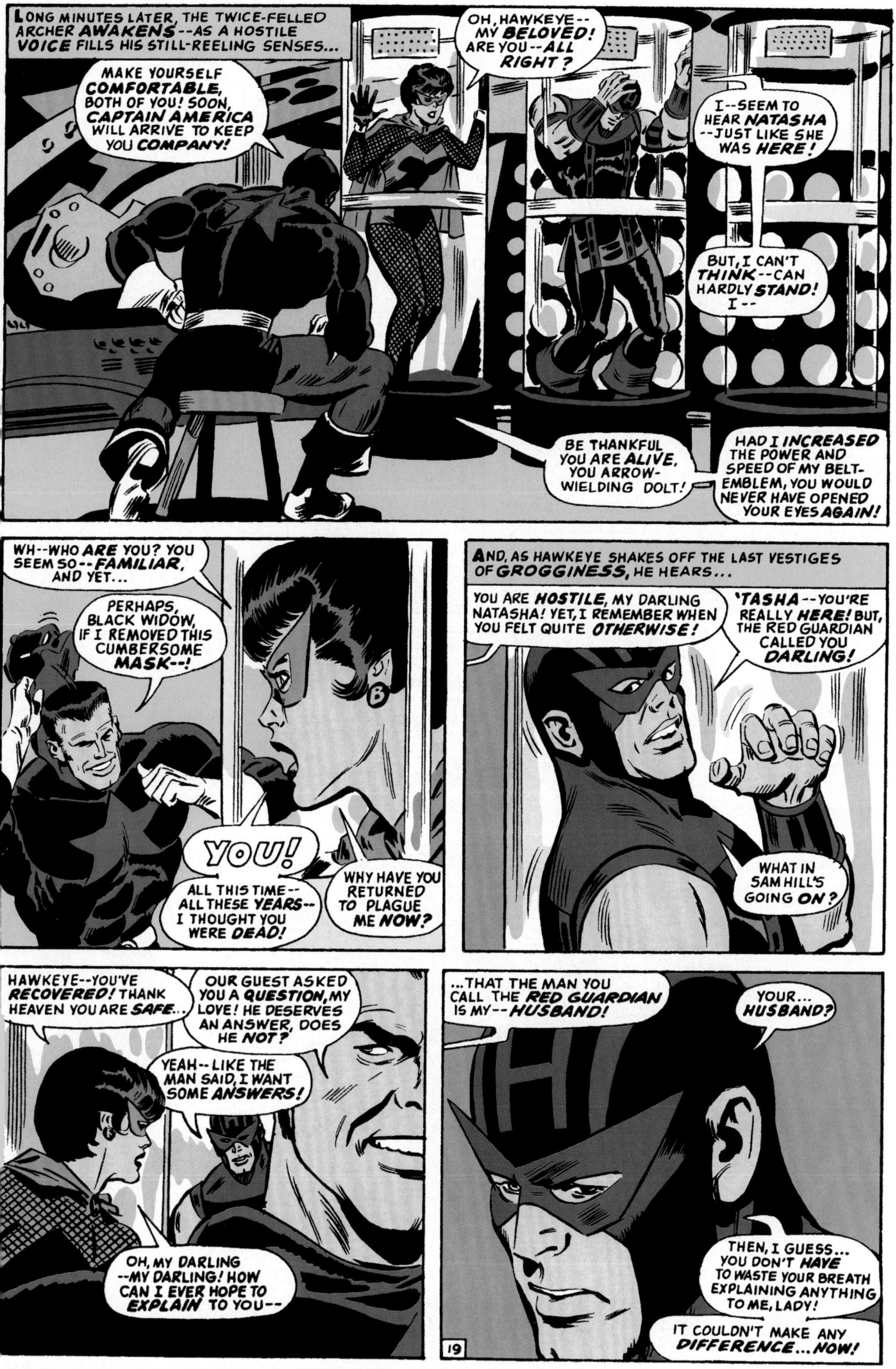

LONG MINUTES LATER, THE TWICE-FELLED ARCHER AWAKENS--AS A HOSTILE VOICE FILLS HIS STILL-REELING SENSES...
MAKE YOURSELF COMFORTABLE, BOTH OF YOU! SOON, CAPTAIN AMERICA WILL ARRIVE TO KEEP YOU COMPANY!
OH, HAWKEYE--MY BELOVED! ARE YOU--ALL RIGHT?
I--SEEM TO HEAR NATASHA--JUST LIKE SHE WAS HERE!
BUT, I CAN'T THINK--CAN HARDLY STAND! I--
BE THANKFUL YOU ARE ALIVE, YOU ARROW-WIELDING DOLT!
HAD I INCREASED THE POWER AND SPEED OF MY BELT-EMBLEM, YOU WOULD NEVER HAVE OPENED YOUR EYES AGAIN!
WH--WHO ARE YOU? YOU SEEM SO--FAMILIAR, AND YET...
PERHAPS, BLACK WIDOW, IF I REMOVED THIS CUMBERSOME MASK--!
YOU!
ALL THIS TIME--ALL THESE YEARS--I THOUGHT YOU WERE DEAD!
WHY HAVE YOU RETURNED TO PLAGUE ME NOW?
AND, AS HAWKEYE SHAKES OFF THE LAST VESTIGES OF GROGGINESS, HE HEARS...
YOU ARE HOSTILE, MY DARLING NATASHA! YET, I REMEMBER WHEN YOU FELT QUITE OTHERWISE!
'TASHA--YOU'RE REALLY HERE! BUT, THE RED GUARDIAN CALLED YOU DARLING!
WHAT IN SAM HILL'S GOING ON?
HAWKEYE--YOU'VE RECOVERED! THANK HEAVEN YOU ARE SAFE...
OUR GUEST ASKED YOU A QUESTION, MY LOVE! HE DESERVES AN ANSWER, DOES HE NOT?
YEAH--LIKE THE MAN SAID, I WANT SOME ANSWERS!
OH, MY DARLING--MY DARLING! HOW CAN I EVER HOPE TO EXPLAIN TO YOU--
...THAT THE MAN YOU CALL THE RED GUARDIAN IS MY--HUSBAND!
YOUR... HUSBAND?
THEN, I GUESS... YOU DON'T HAVE TO WASTE YOUR BREATH EXPLAINING ANYTHING TO ME, LADY!
IT COULDN'T MAKE ANY DIFFERENCE... NOW!
19

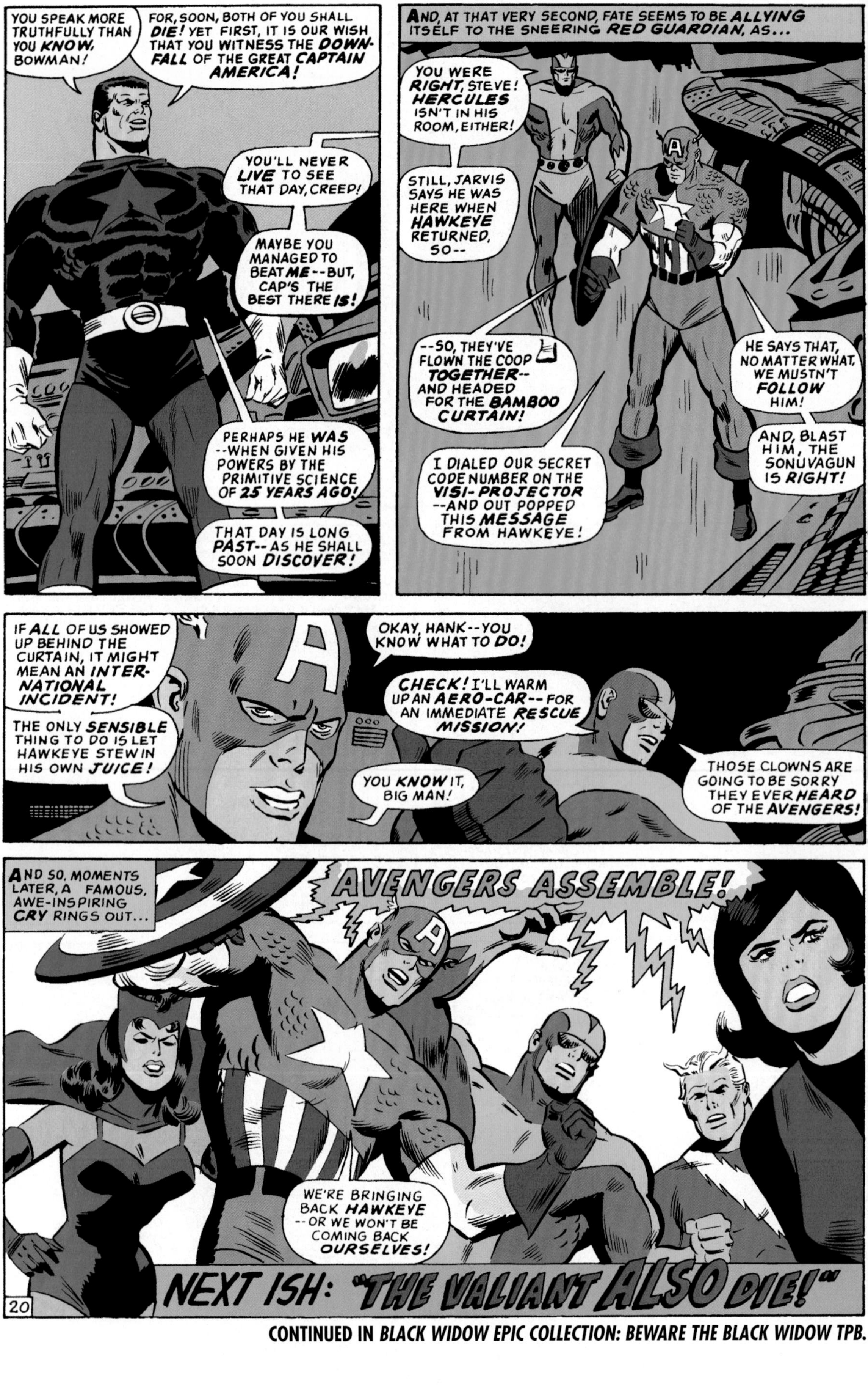
YOU SPEAK MORE TRUTHFULLY THAN YOU KNOW, BOWMAN!
FOR, SOON, BOTH OF YOU SHALL DIE! YET FIRST, IT IS OUR WISH THAT YOU WITNESS THE DOWNFALL OF THE GREAT CAPTAIN AMERICA!
YOU'LL NEVER LIVE TO SEE THAT DAY, CREEP!
MAYBE YOU MANAGED TO BEAT ME--BUT, CAP'S THE BEST THERE IS!
PERHAPS HE WAS--WHEN GIVEN HIS POWERS BY THE PRIMITIVE SCIENCE OF 25 YEARS AGO!
THAT DAY IS LONG PAST--AS HE SHALL SOON DISCOVER!
AND, AT THAT VERY SECOND, FATE SEEMS TO BE ALLYING ITSELF TO THE SNEERING RED GUARDIAN, AS...
YOU WERE RIGHT, STEVE! HERCULES ISN'T IN HIS ROOM, EITHER!
STILL, JARVIS SAYS HE WAS HERE WHEN HAWKEYE RETURNED, SO--
--SO, THEY'VE FLOWN THE COOP TOGETHER--AND HEADED FOR THE BAMBOO CURTAIN!
I DIALED OUR SECRET CODE NUMBER ON THE VISI-PROJECTOR--AND OUT POPPED THIS MESSAGE FROM HAWKEYE!
HE SAYS THAT, NO MATTER WHAT, WE MUSTN'T FOLLOW HIM!
AND, BLAST HIM, THE SONUVAGUN IS RIGHT!
IF ALL OF US SHOWED UP BEHIND THE CURTAIN, IT MIGHT MEAN AN INTERNATIONAL INCIDENT!
THE ONLY SENSIBLE THING TO DO IS LET HAWKEYE STEW IN HIS OWN JUICE!
OKAY, HANK--YOU KNOW WHAT TO DO!
CHECK! I'LL WARM UP AN AERO-CAR--FOR AN IMMEDIATE RESCUE MISSION!
YOU KNOW IT, BIG MAN!
THOSE CLOWNS ARE GOING TO BE SORRY THEY EVER HEARD OF THE AVENGERS!
AND SO, MOMENTS LATER, A FAMOUS, AWE-INSPIRING CRY RINGS OUT...
AVENGERS ASSEMBLE!
WE'RE BRINGING BACK HAWKEYE--OR WE WON'T BE COMING BACK OURSELVES!
NEXT ISH: "THE VALIANT ALSO DIE!"
20

CONTINUED IN *BLACK WIDOW EPIC COLLECTION: BEWARE THE BLACK WIDOW* TPB.

THE AVENGERS HAVE THEIR FIRST RUN-IN WITH THE PHOTO-REALISTIC REFLEXES OF TASKMASTER!

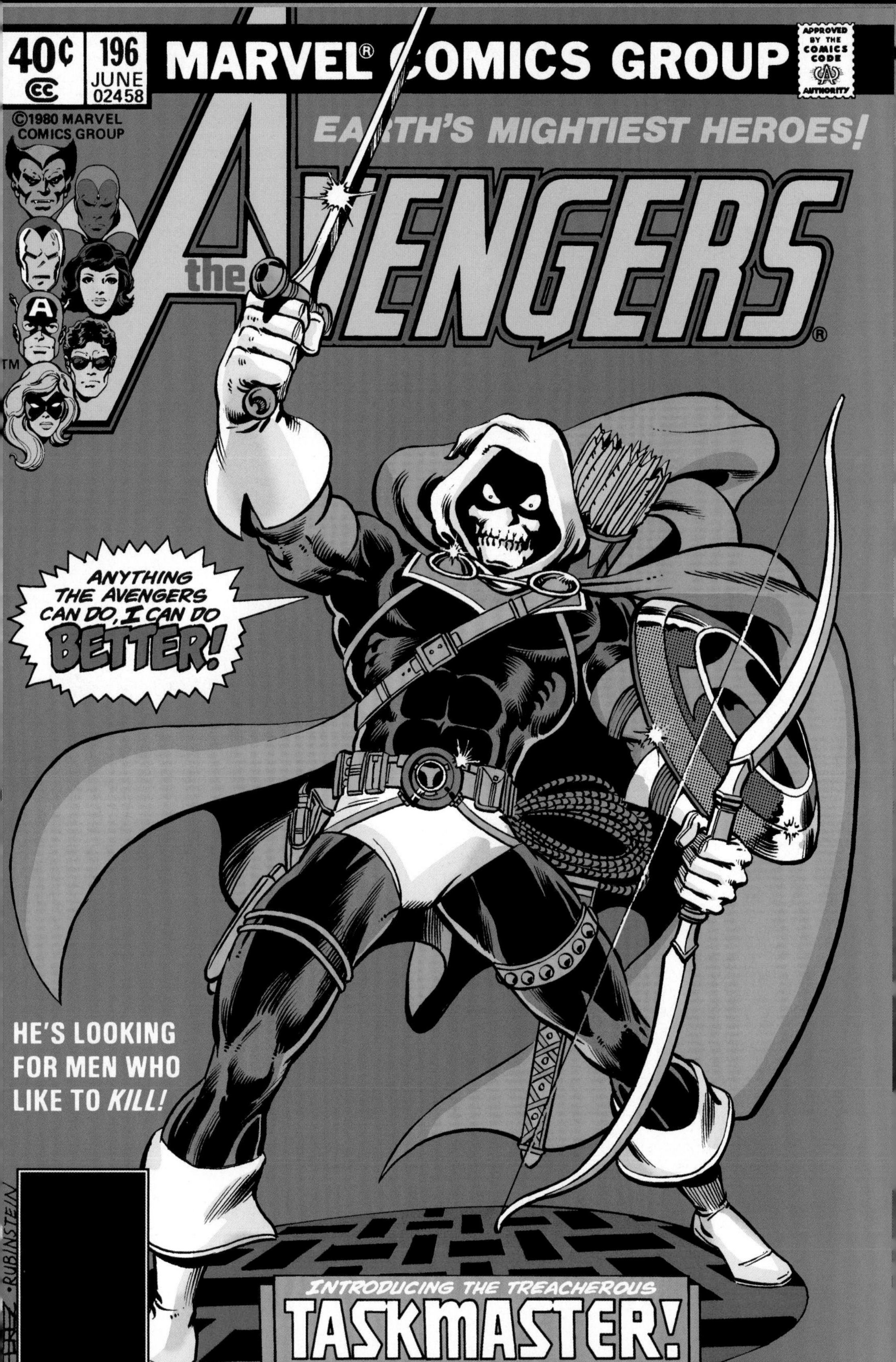
40¢
196
JUNE
02458
MARVEL® COMICS GROUP
APPROVED BY THE COMICS CODE AUTHORITY
©1980 MARVEL COMICS GROUP
EARTH'S MIGHTIEST HEROES!
THE AVENGERS®
ANYTHING THE AVENGERS CAN DO, I CAN DO BETTER!
HE'S LOOKING FOR MEN WHO LIKE TO KILL!
INTRODUCING THE TREACHEROUS
TASKMASTER!
RUBINSTEIN

And there came a day when *Earth's mightiest heroes* found themselves *united* against a common threat. On that day, the *Avengers* were born—to fight the foes no *single* super-hero could withstand!

Stan Lee PRESENTS: THE MIGHTY AVENGERS!

THE FRENCH HAVE A SAYING: CHERCHEZ LA FEMME-- "LOOK FOR THE WOMAN!" AND THAT'S EXACTLY WHAT ANT-MAN AND YELLOWJACKET HAVE DONE, JOURNEYING TO LONG ISLAND, TO THE SOLOMON INSTITUTE FOR THE CRIMINALLY INSANE, IN SEARCH OF THE MISSING WASP.

A SHORT TIME AGO, THEY HAD FOUND HER. UNFORTUNATELY, AN EVEN SHORTER TIME AGO, THE TASKMASTER HAD FOUND THEM!

I SURE HOPE YOU "GET SMALL" TYPES AREN'T PLANNIN' ON USIN' YOUR POWERS TO ESCAPE, 'CAUSE THOSE STASIS CLAMPS MY SCIENCE BOYS COOKED UP BIND DIRECTLY TO THE ATOMIC STRUCTURE OF YOUR WRISTS AN' ANKLES, AN' WHILE THEY CAN'T KEEP YA FROM SHRINKIN' OUTA SIGHT--

--THEY DO MAKE SURE THAT YOUR HANDS AN' FEET DON'T GO WITH YA!

THE TERRIBLE TOLL OF THE TASKMASTER

| DAVID MICHELINIE writer | GEORGE PÉREZ penciler | JACK ABEL inker | JOHN COSTANZA letterer | CARL GAFFORD colorist | JIM SALICRUP editor | JIM SHOOTER editor-in-chief |

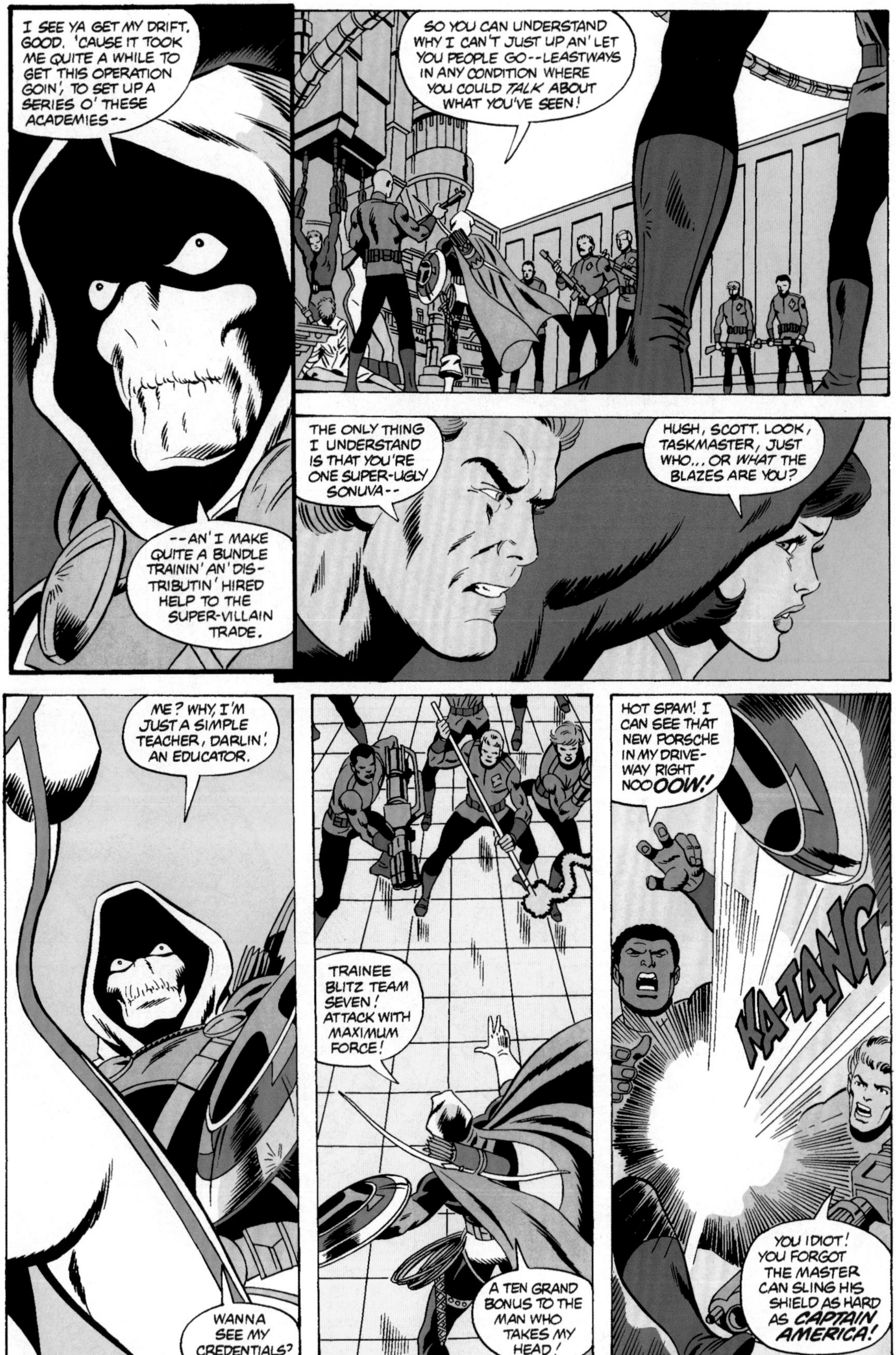
I SEE YA GET MY DRIFT. GOOD. 'CAUSE IT TOOK ME QUITE A WHILE TO GET THIS OPERATION GOIN', TO SET UP A SERIES O' THESE ACADEMIES--
--AN' I MAKE QUITE A BUNDLE TRAININ' AN' DISTRIBUTIN' HIRED HELP TO THE SUPER-VILLAIN TRADE.
SO YOU CAN UNDERSTAND WHY I CAN'T JUST UP AN' LET YOU PEOPLE GO--LEASTWAYS IN ANY CONDITION WHERE YOU COULD TALK ABOUT WHAT YOU'VE SEEN!
THE ONLY THING I UNDERSTAND IS THAT YOU'RE ONE SUPER-UGLY SONUVA--
HUSH, SCOTT. LOOK, TASKMASTER, JUST WHO... OR WHAT THE BLAZES ARE YOU?
ME? WHY, I'M JUST A SIMPLE TEACHER, DARLIN'. AN EDUCATOR.
WANNA SEE MY CREDENTIALS?
TRAINEE BLITZ TEAM SEVEN! ATTACK WITH MAXIMUM FORCE!
A TEN GRAND BONUS TO THE MAN WHO TAKES MY HEAD!
HOT SPAM! I CAN SEE THAT NEW PORSCHE IN MY DRIVEWAY RIGHT NOOOOW!
KA-TANG
YOU IDIOT! YOU FORGOT THE MASTER CAN SLING HIS SHIELD AS HARD AS CAPTAIN AMERICA!

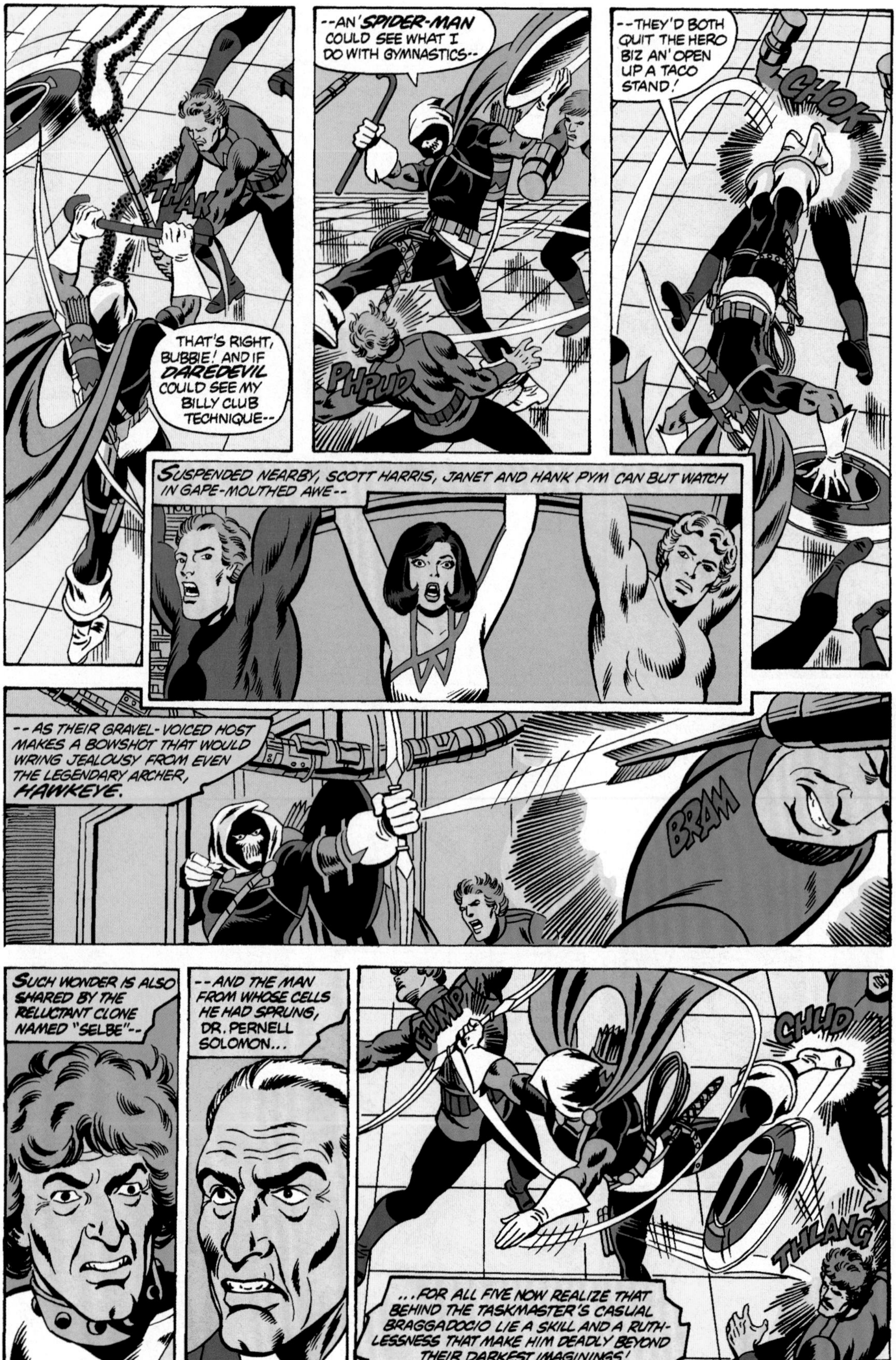
THAK
THAT'S RIGHT, BUBBIE! AND IF DAREDEVIL COULD SEE MY BILLY CLUB TECHNIQUE--
--AN' SPIDER-MAN COULD SEE WHAT I DO WITH GYMNASTICS--
PHPUD
--THEY'D BOTH QUIT THE HERO BIZ AN' OPEN UP A TACO STAND!
CHOK
SUSPENDED NEARBY, SCOTT HARRIS, JANET AND HANK PYM CAN BUT WATCH IN GAPE-MOUTHED AWE--
--AS THEIR GRAVEL-VOICED HOST MAKES A BOWSHOT THAT WOULD WRING JEALOUSY FROM EVEN THE LEGENDARY ARCHER, HAWKEYE.
BRAM
SUCH WONDER IS ALSO SHARED BY THE RELUCTANT CLONE NAMED "SELBE"--
--AND THE MAN FROM WHOSE CELLS HE HAD SPRUNG, DR. PERNELL SOLOMON...
CHUD
THLANG
...FOR ALL FIVE NOW REALIZE THAT BEHIND THE TASKMASTER'S CASUAL BRAGGADOCIO LIE A SKILL AND A RUTHLESSNESS THAT MAKE HIM DEADLY BEYOND THEIR DARKEST IMAGININGS!

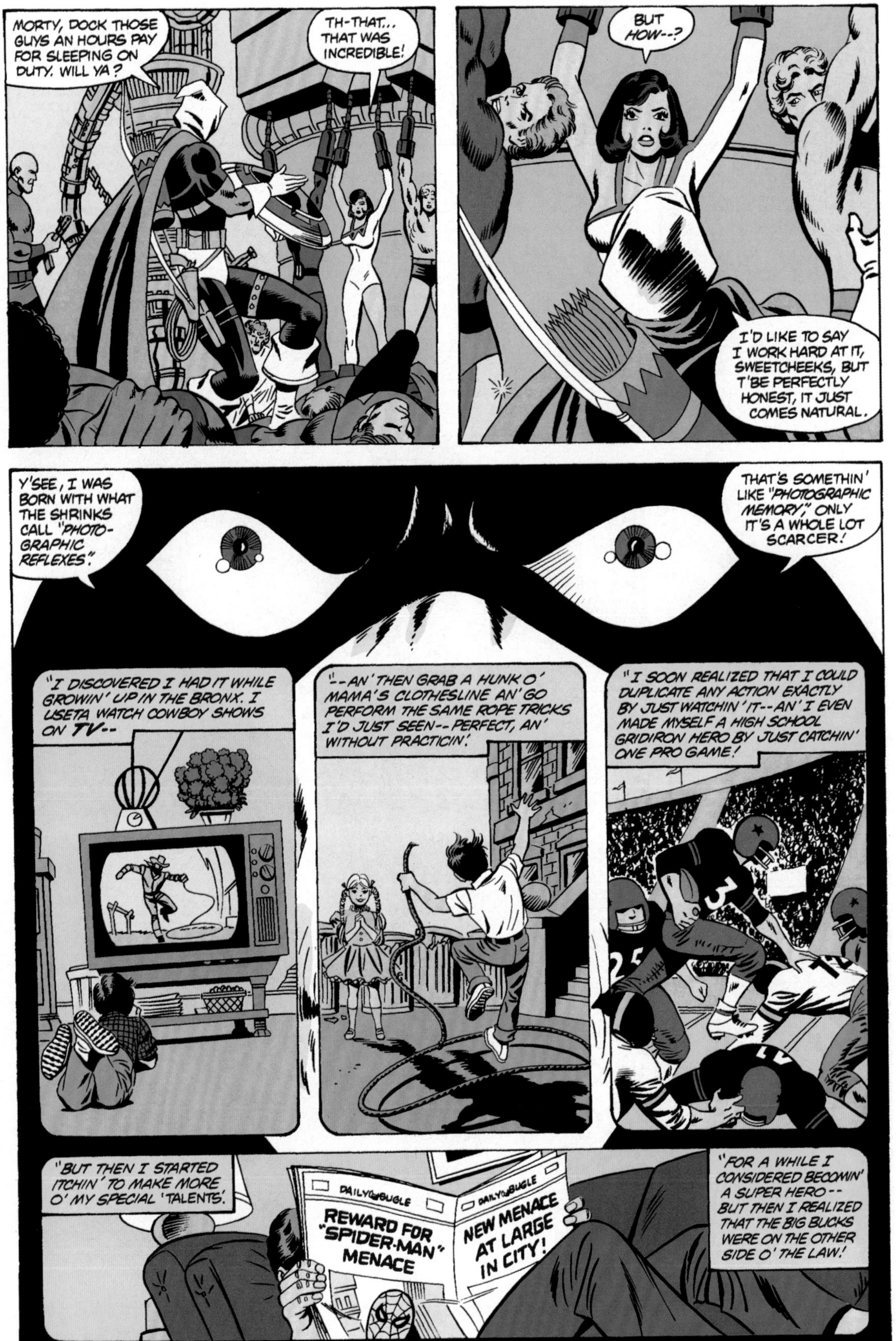
MORTY, DOCK THOSE GUYS AN HOURS PAY FOR SLEEPING ON DUTY. WILL YA?
TH-THAT... THAT WAS INCREDIBLE!
BUT HOW--?
I'D LIKE TO SAY I WORK HARD AT IT, SWEETCHEEKS, BUT T'BE PERFECTLY HONEST, IT JUST COMES NATURAL.
Y'SEE, I WAS BORN WITH WHAT THE SHRINKS CALL "PHOTOGRAPHIC REFLEXES".
THAT'S SOMETHIN' LIKE "PHOTOGRAPHIC MEMORY," ONLY IT'S A WHOLE LOT SCARCER!
"I DISCOVERED I HAD IT WHILE GROWIN' UP IN THE BRONX. I USETA WATCH COWBOY SHOWS ON TV--
"--AN' THEN GRAB A HUNK O' MAMA'S CLOTHESLINE AN' GO PERFORM THE SAME ROPE TRICKS I'D JUST SEEN-- PERFECT, AN' WITHOUT PRACTICIN'.
"I SOON REALIZED THAT I COULD DUPLICATE ANY ACTION EXACTLY BY JUST WATCHIN' IT--AN' I EVEN MADE MYSELF A HIGH SCHOOL GRIDIRON HERO BY JUST CATCHIN' ONE PRO GAME!
"BUT THEN I STARTED ITCHIN' TO MAKE MORE O' MY SPECIAL 'TALENTS'.
DAILY BUGLE
REWARD FOR "SPIDER-MAN" MENACE
DAILY BUGLE
NEW MENACE AT LARGE IN CITY!
"FOR A WHILE I CONSIDERED BECOMIN' A SUPER HERO-- BUT THEN I REALIZED THAT THE BIG BUCKS WERE ON THE OTHER SIDE O' THE LAW!

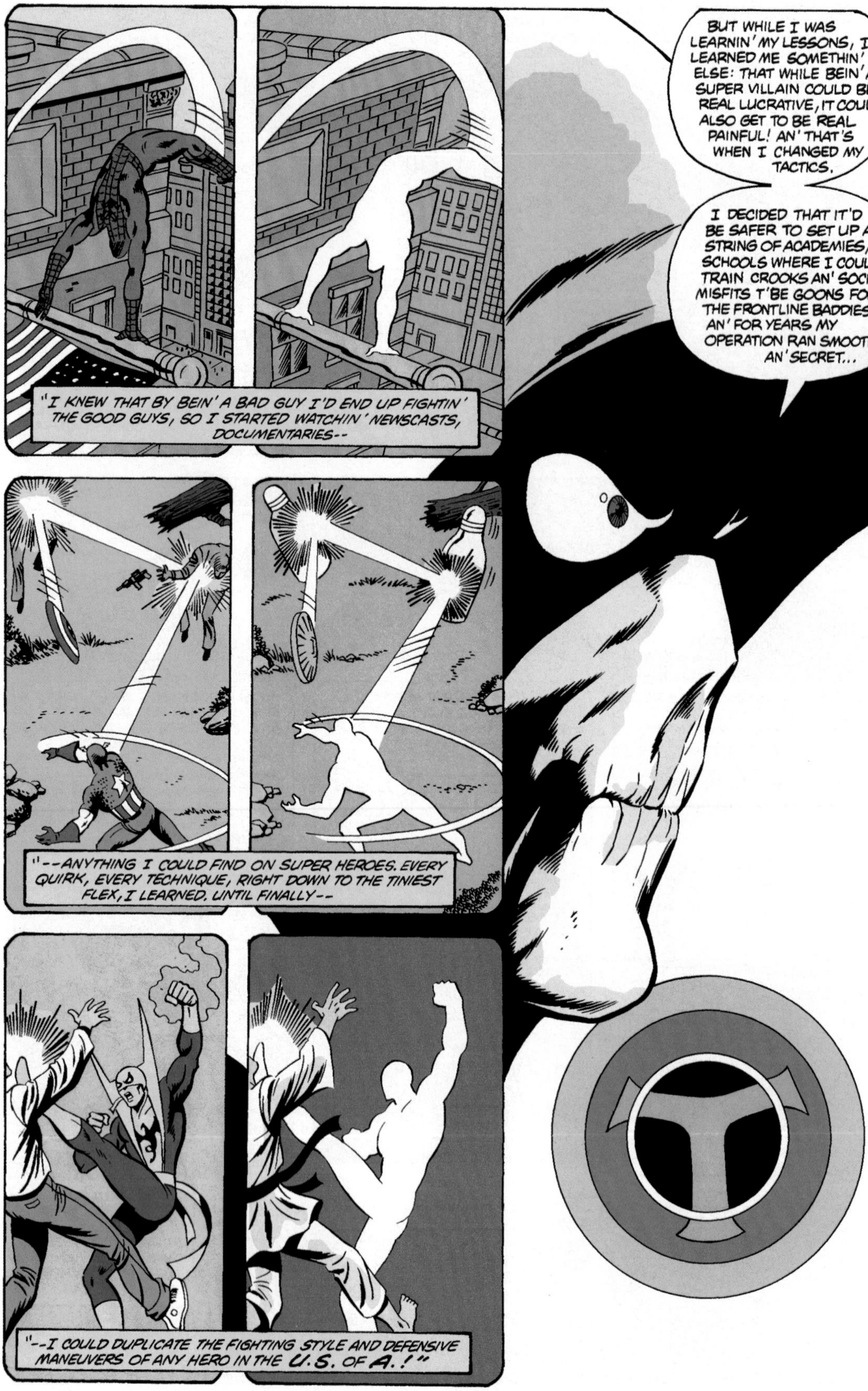
"I KNEW THAT BY BEIN' A BAD GUY I'D END UP FIGHTIN' THE GOOD GUYS, SO I STARTED WATCHIN' NEWSCASTS, DOCUMENTARIES--
"--ANYTHING I COULD FIND ON SUPER HEROES. EVERY QUIRK, EVERY TECHNIQUE, RIGHT DOWN TO THE TINIEST FLEX, I LEARNED. UNTIL FINALLY--
"--I COULD DUPLICATE THE FIGHTING STYLE AND DEFENSIVE MANEUVERS OF ANY HERO IN THE U.S. OF A.!"
BUT WHILE I WAS LEARNIN' MY LESSONS, I LEARNED ME SOMETHIN' ELSE: THAT WHILE BEIN' A SUPER VILLAIN COULD BE REAL LUCRATIVE, IT COULD ALSO GET TO BE REAL PAINFUL! AN' THAT'S WHEN I CHANGED MY TACTICS.
I DECIDED THAT IT'D BE SAFER TO SET UP A STRING OF ACADEMIES, SCHOOLS WHERE I COULD TRAIN CROOKS AN' SOCIAL MISFITS T'BE GOONS FOR THE FRONTLINE BADDIES. AN' FOR YEARS MY OPERATION RAN SMOOTH, AN' SECRET...

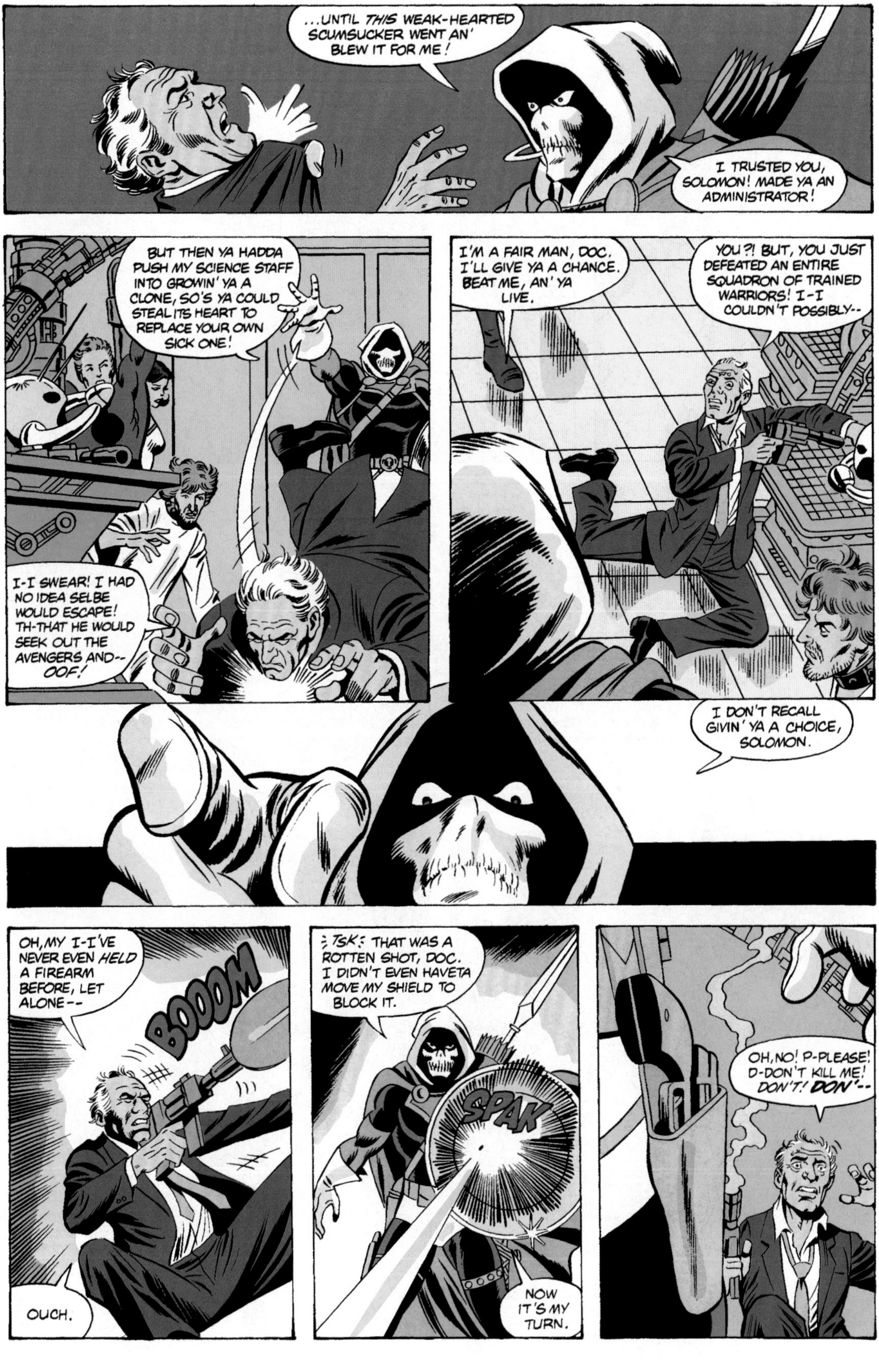
...UNTIL THIS WEAK-HEARTED SCUMSUCKER WENT AN' BLEW IT FOR ME!
I TRUSTED YOU, SOLOMON! MADE YA AN ADMINISTRATOR!
BUT THEN YA HADDA PUSH MY SCIENCE STAFF INTO GROWIN' YA A CLONE, SO'S YA COULD STEAL ITS HEART TO REPLACE YOUR OWN SICK ONE!
I-I SWEAR! I HAD NO IDEA SELBE WOULD ESCAPE! TH-THAT HE WOULD SEEK OUT THE AVENGERS AND-- OOF!
I'M A FAIR MAN, DOC. I'LL GIVE YA A CHANCE. BEAT ME, AN' YA LIVE.
YOU?! BUT, YOU JUST DEFEATED AN ENTIRE SQUADRON OF TRAINED WARRIORS! I-I COULDN'T POSSIBLY--
I DON'T RECALL GIVIN' YA A CHOICE, SOLOMON.
OH, MY I-I'VE NEVER EVEN HELD A FIREARM BEFORE, LET ALONE--
BOOOM
OUCH.
TSK THAT WAS A ROTTEN SHOT, DOC. I DIDN'T EVEN HAVETA MOVE MY SHIELD TO BLOCK IT.
SPAK
NOW IT'S MY TURN.
OH, NO! P-PLEASE! D-DON'T KILL ME! DON'T! DON'--

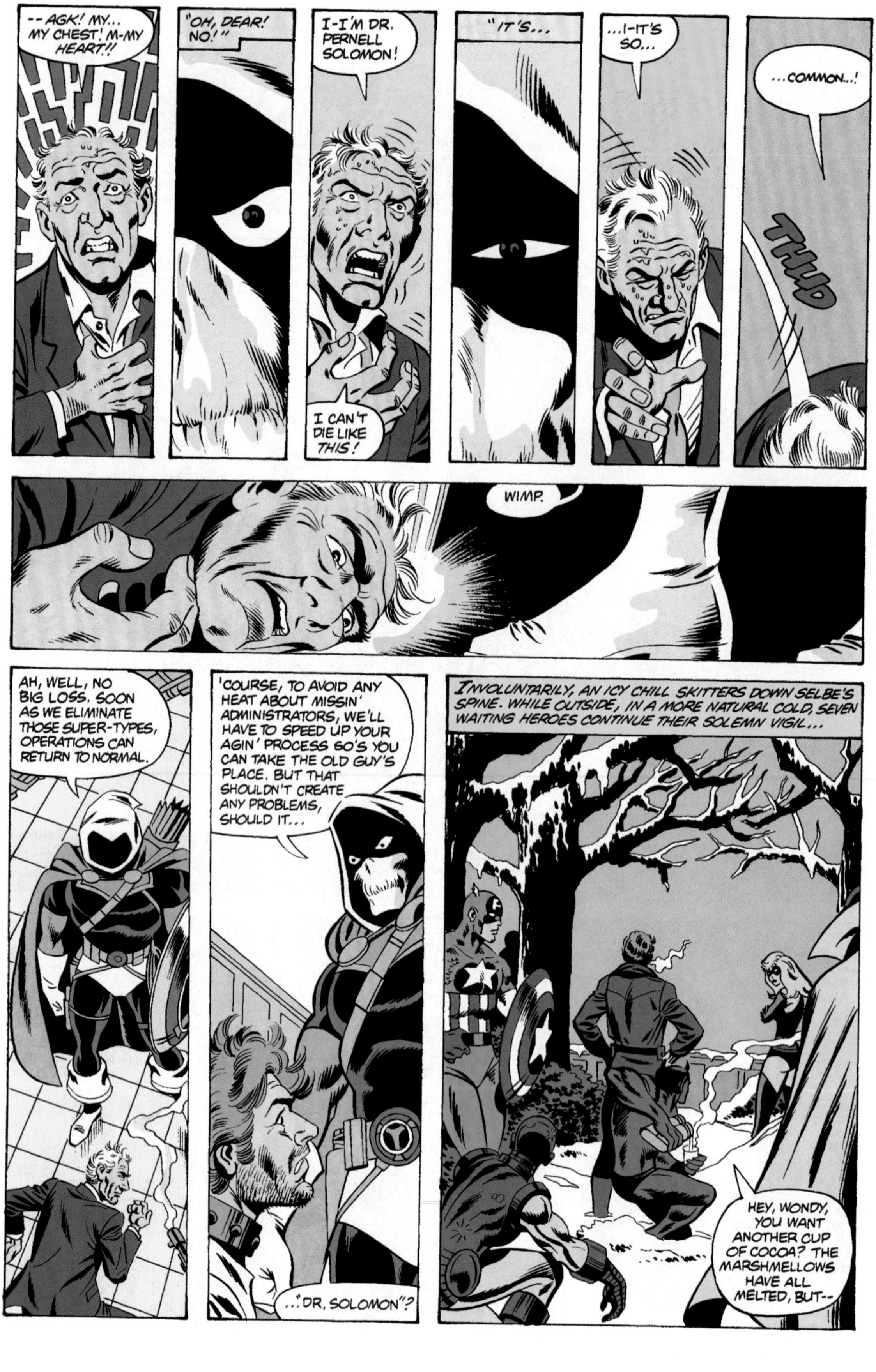
--AGK! MY... MY CHEST! M-MY HEART!!
"OH, DEAR! NO!"
I-I'M DR. PERNELL SOLOMON!
I CAN'T DIE LIKE THIS!
"IT'S...
...I-IT'S SO...
...COMMON...!
THUD
WIMP.
AH, WELL, NO BIG LOSS. SOON AS WE ELIMINATE THOSE SUPER-TYPES, OPERATIONS CAN RETURN TO NORMAL.
'COURSE, TO AVOID ANY HEAT ABOUT MISSIN' ADMINISTRATORS, WE'LL HAVE TO SPEED UP YOUR AGIN' PROCESS SO'S YOU CAN TAKE THE OLD GUY'S PLACE. BUT THAT SHOULDN'T CREATE ANY PROBLEMS, SHOULD IT...
..."DR. SOLOMON"?
INVOLUNTARILY, AN ICY CHILL SKITTERS DOWN SELBE'S SPINE. WHILE OUTSIDE, IN A MORE NATURAL COLD, SEVEN WAITING HEROES CONTINUE THEIR SOLEMN VIGIL...
HEY, WONDY, YOU WANT ANOTHER CUP OF COCOA? THE MARSHMELLOWS HAVE ALL MELTED, BUT--

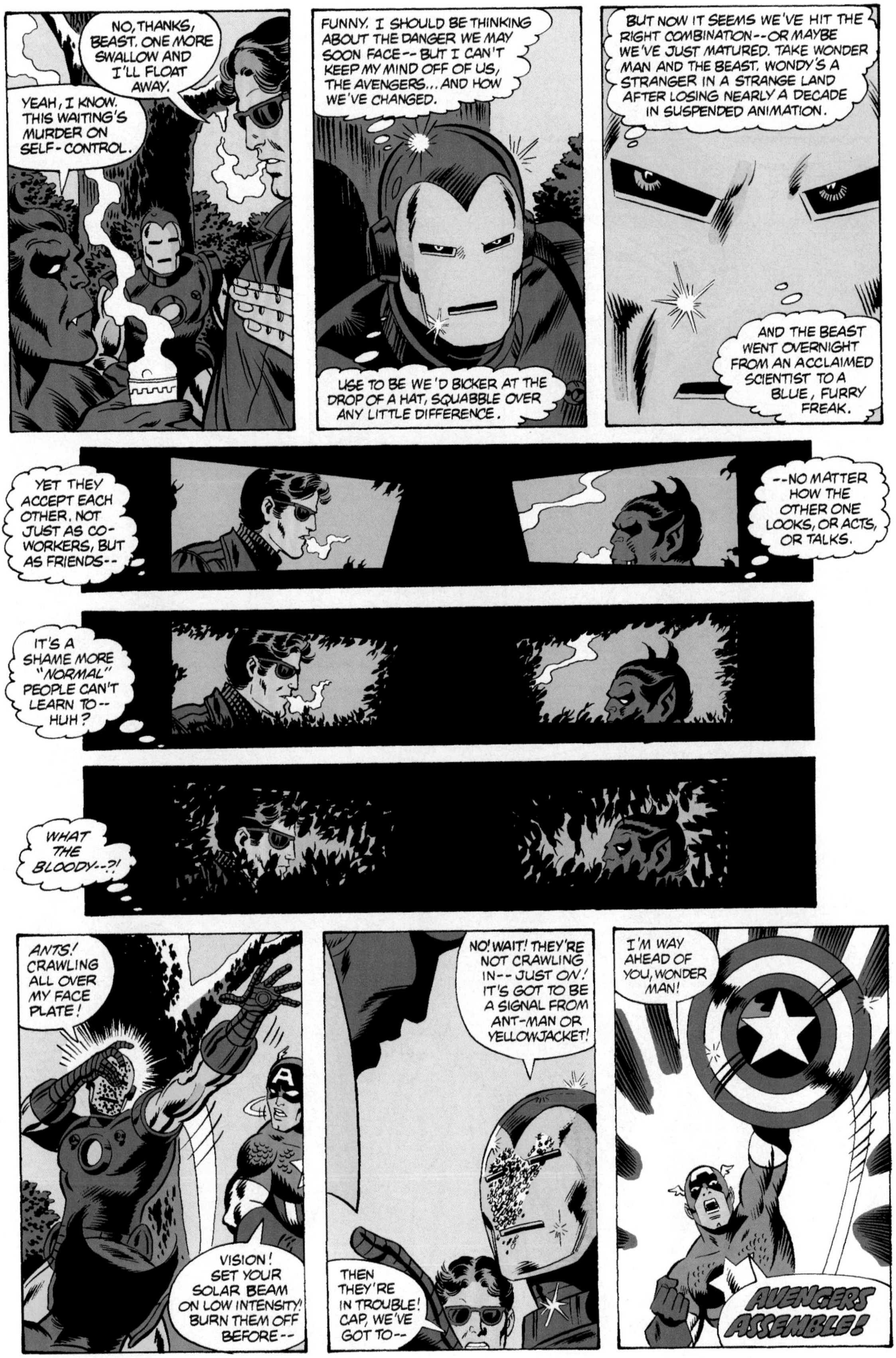
NO, THANKS, BEAST. ONE MORE SWALLOW AND I'LL FLOAT AWAY.
YEAH, I KNOW. THIS WAITING'S MURDER ON SELF-CONTROL.
FUNNY. I SHOULD BE THINKING ABOUT THE DANGER WE MAY SOON FACE-- BUT I CAN'T KEEP MY MIND OFF OF US, THE AVENGERS... AND HOW WE'VE CHANGED.
USE TO BE WE'D BICKER AT THE DROP OF A HAT, SQUABBLE OVER ANY LITTLE DIFFERENCE.
BUT NOW IT SEEMS WE'VE HIT THE RIGHT COMBINATION--OR MAYBE WE'VE JUST MATURED. TAKE WONDER MAN AND THE BEAST. WONDY'S A STRANGER IN A STRANGE LAND AFTER LOSING NEARLY A DECADE IN SUSPENDED ANIMATION.
AND THE BEAST WENT OVERNIGHT FROM AN ACCLAIMED SCIENTIST TO A BLUE, FURRY FREAK.
YET THEY ACCEPT EACH OTHER. NOT JUST AS CO-WORKERS, BUT AS FRIENDS--
--NO MATTER HOW THE OTHER ONE LOOKS, OR ACTS, OR TALKS.
IT'S A SHAME MORE "NORMAL" PEOPLE CAN'T LEARN TO-- HUH?
WHAT THE BLOODY--?!
ANTS! CRAWLING ALL OVER MY FACE PLATE!
VISION! SET YOUR SOLAR BEAM ON LOW INTENSITY! BURN THEM OFF BEFORE--
NO! WAIT! THEY'RE NOT CRAWLING IN-- JUST ON! IT'S GOT TO BE A SIGNAL FROM ANT-MAN OR YELLOWJACKET!
THEN THEY'RE IN TROUBLE! CAP, WE'VE GOT TO--
I'M WAY AHEAD OF YOU, WONDER MAN!
AVENGERS ASSEMBLE!

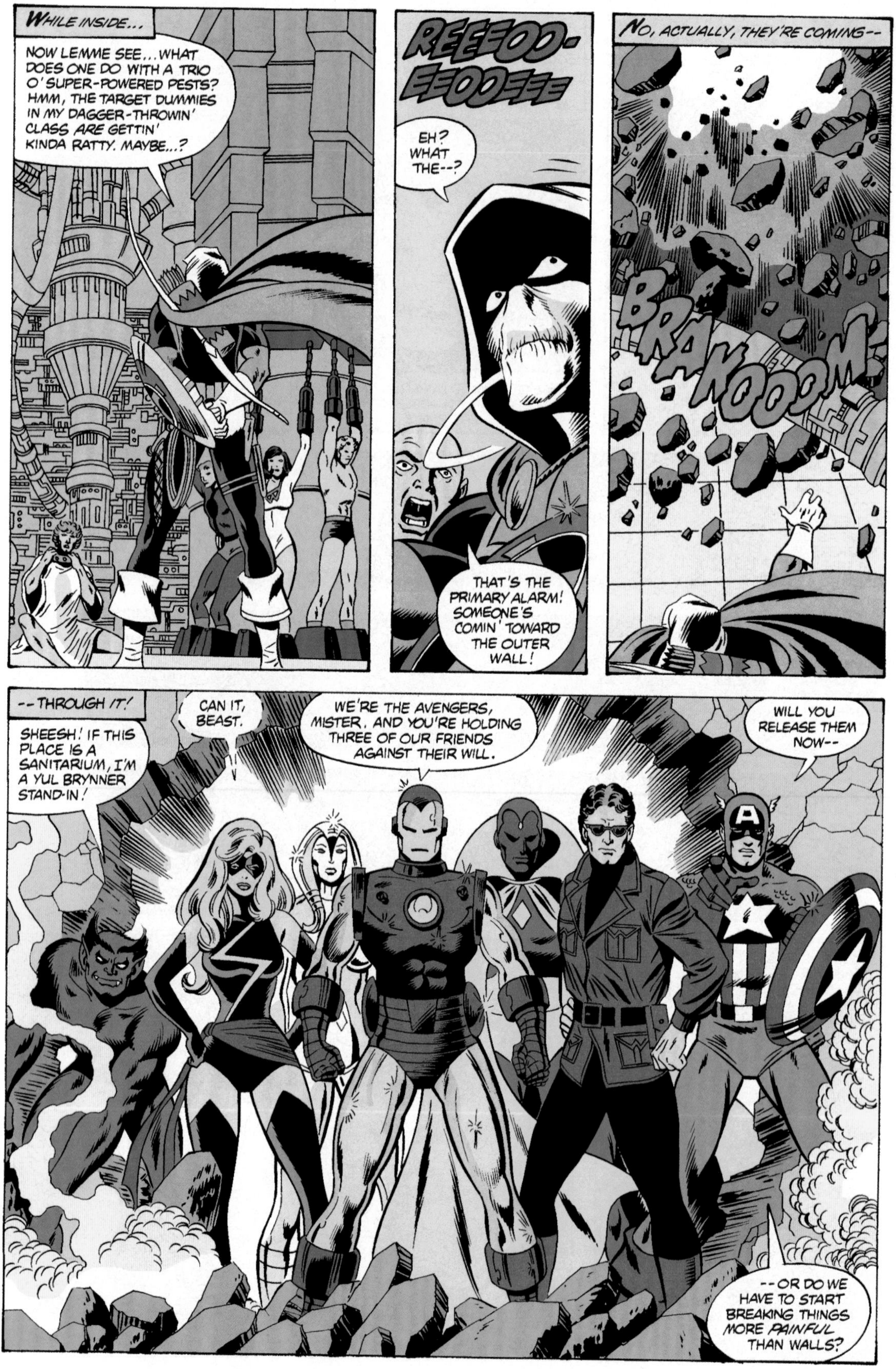
WHILE INSIDE...
NOW LEMME SEE... WHAT DOES ONE DO WITH A TRIO O' SUPER-POWERED PESTS? HMM, THE TARGET DUMMIES IN MY DAGGER-THROWIN' CLASS ARE GETTIN' KINDA RATTY. MAYBE...?
REEEOO-EEOOEEE
EH? WHAT THE--?
THAT'S THE PRIMARY ALARM! SOMEONE'S COMIN' TOWARD THE OUTER WALL!
NO, ACTUALLY, THEY'RE COMING--
BRAKOOOM!
--THROUGH IT!
SHEESH! IF THIS PLACE IS A SANITARIUM, I'M A YUL BRYNNER STAND-IN!
CAN IT, BEAST.
WE'RE THE AVENGERS, MISTER, AND YOU'RE HOLDING THREE OF OUR FRIENDS AGAINST THEIR WILL.
WILL YOU RELEASE THEM NOW--
--OR DO WE HAVE TO START BREAKING THINGS MORE PAINFUL THAN WALLS?

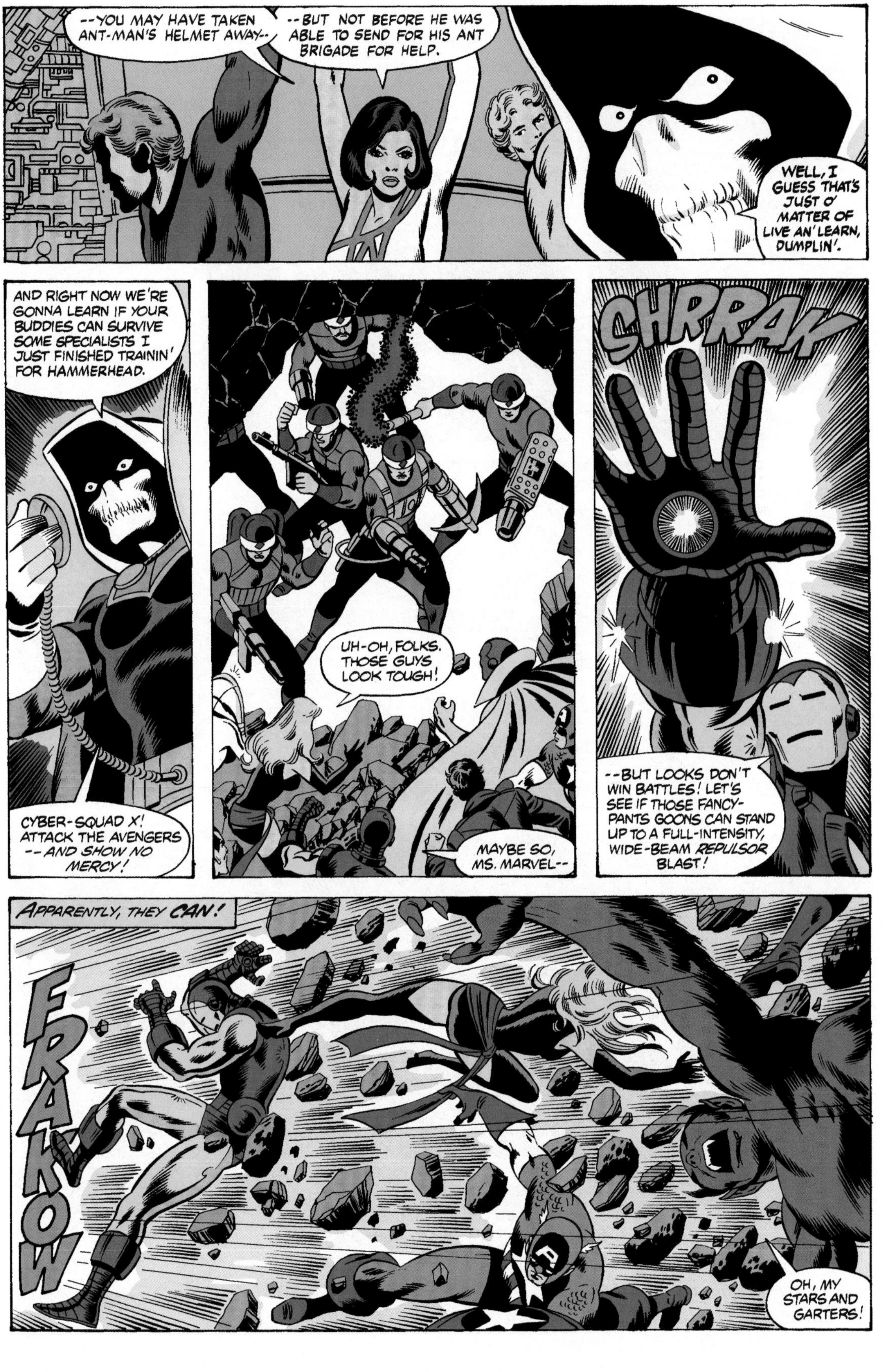
--YOU MAY HAVE TAKEN ANT-MAN'S HELMET AWAY--
--BUT NOT BEFORE HE WAS ABLE TO SEND FOR HIS ANT BRIGADE FOR HELP.
WELL, I GUESS THAT'S JUST O' MATTER OF LIVE AN' LEARN, DUMPLIN'.
AND RIGHT NOW WE'RE GONNA LEARN IF YOUR BUDDIES CAN SURVIVE SOME SPECIALISTS I JUST FINISHED TRAININ' FOR HAMMERHEAD.
CYBER-SQUAD X! ATTACK THE AVENGERS --AND SHOW NO MERCY!
UH-OH, FOLKS. THOSE GUYS LOOK TOUGH!
MAYBE SO, MS. MARVEL--
SHRRAK
--BUT LOOKS DON'T WIN BATTLES! LET'S SEE IF THOSE FANCY-PANTS GOONS CAN STAND UP TO A FULL-INTENSITY, WIDE-BEAM REPULSOR BLAST!
APPARENTLY, THEY CAN!
FRAKOW
OH, MY STARS AND GARTERS!

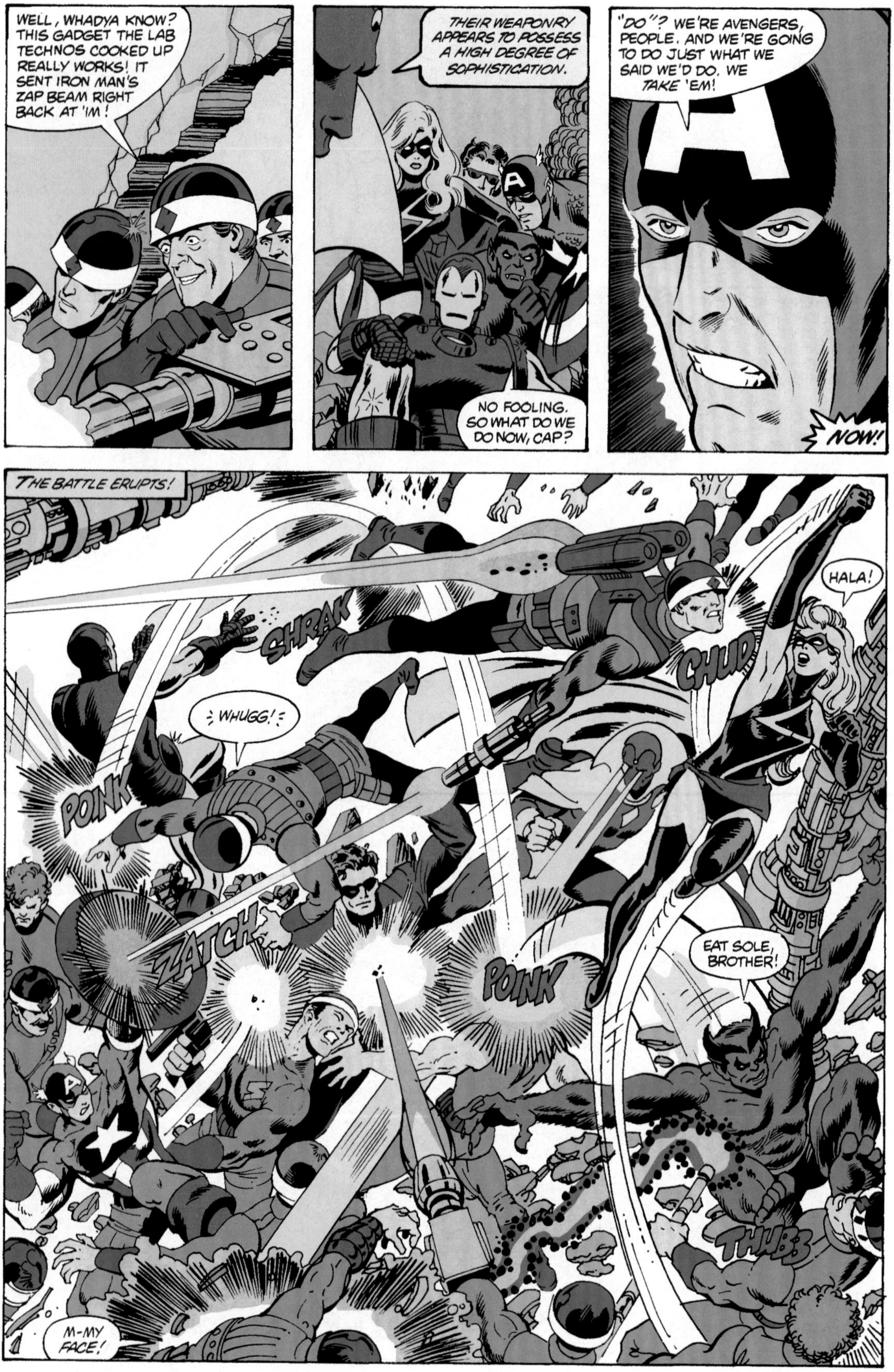
WELL, WHADYA KNOW? THIS GADGET THE LAB TECHNOS COOKED UP REALLY WORKS! IT SENT IRON MAN'S ZAP BEAM RIGHT BACK AT 'IM!
THEIR WEAPONRY APPEARS TO POSSESS A HIGH DEGREE OF SOPHISTICATION.
NO FOOLING. SO WHAT DO WE DO NOW, CAP?
"DO"? WE'RE AVENGERS, PEOPLE. AND WE'RE GOING TO DO JUST WHAT WE SAID WE'D DO. WE TAKE 'EM!
NOW!
THE BATTLE ERUPTS!
HALA!
SHRAK
CHUD
WHUGG!
POINK
ZATCH
POINK
EAT SOLE, BROTHER!
THUBB
M-MY FACE!

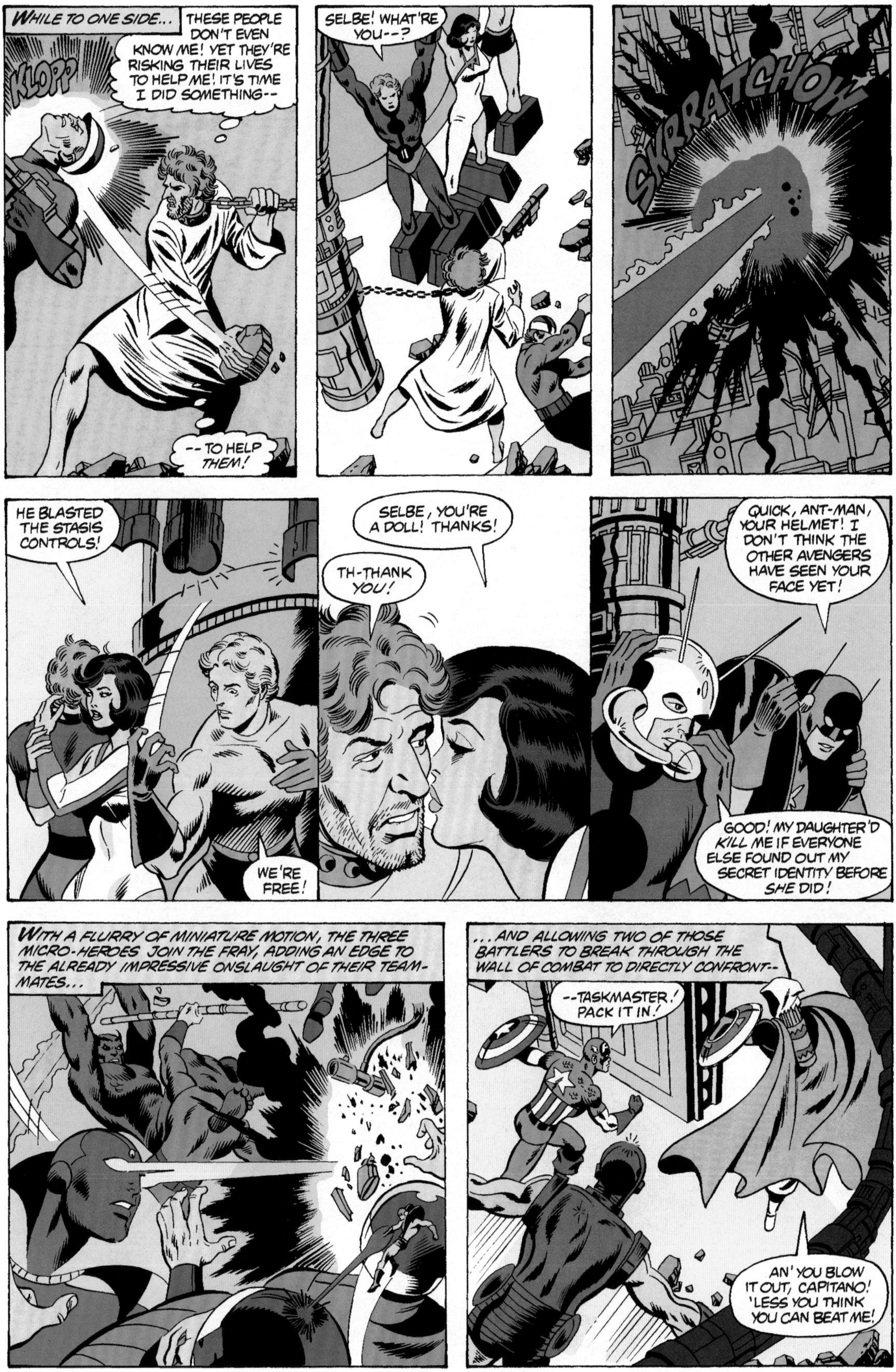
WHILE TO ONE SIDE...
THESE PEOPLE DON'T EVEN KNOW ME! YET THEY'RE RISKING THEIR LIVES TO HELP ME! IT'S TIME I DID SOMETHING--
KLOPP
--TO HELP THEM!
SELBE! WHAT'RE YOU--?
SKRRATCHOW
HE BLASTED THE STASIS CONTROLS!
WE'RE FREE!
SELBE, YOU'RE A DOLL! THANKS!
TH-THANK YOU!
QUICK, ANT-MAN, YOUR HELMET! I DON'T THINK THE OTHER AVENGERS HAVE SEEN YOUR FACE YET!
GOOD! MY DAUGHTER'D KILL ME IF EVERYONE ELSE FOUND OUT MY SECRET IDENTITY BEFORE SHE DID!
WITH A FLURRY OF MINIATURE MOTION, THE THREE MICRO-HEROES JOIN THE FRAY, ADDING AN EDGE TO THE ALREADY IMPRESSIVE ONSLAUGHT OF THEIR TEAM-MATES...
...AND ALLOWING TWO OF THOSE BATTLERS TO BREAK THROUGH THE WALL OF COMBAT TO DIRECTLY CONFRONT--
--TASKMASTER! PACK IT IN!
AN' YOU BLOW IT OUT, CAPITANO! 'LESS YOU THINK YOU CAN BEAT ME!

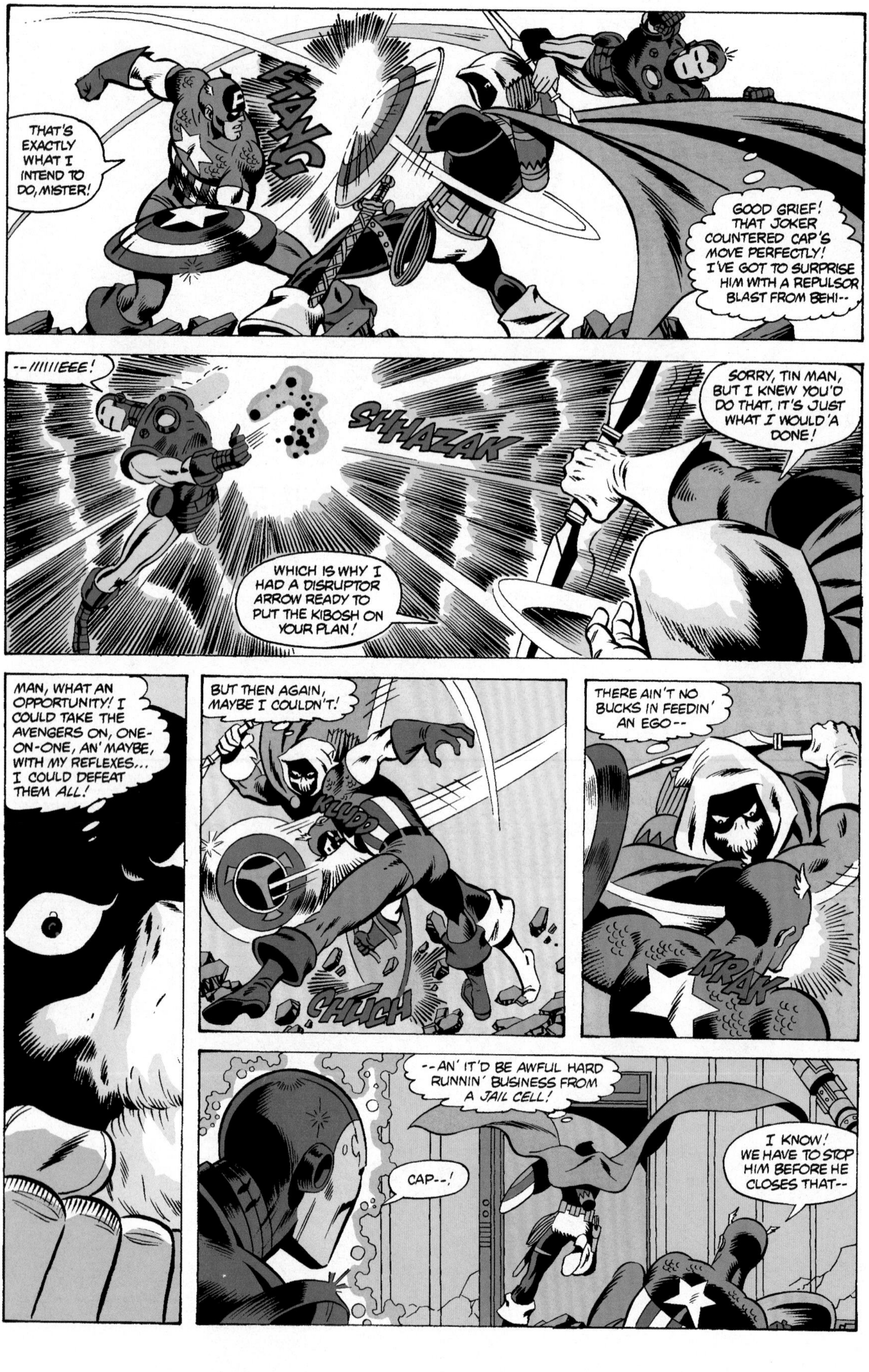
THAT'S EXACTLY WHAT I INTEND TO DO, MISTER!
FTANG
GOOD GRIEF! THAT JOKER COUNTERED CAP'S MOVE PERFECTLY! I'VE GOT TO SURPRISE HIM WITH A REPULSOR BLAST FROM BEHI--
--IIIIIIEEE!
SHHAZAK
SORRY, TIN MAN, BUT I KNEW YOU'D DO THAT. IT'S JUST WHAT I WOULD'A DONE!
WHICH IS WHY I HAD A DISRUPTOR ARROW READY TO PUT THE KIBOSH ON YOUR PLAN!
MAN, WHAT AN OPPORTUNITY! I COULD TAKE THE AVENGERS ON, ONE-ON-ONE, AN' MAYBE, WITH MY REFLEXES... I COULD DEFEAT THEM ALL!
BUT THEN AGAIN, MAYBE I COULDN'T.
CHUCH
THERE AIN'T NO BUCKS IN FEEDIN' AN EGO--
KRAK
--AN' IT'D BE AWFUL HARD RUNNIN' BUSINESS FROM A JAIL CELL!
CAP--!
I KNOW! WE HAVE TO STOP HIM BEFORE HE CLOSES THAT--

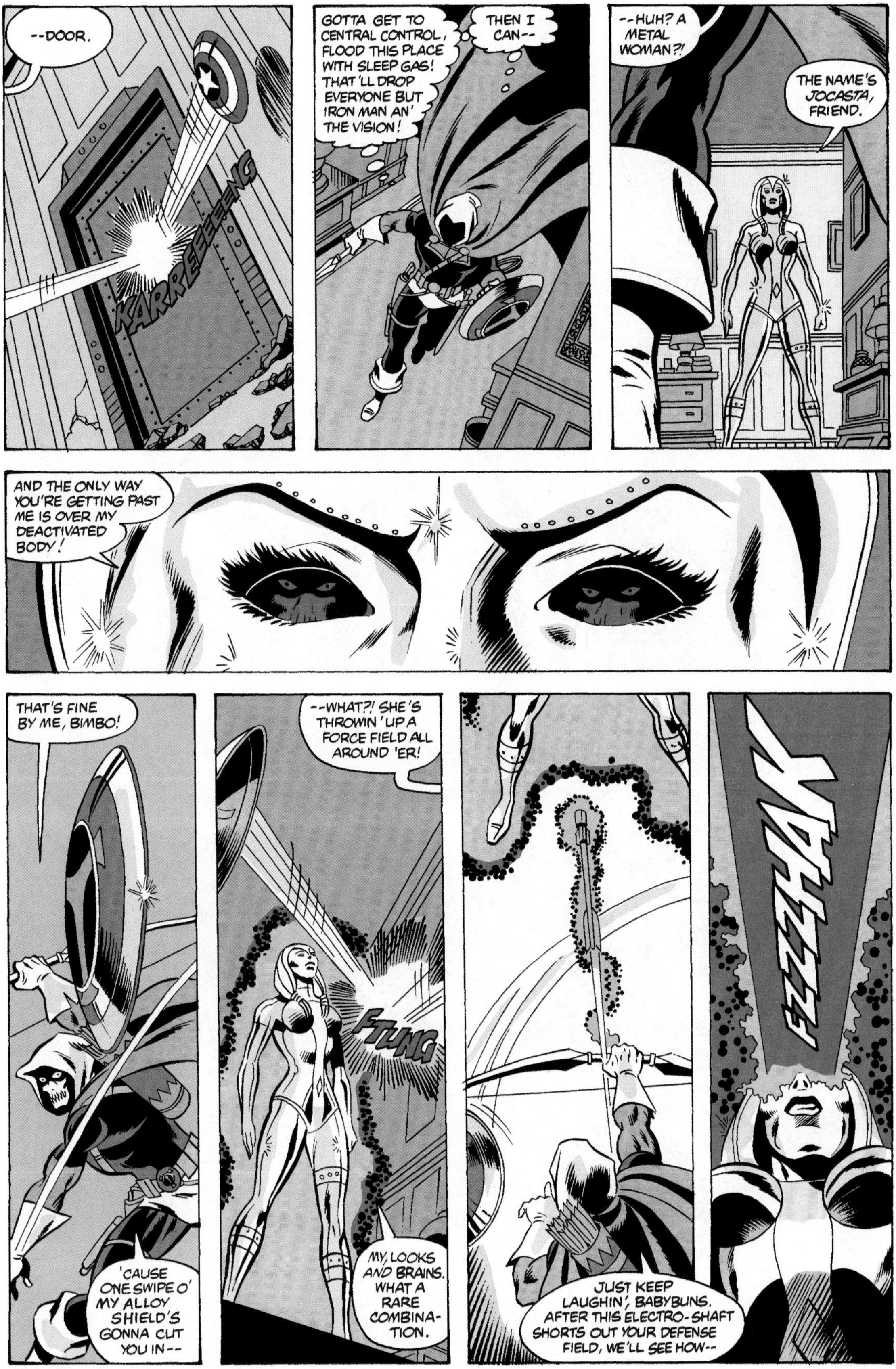
--DOOR.
KARREEEEENG
GOTTA GET TO CENTRAL CONTROL, FLOOD THIS PLACE WITH SLEEP GAS! THAT'LL DROP EVERYONE BUT IRON MAN AN' THE VISION!
THEN I CAN--
--HUH? A METAL WOMAN?!
THE NAME'S JOCASTA, FRIEND.
AND THE ONLY WAY YOU'RE GETTING PAST ME IS OVER MY DEACTIVATED BODY!
THAT'S FINE BY ME, BIMBO!
'CAUSE ONE SWIPE O' MY ALLOY SHIELD'S GONNA CUT YOU IN--
--WHAT?! SHE'S THROWIN' UP A FORCE FIELD ALL AROUND 'ER!
FTUNG
MY, LOOKS AND BRAINS. WHAT A RARE COMBINATION.
JUST KEEP LAUGHIN', BABYBUNS. AFTER THIS ELECTRO-SHAFT SHORTS OUT YOUR DEFENSE FIELD, WE'LL SEE HOW--
FFZZZZAKK

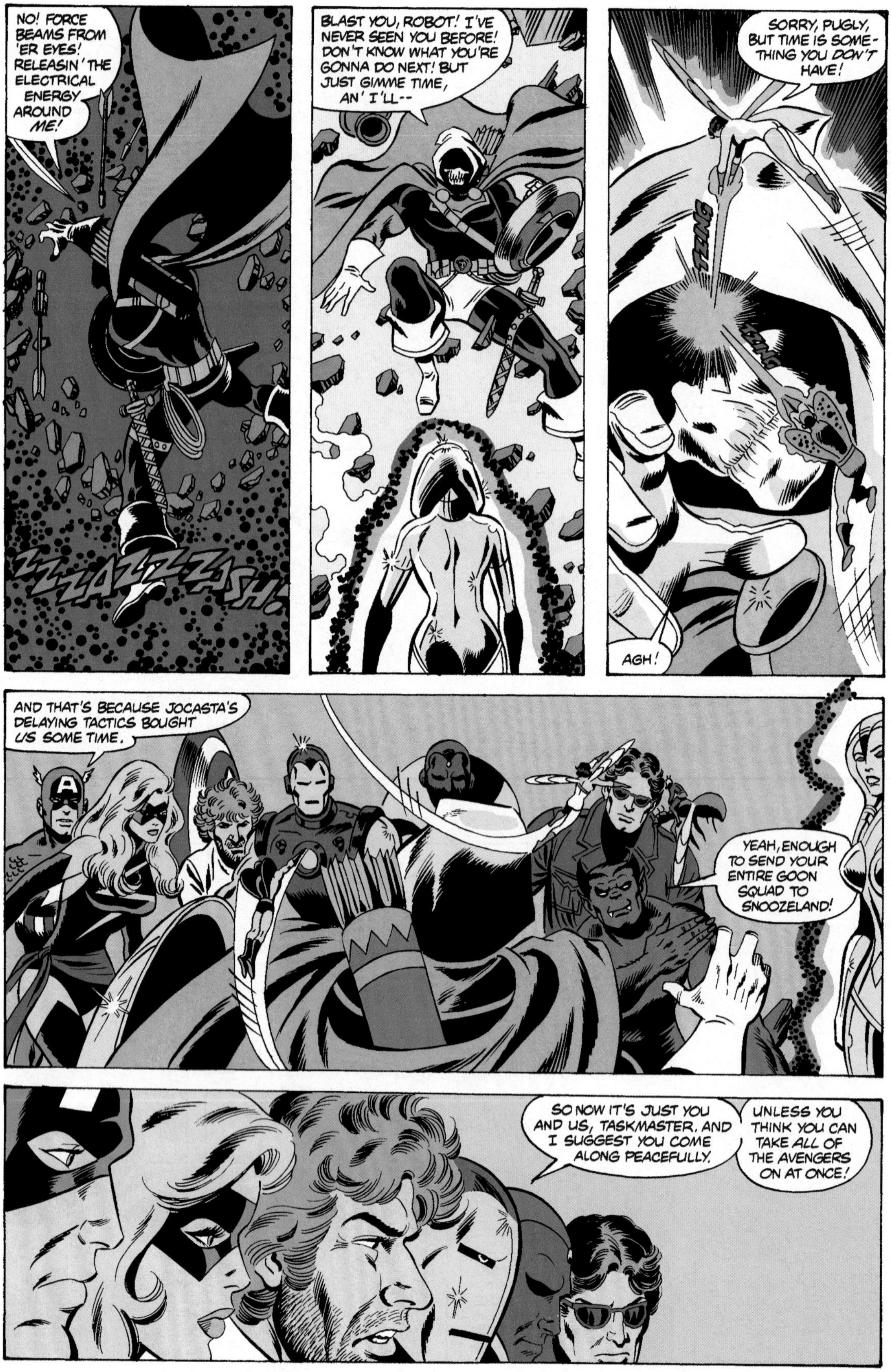
NO! FORCE BEAMS FROM 'ER EYES! RELEASIN' THE ELECTRICAL ENERGY AROUND ME!
ZZZAZZZZSH!
BLAST YOU, ROBOT! I'VE NEVER SEEN YOU BEFORE! DON'T KNOW WHAT YOU'RE GONNA DO NEXT! BUT JUST GIMME TIME, AN' I'LL--
SORRY, PUGLY, BUT TIME IS SOMETHING YOU DON'T HAVE!
THING
TOING
AGH!
AND THAT'S BECAUSE JOCASTA'S DELAYING TACTICS BOUGHT US SOME TIME.
YEAH, ENOUGH TO SEND YOUR ENTIRE GOON SQUAD TO SNOOZELAND!
SO NOW IT'S JUST YOU AND US, TASKMASTER. AND I SUGGEST YOU COME ALONG PEACEFULLY.
UNLESS YOU THINK YOU CAN TAKE ALL OF THE AVENGERS ON AT ONCE!

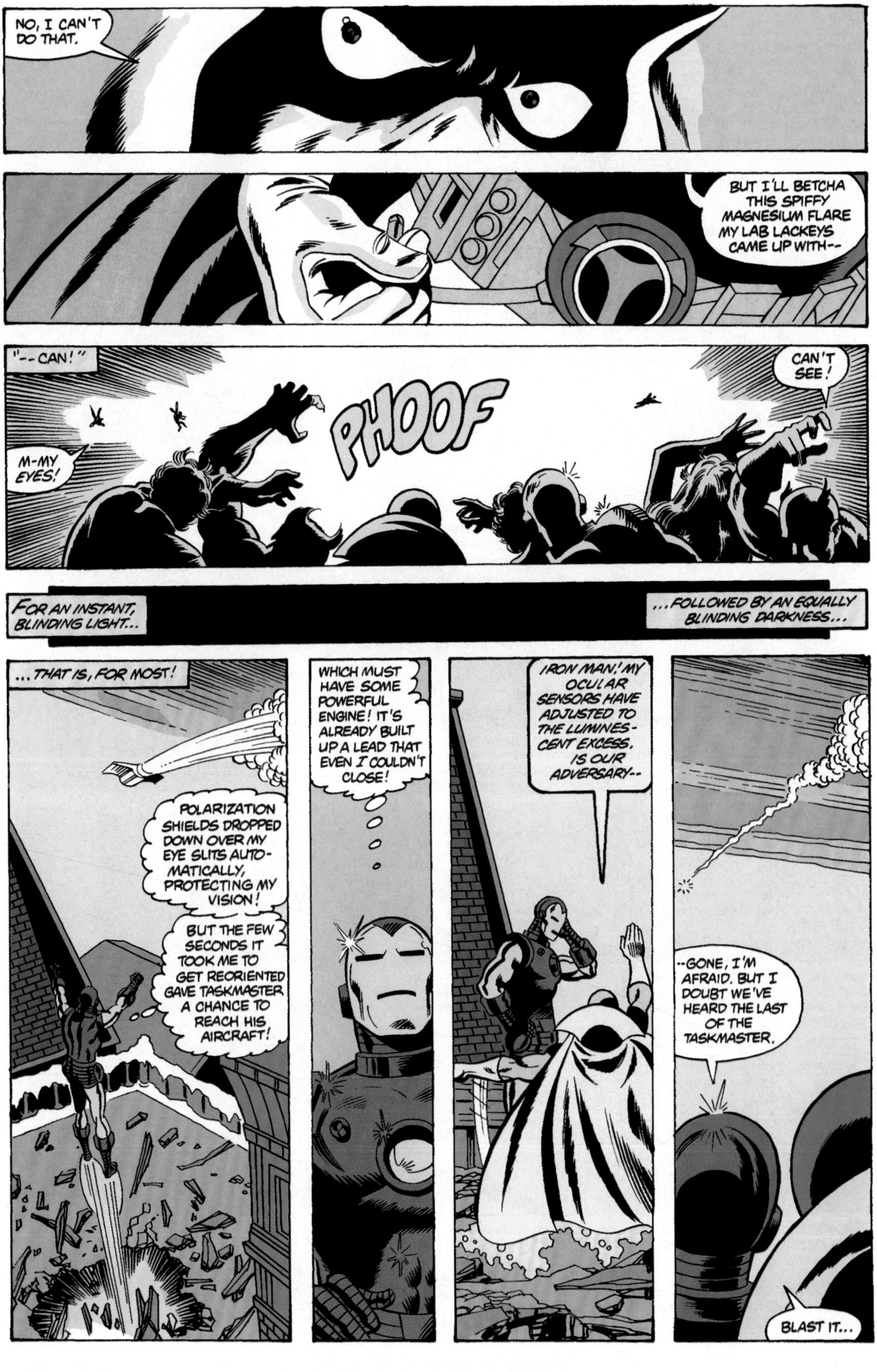

NO, I CAN'T DO THAT.
BUT I'LL BETCHA THIS SPIFFY MAGNESIUM FLARE MY LAB LACKEYS CAME UP WITH--
"--CAN!"
PHOOF
CAN'T SEE!
M-MY EYES!
FOR AN INSTANT, BLINDING LIGHT...
...FOLLOWED BY AN EQUALLY BLINDING DARKNESS...
...THAT IS, FOR MOST!
POLARIZATION SHIELDS DROPPED DOWN OVER MY EYE SLITS AUTO-MATICALLY, PROTECTING MY VISION!
BUT THE FEW SECONDS IT TOOK ME TO GET REORIENTED GAVE TASKMASTER A CHANCE TO REACH HIS AIRCRAFT!
WHICH MUST HAVE SOME POWERFUL ENGINE! IT'S ALREADY BUILT UP A LEAD THAT EVEN I COULDN'T CLOSE!
IRON MAN! MY OCULAR SENSORS HAVE ADJUSTED TO THE LUMINES-CENT EXCESS. IS OUR ADVERSARY--
--GONE, I'M AFRAID. BUT I DOUBT WE'VE HEARD THE LAST OF THE TASKMASTER.
BLAST IT...

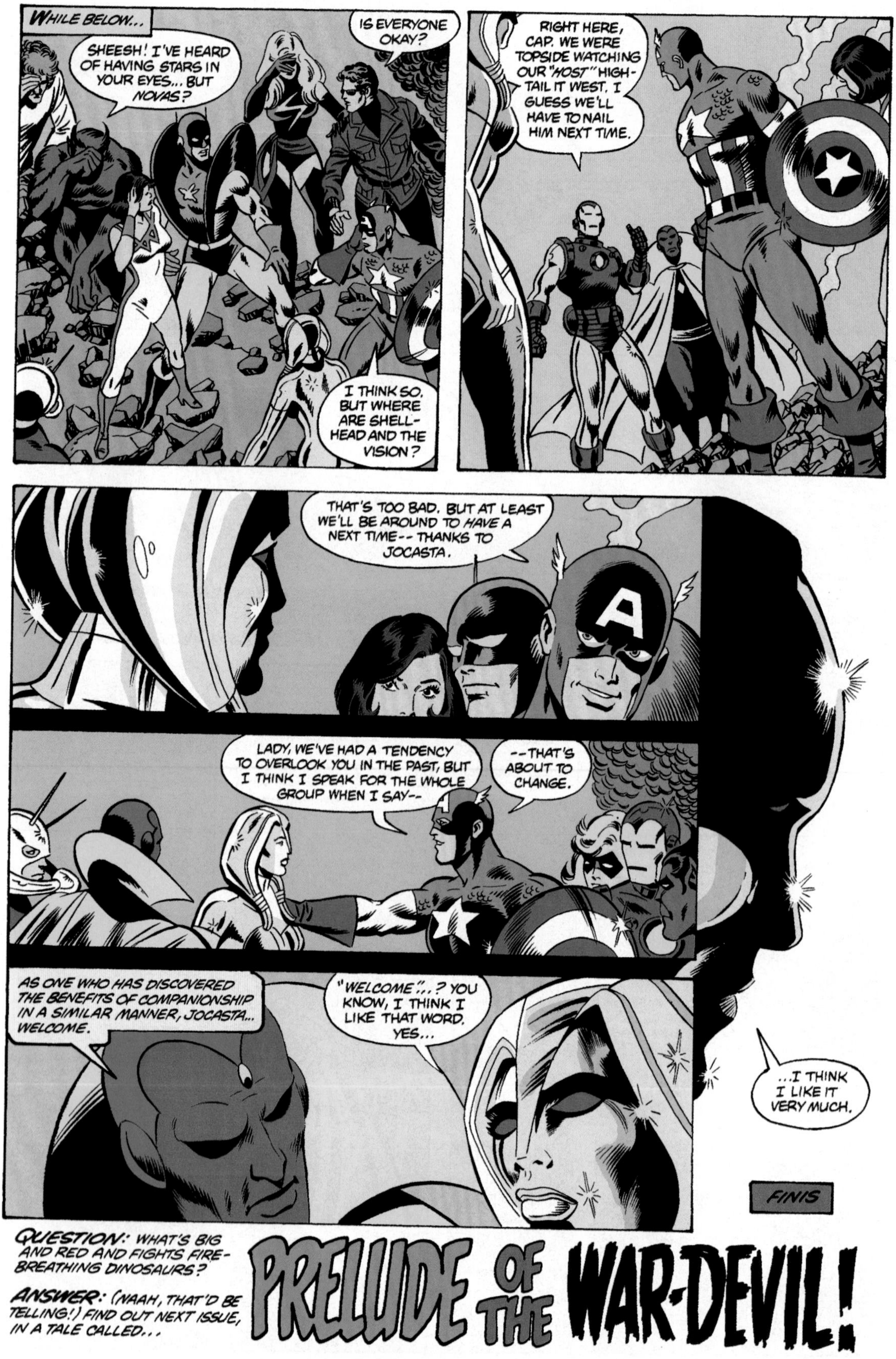

WHILE BELOW...
SHEESH! I'VE HEARD OF HAVING STARS IN YOUR EYES... BUT NOVAS?
IS EVERYONE OKAY?
I THINK SO. BUT WHERE ARE SHELL-HEAD AND THE VISION?
RIGHT HERE, CAP. WE WERE TOPSIDE WATCHING OUR "HOST" HIGH-TAIL IT WEST. I GUESS WE'LL HAVE TO NAIL HIM NEXT TIME.
THAT'S TOO BAD. BUT AT LEAST WE'LL BE AROUND TO HAVE A NEXT TIME-- THANKS TO JOCASTA.
LADY, WE'VE HAD A TENDENCY TO OVERLOOK YOU IN THE PAST, BUT I THINK I SPEAK FOR THE WHOLE GROUP WHEN I SAY--
--THAT'S ABOUT TO CHANGE.
AS ONE WHO HAS DISCOVERED THE BENEFITS OF COMPANIONSHIP IN A SIMILAR MANNER, JOCASTA... WELCOME.
"WELCOME"...? YOU KNOW, I THINK I LIKE THAT WORD. YES...
...I THINK I LIKE IT VERY MUCH.
FINIS
QUESTION: WHAT'S BIG AND RED AND FIGHTS FIRE-BREATHING DINOSAURS?
ANSWER: (NAAH, THAT'D BE TELLING!) FIND OUT NEXT ISSUE, IN A TALE CALLED...
PRELUDE OF THE WAR-DEVIL!

FOLLOW TASKMASTER IN *TASKMASTER: ANYTHING YOU CAN DO...* TPB.

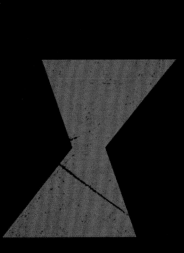

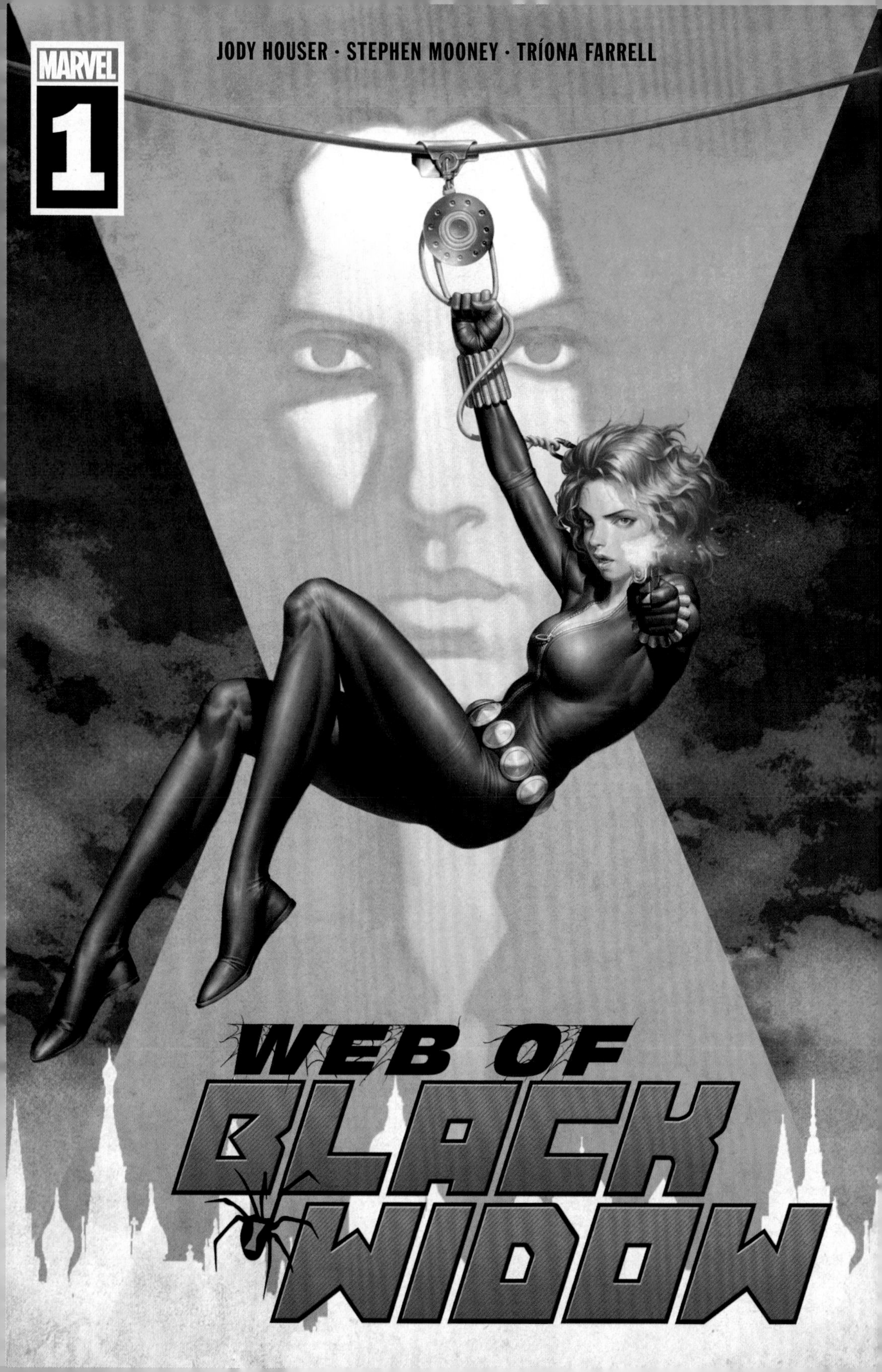

MARVEL
1
JODY HOUSER · STEPHEN MOONEY · TRÍONA FARRELL
WEB OF BLACK WIDOW

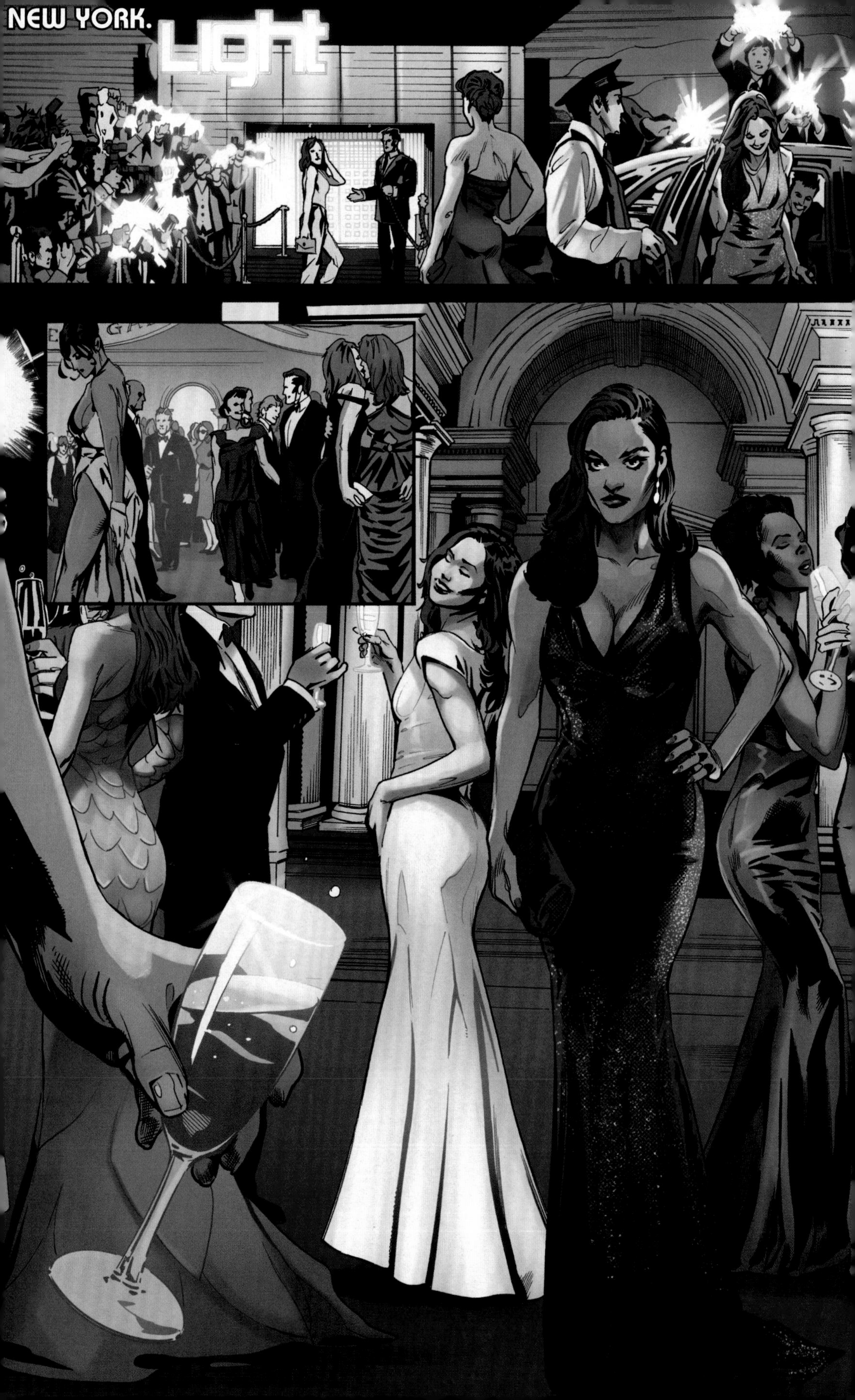
NEW YORK.
Light

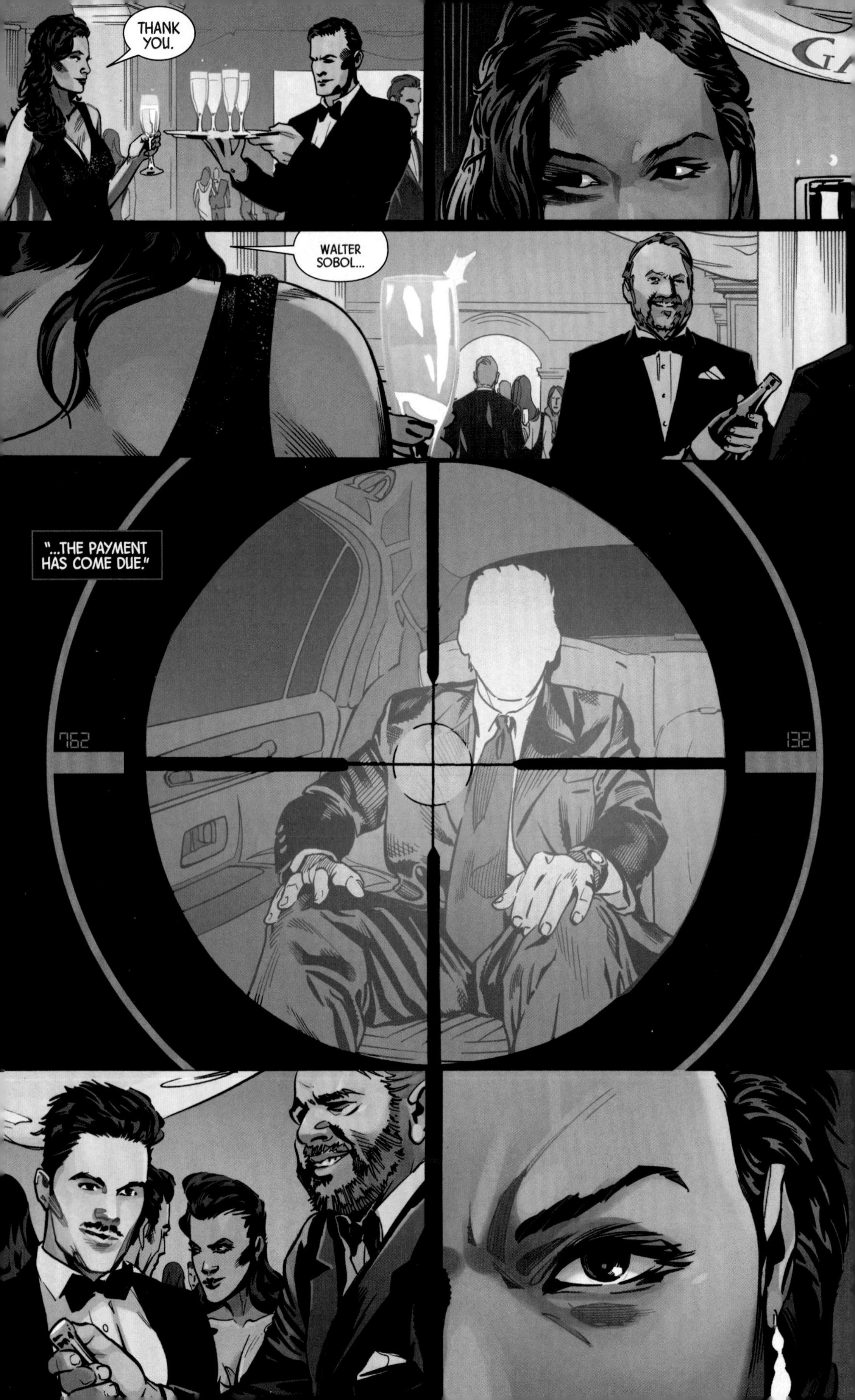
THANK YOU.
WALTER SOBOL...
"...THE PAYMENT HAS COME DUE."
762
132

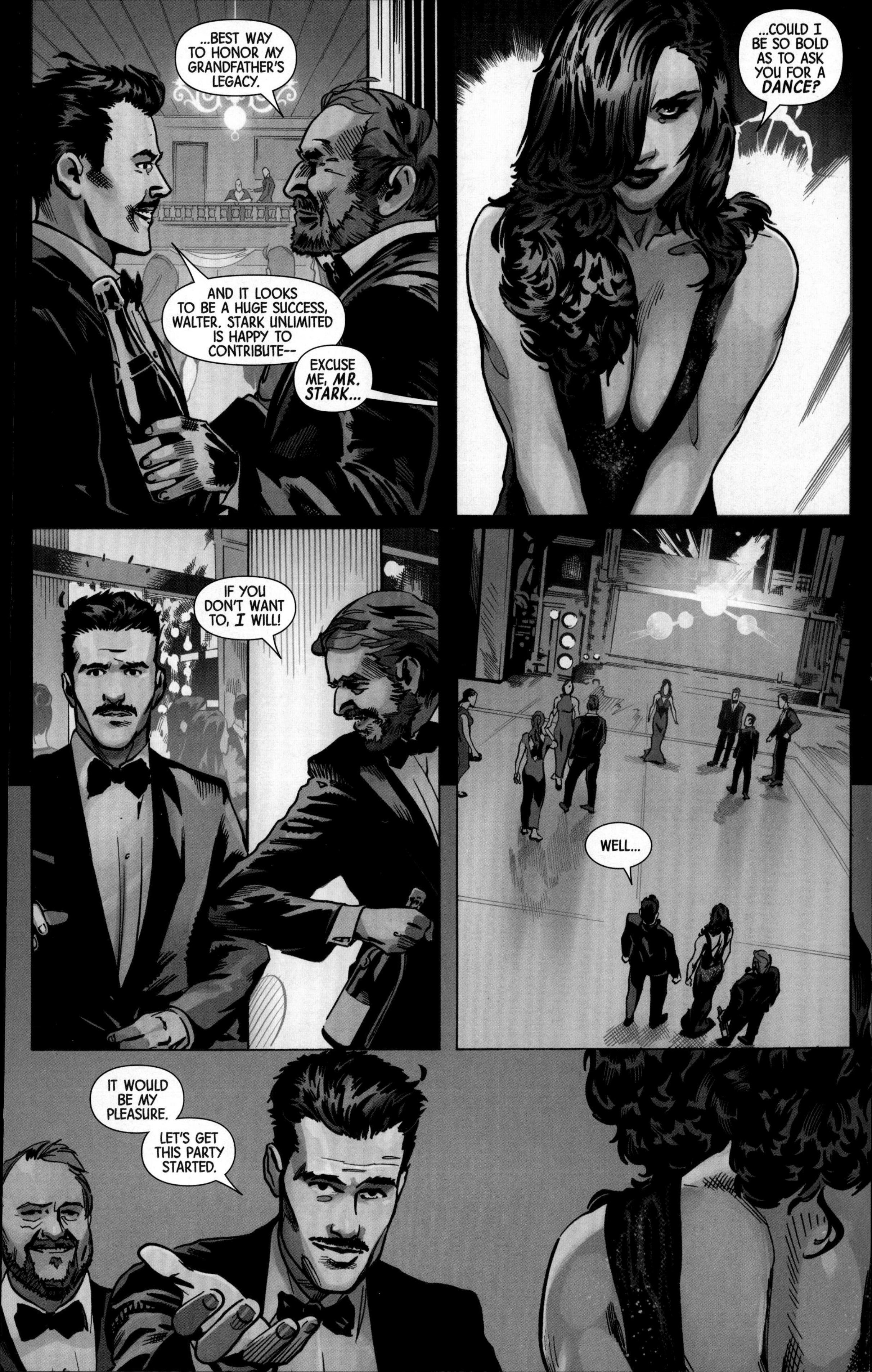
...BEST WAY TO HONOR MY GRANDFATHER'S LEGACY.
AND IT LOOKS TO BE A HUGE SUCCESS, WALTER. STARK UNLIMITED IS HAPPY TO CONTRIBUTE--
EXCUSE ME, MR. STARK...
...COULD I BE SO BOLD AS TO ASK YOU FOR A DANCE?
IF YOU DON'T WANT TO, I WILL!
WELL...
IT WOULD BE MY PLEASURE.
LET'S GET THIS PARTY STARTED.

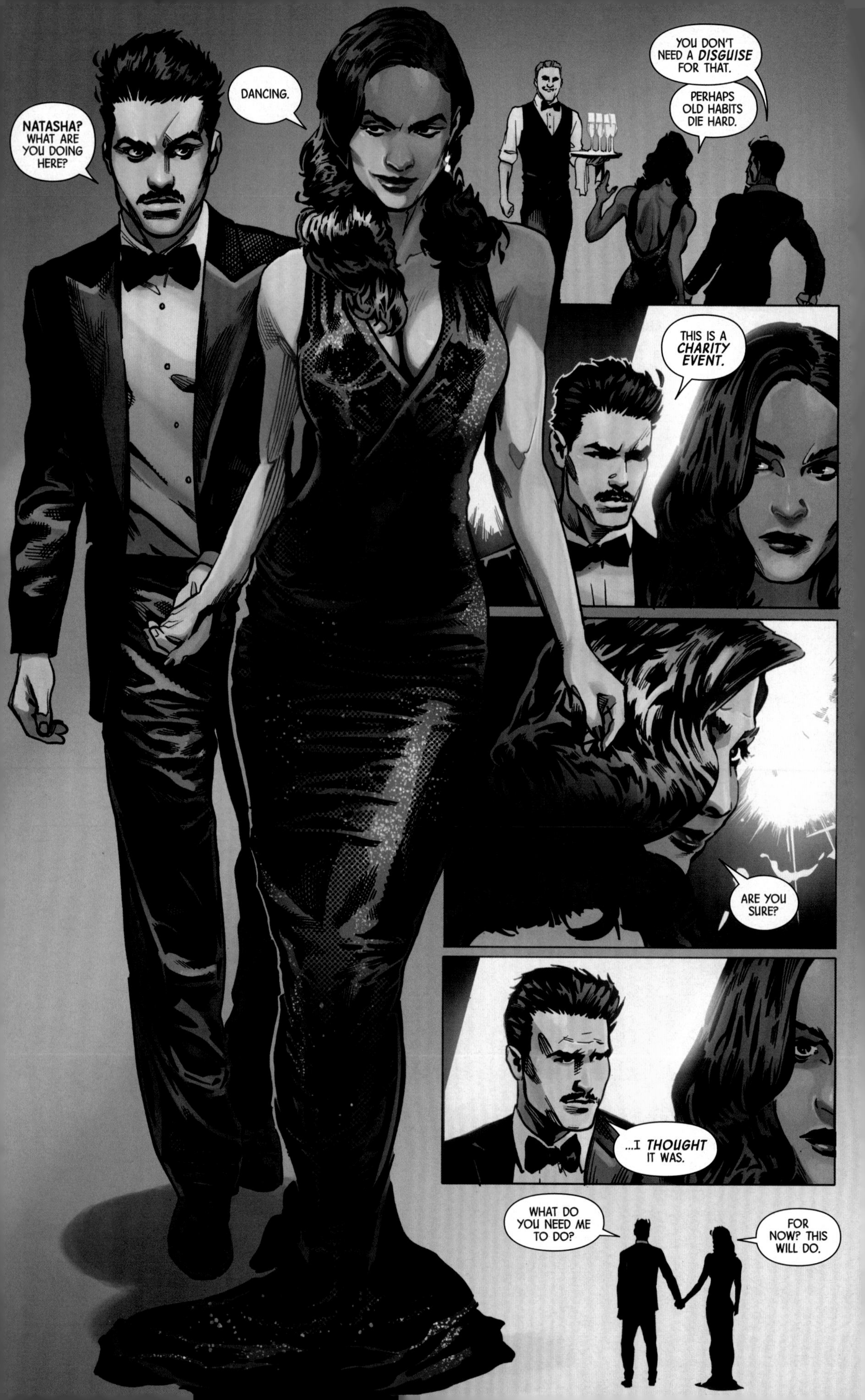
NATASHA? WHAT ARE YOU DOING HERE?
DANCING.
YOU DON'T NEED A DISGUISE FOR THAT.
PERHAPS OLD HABITS DIE HARD.
THIS IS A CHARITY EVENT.
ARE YOU SURE?
...I THOUGHT IT WAS.
WHAT DO YOU NEED ME TO DO?
FOR NOW? THIS WILL DO.

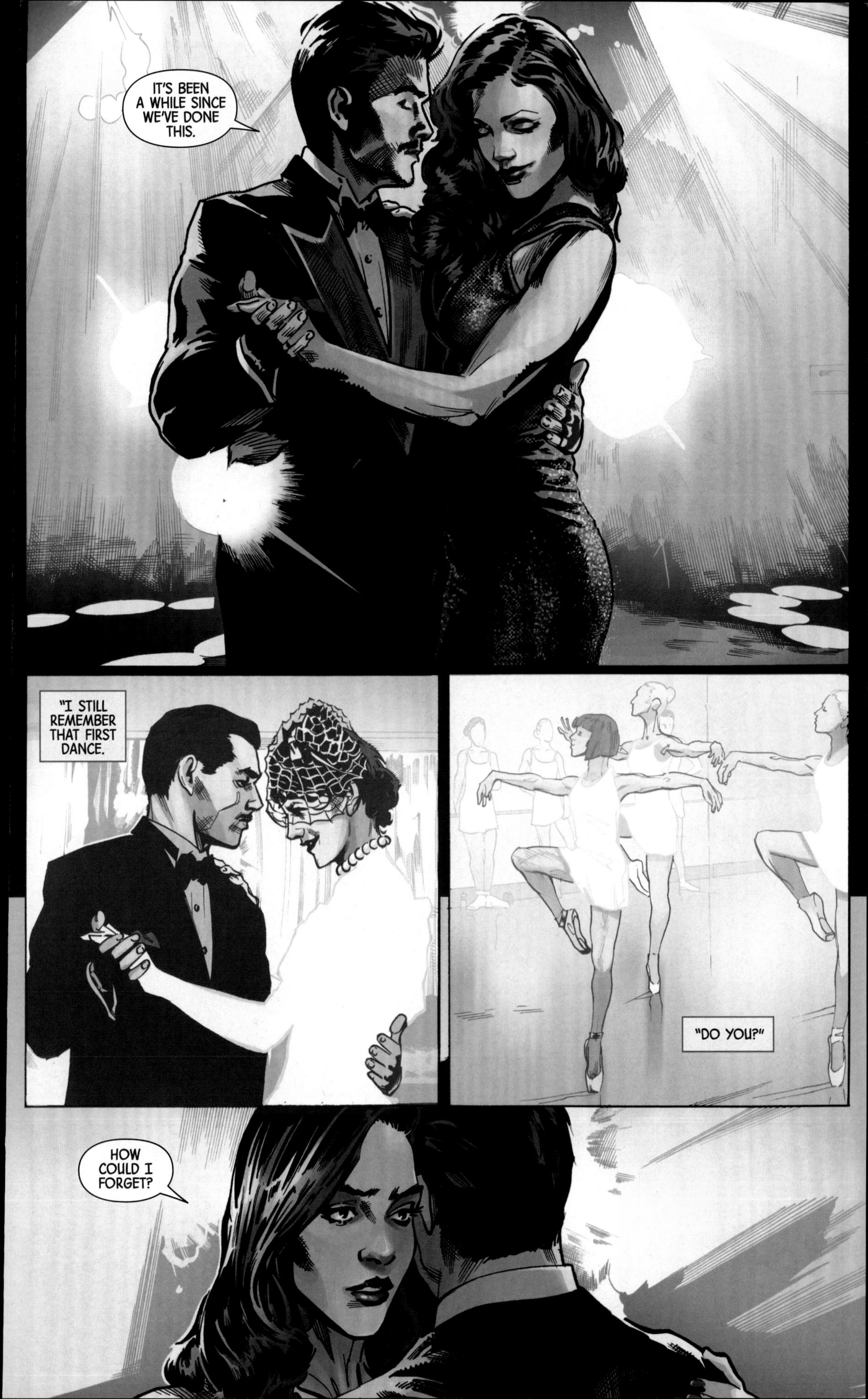
IT'S BEEN A WHILE SINCE WE'VE DONE THIS.
"I STILL REMEMBER THAT FIRST DANCE.
"DO YOU?"
HOW COULD I FORGET?

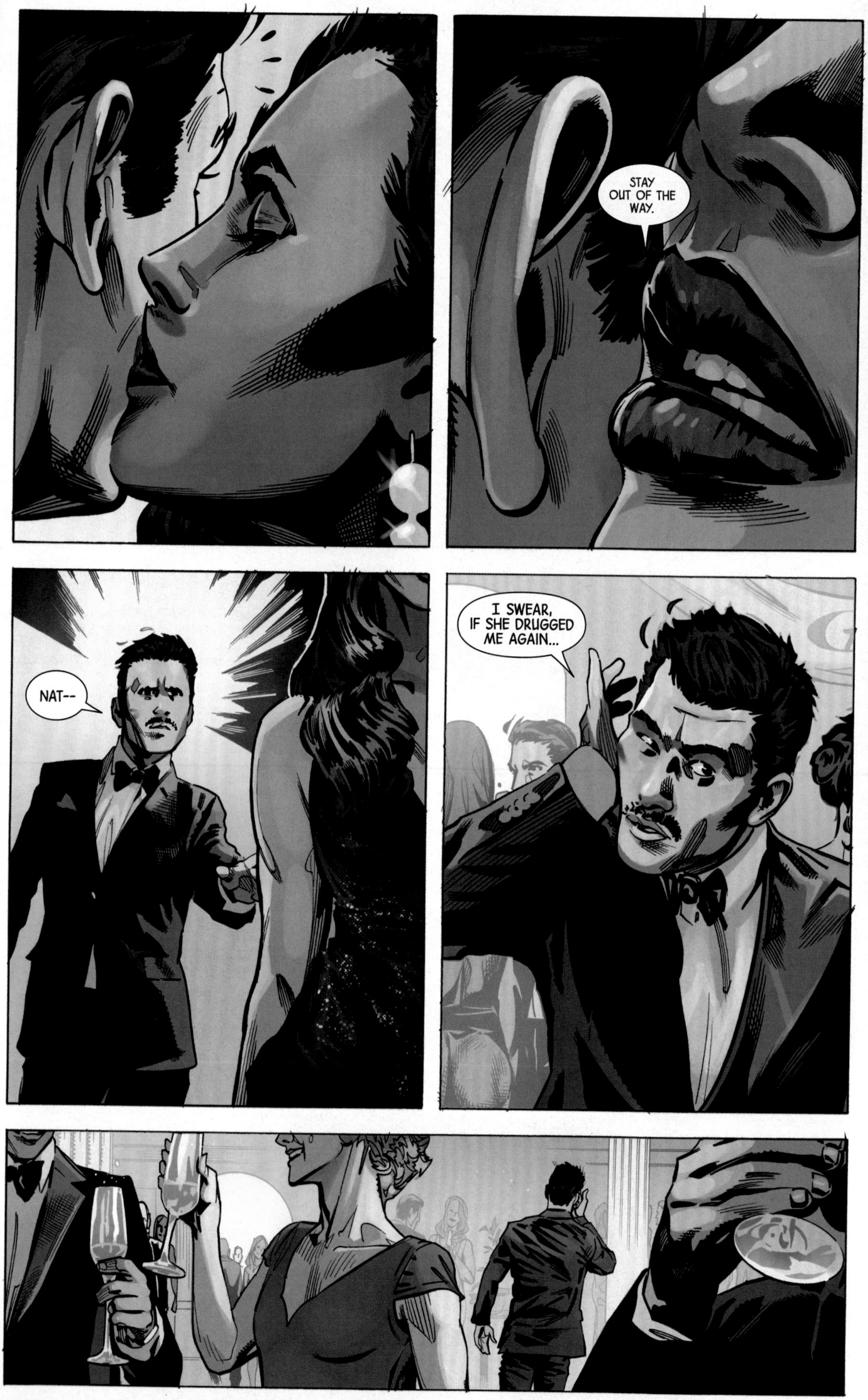
STAY OUT OF THE WAY.
NAT--
I SWEAR, IF SHE DRUGGED ME AGAIN...

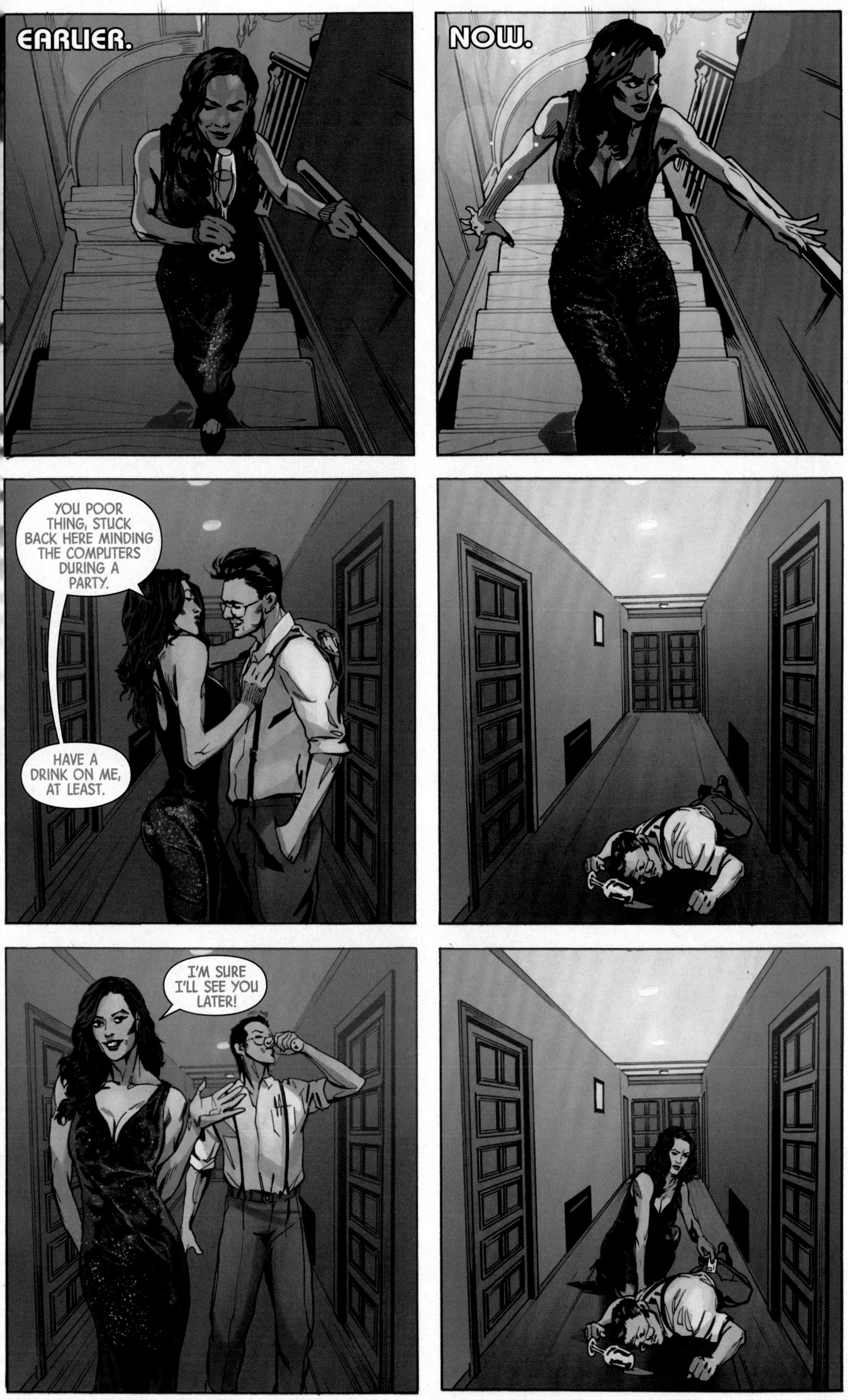
EARLIER.
NOW.
YOU POOR THING, STUCK BACK HERE MINDING THE COMPUTERS DURING A PARTY.
HAVE A DRINK ON ME, AT LEAST.
I'M SURE I'LL SEE YOU LATER!

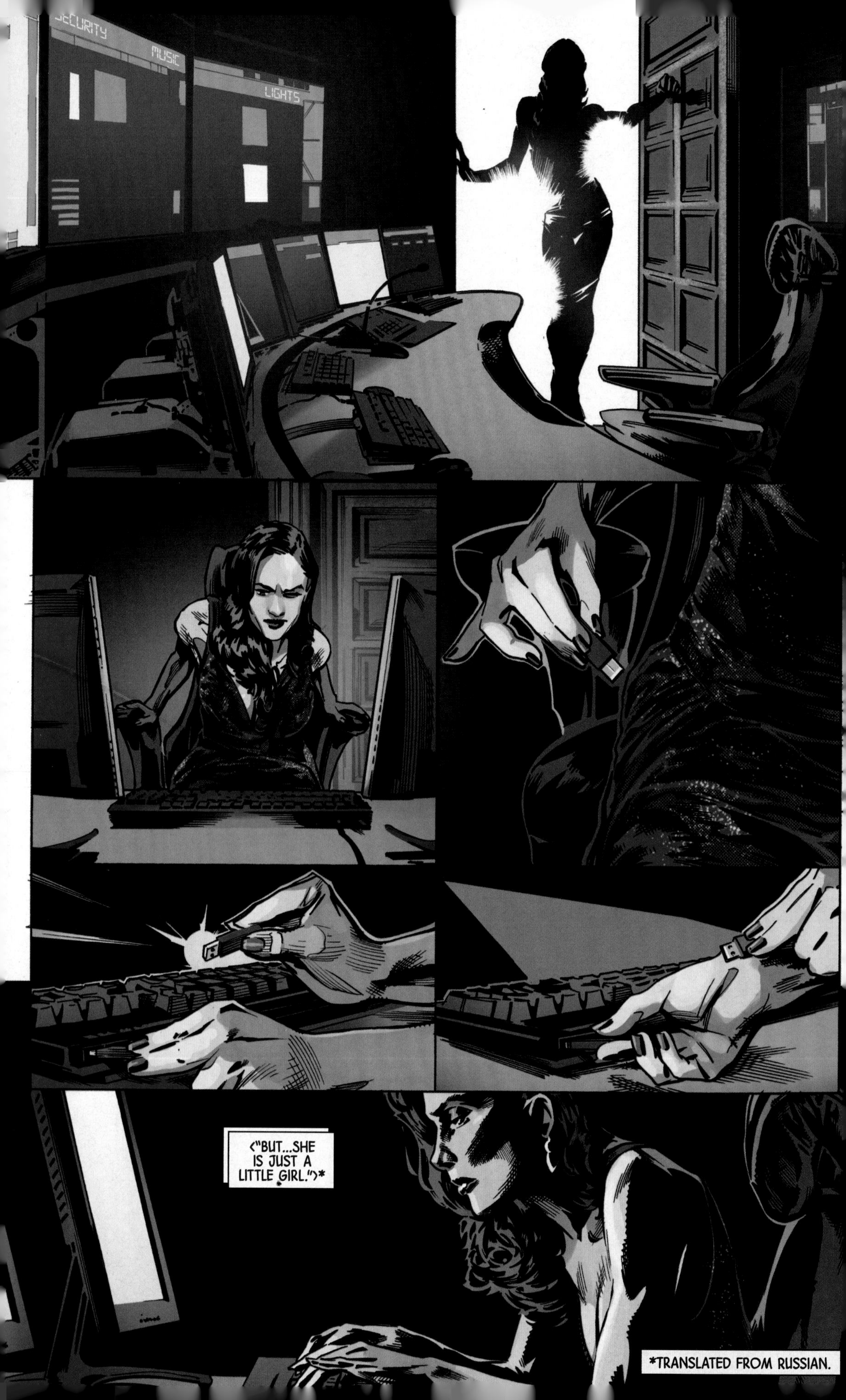
SECURITY
MUSIC
LIGHTS
<"BUT...SHE IS JUST A LITTLE GIRL.">*
*TRANSLATED FROM RUSSIAN.

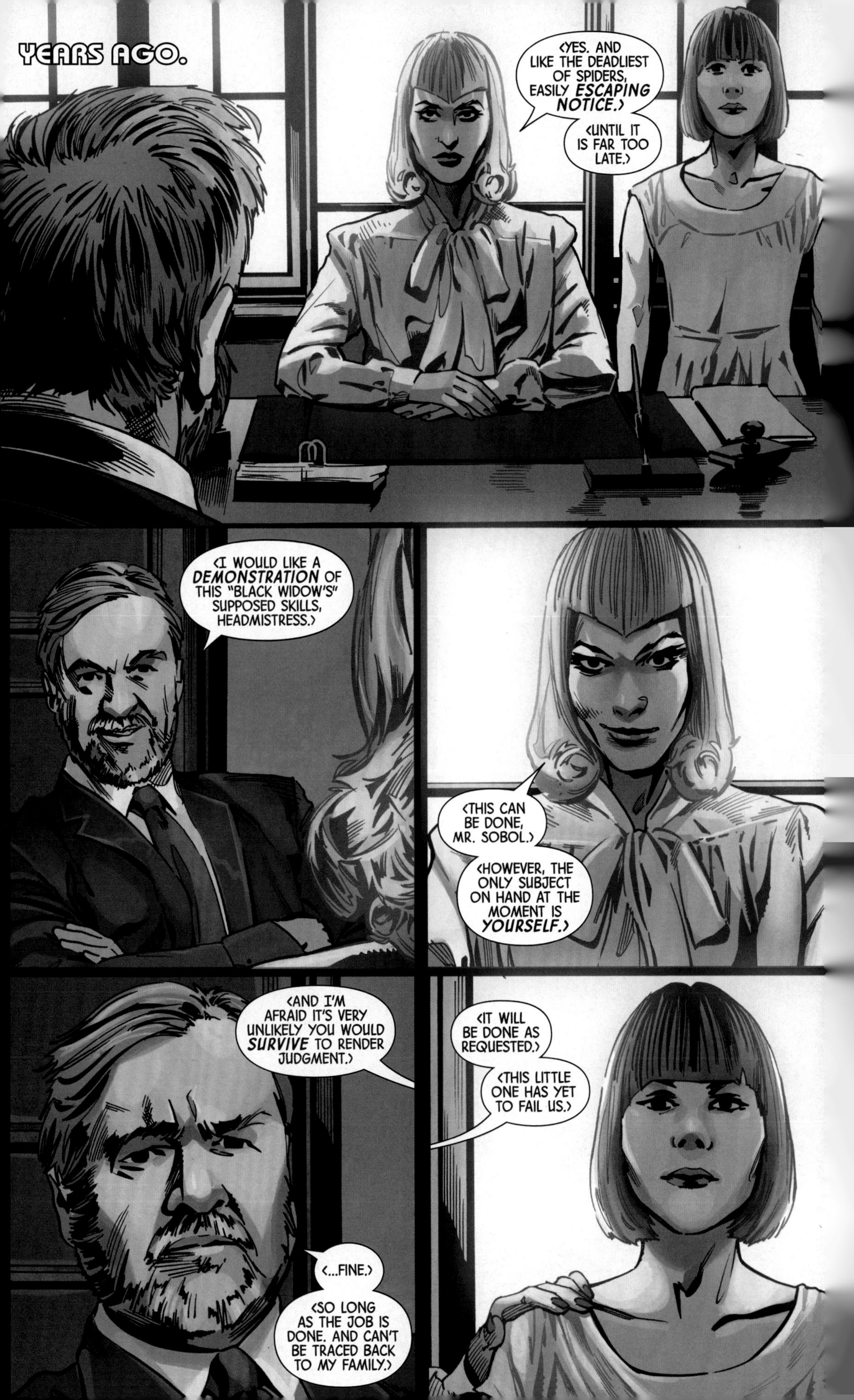
YEARS AGO.
‹YES. AND LIKE THE DEADLIEST OF SPIDERS, EASILY ESCAPING NOTICE.›
‹UNTIL IT IS FAR TOO LATE.›
‹I WOULD LIKE A DEMONSTRATION OF THIS "BLACK WIDOW'S" SUPPOSED SKILLS, HEADMISTRESS.›
‹THIS CAN BE DONE, MR. SOBOL.›
‹HOWEVER, THE ONLY SUBJECT ON HAND AT THE MOMENT IS YOURSELF.›
‹AND I'M AFRAID IT'S VERY UNLIKELY YOU WOULD SURVIVE TO RENDER JUDGMENT.›
‹...FINE.›
‹SO LONG AS THE JOB IS DONE. AND CAN'T BE TRACED BACK TO MY FAMILY.›
‹IT WILL BE DONE AS REQUESTED.›
‹THIS LITTLE ONE HAS YET TO FAIL US.›

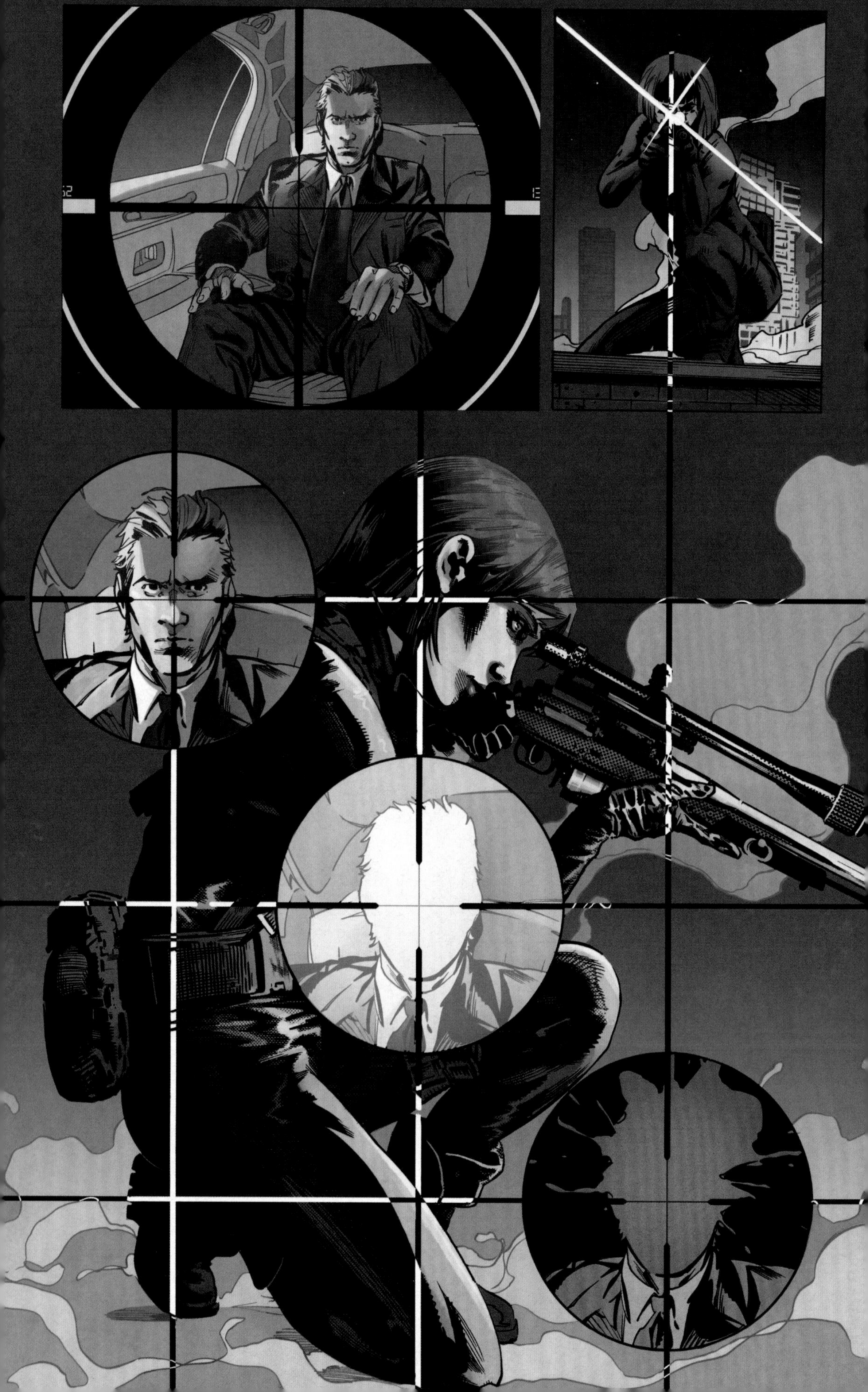

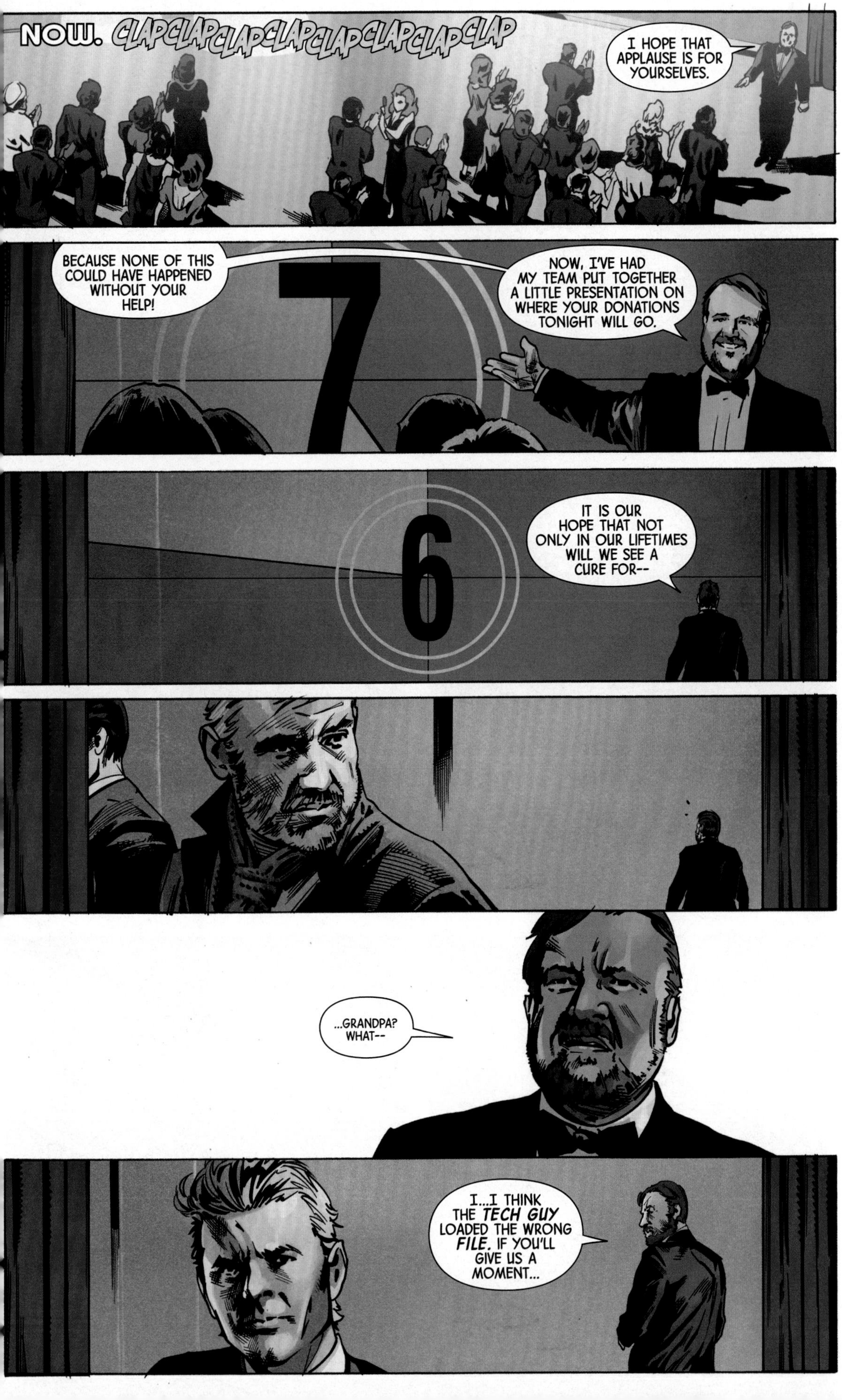
NOW.
CLAPCLAPCLAPCLAPCLAPCLAPCLAPCLAP
I HOPE THAT APPLAUSE IS FOR YOURSELVES.
BECAUSE NONE OF THIS COULD HAVE HAPPENED WITHOUT YOUR HELP!
NOW, I'VE HAD MY TEAM PUT TOGETHER A LITTLE PRESENTATION ON WHERE YOUR DONATIONS TONIGHT WILL GO.
7
6
IT IS OUR HOPE THAT NOT ONLY IN OUR LIFETIMES WILL WE SEE A CURE FOR--
...GRANDPA? WHAT--
I...I THINK THE TECH GUY LOADED THE WRONG FILE. IF YOU'LL GIVE US A MOMENT...

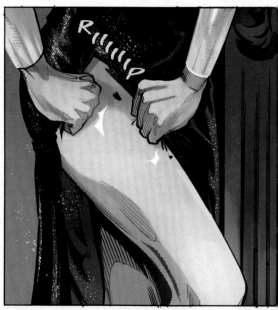

R...iiiiiiP

SLOW...

TROMP TROMP TROMP

THERE
THEY ARE...

THUUD
THUUD
THUUD

HEY!
WHO'S IN
THERE?!

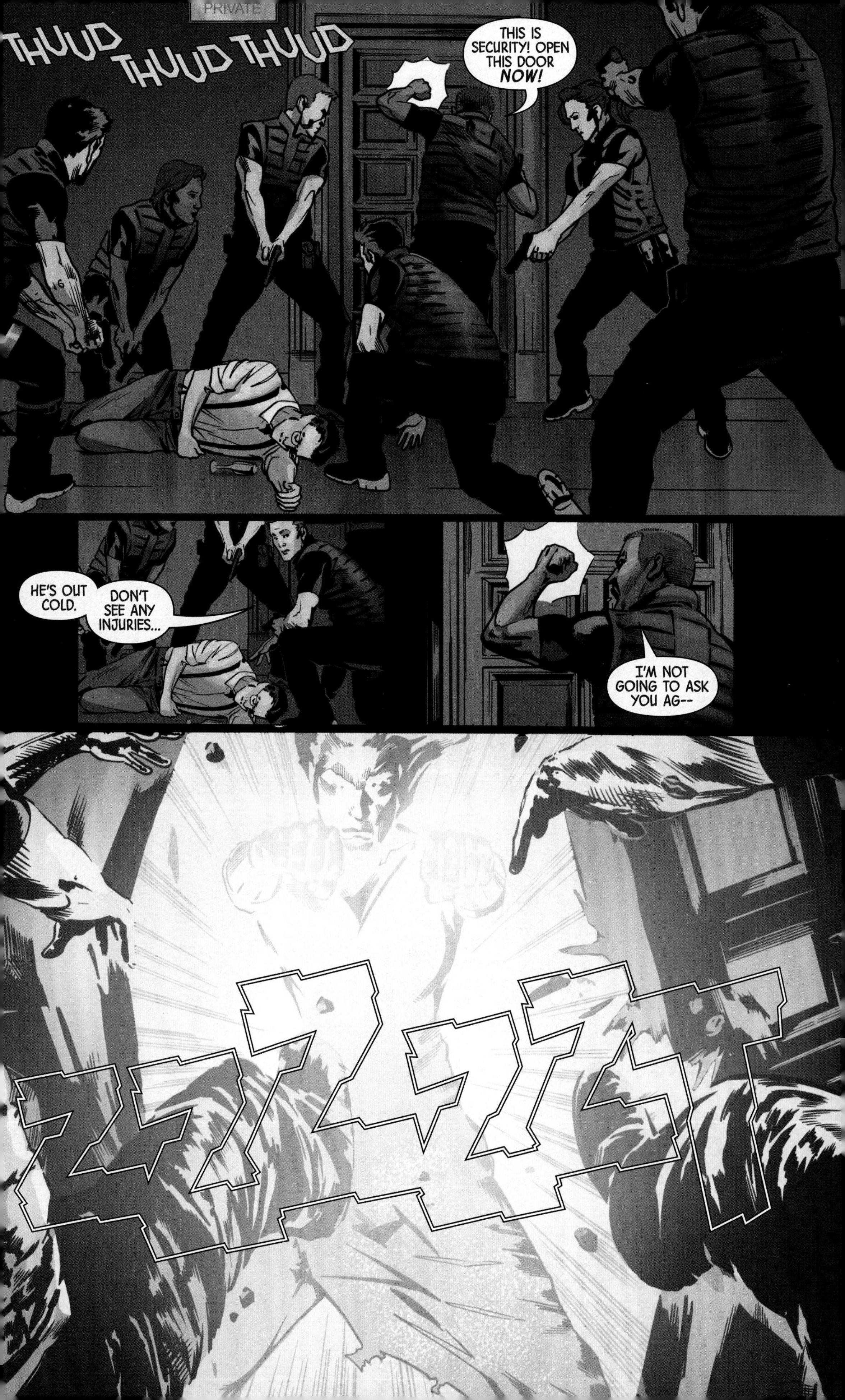
PRIVATE
THUUD THUUD THUUD
THIS IS SECURITY! OPEN THIS DOOR NOW!
HE'S OUT COLD.
DON'T SEE ANY INJURIES...
I'M NOT GOING TO ASK YOU AG--

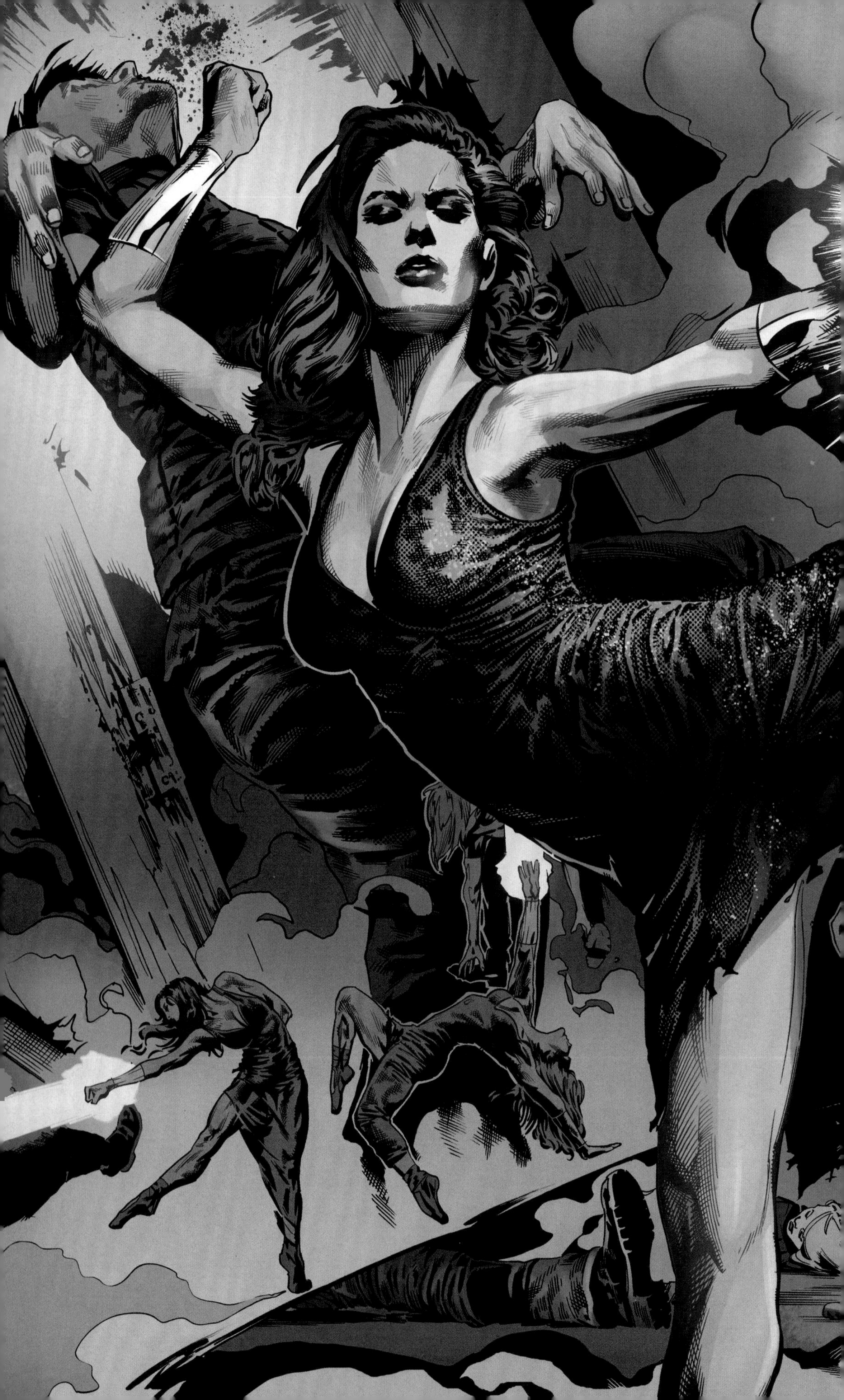

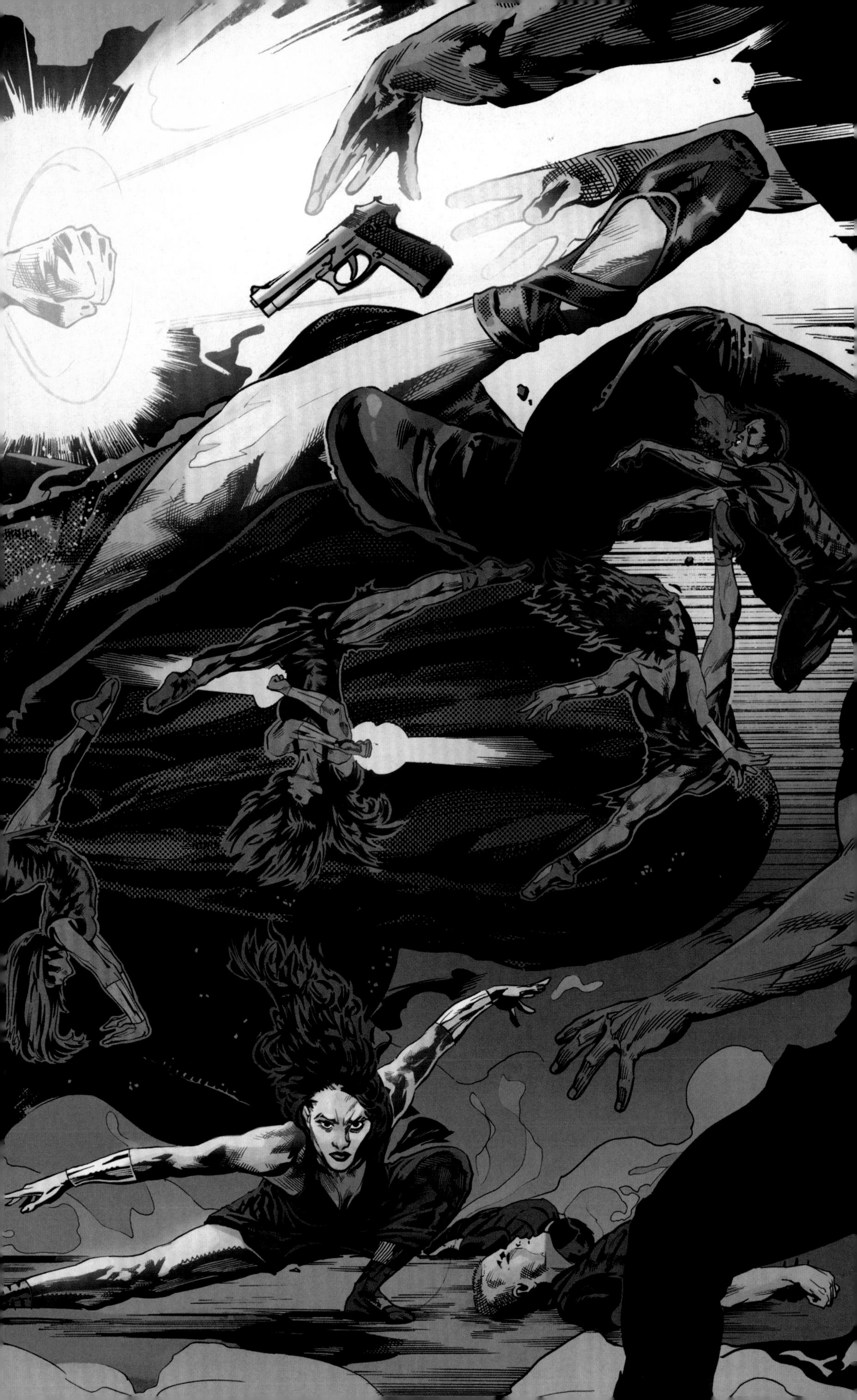

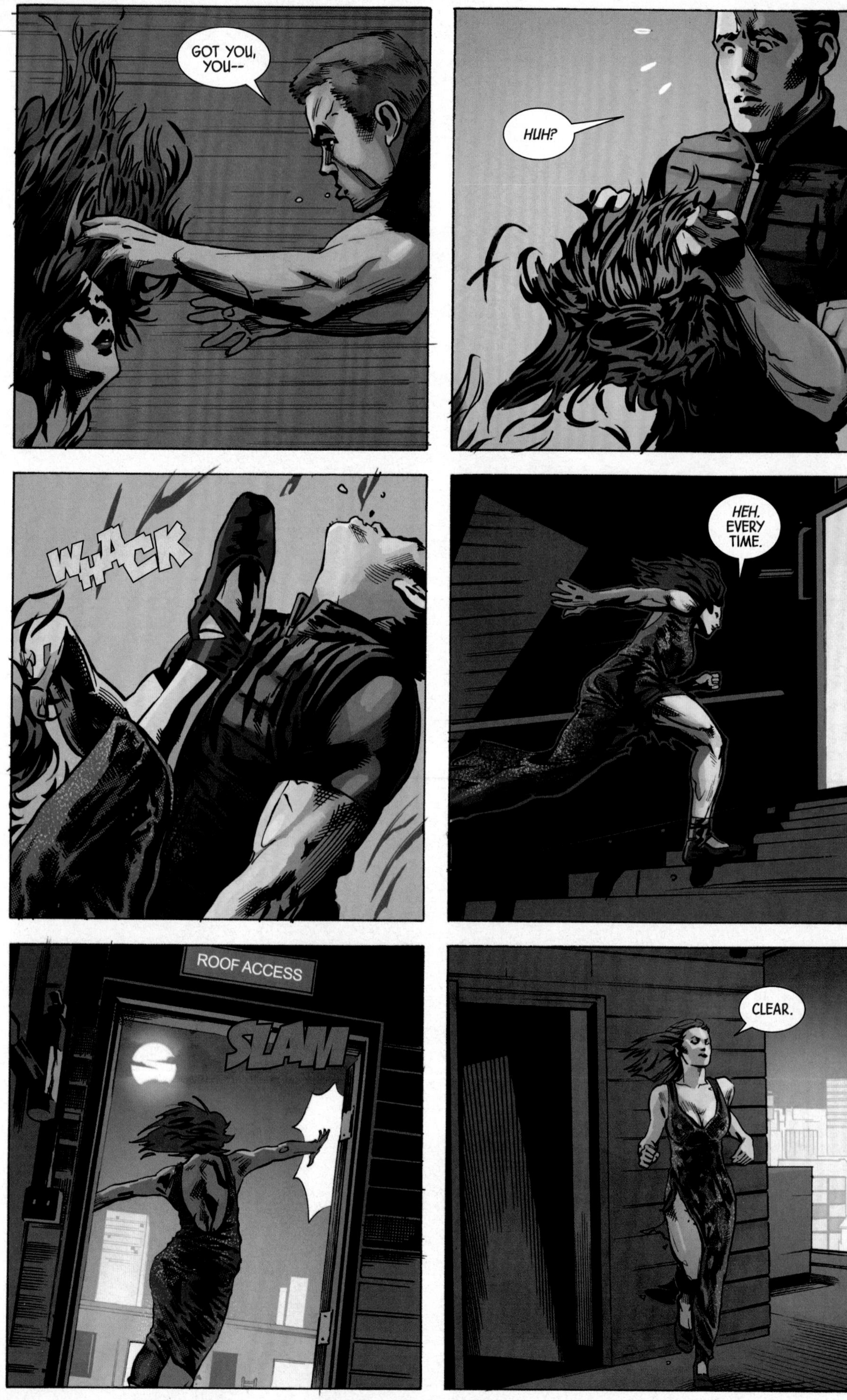
GOT YOU, YOU--
HUH?
WHACK
HEH. EVERY TIME.
ROOF ACCESS
SLAM
CLEAR.

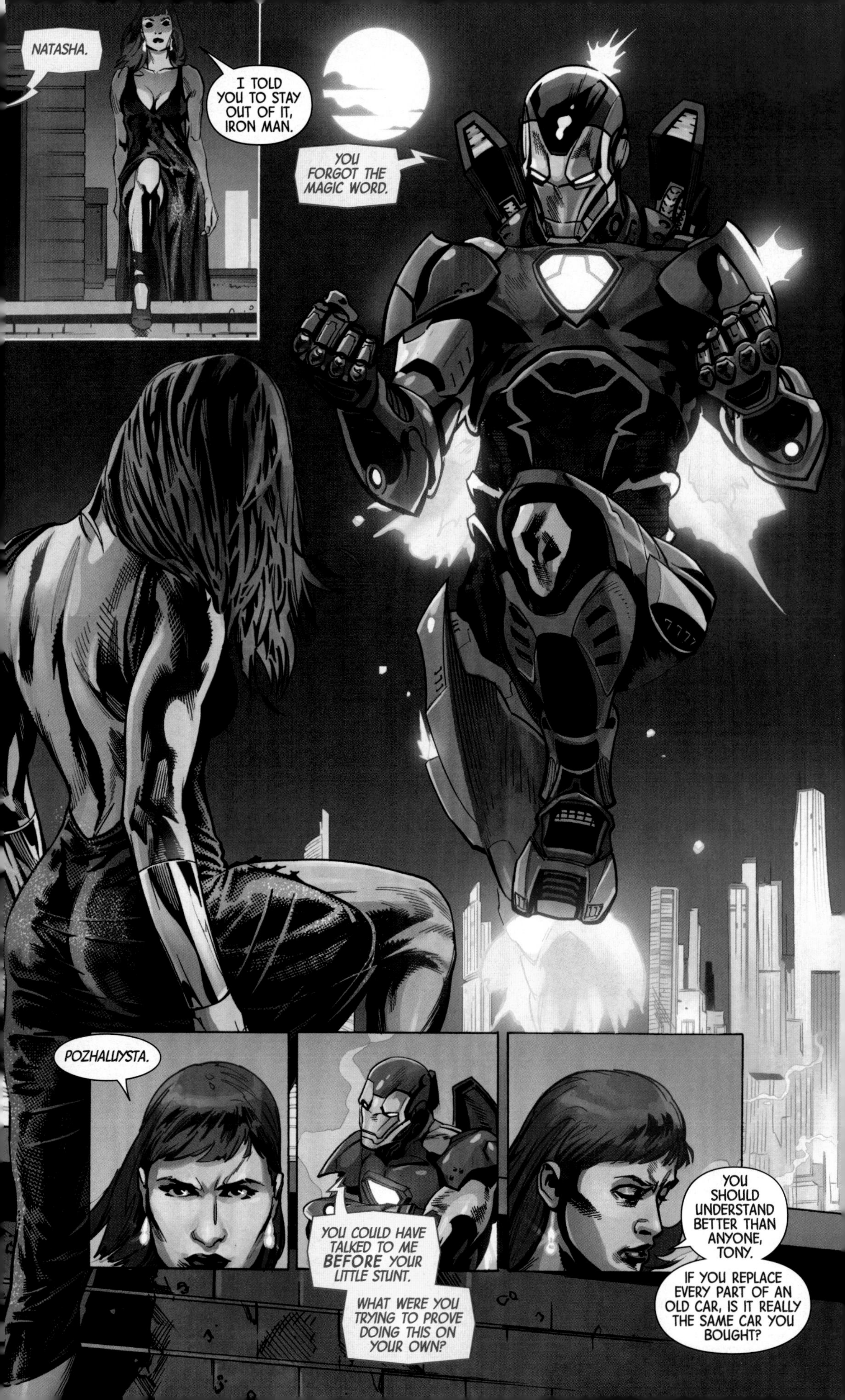
NATASHA.
I TOLD YOU TO STAY OUT OF IT, IRON MAN.
YOU FORGOT THE MAGIC WORD.
POZHALUYSTA.
YOU COULD HAVE TALKED TO ME BEFORE YOUR LITTLE STUNT.
WHAT WERE YOU TRYING TO PROVE DOING THIS ON YOUR OWN?
YOU SHOULD UNDERSTAND BETTER THAN ANYONE, TONY.
IF YOU REPLACE EVERY PART OF AN OLD CAR, IS IT REALLY THE SAME CAR YOU BOUGHT?

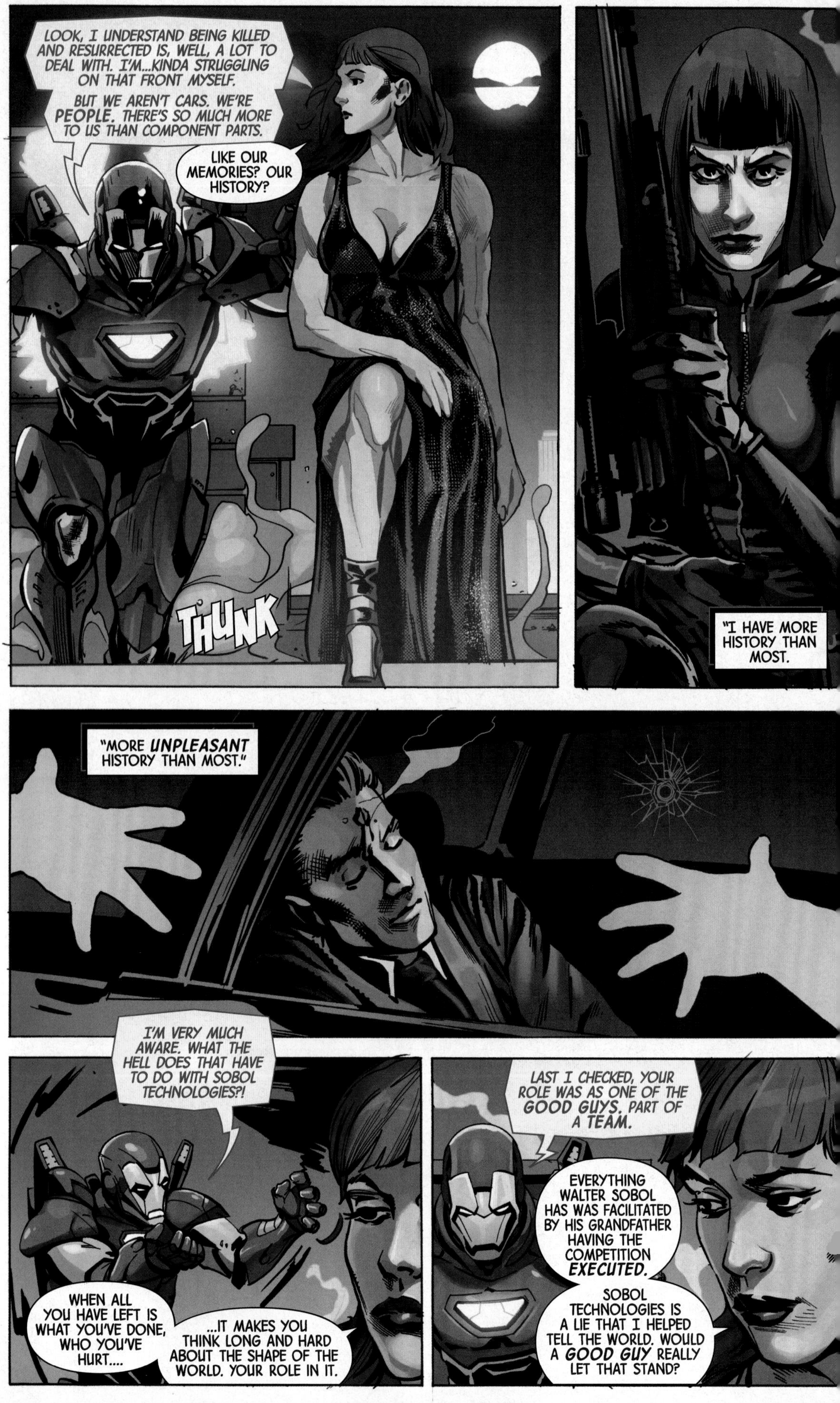
LOOK, I UNDERSTAND BEING KILLED AND RESURRECTED IS, WELL, A LOT TO DEAL WITH. I'M...KINDA STRUGGLING ON THAT FRONT MYSELF.
BUT WE AREN'T CARS. WE'RE PEOPLE. THERE'S SO MUCH MORE TO US THAN COMPONENT PARTS.
LIKE OUR MEMORIES? OUR HISTORY?
THUNK
"I HAVE MORE HISTORY THAN MOST.
"MORE UNPLEASANT HISTORY THAN MOST."
I'M VERY MUCH AWARE. WHAT THE HELL DOES THAT HAVE TO DO WITH SOBOL TECHNOLOGIES?!
WHEN ALL YOU HAVE LEFT IS WHAT YOU'VE DONE, WHO YOU'VE HURT....
...IT MAKES YOU THINK LONG AND HARD ABOUT THE SHAPE OF THE WORLD. YOUR ROLE IN IT.
LAST I CHECKED, YOUR ROLE WAS AS ONE OF THE GOOD GUYS. PART OF A TEAM.
EVERYTHING WALTER SOBOL HAS WAS FACILITATED BY HIS GRANDFATHER HAVING THE COMPETITION EXECUTED.
SOBOL TECHNOLOGIES IS A LIE THAT I HELPED TELL THE WORLD. WOULD A GOOD GUY REALLY LET THAT STAND?

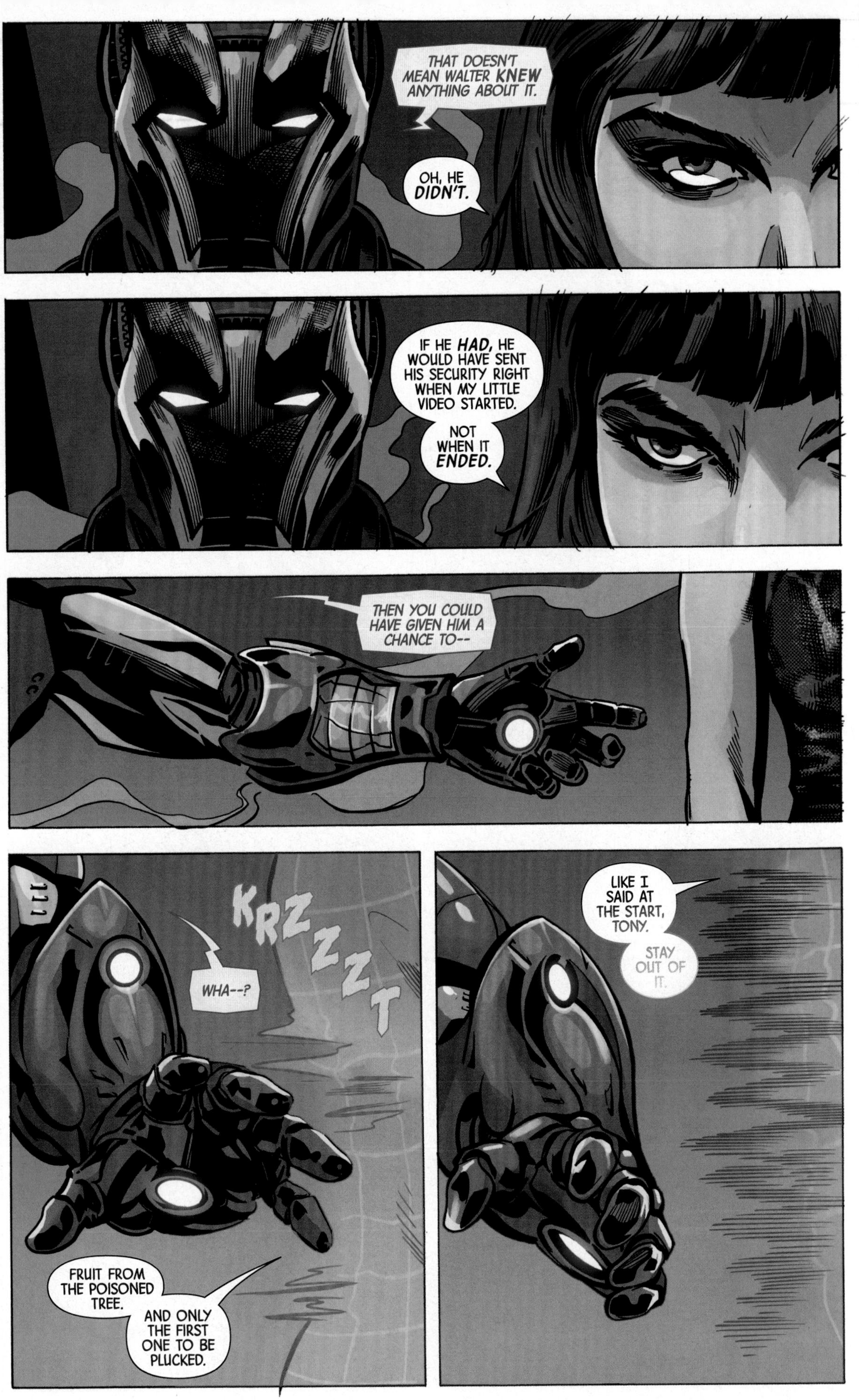
THAT DOESN'T MEAN WALTER KNEW ANYTHING ABOUT IT.
OH, HE DIDN'T.
IF HE HAD, HE WOULD HAVE SENT HIS SECURITY RIGHT WHEN MY LITTLE VIDEO STARTED.
NOT WHEN IT ENDED.
THEN YOU COULD HAVE GIVEN HIM A CHANCE TO--
KRZZZZT
WHA--?
FRUIT FROM THE POISONED TREE.
AND ONLY THE FIRST ONE TO BE PLUCKED.
LIKE I SAID AT THE START, TONY.
STAY OUT OF IT.

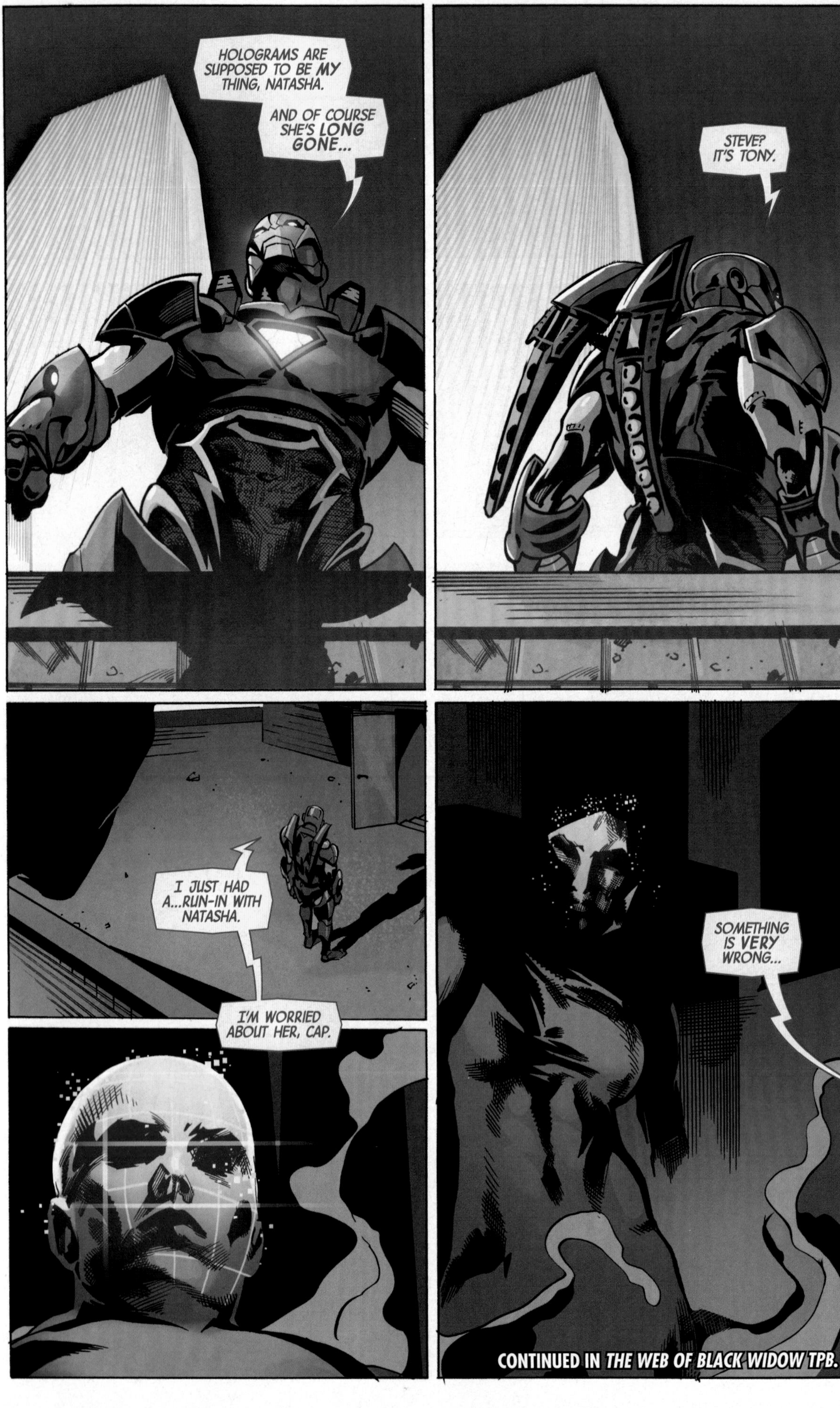

HOLOGRAMS ARE SUPPOSED TO BE MY THING, NATASHA.
AND OF COURSE SHE'S LONG GONE...
STEVE? IT'S TONY.
I JUST HAD A...RUN-IN WITH NATASHA.
I'M WORRIED ABOUT HER, CAP.
SOMETHING IS VERY WRONG...

CONTINUED IN *THE WEB OF BLACK WIDOW TPB.*

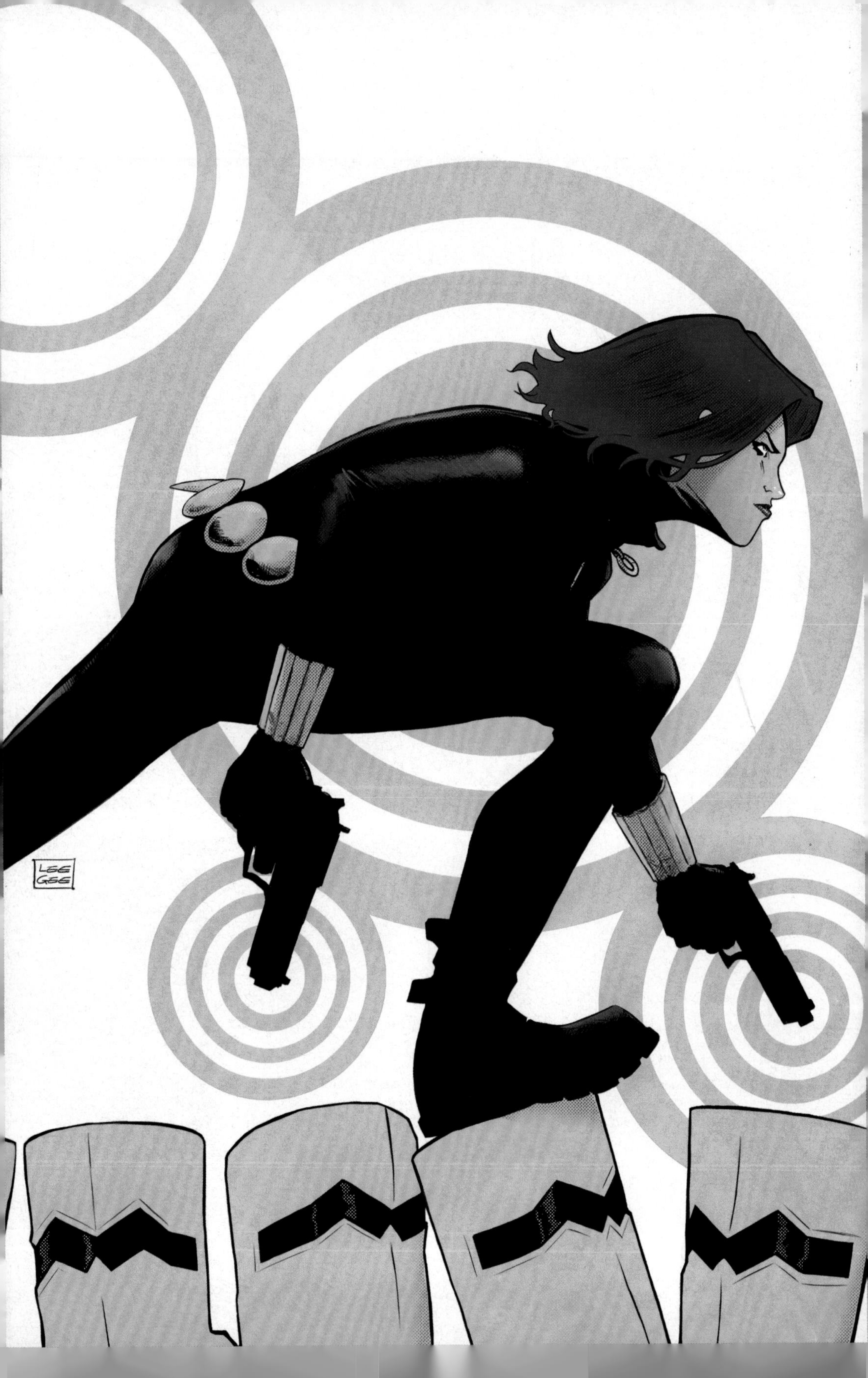

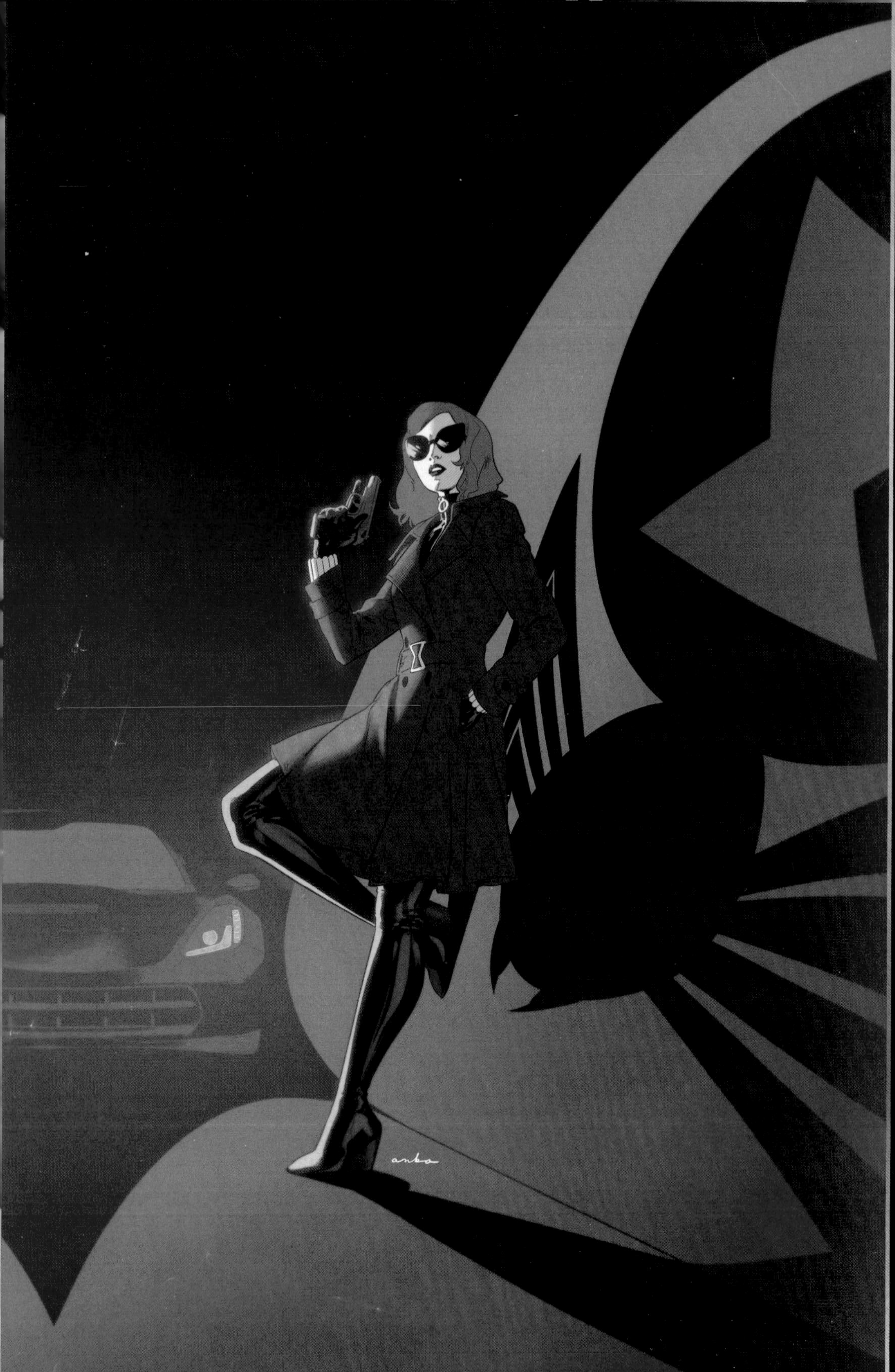
anka